POLISH
COOKERY

Uniwersalna Książka Kucharska

by MARJA OCHOROWICZ-MONATOWA
translated and adapted by Jean Karsavina

CROWN PUBLISHERS, Inc. *New York*

Preface

POLAND, LIKE FRANCE, is a country where people really know food. One can stop at a peasant house in the country, a wayside inn, a modest restaurant in a working-class city neighborhood, and be served a meal worth remembering. Good food is a tradition. Polish hospitality is legendary.

Polish cookery, about which so little is known in this country, evolved slowly over the centuries, a combination of East, West, and native preferences. Foreign princes and princesses making alliances with Poland's rulers, visiting ambassadors and church dignitaries, often brought their own chefs as members of their retinues. In the sixteenth century, for instance, when the Italian Queen Bona came to be married to the Polish king, she brought to the "barbarian country" not only her own cooks, but her produce gardeners as well, thus introducing hitherto unknown vegetables like tomatoes. And ever since, vegetables have been known by a word coined at the time—"wloszczyzna," which, translated literally, means "things Italian." And while the French dandy who later became Henry III of France was a disastrous ruler during his brief tenure of the Polish throne, his influence on sauces was most salutary.

Poland's own aristocracy, living in semi-royal, quasi-feudal splendor, was famous throughout Europe for lavish entertainment. On their vast landed estates, a hundred guests would come together for boar hunts followed by banquets, by week-long entertainments, and the tables would groan with food. Moreover, the special embattled nationalism of the Poles made it a point of pride to maintain, along with a fashionable elegance imported from France, the tradition of purely national dishes. In the kitchen, this made for a happy duality.

Manufactured in the United States of America
Library of Congress Catalog Card Number 58-8317
ISBN 0-517-50526-6
30   29   28   27

Paradoxically, the enormous variety of Polish cooking is due not only to the princely wealth of the wealthy, but also to the poverty of the poor. The country folk incorporated into their diet whatever was at hand or easily come by. Folk songs tell of boys and girls courting while going to the woods to pick berries and wild mushrooms, to gather wild honey of a dozen varieties, to trap wild birds or to hunt. Children's songs repeat this theme. Mushroom picking, in fact, is something of a national pastime, and since everyone knows his mushrooms the picking is entirely safe.

It is necessity, too, which has taught the frugal housewife to make a feast out of the cheapest cut of meat. The crayfish trapped in swamps is turned into a dish fit for a king. Even the lowly herring, in over-supply because it is so abundant in the Baltic, is handled with imagination. Sour cream is put to a hundred uses—in cabbage soup (kapuśniak), barley soup (krupnik), with kasza (buckwheat groats), and in sauces. All of these are distinctive, authentic, and surprisingly easy to prepare.

UNIWERSALNA KSIĄŻKA KUCHARSKA (The Universal Cook Book) by Mme. Marja Ochorowicz-Monatowa, on which this book is based, is the bible of Polish cookery. It was first published at the turn of the century; my own copy, its pages yellow and brittle, is dated 1911 and marked "third printing." Its original purpose, stated rather primly by the author, is to "give brides a knowledge of how cooking is done, so that they may supervise the servants properly." This, the lady tells us, is a *sine qua non* in any properly-run household, be it palatial or modest, since "everyone knows how apt the servants are to cheat, especially if the lady of the house makes no attempt to interest herself in planning menus or fails to check bills and accounts." Mme. Monatowa adds, rather pettishly, that she sees no excuse for any young woman to refuse to assume her proper responsibilities, and that to plead a lack of time is plain malingering. "If," she concludes, "there is room on one's schedule for singing lessons, piano practice, water coloring and fine embroidery, surely there is also a half-hour each day which can be made available for one's housewifely duties . . ."

A book compiled according to such a credo obviously has needed judicious pruning before it could serve the modern housewife in her modern kitchen. One of the main problems was to pick and choose among its twenty-two hundred recipes. Some of these were so extravagant, so complicated and time-consuming, that they sounded like passages out of a fairy tale. So the reader will *not* find the recipe for Roast Boar's Head, or for Turkey Garnished with Two Dozen Roast Field Thrushes. Nor have we included the recipe for peacocks, "highly prized because they are so rare." This recipe begins with the information that "at royal banquets, a favorite dish was a pâté made of peacocks' brains, and two to three thousand birds had to be slaughtered at one time." We assume that, like ourselves, you prefer to look at peacocks rather than eat them, if there are any strutting around in your vicinity.

We do include a recipe for "Bigos," or Hunters' Stew, for all that good Bigos takes a week to prepare properly. But this is an adaptable dish, and in any case no Polish cookbook would be complete without it. The Bigos recipe, like all the others in this book, has been translated into modern terms and has been adapted to the tempo of our own living. There is also a representative sampling, a cross section of dishes most typically Polish, dishes that native Poles on foreign soil grow nostalgic about, dishes which have made Warsaw famous as "the Paris of the East."

JEAN KARSAVINA

Contents

General Information

A good cook learns to handle both meats and vegetables with a minimum of water. Many vegetables, such as onions and fresh mushrooms, contain a great deal of moisture and require no water at all beyond the little that clings to them after washing, provided they are sautéed in butter or a little oil. The secret is to cover them tightly and to cook over low heat; stir occasionally but not so often that moisture evaporates.

Most meats may be cooked according to the same principle. A pot roast will require no water or, at most, a few spoonfuls of bouillon or soup stock if it is cooked with onions and other vegetables. Again, the secret is to seal in moisture by cooking tightly-covered over low heat. If the natural meat juices, fats, and vegetables do not yield enough pan gravy, it is always better to add more liquid to the pan after the meat is done. Add just enough liquid for the amount of gravy required, then simmer a few minutes and, if too thin, reduce again over high heat.

When basting meat or fowl, always use *cold* water. This helps break down the tissues and makes the roast more tender. Baste sparingly and frequently. Never add water to the pan in which meat or fowl is roasting, not even if a rack is being used. Water in the bottom of the pan will steam the meat.

Always roast meats uncovered, preferably in a shallow pan to avoid any "steamed" effect.

Certain foods and ingredients called for in the book may not be familiar to all readers. An effort has been made, whenever possible, to indicate what these are and where they may be obtained. Specialty stores dealing in so-called "exotic" ingredients generally have the items mentioned or can direct one to their source. Such stores carry fresh vanilla beans; whole (rather than ground) spices such as peppercorns, cloves, nutmeg, juniper berries, etc.; bitter almonds, and herbs.

The dried anchovies called for in a number of meat, fish, and sauce recipes may be obtained in any Italian food market. They are highly salted and should be soaked in water until soft, then boned. Canned anchovy fillets are an excellent substitute, though considerably more expensive.

Fresh dill is, of all herbs, the one most extensively used in Polish cookery. In large cities dill is readily available in Italian and Jewish neighborhoods, or may be ordered in advance from any fresh produce market. It is also extremely easy to grow: a dozen seeds taken from the package of dill seed on the spice shelf will produce worthwhile results. Dill is a biennial, although it is not as tender the second year.

Paprika, like curry powder, is one of those condiments that is only a pale second-cousin to itself when bought in the average grocery store. The commercially-available paprika with which most of us are familiar is used mainly for its attractive bright-red color. It has a minimum of taste, since it is mixed generously with flour before it is packaged. The discriminating cook will find it worthwhile to shop around in specialty stores for genuine Hungarian paprika. This, while not a particularly sharp seasoning, has a distinctive flavor that adds immeasurably to the recipes where it is called for. The amounts of paprika called for in the recipes in this book, it should be added, are for the original Hungarian, nonadulterated product.

Rings of Polish sausage—actually Cracow sausage but known here by the generic name for sausage, *kiełbasa*—have become so popular that they are now available in most supermarkets throughout the country. They are a domestic product and inexpensive.

Another food gaining in popularity and imported from Poland is Polish ham, available in both small and large cans. This is distinctive in flavor and is worth tracking down even where not readily available. It may be sliced and used cold like ordinary canned ham, or used in recipes calling for boiled (precooked) ham.

Imported dried mushrooms from Poland differ in taste from those imported from Italy and from the domestic variety available in Italian food markets. The latter are made from cultivated mushrooms; the former from wild mushrooms, which have a much stronger, more distinctive taste. To use sparingly as flavoring for sauces or pot roast, the genuine Polish mushrooms are worth splurging on, expensive as they are. However, where more than a few are needed, the Italian ones will provide a very adequate substitute. Dried mushrooms and fresh mushrooms are not altogether inter- changeable—fresh cultivated mushrooms have a much more delicate flavor which is often lost in a recipe calling for dried mushrooms.

A larding needle is an indispensable kitchen tool for the cook who is serious about her meats. Veal, venison, game, turkey—any meat likely to be dry—is improved both in texture and flavor by larding; and without a larding needle the process is laborious. Larding needles may be purchased in stores specializing in gadgets for the gourmet. A piece of lard or bacon must be cut into thin strips to thread the needle. When a piece of meat is to be cut into thin steaks or slices and these are to be larded, the best method is to lard the whole piece first, running the strips of lard lengthwise, and then to slice across them.

Electric blenders and mixers may be used to shorten work time. For speeds and timing, follow the general rules for the use of elec- tric appliances.

For casserole dishes, stews, and braising, it is best to use the heaviest kitchenware available. Old-fashioned earthenware casseroles and cast-iron pans, and the now-popular enameled cast-iron or heavy cast-aluminum utensils are recommended, since food does not scorch or burn in these. Thin enamel or aluminum pots are seldom satis- factory, and an initial investment in good cooking utensils is, in the end, the best economy.

Soups

Meat and Poultry Soups

GENERAL DIRECTIONS: While many variations are possible in making good basic soup stock, best results are obtained when certain simple rules are followed. Meat and bones should be rinsed off in cold water, never soaked. Soup should always be started with *cold* water, brought to a boil, then allowed to simmer a minimum of 3 hours. The proportions are 1 lb. of meat to 5 cups of water. It is better to start with too much water and let it simmer down, than to start with too little and add water during the cooking. If marrow bone is added, ask the butcher to split it whenever possible. Start cooking without salt; skim and keep skimming the scum and fat. When no more comes to the surface, add salt to taste. Add soup greens, which generally include one or two carrots, celery root, parsley root, a stalk of celery, a leek, fresh parsley, and a medium-size onion. The onion is most tangy if previously baked to a light golden-brown in the oven, or cut in quarters and lightly browned with a bit of butter in a covered skillet. Half an hour before the soup is ready, half a head of savoy cabbage or a half-dozen Brussels sprouts may also be added. Once all the vegetables are in, the soup should be covered tightly and *simmered,* never boiled hard. A few minutes before serving, it should be taken off the flame and a spoonful of cold water added. This will help it settle and make it easier to skim unwanted fat.

THICKENINGS: A paste or *roux* made of butter and flour and slowly diluted with a few spoonfuls of the soup stock is used to thicken many soups. There are three ways to make this thickening.

1. Melt the butter *without browning,* slowly stir in the flour as for white sauce, dilute with enough soup to make sure no lumps form, and then pour into the soup kettle.

3

2. Melt *and brown* the butter. Then add flour, and proceed as above.
3. *Brown* the flour *first*. This is done by heating the necessary amount in a heavy, dry skillet, being careful not to have the heat too high and stirring constantly to avoid sticking. When flour is a light golden-brown, add the butter, continue stirring, and proceed as above.

Since many of the following recipes are made from basic soup stock, to save space we will not repeat this basic recipe. Where additions of other ingredients make for especially rich fare, the use of light stock made with soupbones alone is often indicated. When no stock is available and time is at a premium, bouillon cubes, beef extract, or canned broth may be used as substitutes. The perfectionist may shudder, but the results will nevertheless be reasonably satisfactory, especially if there is time to simmer the bouillon at least a half-hour so that the artificial taste disappears.

1. BEEF BOUILLON (*Rosół z Wołowiny*)
Basic Recipe for Soup Stock and Boiled Beef

2 lbs. brisket or plate of beef	few sprigs of parsley
10 cups cold water	½ head savoy cabbage
piece of marrow bone	(optional)
2 or 3 carrots	1 bay leaf (optional)
1 celery root	3–4 dried mushrooms (optional)
1 parsley root	6 peppercorns
1 large leek	salt to taste
2 med. onions, preferably baked	1 tbs. chopped fresh dill or
(see directions at beginning of	parsley
chapter)	

Have the butcher saw the soupbone in half in order to get the most out of the marrow. Cover meat, which should be cut in one thick, short piece, and soupbone with *cold* water (proportions 5 cups to 1 lb. meat) and bring to a boil. Skim carefully. When no more scum comes to the surface, lower flame, add salt to taste, a dash of fresh-ground pepper, and finally the soup greens. Cover and let simmer for at least 3 hours. Fifteen minutes before serving, set aside and add 1 or 2 tbs. cold water to clarify the soup. Skim excess fat. Strain if clear soup is desired.

Soup can be made still tastier by adding the following to the clear bouillon:

¼ lb. beef liver	½ med. carrot, diced
1 tbs. butter	¼ celery or parsley root, diced
1 small diced onion	

Dice liver and sauté in butter in heavy skillet. When it begins to brown add diced vegetables, and when these too are slightly brown, add enough soup stock to cover. Simmer until vegetables are soft. Pour the rest of the strained soup over this mixture and continue simmering another half-hour. When serving, sprinkle with chopped fresh dill or parsley.

If soup is to be used for stock only, omit the second part of recipe. If a more economical stock is desired, use bones alone or bones and meat scraps. Still another way is to utilize chicken giblets and feet, if available, along with soup bones. Strained stock can be poured into jars or bottles, covered tightly, and stored in refrigerator to be used as needed.

Yield: 4 to 5 helpings each of soup and of soup meat, which is served as a second course with boiled potatoes; another 4 or 5 cups of stock left over for later use.

2. CLEAR CONSOMMÉ (Rosół Czysty)

2 lbs. brisket or plate beef	10 cups cold water
¼ lb. veal	1 bouillon cube
¼ lb. chicken giblets, or chicken meat cut in small pieces	soup greens as in No. 1

Start soup as for Beef Bouillon, adding the chicken and the veal, which should first be dipped in boiling water. Proceed as in No. 1, simmering 3 hours. Skim fat, strain, serve with crackers or meat pastries. (See Index.) Serves 8 to 10.

3. CHICKEN OR VEAL BROTH
(Rosół z Kury Lub Cielęciny)

Substitute veal or chicken for beef, and cook according to directions for Beef Bouillon, No. 1, being careful, however, to cook veal stock no longer than 1½ hours and chicken stock from 2 to 2½ hours, and taking care not to let the meat fall apart. The meat may be served as a second course with a White Sauce (see Index). All veal must be blanched (dipped in boiling water) first; otherwise the soup will have a whitish appearance.

4. RICE AND VEAL SOUP (Zupa z Cielęciny i Ryżu)

2 lbs. veal with bones (shank, neck, etc.)	dash of nutmeg
cold water, 5 cups per lb. meat	3 egg yolks
soup greens as in No. 1	2 cups milk
6 peppercorns	salt and pepper to taste
1 bay leaf	½ cup rice, cooked separately

Cook the soup the same as in No. 1, allowing 1½ hours. When done, pick all the meat off the soupbones, add cooked rice, chop fine, and put through sieve or ricer. Return to bouillon, which has been strained in the meantime. Reheat. Beat up raw egg yolks with milk and add to soup, stirring and taking care not to boil again lest the eggs curdle. Serve with croutons or cooked inch-long pieces of macaroni. Serves 10.

5. VEGETABLE PURÉE *(Zupa Jarzynowa)*

1 large marrow bone, cut and split	Brussels sprouts (optional)
2 med. onions	other vegetables to taste
1–2 med. carrots	small bunch fresh parsley and,
1 celery root	if available, fresh dill
1–2 celery stalks with leaves	salt and pepper to taste
1 parsley root	1 tbs. butter
1 parsnip	½ tbs. flour
½ head savoy cabbage or 1 cup	8 cups cold water

Cover soupbones with cold water and simmer one hour, skimming as necessary. Add salt. Peel and cook vegetables separately, tightly covered, using just enough water to cook without scorching. When thoroughly done, chop and put through meat grinder or sieve together with cooked bone marrow, saving all the juices. Moisten with soup stock as needed to make sure all vegetable pulp is utilized. Combine with strained soup stock. Melt butter in heavy skillet; blend in flour, stirring constantly; dilute with a few spoonfuls of stock and return to pot. Season to taste and serve with croutons and grated Parmesan. Serves 6.

6. POLISH MUSHROOM AND BARLEY SOUP
(Krupnik Polski)

6 cups soup stock made with bone and meat scraps	1½ tsp. butter
½ bouillon cube	1 tbs. chopped parsley
6 dried mushrooms	2–3 med. potatoes, cooked and diced
6 green beans	salt and pepper to taste
½ cup barley, cooked separately	

Make soup stock according to directions in No. 1, adding ½ bouillon cube if stock is thin. Cook barley separately in heavy covered pot, adding a little of the stock as necessary to separate grains. (See Index.) When done, add butter, stir well, pour barley into soup pot and let boil up. Remove bones and serve the rest without straining, adding diced potatoes and chopped parsley. Serves 6.

7. BARLEY SOUP WITH GIBLETS
(Krupnik z Podróbkami)

6 cups soup stock or enough meat scraps, soupbones, and soup greens for 6 cups of basic stock

chicken, duck, or turkey giblets from one bird
2 egg yolks (optional)

Cook Krupnik like Beef Bouillon, No. 1, substituting giblets for beef. When done (2 to 3 hours) dice the giblets and return to soup. For added taste, beat up two egg yolks and slowly dilute with hot soup, a spoonful at a time to prevent curdling. Add to soup, stirring constantly, and serve at once. Serves 6.

8. SAUERKRAUT SOUP *(Kapuśniak)*

1 lb. sauerkraut
½ lb. pork meat (head or rump) marrow bone
8 cups cold water
1 med. onion (preferably baked; see basic directions) soup greens consisting of 1 celery root, 1 parsley root, 1 parsnip, 2 carrots, 1–2 celery stalks, few sprigs of parsley
4–6 dried mushrooms

1 bay leaf (optional)
6 peppercorns
2 strips bacon, or equivalent amount of salt pork, diced
½ med. onion, diced
1 tbs. flour, browned (see basic directions)
1 lump sugar (optional) salt and pepper to taste
1–2 frankfurters or several slices salami, diced (optional)

Cover sauerkraut, meat, and marrow bone with cold water. Boil and skim. Add browned onion, soup greens, and mushrooms and let simmer, skimming as necessary, for at least 2 hours. When meat is soft, remove from bones and cut into small pieces; cut mushrooms into strips. Remove marrow from marrow bones. Strain soup or not, according to preference. Return meat, mushrooms, and marrow to pot. In heavy skillet brown the bacon or salt pork together with chopped onion and browned flour, adding stock a little at a time until lumps are dissolved. Add to soup and boil up once. Season to taste, adding sugar if soup is too sharp. Add diced sausage if desired. Serves 8.

9. FRESH CABBAGE SOUP *(Kapuśniak)*

Follow recipe for Sauerkraut Soup, No. 8, substituting the following:

1 lb. fresh cabbage for the sauerkraut

½ lb. beef for the pork
1 tbs. vinegar instead of sugar

Both types of cabbage soup may be served with one tablespoon sour cream per portion as topping. In this case, omit the diced sausage.

10. GRUEL *(Kleik)*

1 cup barley or whole-wheat
  groats
2 cups boiling water
¼ tsp. salt

2 tbs. butter
4 cups soup stock or clear
  bouillon

Wash cereal and put in boiling water to which salt and 1 tbs. of the butter have been added. Let boil up, stir, and reduce heat. Let simmer until grains are done (½ hour to 45 min.), being careful to skim and save the glue-like substance which settles around edges of pot. Stir frequently to avoid scorching. When grain is done and the water absorbed, put the cereal through a sieve or ricer. Dilute with soup stock, add skimmings, and top with remaining butter. Serves 6. The proportion of cooked cereal to clear soup may be varied according to whether a thicker or thinner gruel is desired. Bouillon cubes may be substituted for homemade bouillon.

11. PICKLED BEET SOUP
(Barszcz Kwaszony z Buraków)

6 large or 10 small beets
1 slice sour rye bread or buttermilk
  rye

4 cups lukewarm water
salt and pepper to taste
dash of sugar (optional)

Scrape and dice the beets. Cover with water and place slice of bread on top. Cover loosely and let stand for 4 days in the warmest spot in the kitchen. The liquid should be sufficiently sour and tasty by that time (depending on the weather). Should mold appear, carefully skim it off. Discard bread, and season soup to taste. May be served hot or cold, with topping of sour cream if desired. Tightly covered, it may also be stored in refrigerator for later use. Serves 4.

12. CLEAR, HOT *BARSZCZ* *(Barszcz Czysty)*

4 cups soup stock, preferably
  made with equal amounts of
  pork and beef
2–3 beets
4 cups Pickled Beet Soup
3–4 dried mushrooms ⎫
1 tsp. Maggi extract ⎬ when commercial beef extract is used
sugar to taste (optional) ⎭

Make stock according to basic directions, adding beets during last half-hour. When beets are soft, remove and dice. Strain remaining liquid; combine in equal parts with pickled beet liquid. (See preceding recipe.) Add diced beets. Heat, being careful not to overcook lest the beets lose their fresh red color. Season with salt, pepper, and enough sugar for a sweet-and-sour taste. Serve in bouillon cups with croutons or meat pastries. Serves 8.

If commercial beef broth or bouillon cubes are used, cook for half an hour with the addition of dried mushrooms and Maggi extract. Then add beets and continue cooking until both beets and mushrooms are tender.

13. POLISH *BARSZCZ* WITH MEAT POCKETS
(*Barszcz Polski z Uszkami*)

Prepare the same as No. 12. In addition to diced beets, add the following to the strained soup:

¼ lb. diced Polish sausage (salami or frankfurters may be substituted)

¼ lb. cooked pork meat, diced

meat pockets (Use 2 or 3 pockets per person—see Index—or 1 med. potato per serving may be substituted; prepared ravioli may also be substituted.)

Serves 8.

14. UKRAINIAN *BARSZCZ* (*Barszcz Ukraiński*)

6 cups soup stock cooked as in No. 1, with pork meat, dry mushrooms, and beets added

¼ cup fresh Lima or green beans

½ head savoy cabbage

5 med. tomatoes, quartered

2 strips raw bacon

½ med. grated onion

1 tsp. fresh dill

1 tsp. fresh parsley

1 tbs. butter

2 hard-cooked eggs (optional)

¼ lb. diced sausage (optional)

salt and pepper to taste

Dice cabbage and beans, and cook, covered, in very little water until tender. In heavy skillet simmer the tomatoes in butter until they can be easily puréed. Dice beets and mushrooms as well as pork meat, and combine all ingredients. Remove bones and unsightly pieces of soup greens from soup pot, but do not strain. Chop bacon; mix with grated onion and fresh herbs and add to soup. Boil up once. Add diced sausage and quartered hard-cooked eggs. Serves 6 to 8.

15. *BARSZCZ* MADE OF HARE OR RABBIT
(*Barszcz z Przodków Zajęczych*)

forepaws, lungs, livers, and other scrap meat from 1 hare or 2 rabbits

8 cups cold water

2 med. onions, preferably baked (see general directions)

6 peppercorns

1 bay leaf

1 stalk celery

1 celery root

2 med. carrots

1 leek

1 parsnip

few sprigs of parsley

salt to taste
3 dried mushrooms
1 tbs. butter
1 tbs. flour

Fermented rye liquid (see recipe following) in proportion of 1 cup to 1 cup soup stock

This is an excellent way to utilize those parts of the hare or rabbit which are ordinarily discarded in the preparation of a main dish. Carefully wash the meat; cover with cold water, bring to a boil, and skim. Add all remaining ingredients except butter and flour, and if meat seems scanty, a marrow bone. Simmer from 2 to 3 hours. Strain and combine with rye liquid according to taste, usually in 1 to 1 proportion. Dice good pieces of meat and liver, as well as mushrooms. Return to soup and heat thoroughly. In heavy skillet brown 1 tbs. butter, stir to a paste with flour, and add enough soup liquid to prevent lumping. Pour back into soup and boil up once. Then simmer another 10 minutes to thicken. Serve with boiled potatoes. Serves 6, with 3 cups soup (undiluted) left over for future use. This may be stored, tightly covered, in refrigerator.

16. FERMENTED RYE *BARSZCZ*
(*Barszcz Kwaszony Żytni*)

4 cups rye grits or flour   4 cups boiling water

In a heavy bowl or crock, combine flour and boiling water to a thick dough. Let stand, loosely covered, in a warm spot in the kitchen for at least 48 hours. When dough begins to ferment and rise, add a quart of *cold* water. Let stand until the liquid is completely clear. Store in cool spot and use as necessary, taking care to remove liquid without stirring. Fresh water may be poured over the dough and new brew made, to be utilized as needed. Discard when the dough becomes slimy.

Rye *barszcz* may be used instead of fermented beet *barszcz* in all the preceding recipes, or added to soup stock to lend its own special flavor; 3 or 4 freshly-boiled beets may be added for color.

17. VENISON OR HUNTERS' SOUP
(*Zupa z Dziczyny, Myśliwska*)

1 small game bird, or
1 lb. venison meat, or
  rabbit or hare forepaws and
  livers, or
  combination of any of the
  above

1 med. onion, diced
2 tbs. butter
1 carrot
1 parsnip
1–2 stalks celery
1 celery root

1 leek
few sprigs parsley
6 peppercorns
bay leaf (optional)
salt to taste

cold water (5 cups to each
pound of meat)
2-3 egg yolks
1 cup sweet cream
¼ cup dry white wine

(This is an excellent way to utilize venison scraps when venison is in season.) Cut meat in small pieces and sauté in heavy covered pot with butter and onion until lightly brown. Add diced vegetables and seasonings and continue sautéing until meat is tender, adding a little cold water as needed to prevent scorching. When done, clean meat off the bones, and put through meat grinder. Return bones to pot, together with vegetables. Add water and simmer another hour. Strain and combine with ground meat. Thicken with 1 tbs. flour and 1 tbs. browned butter stirred to a paste and diluted with stock. Add ¼ cup white wine and boil up once. Beat 2 or 3 egg yolks into 1 cup sweet cream, and slowly add to hot soup, stirring constantly to prevent curdling. Serve with croutons. Serves 6 to 7.

18. LIVER SOUP (Zupa Wątrobiana)

1 lb. calf's liver or equivalent
amount beef or lamb liver
2 med. onions
1 carrot
1 stalk celery
1 celery root

1 leek
few sprigs parsley
2 strips lean bacon, diced
2 tbs. butter
6 cups light soup stock
2 egg yolks

Cut meat in strips and sauté in heavy covered skillet together with diced vegetables and bacon and butter, omitting salt, since salt toughens the liver. When meat and vegetables are tender (about 45 minutes) put through meat grinder or ricer. Then combine with soup stock and heat thoroughly. Beat up the egg yolks, dilute with soup stock, being careful not to curdle. Pour into soup and stir well. Season to taste. Serves 6 to 8.

19. CAULIFLOWER SOUP (Zupa Kalafjorowa)

6 cups light soup stock
1 med. cauliflower
1 tbs. butter
1 tbs. flour
2-3 egg yolks

½ cup cream
6 fresh mushrooms (optional) cut
into strips and sautéed in butter
salt and pepper to taste

Cook cauliflower in salted boiling water until tender—about 20 minutes. Reserve 6 to 8 flowerets. Mash the rest, combine with hot meat stock, thicken with the flour and butter stirred to a paste and diluted until smooth. Let simmer another few minutes. In the meantime beat the egg yolks with cream. Add, a little at a time, stirring constantly to avoid curdling. Season to taste. Add the whole flowerets, mushrooms if desired, and serve with croutons. Serves 6 to 8.

20. BRUSSELS SPROUT SOUP *(Zupa z Brukselki)*

¼ lb. smoked pork	few sprigs fresh parsley
1 med. onion	1 pt. Brussels sprouts
1 leek	7–8 cups water
1 celery stalk	salt and pepper to taste
1 celery root	1 tbs. flour
1 parsnip	1 tbs. bacon fat

Start pork and vegetables in cold water; simmer until done—about 45 minutes. Reserve half the sprouts (choosing the most tightly closed ones) and put remaining vegetables through sieve or ricer. Dice the meat. Return to pot, add the whole sprouts, and heat through. Brown the flour, make paste of flour and bacon drippings, add a little soup, and stir until smooth. Add to soup, let bubble up, and serve. Serves 6.

21. SORREL SOUP WITH MEAT STOCK
(Zupa Szczawiowa na Rosole)

6 cups beef stock or bouillon made from cubes	an adequate substitute when sorrel is unavailable. Season spinach with 1 tsp. lemon juice.)
1 lb. sorrel leaves (A package of frozen chopped spinach makes	6 eggs, poached separately

Wash, clean, and then dry the sorrel. Chop before cooking. Cook in the broth for 20 to 25 minutes or until tender. Season and serve, adding one poached egg per serving. Serves 6.

22. BREAD SOUP *(Zupa Chlebowa)*

6 cups strong beef bouillon	2 frankfurters, or equivalent amount of salami or Polish sausage, diced (optional)
1 tbs. flour	
1 tbs. butter	
6 slices rye or corn bread	6 poached eggs
butter to spread on bread	salt and pepper to taste

Thicken the beef bouillon with paste made of dry-browned flour and butter stirred smooth with a little of the broth. Let simmer. Butter the bread slices and toast in oven or under broiler. Dice sausage and add to soup. Pour into individual dishes and top each with piece of toast on which has been placed one poached egg. Serves 6.

23. CARAWAY SOUP *(Zupa Kminkowa)*

Cook beef broth as usual. For six servings, add 1 heaping tbs. of caraway seed to pot at the same time as vegetables. Strain, thicken with paste made of browned flour and butter stirred until smooth. Serve with croutons. For added flavor, ¼ lb. diced Polish sausage or salami may be added if desired. Serves 6.

24. FRESH MUSHROOM SOUP *(Zupa Pieczarkowa)*

12–15 fresh mushrooms	6 cups soup stock made with
1 med. onion, chopped	marrow bone
2 tbs. butter	salt and pepper to taste

Dice mushrooms and sauté with onion and butter until tender (about 25 minutes), adding a little soup stock if necessary to keep thoroughly moist. Season with salt and pepper to taste. Combine marrow extracted from bones, with the mushrooms. Purée together, combine with soup stock, and let simmer for another 15 to 20 minutes. Thicken with paste made of melted butter and flour diluted with a few tbs. soup and stirred until smooth. Let stand another 10 minutes so that it will thicken thoroughly. Season to taste. Serve with grated cheese and croutons or hot rolls. Serves 6.

25. CLEAR TOMATO BOUILLON
(Zupa Pomidorowa Czysta)

1 lb. tomatoes, sliced	½ cup dry white wine
2 tbs. butter	1 egg white, unbeaten, and
6 cups soup stock, preferably	crushed eggshell
cooked with addition of ½ lb.	salt and pepper to taste
veal and chicken giblets	

Simmer tomatoes in butter until thoroughly done and the melted butter floats to the surface. Purée the tomatoes, combine with strained soup stock, add wine and the egg white and shell, which will help clear the soup. Remove egg and shell with strainer spoon. Serve with cheese croutons or meat patties. Serves 6 to 7.

26. TOMATO SOUP WITH SOUR CREAM
(Zupa Pomidorowa ze Śmietaną)

Cook like No. 25. Soup stock may be made with bones and soup greens alone, omitting soup meat. Omit wine. When combining stock and tomato purée, add 1 cup sour cream and ½ tsp. flour. Simmer another 30 minutes. Serve with cooked rice or croutons. A dash of sugar may be added for more piquant taste. Serves 6 to 7.

27. LEMON SOUP *(Zupa Cytrynowa)*

2 egg yolks
1 tbs. flour
⅓ cup sour cream

6 cups stock made with veal bones
juice and grated rind of ½ lemon

Beat raw egg yolks and flour into sour cream until thoroughly smooth. Slowly add hot, strained soup stock, being careful not to let the liquid curdle. Add lemon rind and juice, stirring constantly. Since tastes differ, it is important to add the lemon juice a little at a time, or soup may turn out too tart. Heat thoroughly on very low heat, being careful not to boil and curdle. Serve with croutons or hot boiled rice. Serves 6 to 7. (For thinner soup, use less sour cream.)

28. SORREL SOUP WITH SOUR CREAM *(Zupa Szczawiowa)*

1 lb. sorrel leaves, cleaned, washed, and dried (1 pkg. frozen spinach may be substituted, with addition of few drops of lemon juice)
2 tbs. butter

6 cups light soup stock
⅓ cup sour cream
1 tbs. flour
salt and pepper to taste
4–6 hard-cooked eggs (optional)

Chop sorrel raw; add salt to taste, and sauté in butter until done—about 20 minutes. Combine with strained soup stock. Beat flour into the sour cream and combine with soup; stir thoroughly and let simmer 5 to 10 minutes. Serve with quartered hard-cooked or deviled eggs on strips of toast. Serves 6 to 7. (May be served with croutons alone.)

29. FRESH DILL SOUP *(Zupa Koprowa)*

Made like Sorrel Soup (No. 28), with the following changes:

1 large bunch dill, chopped fine, is substituted for sorrel.
3 raw egg yolks (optional), substituted for the cooked eggs.

Sauté the dill in butter for 3 to 4 minutes, no longer. Beat the raw egg yolks into the sour cream until thoroughly blended. Combine dill, soup stock, and sour cream and egg mixture, being careful not to let curdle. Heat thoroughly without boiling. Season to taste and serve with croutons. Serves 6 to 7.

30. DILL PICKLE SOUP *(Zupa Ogórkowa)*

3–4 dill pickles, depending on size
2 tbs. butter
6 cups light meat stock

⅓ cup sour cream
1 tbs. flour

Peel the pickles, slice thin, and cook in butter and one cup of stock until transparent and completely tender (about 30 minutes). Combine with remaining strained soup stock and the sour cream into which the flour has been thoroughly blended. Season sparingly, since salt tends to accentuate the sour taste. If not tart enough, add a little of the pickling liquid or a few drops lemon juice. Serves 6 to 7.

31. CRAYFISH SOUP (*Zupa Rakowa ze Śmietaną*)

20 large or 30 small live crayfish (fresh shrimp may be substituted for approximate results)	6 cups clear soup stock
	½ cup sour cream
	1 tbs. flour
1 bunch fresh dill	fresh-ground pepper
salted water to cover	1 tbs. chopped fresh dill
2–3 tbs. butter	

Scrub crayfish and rinse thoroughly. Add bunch of fresh dill to boiling water and throw in the crayfish. Let water come to a boil again, and cook 8 to 10 minutes, depending on size. Drain, reserving liquid, and clean as follows: With a sharp knife cut away edges of tails and claws for easiest cleaning. Carefully remove meat, keeping pieces as large as feasible. On the under side of tail (or neck, as it is sometimes called) is a black thread which should be removed, as in cleaning shrimp. Reserve tail shells for stuffing. Discard only the eyes and bile. Pound remaining shell bits, claws, fat, etc., to a mass, using a mortar and pestle. Sauté this mass in heavy skillet, with butter, for half an hour.

Combine with liquid in which crayfish cooked, and simmer, skimming the butter into a separate cup as it comes to the surface. Continue until all butter has been skimmed. Then reduce liquid to 1 cup, strain, and combine with soup stock. Add sour cream blended with the flour and bubble up once. Add the cleaned crayfish meat, the skimmed butter, and the chopped fresh dill. Season to taste, stir, and serve with stuffed crayfish shells floating on top. Serves 6 to 7.

Note: Crayfish Butter for Storing: While the crayfish mixture is simmering, the skimmed butter, sometimes also called Coral Butter, may be prepared in larger quantities, then stored, tightly covered, in the refrigerator for later use. Up to a half-pound of Coral Butter may be prepared at one time.

Stuffed Crayfish Shells:

1 tbs. butter	1 tsp. chopped fresh dill
2 egg yolks	salt and pepper to taste
2–3 tbs. bread crumbs	

Cream butter and egg yolks, add bread crumbs and chopped dill, and mix thoroughly. Season to taste and stuff shells with this mixture. Add to soup for final minute of cooking.

32. CALF'S BRAIN SOUP *(Zupa z Móźdźku)*

1 set of calf brains	1 stalk of celery, diced
1 tbs. butter	2–3 tbs. green beans, Limas, or
1½ tsp. flour	peas
1 stale roll or slice of bread,	2–3 fresh mushrooms (optional),
soaked in milk	cut fine
salt and pepper to taste	butter for cooking
1 med. onion, chopped	5–6 cups light soup stock
1 carrot, diced	2 egg yolks, lightly beaten

Rinse and clean the brains, cut up coarsely, and cream with butter and flour. Add roll or bread, mix thoroughly, and season with salt and pepper. In the meantime, sauté the onion and vegetables in butter, adding a few spoonfuls of stock, if necessary, to keep from sticking, until quite soft (about 30 minutes). Combine with soup stock. Purée by putting through sieve or ricer. Heat thoroughly. Dilute egg yolks with a little of the hot soup and pour into soup pot, being careful not to let the eggs curdle. Serves 6.

Meatless Soups

33. CHRISTMAS EVE *BARSZCZ (Barszcz Wigilijny)*

2 med. onions, preferably baked	1 bay leaf (optional)
(see general directions)	6 peppercorns
1 oz. dried mushrooms	1 tsp. salt
2 carrots	3–4 cups water
2 stalks celery	3 cups pickled beet liquid (see
1 parsnip	No. 11; canned beets and juice
2 med. leeks	may be substituted)
1 celery root	1 tbs. browned flour (see gen-
3–4 beets	eral directions)
1 small bunch parsley, or parsley	1 heaping tbs. butter
and fresh dill combined	

Cut up all vegetables except beets and mushrooms, which go in whole. Let simmer with bay leaf and peppercorns in 3 to 4 cups salted water for about an hour. Strain vegetables if desired, or serve in soup. In the latter case, cut mushrooms into strips and slice beets matchstick-thin. Return to pot. Combine stock with pickled beet liquid, and thicken with paste made of flour and butter, stirring contantly to prevent lumps. Serve with Mushrooms Pockets (see Index). Serves 6.

34. WHITE *BARSZCZ* (*Barszcz Zabielany*)

Cook like Christmas Eve Barszcz, adding half the quantity of dried mushrooms. Add ½ to 1 cup sour cream, depending on the thickness desired. Blend and heat thoroughly. Serve with sliced hard-cooked eggs or with boiled potatoes. Serves 6 to 7.

35. BREAD SOUP (*Zupa Chlebowa*)

2 cups stale dark bread (rye, whole wheat, etc.) moistened with water	1 celery stalk
	1 celery root or parsnip
2 med. onions	5 cups salted water
1-2 carrots	dash of nutmeg
1 leek	1 cup milk
few sprigs parsley	3 egg yolks
6 green beans or 2-3 tbs. Lima beans or peas	salt and pepper to taste

Make light broth of all the vegetables and the bread. When vegetables are soft (30 to 45 minutes), put through sieve or ricer and return to broth. Add nutmeg and milk; stir thoroughly and bring to a simmer but do not boil. Dilute beaten egg yolks with a few spoonfuls of the broth and blend into soup, being careful not to curdle. Season to taste and serve with croutons or slices of hard-cooked egg. Serves 6.

36. DRIED MUSHROOM SOUP (*Zupa Grzybowa Czysta*)

½ oz. dried mushrooms	7 cups water
2 med. onions	1 tbs. browned flour (see general directions)
1 leek	
2 stalks celery	1 tbs. butter
2 carrots	salt and pepper to taste
1 parsnip or celery root	

Simmer mushrooms and vegetables until thoroughly done, about an hour. Cut mushrooms into thin strips and return to pot. Thicken soup with paste made of browned flour and butter, blend well, and season to taste. Flat noodles or macaroni may be added (see Index). Serves 6.

37. DRIED MUSHROOM AND SOUR CREAM SOUP
(*Zupa Grzybowa ze Śmietaną*)

Cook the same as Dried Mushroom Soup, omitting butter and browned flour. Instead of these, add:

¾–1 cup sour cream, depending on
     taste
1 tbs. white flour

¼ cup barley, cooked separately
     (see Index)

Combine barley, sour cream, and flour, and stir into the mushroom broth. Heat thoroughly, allow to bubble up, and serve. Serves 6.

38. CARAWAY AND SOUR CREAM SOUP
(Zupa Kminkowa ze Śmietaną)

1 med. onion
2 carrots
1 celery root or 1 parsnip
1 celery stalk
2 leeks

1 heaping tbs. caraway seed
5–6 cups water
1 cup sour cream
1 tbs. flour
salt and pepper to taste

Simmer vegetables and caraway seed until vegetables are tender, about 45 minutes. Put through sieve, using stock to dilute. Return to soup pot, blend in sour cream and flour, and heat until the soup bubbles. Serves 6.

39. BEER SOUP *(Zupa Piwna)*

3 pts. beer
1 pt. sour cream
2 tsp. flour

½ lb. farmer cheese or pot cheese
sugar to taste (optional)

Heat the beer, tightly covered. Blend flour into sour cream and stir into beer. Let bubble up once and pour over farmer cheese cut into small pieces or over lumps of pot cheese. Sweeten to taste. Serve at once. Serves 6 to 8.

40. BEER SOUP WITH EGG *(Zupa Piwna)*

3 pts. beer
6 egg yolks

1 tbs. sugar

Cream raw egg yolks and sugar. Bring beer, tightly covered, to a boil. Dilute egg mixture with a few spoonfuls of hot liquid, a little at a time, and then pour the rest of the beer over the eggs, stirring vigorously or using rotary egg beater to avoid curdling. Serve at once. Serves 6.

41. WINE SOUP *(Polewka z Wina)*

1 cup water
6 cloves
1 stick cinnamon

2 cups white table wine
2–3 egg yolks (depending on size)
sugar, 1 tbs. to each egg yolk

Boil water with cloves and cinnamon, covered, for 15 minutes. Add wine, and bring to boil and strain. Combine egg yolks and sugar, and cream thoroughly. Place on asbestos over low heat and slowly add the boiling wine mixture, beating constantly with whisk or rotary beater until foamy and thick, taking care not to let eggs curdle. Serve in cups with dry biscuits or Melba toast. Serves 3 to 4.

42. ALMOND SOUP *(Zupa Migdałowa)*

½ lb. sweet almonds	sugar to taste
10 bitter almonds	½ cup rice, cooked separately
7 cups milk	2 tbs. seedless raisins

Blanch and peel almonds. Grind or chop them and then mash to a paste with a little milk. Put through fine sieve, using hot milk to help with the process. Scald remaining milk, combine with almond paste, and stir thoroughly. Add sugar to taste and let bubble up once. Add cooked rice and raisins, and serve at once. Serves 8.

43. MILK SOUP WITH HOMEMADE NOODLES AND DUMPLINGS
(Zacierki, Kluski Kładzione, Lane Ciasto na Mleky)

Make noodles according to Recipe No. 1 or 2 under Garnishes. Scald milk in proportion of 1 cup per serving. Add noodles, cover, and let simmer until noodles rise to the top. Salt sparingly and serve at once, before crust forms. For added taste and nourishment, add small pat of butter per serving.

Cold Summer Soups

44. "NOTHING" SOUP *(Zupa Nic)*

6 cups milk	5 eggs, separated
2″ piece vanilla bean	6 tbs. sugar

Scald milk and vanilla bean; cool, and then discard the bean. Cream egg yolks and sugar, reserving egg whites. When egg yolks look almost white, place over low heat, preferably in double boiler, and beat vigorously with whisk or rotary beater while slowly adding cooled milk.

Cool in refrigerator until ready to serve. Top with "Kisses" made with the egg whites (see Index). Serves 6.

45. CLEAR BERRY SOUP *(Zupa Jagodowa Czysta)*

1 qt. blueberries (huckleberries or blackberries may be substituted)	1½ qts. water sugar to taste 1 tbs. potato flour

Clean berries and bring to a boil. When fruit is soft—about 10 or 15 minutes—press through a sieve and then return to liquid. Add sugar to taste and the potato flour dissolved in cold water. Stir thoroughly. Serve hot or iced. Serves 6.

46. BERRY SOUP WITH SOUR CREAM
(Zupa Jagodowa ze Śmietaną)

Proceed as for Clear Berry Soup, dissolving flour in 1 to 2 cups sour cream instead of cold water. Add to fruit liquid, boil up once, and serve hot. Do not boil if soup is to be served cold. Serves 7 to 8.

47. RASPBERRY AND STRAWBERRY SOUP
(Zupa Malinowa z Poziomkami)

1 pt. raspberries	sugar to taste
1 pt. garden or wild strawberries	1 tbs. potato flour or cornstarch
3 pts. water	

Clean berries. Bring raspberries to a boil and simmer about 10 minutes. Pass through sieve, together with cleaned and hulled raw strawberries. Return to liquid. Dissolve potato flour in a little cold water, stir into soup, add sugar to taste, and serve hot or iced. Serves 6.

As a variation, add 1 cup sour cream, following recipe for Berry Soup with Sour Cream, No. 46.

48. STRAWBERRY SOUP WITH WINE
(Zupa Poziomkowa z Winem)

4 cups fresh strawberries	juice of half a lemon
5 cups water	dash of grated lemon rind
1 cup dry white wine	½ cup sugar

Wash and hull berries. Reserve one cup, and press the rest through a sieve, pouring water over them a little at a time to facilitate the process. Add lemon juice, lemon rind, wine, and sugar to taste. Add reserved whole berries, chill, and serve. Serves 6.

49. PLUM OR APRICOT SOUP
(Zupa ze Śliwek lub Moreli)

fruit in proportion of 1 cup to
1¼ cups water
sugar to taste
dash of lemon juice

dash of lemon rind
1 tbs. potato flour
sour cream for topping (optional)

Cook fruit until thoroughly done (20 minutes to half an hour). Discard pits and put fruit through sieve. Fruit may be pitted raw for easier handling, but the taste will be less subtle. Combine fruit pulp, sugar, lemon juice and rind, and potato flour with the water in which fruit has boiled. Serve hot or cold, with buttered croutons.

If sour cream is added, allow ⅛ cup for each two servings.

This basic recipe may be used for other fruit, or several different kinds in combination. Cherries, apples, and pears are all suitable. A winter variation is hot fruit soup made of soaked dried fruit. Prunes or apricots, thoroughly cooked and puréed and thickened with cornstarch, are especially good. Use the same basic proportions as in other fruit soups. Serve hot with croutons.

50. SWEET-AND-SOUR BEER SOUP (Kalteszal)

3 pts. beer
1 cup sugar, or less, to taste
4 egg yolks
juice of 2 lemons

grated rind of 1 lemon
2″ stick cinnamon
1 jigger rum
2 tbs. seedless raisins

Beat egg yolks and half the sugar until very light. Add lemon juice and rind. Bring beer to a boil, covered, with cinnamon and the rest of the sugar. Let cool slightly. Then place in double boiler over boiling water and stir in eggs, stirring constantly. Add rum and raisins and chill. Serve with croutons. Serves 6.

51. LITHUANIAN SOUP (Chłodnik Litewski)

3 pts. clabber (buttermilk may be substituted)
1 pt. light sour cream
1 cup dill pickle juice or cold beet juice
2 cups young beet tops, diced and steamed
2 cucumbers, peeled, sliced thin, and allowed to stand

in 2 tbs. salt for two hours
3–4 tbs. chopped fresh dill
3–4 hard-cooked eggs
12–15 crayfish tails (see Index), or equal amount of cooked, peeled shrimp
1″ slice of cold roast veal, diced
salt and pepper to taste

Have all ingredients thoroughly chilled. When preparing cucumbers, place in mixing bowl, mix the salt in thoroughly, and press down with a saucer on which some other weight can conveniently rest. When ready for use, discard salty cucumber juice. Beat clabber and sour cream together until bubbly. Add pickle or beet juice, beet tops, cucumber, and dill. Mix thoroughly. Add more salt if necessary, and fresh-ground pepper to taste. Peel and slice eggs, and add these, as well as diced meat and crayfish. Serve each portion over a piece of ice. Makes 8 generous servings, and a complete summer meal.

52. COLD MEAT SOUP *(Chłodnik Gotowany)*

6-8 cups light soup stock made with bones and meat scraps (see Index)

2 cups fermented rye, pickled beet, or dill pickle juice (approx.)

1-2 cups light sour cream

2 tbs. flour

2 cups diced, steamed, young beet tops

1 cooked beet (canned beet and juice may be used)

3-4 tbs. chopped fresh dill

3-4 hard-cooked eggs

12-15 crayfish tails (see Index), or equal amount cooked, peeled shrimp

1" slice cold roast veal, diced

2 cucumbers, peeled and marinated as in recipe for Lithuanian Soup

Have all ingredients thoroughly chilled. Combine all except the beet. Use enough juice to give a winey taste. Grate cooked beet and add to soup for a light pink color. Season to taste and serve each portion over a piece of ice. Makes 10 to 12 generous servings.

53. RUSSIAN RYE SOUP *(Ochroszka)*

3 cups fermented rye *barszcz* (see Index)

1 cup light sour cream sugar and salt to taste

1 tsp. dry mustard

1 tbs. flour

2-3 tbs. chopped fresh dill

2-3 hard-cooked eggs

10-12 crayfish tails (see Index) or equivalent amount cooked, peeled shrimp

½" slice cold roast pork or ham

1 cucumber, sliced and marinated in salt for two hours

Have all ingredients thoroughly chilled. Combine as above, making sure that the mustard and flour are thoroughly blended into the liquid before adding eggs, fish, and meat. Add sugar and salt for a sweet-sour taste. Serve over ice. Serves 4.

Soup Garnishes

1. BATTER NOODLES (*Lane Ciasto*)

2 whole eggs   4 tbs. flour

Beat eggs, and add flour gradually to make a smooth batter just thick enough to pour from spoon like a heavy rope. Pour into simmering soup and let cook 2 to 3 minutes. Makes 6 servings.

2. FRENCH DUMPLINGS (*Kluski Francuskie*)

1 tbs. salt butter   1 tbs. flour
2 eggs, separated

Cream butter and egg yolks until very light. Fold in beaten egg whites and the flour. To avoid unnecessary stirring, the flour is best shaken in through a strainer. Mix lightly. Test batter by dropping a small blob into the simmering soup; if it dissolves, add another teaspoon of flour. (The exact amount of flour is determined by the size of the eggs.) Drop into soup from a demitasse spoon, dipping the spoon in soup each time to avoid sticking. Cover the pot and steam 2 to 3 minutes. Makes 6 servings.

3. LIVER DUMPLINGS (*Kluski Wątrobiane*)

1 tbs. salt butter   2 tbs. cracker meal or finely
2 eggs, separated   ground bread crumbs
2 tbs. ground chicken or calf's
liver

Cream egg yolks and butter until very light. Add raw liver and mix to smooth paste. Add cracker crumbs, fold in beaten egg white, and stir lightly. Proceed as for French Dumplings. Serves 6.

4. MUSHROOM DUMPLINGS (*Kluski z Grzybami*)

Proceed as for Liver Dumplings, substituting 2 tbs. cooked chopped mushrooms for the liver.

5. ROYAL DUMPLINGS FOR CONSOMMÉ
(Kluski "Royal")

3 eggs
1 cup light cream

2 tbs. grated Parmesan
butter and flour for molding

Beat the whole eggs and cream to a light froth. Fold in the cheese, and pour into mold which has been greased and dusted with flour. Steam, tightly covered, over boiling water for 30 minutes. Test with straw to determine whether it is done—when inserted into the center, straw should come out dry. Cool, unmold, and cut into strips. Add to soup.

6. SUET OR MARROW BALLS
(Pulpety z Łoju lub Szpiku)

¼ lb. beef suet or marrow, or a
  mixture of both
2 eggs, separated
  salt and pepper to taste
2 tbs. cracker meal or bread
  crumbs

1 tbs. chopped fresh dill or parsley
  (optional)
flour for rolling

Put the suet or marrow through meat grinder, and cream with egg yolks, salt, and pepper. Add cracker meal and fold in beaten egg whites. Knead lightly with hands, and shape into small balls, the size of a quarter in diameter. Roll in flour and cook in boiling water or in the soup pot for about 30 minutes. The marrow balls are done when they rise to the surface. Serve with soup or with tripe.

7. MEAT CROQUETTES (Pulpety z Mięsa)

¼ lb. meat (beef, pork, veal, or
  venison)
1–2 tbs. marrow and/or suet
1 stale roll, moistened in milk

2 eggs
salt and pepper to taste
flour for rolling

Put meat, marrow, and roll through meat grinder. Add beaten whole eggs and seasoning, and stir thoroughly. Roll in flour. Proceed as for Marrow Balls, No. 6.

8. CROQUETTES FROM LEFTOVER VEAL
(Pulpety z Pieczeni Cielęcej)

1 cup leftover lean meat
1 stale white roll, moistened
  with milk
3–4 fresh mushrooms, chopped
½ small onion, chopped

2 tbs. butter
2 eggs
1 tsp. chopped parsley
  salt and pepper to taste
flour for rolling

Put meat and roll through meat grinder. Sauté mushrooms and onion in some of the butter until golden brown. Add to meat. Add egg yolks which have been creamed with remaining butter, parsley, and seasoning. Fold in beaten egg whites. Proceed as for Marrow Balls, No. 6.

9. CALF'S BRAIN CROQUETTES *(Pulpety z Mózgu)*

1 set of calf brains	1 tbs. butter
1 med. onion	salt and pepper to taste
1 bay leaf	dash of fresh-ground nutmeg
6 peppercorns	2 tsp. chopped fresh parsley, or
½ lemon	parsley and dill mixed
4-5 mushrooms, chopped	4 tbs. bread crumbs
½ small onion, chopped	flour for rolling
2 eggs	

Parboil brains with onion, bay leaf, peppercorns, and lemon for about 10 minutes. Drain, remove membranes, and mash with a fork. Sauté onion in butter until golden brown; add mushrooms and sauté 5 minutes longer. Add to brains. Add eggs, lightly beaten, bread crumbs, chopped parsley, and nutmeg. Mix thoroughly, season to taste, and shape into small croquettes or round balls. Roll in flour, and cook in salted boiling water or soup stock for 30 minutes, or until croquettes rise to the surface. Serve as garnish with consommé, or with a White Sauce as a luncheon dish. Serves 6 as garnish; 2 as main dish.

10. FISH QUENELLES *(Knelki z Ryb)*

1 cup cooked fish, leftovers or freshly boiled (see Index)	1 tbs. butter
4 tbs. bread crumbs	dash of nutmeg
2 eggs	salt and pepper to taste
	flour for rolling

Carefully remove all fish bones. Mash the fish meat, add bread crumbs, season with salt and pepper and nutmeg. Cream egg yolks and butter to a light color, add to fish mixture, and mix thoroughly. Fold in beaten egg whites and shape into croquettes, making tiny ones if they are to be used in soup, larger ones if to be served as main dish. Roll in flour and cook in boiling water or soup stock for 30 minutes, or until they rise to the surface. Serves 6 as soup garnish; serves 2 as main dish.

11. VEAL OR CHICKEN QUENELLES
(Knelki z Cielęciny lub Drobiu)

½ lb. raw veal or breast of chicken without skin	1 soft white roll or equivalent in white bread, moistened in milk

salt and pepper to taste   1 cup heavy cream
dash of nutmeg (optional)

Chop the meat raw; then force through sieve together with roll.
Season to taste, being careful not to over-season since the meat has
a delicate taste. Place in deep bowl and pour in the cream, a little
at a time, beating vigorously with a whisk. When thoroughly
blended and stiff, drop by teaspoonfuls into boiling water. Reduce
heat to a gentle boil and allow 30 minutes cooking time. Handle
carefully when done, using a strainer spoon. Serve at once. Used
as garnish for special-occasion soup or with meat ragout.

12. CROUTONS *(Grzanki)*

stale bread or rolls   1–2 tbs. butter

Melt butter in skillet. Cut bread into thin slices, cube, and mix with
the melted butter. Place in medium oven until dry and golden
brown (about 20 to 30 minutes), taking care not to burn. Thinly-
sliced black pumpernickel is an excellent variation. May be stored
and reheated.

13. CHEESE CROUTONS *(Diablotki)*

1 tbs. butter   dash of paprika
2 egg yolks   2" squares of thinly sliced bread
2 tbs. grated Parmesan

Cream egg yolks and butter. Combine with grated cheese and
spread thickly on the bread slices. Arrange on cooky sheet, sprinkle
with paprika, and place in hot oven for 5 minutes directly before
they are to be served. Other cheeses may be substituted. French
bread, "hero" rolls, and the thinly sliced icebox ryes are especially
good for this.

14. GRATED DOUGH *(Zacierki)*

1 cup unsifted flour   1 egg

This dough is best when made with egg alone, but may also be
made with water. Break whole egg into bowl, beat lightly, and add
flour. If too dry to work, add cold water, a little at a time. Turn
onto floured board, roll in flour, and knead lightly. The dough
should be so dry that after kneading, it may be grated on a coarse
grater or chopped to the consistency of rice. Do not handle until
gratings are dry. Use in proportions of ½ cup to 8 cups of soup,
storing the rest in refrigerator for future use. Sprinkle into soup
during last 5 minutes of cooking time.

15. STUFFED EGGS *(Jajka Faszerowane)*

1 hard-cooked egg per person chopped chives, parsley, or dill, or a combination of these, ½ tsp. per egg	salt and pepper to taste butter for cooking bread crumbs

Run cold water over hard-cooked eggs to facilitate handling. With a very sharp knife, slice each *unpeeled* egg in half lengthwise, being careful not to crush the shell. Extract both yolks and whites; chop fine, adding the herbs and seasoning, and brown lightly in butter, allowing about 1 tsp. per egg. Return to shells and sprinkle with bread crumbs. Place in skillet, shell side up, and brown another minute, so that the bread crumbs will be a golden brown. Serve hot as a side dish.

16. MEAT POCKETS FOR *BARSZCZ (Uszka do Barszczu)*

Dough:
2 cups flour
1 large or 2 small eggs
few teaspoons water
Filling:
2 cups leftover beef or veal with all fat removed

1 hard roll, moistened in milk
salt and pepper to taste
2 tsp. fresh-chopped herbs (optional)
1 small or ½ med. onion, chopped and browned in butter
1 tbs. butter

Make dough, mixing flour, eggs, and water together well. Work until firm. Roll into a very thin sheet. Cut into 3-inch squares. Put meat and roll through meat grinder, season with salt and pepper, and add herbs if desired. Mix well and cook with the browned onion for 3 to 5 minutes. Place a teaspoon of this mixture on each dough square. Fold over into a triangle and press sides firmly together. Cook in large amount of boiling salted water 20 to 30 minutes. They are done when they float to the surface.

17. MUSHROOM POCKETS *(Uszka Postne)*

Make dough as for Meat Pockets. Fill as follows:

Filling:
¼ lb. fresh mushrooms, chopped fine (if soup was made with dried mushrooms, utilize these)
1 small or ½ med. onion, chopped fine

1 tbs. butter
2 tbs. bread crumbs
salt and pepper

Sauté all ingredients together until mushrooms are done and the onions a golden brown, taking care not to burn (about 15 minutes). Proceed as for Meat Pockets, No. 16.

18. KISSES TO GARNISH "NOTHING" SOUP
(Pianki do Zupy "Nic")

5 egg whites   5 heaping tbs. sugar

Beat egg whites until stiff enough to cut. Add sugar (less sugar than recipe calls for, for those who do not have a sweet tooth), stir, and beat again. Arrange by spoonfuls on cooky sheet greased with olive oil. Bake in slow oven until crisp on top (30 to 40 minutes). Do not allow to brown. These kisses are best prepared a day in advance or in the morning, to let them dry out. Serve separately with "Nothing" Soup.

A timesaving variation is to beat the egg whites and sugar and float uncooked in the soup, in which case the preparation should be left until the last minute.

Meat Pastries, Pâtés, Dumplings, and Croquettes

The preparation of meat for pâtés and pastry fillings is most successful when three simple rules are followed:

1. The meat should be thoroughly cooked and tender, but never browned while cooking or the pastry filling will be dry, hard, and too dark.
2. It should be put through a meat grinder at least twice, then preferably pounded or forced through a sieve. To facilitate the process add bacon drippings, a bit of chopped salt pork, or chicken fat. (Beef suet is least tasty.) Have meat and fat at room temperature, since they will be easier to handle than when taken straight from a refrigerator.
3. Pâtés may be baked in the oven, but are best steamed. Baking dries and toughens them somewhat. Doneness should be tested by inserting a straw: if straw comes out dry, the pâté is done. Unmold when cool.

1. FRENCH PASTRY DOUGH FOR SHELLS

3 cups sifted flour	1 cup water
1 egg	2 tsp. white vinegar
¼ tsp. salt	1 lb. unsalted butter

In a mixing bowl combine flour with lightly beaten egg, salt, water, and vinegar, and knead until dough no longer sticks to the hands. Cover and let stand half an hour.

Flatten the butter, which should be very cold, between two sheets of wax paper into a square about ½ inch thick. Roll the dough into a piece a little more than twice the size of the butter. Place butter on the dough, fold dough over to form an envelope, and press edges together. Roll this out very thin, fold in three, and let stand about 10 minutes. Fold three more times and roll again (nine layers in all) to thickness of a finger. For best results always roll in one direction, away from the body, and work if possible in a cool room.

When bubbles begin to form in the dough, it has been sufficiently rolled. Let stand another 15 minutes. Cut out pastry shells with pastry cutter as follows: Cut four rounds for each finished shell. One round should be left whole for the bottom layer. Using a smaller cutter, hollow out the centers of the remaining three. Pile these three rounds, one after another, on the bottom one, spreading each with raw egg white, and then brushing the outside with egg white to make the whole thing stick together. Brush the tops of the center cutouts with egg white too, and use them for covers. Bake in medium-hot oven for 15 to 20 minutes until a golden brown. Any remaining tops (there will be two left over from each completed pastry) may be served instead of croutons with soups or hors d'oeuvres.

2. FRENCH PUFF PASTRY *(Modernized Recipe)*

½ cup butter (1 bar)	¼ tsp. salt
¾ cup *sifted* flour	¼ cup ice water

Slice bar of butter in three parts lengthwise. Wrap in foil and store in refrigerator until ready to use. Sift flour and salt together. Stir in water with a fork, and then knead until dough is smooth and satiny. Roll dough into a neat rectangle about 6 by 11 inches on a floured board. Put the three slices of butter on one half of the rectangle, leaving a half-inch margin all around. Fold the second half of dough over butter and press edges together. Wrap in foil and refrigerate 30 minutes. Remove from refrigerator and unwrap on floured board. Bang top half of dough with a rolling pin several times to flatten. Be sure that dough is placed in a different direction from the way you rolled it last time (turned ¼ way round). Roll out dough to a rectangle 6 inches wide and 18 inches long. Fold over from each end, making a square. Wrap and refrigerate again for 30 minutes. Repeat this operation five times. Each rolling and folding is called a turn. Shape pastry shells and bake the same as French Pastry Dough.

3. SEMI-FRENCH PASTRY DOUGH
(Ciasto Pół Francuskie)

1 ounce yeast	¼ teaspoon salt
1 cup lukewarm milk	3 egg yolks and 1 whole egg
4 cups *sifted* flour	½ lb. butter

Dissolve yeast in milk. Add flour, salt, the well-beaten eggs, and continue mixing until bubbles appear. Cover and let stand in a warm spot until dough rises. Set aside to cool. Roll out the dough and the butter and proceed as for French Pastry Dough.

4. BUTTER DOUGH (Ciasto Maślane)

4 cups sifted flour	2–3 tbs. sour cream or water
½ lb. butter	¼ tsp. salt
2 eggs	

Work all the ingredients to a dough. (Start with 2 tbs. of liquid and add more if dough is very dry.) Roll out into a square on a pastry board, fold again, and continue rolling and folding as for French Pastry Dough. This dough is used for most meat pastries and pies.

5. PASTRY DOUGH (Ciasto Kruche)

2 cups sifted flour	¼ tsp. salt (optional) *
¼ lb. butter (preferably unsalted)	2 tbs. sugar and dash of lemon
1 egg yolk	rind (optional) *

Work butter into flour with pastry cutter. Add egg yolk, and work with fingers until thoroughly blended (longer if patience permits). Let stand in a cool spot for half an hour. Roll out thin for pastries or pies, or use to line large pastry forms.

* Depending on whether dough is to be used for meat or dessert pastry. Add salt for a meat pastry; sugar and a dash of lemon rind for a dessert.

6. YEAST DOUGH FOR RUSSIAN PIROGEN (Ciasto Drożdżowe do Pierogów)

½ oz. yeast	½ tbs. sugar
1 cup lukewarm milk	¼ tsp. salt
4 cups flour	1 tbs. melted butter
2 egg yolks and 1 whole egg	beaten egg for brushing

Dissolve yeast in milk, and combine with flour. When dough begins to rise, add the beaten eggs, sugar, salt, and melted butter, and work with fingers until the dough no longer sticks to the hands. Cover and let stand in a warm spot. When dough rises and the surface begins to crack, roll out on a floured pastry board to half-inch thickness. Fill with meat and hard-cooked eggs, or with cooked cabbage (see Index). Fold over and press edges firmly together to form one large cake. For individual pastries, cut dough into small strips, fill and press individually. Place on greased, floured pastry pan and let stand in a warm spot for half an hour longer to let dough rise again. Brush with beaten egg and bake in a hot oven (450°) until golden brown (30 to 45 minutes).

7. RUSSIAN PASTRY WITH MEAT
(Pieróg Ruski z Mięsem)

French, Semi-French, or Yeast
Dough (see Index)
Filling:
2 cups leftover boiled or roast
  meat (preferably beef, with
  addition of a small piece of
  pork)

1 stale roll, moistened with milk
½ med. onion, minced
1 tbs. butter
2 hard-cooked eggs, coarsely
  chopped
  salt and pepper to taste
1 raw egg yolk

Chop meat or put it through meat grinder together with the roll.
Brown the onion lightly in butter, and then add meat and bread,
chopped hard-cooked eggs, salt and pepper. Continue browning
lightly, stirring constantly to avoid sticking and scorching. When
cool, blend in the raw egg yolk and use as filling for pastry, as
follows:

Roll out the dough on a floured pastry board to half-inch thickness.
Spread half with the filling, fold over, and press edges firmly together. Let stand in a warm place for half an hour to rise. Before
baking, brush top with beaten egg. Bake in a hot oven (450°) for
30 to 45 minutes, testing with straw. Serve with clear consommé
or clear beet soup. (Small individual pastries may be formed in
the same way, in which case the dough should be rolled out thinner.)

8. CABBAGE PASTRY (Pieróg Ruski ze Słodką Kapustą)

French, Semi-French, or Yeast
Dough (see Index)
Filling:
2 cups shredded cabbage, parboiled in salted water (measure after cooking)
½ tsp. sugar

1 tbs. butter
1 med. onion, minced
1 tbs. cooked, chopped dried
  mushrooms
2 hard-cooked eggs, chopped
  (optional)
  salt and pepper to taste

Drain the cabbage thoroughly and chop fine. Add sugar, the onion
browned lightly in butter, the cooked chopped mushrooms (fresh
mushrooms may be substituted, in which case the amount can be
increased since the flavor is much less pronounced) and hard-
cooked, coarsely-chopped eggs. Add salt and pepper, mix thoroughly, and proceed as for meat pastry. (Eggs may also be used as
a substitute for the mushrooms.)

9. MEAT PATTIES (Paszteciki w Francuskiem Cieście)

Pastry Shells: see Index or buy prepared pastry shells.

Filling:
½ lb. leftover veal

½ lb. leftover pork
2 generous tbs. bread crumbs
½ med. onion, minced

2 tbs. butter
1 egg yolk
2 tbs. sweet cream

Chop meat fine or put through grinder. Season to taste and mix well with bread crumbs. Simmer minced onion in butter until a light golden-brown; add meat and bread crumbs and brown very lightly. Allow to cool, and then add raw egg yolk and cream, and mix thoroughly to a paste. Fill the shells.

10. CALF'S BRAIN PATTIES *(Paszteciki z Mózgu)*

Pastry Shells: see Index or buy pre-
  pared pastry shells.
Filling:
1 set of calf brains
1 onion
1 bay leaf
½ lemon
1 stalk celery
  salt and pepper to taste

½ med. onion, minced
1 tbs. butter
½ tbs. flour
2–3 tbs. soup stock
  salt, pepper, and lemon juice
2 egg yolks
1 tbs. chopped fresh dill (op-
  tional)

Parboil brains in salted water to which the onion, bay leaf, lemon, celery, salt, and pepper have been added. (Always start brains in boiling water and allow 5 to 10 minutes after water starts boiling again.) Drain, remove membranes, and chop or mash with fork. Sauté minced onion in butter until transparent but not brown. Sprinkle in flour, blend, add soup stock, and blend again. Season to taste with salt, fresh-ground pepper, and lemon juice. When cool, blend with raw egg yolks and brains. Chopped fresh dill may be added for extra flavor. Put into heated pastry shells.

Serve with clear consommé or beet soup, as hors d'oeuvres or a luncheon snack.

11. PATTIES *À LA REINE (Paszteciki Królewskie)*

Pastry Shells: see Index or buy pre-
  pared patty shells.
Filling:
  meat from 1 raw chicken
  salt and pepper to taste
2–3 tbs. butter

6 fresh mushrooms (truffles if
  available)
  lemon juice to taste
¼ cup white wine
2 egg yolks

Bone the chicken and remove all skin. Chop meat fine or put through grinder, and season to taste. Sauté in butter together with chopped mushrooms for about 15 minutes. Add lemon juice to taste. Add wine, mix thoroughly, and let cool just enough so that the beaten egg yolks may be added without curdling. Blend again thoroughly and put into heated pastry shells or fried pastries (see Index). Serve with clear soups or as hors d'oeuvres or side dish.

12. CRAYFISH PATTIES *(Pasxteciki z Raków)*

French Pastry Shells (see Index)
Filling:
  30 crayfish (shrimp may be sub-
    stituted)
  1 bunch fresh dill
  2 tbs. butter

½ tbs. flour
2–3 tbs. soup stock
1 tbs. each of chopped fresh
  parsley and dill
2 egg yolks
salt and pepper to taste

Cook crayfish in boiling salted water with the dill, reserving enough dill for chopping. Clean crayfish and chop the shells. Then simmer in butter, following directions under Crayfish Soup (see Index for this and the Crayfish Butter in the next step). Brown the flour lightly in the Crayfish Butter. Dissolve with soup stock, add chopped crayfish meat, dill, and parsley. Let cool slightly, add beaten egg yolks, season to taste, and mix thoroughly. Fill pastry shells. May be used as filling for baked pastries.

13. MUSHROOM PATTIES *(Pasxteciki z Grzybów)*

French Pastry Shells
Filling:
  ½ lb. fresh mushrooms
  1 med. onion, minced
  salt and pepper to taste

1 tbs. butter
½ tbs. flour
2–3 tbs. sour cream
2 egg yolks

Slice mushrooms very thin, season, and simmer with onion, tightly covered, until transparent. Add butter, and when this has melted and been absorbed, dust with flour. Add sour cream and blend thoroughly. Cool slightly and then beat in the egg yolks. Use as filling for French Pastry Shells or in baked pastries. Serve with clear soups.

14. FISH PATTIES *(Pasxteciki Z Ryb)*

3–4 French Pastry Shells or French
  Puff pastry (see Index)
Filling:
  ½ lb. raw boned fish, coarsely
  chopped
  1 med. onion, grated
  1 tbs. butter

½ stale white roll or equivalent
  amount in bread crumbs,
  moistened with milk
salt and pepper to taste
dash of nutmeg
1 tbs. fish or vegetable stock
2 egg yolks, slightly beaten

Sauté onion in butter until a light golden-brown. Add chopped fish, roll or bread crumbs, seasoning, and stock. Simmer, tightly covered, for 15 to 20 minutes. Add beaten egg yolks, mix thoroughly, and fill pastry shells. Serve at once, as a luncheon dish or as garnish for fish soup. Serves 3 to 4 as entree. For garnish, use small patties or puffs.

15. PANCAKES WITH MEAT OR CALF'S BRAIN FILLING (*Naleśniki z Mięsem Albo Mózgiem*)

Pancake Batter: see Index.
1 beaten egg
½ cup bread crumbs
  butter for frying
  bunch of fresh parsley

Filling:
  Same as for Meat or Calf's Brain
  Patties (see Index), plus
2 tbs. sour cream

Add sour cream to other ingredients for a thinner filling than required for patties. Make pancakes with very thin batter, spread with filling, fold in edges of each cake to form a square; then fold square twice to form an oblong. Dip in beaten egg, roll in bread crumbs, and fry in butter until golden brown. Garnish with sprigs of fried parsley. Serve with clear soups or as a side dish.

16. DEEP-FRIED PATTIES (*Pierożki Smażone*)

Filling: same as for Russian Meat
  Pastry (see Index).
Dough:
  1 cup lukewarm milk
  ½ oz. yeast
  4 cups flour

2 eggs
½ tsp. salt
1 tbs. melted butter
1 tsp. sugar
  deep fat for frying

Dissolve the yeast in the milk, add 2 cups of flour, mix thoroughly, and let stand in a warm place until dough rises. Add remaining 2 cups of flour, the eggs, slightly beaten, salt, sugar, and melted butter, and knead until the dough no longer sticks to fingers. Let rise again. Roll small balls of dough in flour and then flatten out. Place a spoonful of filling on each, and press edges firmly together to form a pocket. Let stand another half-hour if possible. Then fry in deep fat, turning to brown evenly.

17. POTATO CROQUETTES (*Krokiety Kartoflane*)

2 large or 3 med. potatoes
  soup stock
2 eggs
4 tbs. bread crumbs
1 med. or ½ large onion, minced
  and browned in butter

1 tbs. butter
  bread crumbs for rolling
  more butter for frying
  few sprigs of parsley
  salt to taste

Cook potatoes in soup stock (water will do), put through a sieve, add beaten eggs, bread crumbs, and the onion. Mix thoroughly. Season to taste and then fry lightly in 1 tbs. of butter. When cool enough to handle, shape into croquettes not more than 3 inches long, roll in bread crumbs, and fry in butter. Garnish with fried parsley sprigs. Serve with clear soups or as a side dish.

Ramekin Patties
(Paszteciki w Muszelkach)

Ramekin dishes have the advantage that they may be prepared well in advance, stored in the refrigerator, and browned or heated at the last minute before serving. Scallop shells make an attractive and inexpensive substitute for ramekins.

18. CALF'S BRAIN PÂTÉ (Paszteciki z Mózgu)

1 set of calf brains	½ onion, minced
1 small onion	2 tbs. butter
1 bay leaf	1 tbs. flour
6 peppercorns	2–3 tbs. soup stock
1 carrot	¼ cup sour cream
1 celery stalk	2 egg yolks (optional)
1 lemon (approx.)	salt and pepper to taste
salt to taste	bread crumbs to cover

Start brains in boiling salted water to which the onion, bay leaf, peppercorns, carrot, celery, and half the lemon have been added. Cook about 10 to 15 minutes, counting from the time when water boils again. Drain, remove membranes, and dice the brains. Sauté minced onion in half the butter, add flour, and blend in soup stock. When smooth, add the sour cream, lemon juice to taste, and a little grated lemon rind. Add the diced brains, and the egg yolks if desired. Mix thoroughly, season to taste with salt and pepper, and sauté in remaining butter until cooked through. Fill the ramekins with the mixture, sprinkle with bread crumbs, brush with butter, and set in oven or under the broiler until brown on top. Serves 4 as a side dish, 2 as an entree.

19. PÂTÉ OF LEFTOVER POULTRY OR VEAL ROAST
(Paszteciki z Drobiu lub Cielęciny)

2 cups leftover meat, diced	grated Parmesan cheese (½ tbs.
½ cup Béchamel Sauce (see Index)	per serving)
salt and pepper to taste	2 tbs. melted butter

Mix the meat and sauce, season to taste, and fill ramekins with the mixture. Sprinkle with Parmesan cheese and melted butter, and bake in hot oven for 15 minutes. Serves 4.

20. SPINACH POCKETS *(Paszteciki ze Szpinakiem)*

Dough: the same as No. 16 in Soup
   Garnishes
Filling:
   ½ pkg. frozen chopped spinach
   (2 cups fresh spinach)

3 tbs. butter
1 tbs. flour
salt and pepper to taste
2 tbs. bread crumbs

Simmer spinach in very little water until tender, about 15 minutes Put through sieve. Melt 1 tbs. butter, add flour, stir until smooth, add the spinach, and season with salt and pepper. Cook together for another 5 minutes, or until flour has thickened. Roll the dough out very thin. Place the spinach by the spoonful on one sheet of dough. Then cover with a second sheet and, using a glass or pastry cutter, cut out the spinach pockets, taking care that their edges are pressed tightly together. Cook in boiling salted water until the pockets float to the top. Place each on a scallop shell, sprinkle with the bread crumbs browned in the rest of the butter, and set in oven or under a medium-hot broiler for 5 minutes.

21. MEATLESS OR LENTEN PATTIES *(Paszteciki Postne)*

3 tbs. butter
¼ med. onion, minced
1½ ozs. dried mushrooms, cooked in
   very little water and chopped
¼ lb. fish roe (any roe may be
   used, as well as the milts),
   chopped

4 tbs. bread crumbs
2 tbs. sour cream
2 egg yolks
salt and pepper to taste

Cook onion in half the butter until golden brown. Add the fish roe, mushrooms, 2 tbs. bread crumbs, and season to taste. Sauté about 10 minutes, taking care mixture does not stick to pan. Add sour cream and blend well. Add beaten egg yolks and then fill greased scallop shells with this mixture. Brown remaining bread crumbs and butter. Sprinkle on top. Bake or broil for 5 minutes. Serves 4.

22. ROE AND MILT PATTIES
(Paszteciki z Mleczka i Ikry)

¼ lb. of roe, milt, and fish livers
   mixed
vegetable soup stock to cover
¼ med. onion, minced
3 tbs. butter

1 tbs. flour
¼ cup sour cream
salt and pepper to taste
2 tbs. bread crumbs

Cook the roe and other fish parts in soup stock for about 10 minutes. Dice or chop coarsely. Simmer the chopped onion in 1 tbs. butter until transparent. Blend in flour, add 2 to 3 tbs. stock, and blend until smooth. Add sour cream, and season sauce to taste. Add fish, mix thoroughly, and fill the shells with the mixture. Brown bread crumbs in remaining butter, sprinkle over the top, and bake in hot oven for 10 minutes. Serves 2 to 3.

23. LEFTOVER FISH SHELLS *(Kokilki z Ryb)*

1 cup leftover cooked fish
4–6 fresh mushrooms (depending on size), sliced
2 tbs. butter
salt and pepper to taste

½ cup Béchamel Sauce (see Index)
1 tbs. grated Parmesan cheese
1 tbs. bread crumbs

Bone the fish and dice or mash with fork. Sauté sliced mushrooms in half the butter, tightly covered, until transparent (not more than 10 minutes). Mix with fish, season to taste, and fill the shells. Pour Béchamel Sauce over the mixture, sprinkle with Parmesan, then with bread crumbs which have been browned in remäining butter. Bake in hot oven for 15 minutes. Serves 2 to 3.

24. SCRAMBLED EGG AND SMOKED FISH PATTIES
(Paszteciki z Wędzoną Rybą z Jajecznicą)

8 eggs
3 tbs. sweet cream
1 tbs. butter
salt and pepper to taste

¼ lb. smoked salmon or sturgeon
butter for shells
1 tbs. chopped fresh parsley

Beat eggs and cream lightly. Season to taste and scramble in butter until medium done. Butter the shells, fill with scrambled egg mixture, and garnish with strips of smoked fish. Sprinkle with chopped fresh parsley and serve at once. Serves 6.

25. SCRAMBLED EGG AND ANCHOVY PATTIES
(Paszteciki z Sardelami)

Follow the directions for Smoked Fish Patties (No. 24), substituting crisscrossed anchovy fillets for smoked fish, and chopped chives for parsley.

26. EGGS BAKED IN ANCHOVY PASTE
(Jaja z Masłem Sardelowem)

1 egg
1 tbs. (level) anchovy paste
1 tsp. grated Parmesan
1 tsp. butter

1 tsp. bread crumbs
salt and pepper
dash of lemon juice

Spread ramekin or shell heavily with anchovy paste. Break an egg into shell, sprinkle with grated Parmesan and with bread crumbs browned in melted butter. Season with salt and pepper and a dash of lemon juice, and place in hot oven or under broiler just long enough for the egg white to cook (about 5 minutes). Serves 1. (Excellent Sunday brunch dish.)

27. CRAYFISH PATTIES *(Paszteciki z Raków)*

30 crayfish (shrimp may be substituted)	1 cup sour cream
	salt and pepper to taste
10 med. mushrooms, sliced thin	3 egg yolks
½ med. onion, minced	1 tbs. each of chopped fresh dill
2 tbs. butter	and parsley
1 tbs. flour	

Clean and cook crayfish as for Crayfish Soup, utilizing the shells as indicated to make Crayfish Butter (see Index). Smother onion and mushrooms with half the Crayfish Butter until transparent, or about 10 minutes. Using the rest of the butter, make a *roux* with the flour. Blend in 2 tbs. of the broth in which the crayfish cooked, add sour cream, and stir until smooth. Add mushrooms, onion, and crayfish meat cut in small pieces. Season to taste and let bubble up once. Add the beaten egg yolks, taking care not to curdle. Fill the shells with this mixture, sprinkle with dill and parsley, and place in hot oven until heated through (about 5 minutes). Serves 5 to 6.

28. VEAL OR POULTRY CROQUETTES
(Krokiety z Drobiu lub Cielęciny)

2 cups leftover meat, boned and chopped	4–6 mushrooms, sliced fine
	salt and pepper to taste
1 tbs. butter	1 whole egg
1 tbs. flour	½ cup bread crumbs
¼ cup soup stock	butter for frying
3 egg yolks	few sprigs parsley
1 tbs. cream	lemon slices

Make a white sauce of half the butter, the flour, and soup stock. Slowly add egg yolks beaten with the cream, taking care not to curdle. In the meantime, simmer the sliced mushrooms in remaining butter for about 10 minutes. Mix mushrooms with sauce, add leftover meat, season, and mix again. (If sauce is too thick, add a little more stock.) Shape into croquettes, dip in beaten egg, roll in bread crumbs, and fry in butter, turning several times until golden brown. Garnish with fried parsley sprigs and lemon slices. Serve with Tomato Sauce, Béchamel, or any other sauce according to personal preference. Serves 4.

29. POULTRY PIE *(Vol-au-Vent z Drobiu)*

1 large French Pastry shell about 9" in diameter, with shell cover (see Index)

Filling:
1 tbs. butter
1 tbs. flour
¼ cup strong bouillon
½ cup heavy sweet cream
2 cups boned roast chicken, turkey, or duck, skinned and diced
liver, heart, and gizzard (roasted or cooked separately), coarsely chopped
¼ lb. sweetbreads (cooked in salted water 10 minutes, skinned, and sliced)
2–3 tbs. cooked peas
10–12 crayfish, cooked and shelled (shrimp may be substituted)
4–6 mushrooms, sliced thin and sautéed in butter
juice ½ lemon (dash of lemon rind, optional)
salt and pepper
3 egg yolks

Cream butter and flour, dilute with bouillon, and add cream. Keeping pan over very low flame, let the mixture heat through and begin to thicken. Add meat, giblets, sweetbreads, crayfish, peas, mushrooms, stirring constantly until everything is thoroughly heated. Add seasoning and lemon juice and, finally, the beaten egg yolks. Pour into heated pastry shell, cover with pastry top, and serve at once. If allowed to stand, the pastry will become soggy. Serves 6 to 8.

30. FISH PIE *(Vol-au-Vent z Ryb)*

Follow recipe for Poultry Pie, No. 29, substituting cooked boned fish and fish roe for poultry.

31. RUSSIAN FISH PASTRY *(Kulebiak z Rybą)*

French or Semi-French Pastry dough, chilled (see Index)
1 whole egg, beaten

Filling:
2-lb. pike or perch
3 tbs. butter
1 onion
1 carrot
1 celery stalk
few sprigs of parsley
1 bay leaf
6 peppercorns
3 hard-cooked eggs
salt and pepper to taste

Stew the fish with half of the butter, the vegetables, and herbs, tightly covered, in very little salted water until thoroughly done (20 to 30 minutes). Remove skin and bones, and shred fish. Slice or chop the eggs. Divide the dough in half and roll out into oblongs on a pastry board. On one piece arrange the fish and the eggs in alternate layers. Season if necessary, sprinkle with remaining melted butter, cover with second piece of dough, and press edges firmly together. Brush with beaten egg and bake in hot oven about 20 minutes. (Traditional.) Serves 6 to 8.

32. CABBAGE AND MUSHROOM PASTRY
(Kulebiak z Kapustą i Grzybami)

Filling:
2 small or 1 med. cabbage
1 med. onion, minced
2 tbs. butter

2 tbs. cooked and chopped dried mushrooms
3 hard-cooked eggs, chopped
salt and pepper to taste

Parboil cabbage in salted water, drain, shred, and stew, tightly covered, with butter and minced onion until tender. Cook mushrooms in as little water as possible without scorching, then chop and add to cabbage. Add chopped hard-cooked eggs. Season to taste, mix thoroughly, and use as a filling for pastry. Makes 6 to 8 slices.

Pastry:

Follow recipe for French or Semi-French Pastry (see Index), and proceed as for Russian Fish Pastry, No. 31.

33. CRAYFISH, FISH, AND EGG PASTRY
(Pasztet z Raków, Jaj i Ryb)

Pastry shell: 1 large shell, about 9″ in diameter, made with French Pastry or ordinary Pastry Dough (see Index), with cover

Filling:
15 crayfish (or shrimp)
1-lb. pike or perch, cooked and boned

3–4 dried mushrooms, cooked and chopped
½ roll, moistened in milk
1 tbs. Crayfish or Coral Butter
salt and pepper to taste
3 tbs. sour cream
2 raw egg yolks
5 hard-cooked eggs

Prepare crayfish and Crayfish Butter as in recipe for Crayfish Soup (see Index). Shred the cooked fish (frozen perch fillets are useful for this purpose), combine with mushrooms, the moistened roll, and the Crayfish Butter. Season to taste and mix thoroughly. Heat in a buttered heavy pan, stirring constantly, until mixture begins to brown. Add sour cream, and when thoroughly heated again, remove from heat. Blend in the well-beaten egg yolks, add diced crayfish and hard-cooked eggs, mix once more, and fill heated pastry shell with the mixture. Serve at once. Serves 4 to 6.

34. VENISON PASTRY (Pasztet ze Zwierzyny)

2 pairs hare forelegs, or 1 whole hare, or equivalent amount of venison
½ lb. salt pork or bacon
1 onion
1 carrot
½ celery root

1 parsley root
1 bay leaf
10 peppercorns
10 whole allspice
1 lb. fat fresh pork
4–5 dried mushrooms
2 cups water

| salt and pepper to taste | 2 tbs. butter |
| 1 lb. calf's liver | 4 whole raw eggs |

Use those parts of the hare which are ordinarily discarded in roasting, including livers. Place slices of salt pork or bacon in bottom of pan. Put meat, vegetables, spices, fresh pork, and mushrooms on top. Add water, cover tightly, and let simmer until meat comes away from the bones. Discard bones, bay leaf, peppercorns, and allspice, and press the meat and remaining vegetables through a meat grinder twice, or combine in a blender.

Separately, sauté the calf's liver in butter for 30 minutes, keeping tightly covered so that liver will remain moist. Skin and vein the liver and press through a sieve. Mix with remaining meat and vegetable mass, blend in the well-beaten eggs, season to taste, and use to fill the pie.

Piecrust:

Follow recipe for Pastry Dough (see Index), or use prepared pie mix. Roll the dough out fairly thin, using half for the pie shell and half for topping. Bake in a well-greased tin in a hot oven for a full hour. Serve with Madeira Sauce or Mushroom Sauce. Serves 8 to 10.

35. PARTRIDGE, SNIPE, OR WOOD THRUSH PIE
(Pasztet z Kuropatw, Bekasów lub Kwiczołów)

5–6 partridges, or double the number of the smaller birds	1 large hard roll, moistened in milk
salt	2 eggs, slightly beaten
juice of 1½ lemons	1 med. onion, blanched and grated
fresh juniper leaves, if available	10–12 juniper berries
¼ lb. calf's liver	salt and pepper to taste
1 lb. raw veal	12 bacon slices
½ lb. salt pork, bacon, or beef marrow	few sprigs of parsley

Clean the birds and cut lengthwise, reserving livers, hearts, gizzards, and heads. Rinse off, sprinkle with salt and lemon juice, and rub with juniper leaves. (When leaves are not available, use half the crushed juniper berries.) Let stand 2 to 3 hours.

Pâté:

Put the calf's liver, veal, salt pork, and roll through a meat grinder together with the giblets, heads, and livers. Combine with grated onion, eggs, and the remaining crushed juniper berries. Season to taste.

Piecrust:

Use recipe for Pastry Dough (see Index) or a prepared piecrust mix. Line greased rectangular mold with a thin layer of dough, put down layer of pâté, then a layer of the halved birds, each on a strip of bacon. Repeat until all the ingredients have been used up, ending with a layer of pâté. Cover with piecrust and, preferably, with a second, inverted mold, in which case tie with string to keep securely in place. Bake in medium-hot oven for two hours. Unmold and serve with lemon slices, sprigs of parsley, and Juniper Sauce (see Index). Serves 6 to 8.

To serve in a French Pastry shell, both the meats for the pâté and the birds must be stewed first. The pastry shell is then filled in layers as above and placed in a hot oven for no longer than 10 minutes, just enough to heat through.

The same recipe may be used for any game birds. Traditional.

36. PASTRY OF WILD OR DOMESTIC DUCK
(Pasztet z Kaczek Dzikich lub Swojskich)

Use recipe for Pastry Dough (see Index) or a prepared piecrust mix. Line greased rectangular mold with dough, and fill according to the following directions:

Filling:

2 ducks, cleaned and salted an hour before cooking	1 celery root
	1 leek
1 onion	2 tbs. red wine (optional)
1 carrot	few strips of bacon or salt pork
1 stalk celery	salt and pepper to taste
1 parsley root	½ cup water

Braise the ducks with all other ingredients, tightly covered, in a heavy pan until soft and lightly brown, or about 1 hour. In the meantime, prepare pâté paste as follows:

2 pairs hare's forelegs or equivalent amount venison	1 bay leaf
	10 peppercorns
½ lb. salt pork or bacon	10 whole allspice
1 lb. fat fresh pork	4–5 dried mushrooms
1 lb. calf's liver	2 cups water
2 tbs. butter	3–4 tbs. strong bouillon
1 onion	salt and pepper to taste
½ celery root	
1 parsley root	

Follow recipe for Venison Pastry (No. 34). Substitute bouillon for raw eggs. (Liquid in which ducks have braised may be used, if enough is left over. In this case, skim the fat.)

Fill piecrust with a layer of pâté. Cut ducks in small pieces and bone or not, as desired. Arrange in layers, alternating with pâté. Cover with piecrust, press edges tightly, and bake in hot oven for 10 minutes. Separately, serve Caper or Madeira Sauce. Serves 12. Recipe may be halved for ordinary household use.

37. TURKEY PIE (Pasztet z Indyka)

1 small turkey (5–6 lbs.), cut in small pieces	1 hard roll, moistened in milk
2–3 cups soup stock	butter for cooking
1 cup white wine	2 tbs. chopped capers
1 lb. salt pork or bacon	2 tbs. chopped anchovy fillets
2 lbs. veal	4 egg yolks
	salt and pepper to taste

Cook turkey in just enough soup stock to half-cover. When bird begins to look done (1 to 1½ hours), add the wine and continue cooking until completely soft. In the meantime, make the pâté as follows: Put salt pork, veal, and roll through meat grinder and fry lightly in butter, stirring constantly and taking care not to brown. Add chopped capers and anchovies and finally the beaten egg yolks. (Do not season until the end, since the capers and anchovies are highly spiced. The amount of these may be varied according to individual taste.) Mix thoroughly.

Piecrust:

Make dough according to directions for French Pastry or ordinary Pastry Dough (see Index) or use a prepared mix. Line one or two greased molds with dough, then with a layer of pâté paste. Alternate layers of pâté and turkey, ending with pâté. Cover with a lattice of dough strips and bake in hot oven for 30 minutes. Serve garnished with lemon slices. Separately, serve Truffle (or Mushroom) Sauce or White Caper Sauce (see Index). Serves 8 to 10. Recipe may easily be halved, or made with leftover roast turkey.

38. SUCKLING PIG PÂTÉ (Pasztet z Prosiaka)

1 suckling pig	4 eggs, separated
1 large onion, grated	salt and pepper to taste
½ lb. salt pork or bacon, diced	pinch of marjoram
1 whole calf's liver	pinch of nutmeg
1 white roll, moistened in milk	¼ cup sherry or Madeira wine
1 tbs. butter	bacon strips for lining mold

Have the butcher clean and quarter the pig. Reserve head and feet for headcheese, and add the liver to pâté ingredients. Line a pan with grated onion and diced salt pork. Arrange the meat on top, and steam, tightly covered, in very little water (no more than ½ cup), sprinkling occasionally with a little cold water to keep it from browning. When thoroughly done, in about 2 hours, cut into small serving pieces.

In the meantime, prepare the following pâté:

Chop both the calf and pork liver raw, and put through a sieve together with the roll. Cream butter and egg yolks, add liver mixture, and mix thoroughly. Add the diced salt pork which has cooked with the meat. Season with salt, pepper, and other spices, and add the wine. Mix again. Fold in beaten egg whites. Line a mold with bacon strips, and arrange meat and pâté in alternating layers, beginning and ending with pâté. Cover tightly and cook over steam for 1½ hours, testing with straw or toothpick for doneness. Allow to cool slightly before unmolding. Garnish with lemon slices, croutons, or hard-cooked egg slices. Serve with Fresh Mushroom, Lemon, or highly-spiced Stroganoff Sauce. (See Index.) Serves 12, with possible leftovers. Traditional.

39. PIGEON SQUAB PASTRY *(Pasztet z Gołębi)*

6 pigeon squabs	2 cloves (optional)
2 lbs. boneless veal	1 bay leaf (optional)
½ lb. salt pork or bacon, diced	soup stock for basting
1 onion	2 rolls, moistened in milk
1 carrot	¼ lb. mushrooms, sliced and sautéed in 1 tbs. butter
1 stalk celery	
1 parsley root	4 eggs
1 celery root	salt and pepper to taste
6 peppercorns	

Have butcher clean and split the squabs, reserving livers and giblets. Cook tightly covered over low heat, together with veal, diced pork, vegetables, and spices, basting frequently with soup stock. When thoroughly done, about 30 minutes, remove the squabs and, if necessary, continue cooking veal a little longer. Put the veal, salt pork, and vegetables through a meat grinder, together with the rolls, discarding cloves, peppercorns, and bay leaf. Add cooked mushrooms and the whole beaten eggs. Season to taste with salt and pepper.

Pastry Shell:

Make one large French Pastry shell with cover (see Index). Arrange pâté mixture and pieces of squab in shell, in alternating layers, beginning and ending with pâté. Cover with greased paper and bake in medium-hot oven for half an hour. Cover with shell cover. Serve with White Caper or Lemon Sauce (see Index). Serves 6 to 8.

40. HUNGARIAN PASTRY *(Pasztet Węgierski)*

French Pastry dough made with
4 cups of flour
1½ lbs. beef fillet (boneless top
sirloin may be substituted)

1 large parsley root
fresh-ground pepper and salt to
taste
beaten egg

Cut the meat, which should be well-veined with fat, into pea-size pieces. (The original recipe recommends that the meat not be chopped.) If meat is lean, add a piece of beef suet. Add seasoning and the parsley root cut in half. Cover tightly and braise over slow heat without any water for about half an hour. Uncover and let cool. While the meat is cooling, roll out the dough, line a greased baking pan with it, and arrange a layer of meat on top. Continue arranging dough and meat in layers, ending with dough. The meat may also be used as a one-layer filling for the pastry, if the mold is large enough. Brush top with beaten egg and bake in a very hot oven for 20 minutes. Serves 4.

Cold Pâtés

41. GAME PÂTÉ *(Pasztet z Dziczyny)*

1½ lbs. shoulder of venison
1 whole small hare or large
rabbit
2 onions
2 carrots
1 parsley root
1 celery root
1 bay leaf
2–3 cloves
10 peppercorns
10 juniper berries

water and vinegar in equal
parts for marinade (about 2
qts.)
2 tbs. olive oil
¼ lb. salt pork or bacon
¼ lb. corned or pickled tongue
½ cup red wine
4 eggs, slightly beaten
salt and pepper
bacon slices for lining mold

Boil vegetables and spices in enough of the water and vinegar mixture to half-cover meat. Pour boiling mixture over the meat, add olive oil, and let stand in the marinade for 2 to 3 days, turning occasionally. Add half the salt pork and simmer, tightly covered, in the marinade until the meat is very tender and comes away from the bones (about 1½ hours). Let cool for easy handling. Then bone meat and put through meat grinder, together with the marinated salt pork. Press through a sieve, dice, and add the rest of the salt pork and the tongue, the wine, and the eggs. Season and mix thoroughly. Line a mold with bacon strips, pour in pâté mixture, cover, and cook over steam or in a kettle of boiling water for a full 2 hours. Let cool before unmolding. Chill and cut into thin slices.

42. CHAUD-FROID OF THRUSHES (*Pasztet z Kwiczołów*)

12 thrushes (any small game birds may be substituted)	10 peppercorns
¼ lb. calf's liver	10 juniper berries
1 lb. boneless veal or pork	salt and pepper to taste
¼ lb. salt pork or bacon fat (optional)	¼ cup bouillon
3–4 dried mushrooms (optional)	¼ cup Madeira
1 onion	olive oil
1 bay leaf (optional)	watercress
	bacon strips and sliced raw vegetables to line casserole

Clean the birds, skin carefully, and remove backbone. Sprinkle with salt inside and out, and return hearts and livers before stuffing.

Stuffing:

Braise calf's liver, veal, salt pork, thrush gizzards, and dried mushrooms in very little water, tightly covered, together with onion and spices, until very tender. (Liver will be done after 20 to 30 minutes. Meat will cook twice that long.) Discard bay leaf and peppercorns and remove mushrooms. Grind remaining mixture; press through sieve. Cut mushrooms in small pieces; add to pâté mixture. Add 2 tbs. of the bouillon, the wine, and a pinch of ground juniper berries. Season and mix thoroughly. Stuff the birds, reserving sufficient stuffing for spreading, later on. Secure with toothpicks or sew up with coarse cotton. Roll each in a piece of paper rubbed with olive oil and arrange in pan which has been lined with bacon strips and raw vegetable slices. Cover with another sheet of paper rubbed with oil and sprinkle with remaining bouillon. Roast in hot oven for 30 minutes.

While birds are in the oven, prepare the following aspic:

1 pkg. gelatin dissolved in ¼ cup cold water	1 bouillon cube
1 tbs. potato flour or cornstarch	1 cup hot water *

Let the roast birds cool, and then spread each with remaining stuffing, leaving them as smooth as possible. Dip individually in the aspic liquid, holding on fork long enough for aspic to jell a little. Chill; arrange on a bed of very thin dry toast. Garnish with watercress and serve with Tartare Sauce. Serves 6 to 8.

* Dissolve bouillon cube in hot water, stir into gelatin, and add cornstarch. Stir until smooth, and let stand until it begins to thicken.

43. STRASBOURG PÂTÉ *(Pasztet Strasburski)*

1 lb. goose livers (turkey or chicken livers are a good substitute)	salt and pepper to taste
	dash of nutmeg
	6 peppercorns
milk to cover	6 whole allspice
¼ lb. salt pork	2 tbs. strong bouillon
½ med. onion, minced	1 tbs. chopped trufflles (canned)
½ tbs. butter	

Soak the livers in milk overnight. In a heavy covered pan, simmer salt pork until transparent and tender, about half an hour. Slice. Cook minced onion in butter until transparent but not brown. Arrange half the pork slices and onion in bottom of pan, add the goose livers (which have been skinned), cover with the remaining pork and onion, and season lightly with salt and pepper. Add spices and bouillon, cover, and simmer for 15 minutes. Discard spices and put the rest of the ingredients through meat grinder, then through a sieve. Add chopped truffles, mix well, and chill. If pâté is not to be used at once, put into jars, cover with a heavy layer of goose fat, then with wax paper. Cover tightly and store in refrigerator.

44. PÂTÉ FOR QUICK USE *(Pasztet do Prędkiego Użycia)*

1 lb. goose livers (calf's liver makes a satisfactory substitute)	6 whole allspice
	1–2 cloves
	salt and pepper to taste
milk to cover	¼ cup bouillon
½ med. onion, chopped	2 egg yolks
¼ lb. salt pork	1 whole egg
½ lb. boneless veal	dash of nutmeg
6 peppercorns	

Soak livers in milk overnight. (If calf's liver is used, it should soak 24 hours.) In heavy pan, cook chopped onion in a little salt pork until onion is transparent but not brown. Arrange onion and sliced salt pork in bottom of pan. Add veal and spices and a tablespoon of bouillon. Cover tightly and braise until veal is soft, basting occasionally with more bouillon. Add liver and simmer another 15 minutes. Allow to cool. Discard spices and put everything else through meat grinder twice; press through a sieve. Add beaten egg yolks and whole egg, dash of nutmeg, and salt and pepper to taste, and mix thoroughly.
Separately, prepare:

1 goose liver, soaked overnight in milk	salt to taste
	1 tbs. truffles (canned), sliced thin or chopped
1 tbs. butter	
1 tbs. bouillon	

Sauté goose liver in butter and a little bouillon, covered, for about 10 minutes, taking care not to brown. Do not salt until done. Allow to cool and cut into medium-thick slices.

Arrange the pâté paste and the slices of goose liver and truffles in alternate layers in a greased mold, ending with a layer of pâté. Cover with sheet of paper greased with oil and bake in moderate oven for 80 minutes. Allow to cool; then unmold and pour melted goose fat over the whole surface. Chill, or serve at room temperature. Cut in thin slices for serving.

Fish and Shellfish

Ideally, fish should be bought live in special markets. Since this is seldom possible, care must be taken to choose fresh-caught and well-refrigerated fish. A fresh fish may be recognized by the eyes, scales, and fins: the eyes and scales should be light in color and have luster; the fins should be reddish. Even when refrigerated, the eyes should bulge slightly. Avoid fish with milky, flat eyes—such fish will lack flavor.

To salt fish, it is best to grill the salt by placing a few spoonfuls of ordinary salt in a dry pan and heating until the salt takes on a slightly yellow color and stops sizzling. Shake pan frequently during the process.

1. BOILING:

Fish may be cooked whole or cut into serving pieces, depending on convenience. A large fish served whole looks best when appearance counts. For easiest handling, cooking should be done in a large oblong pan on a rack (a roasting pan with cover can double for a fish kettle); for additional ease, the fish may be wrapped in cheesecloth.

Prepare a court bouillon, using per quart of water:

1 large onion	½ bay leaf (optional)
2–3 carrots	salt and pepper to taste
½ celery root	other spices according to per-
½ parsley root	sonal preference: thyme, oreg-
2–3 celery stalks with leaves	ano, tarragon, etc.
slice of lemon	

Boil the water and vegetables until vegetables are done. Strain. (The other vegetables may later be used to strain for sauce, the carrots for garnish.) Place fish on rack, belly down, and immerse in the liquid, of which there should be enough to cover. Simmer very slowly until done, about 5 minutes per inch of thickness. Remove with rack and drain; cut cheesecloth and remove carefully. Broth may be used as the basis of a fish chowder.

50

2. STEAMING:

1st Method:
Place fish, whole or cut into serving pieces, on rack over enough court bouillon (see No. 1) to allow plenty of steam throughout cooking time, which is a very little longer than boiling time. Cover very tightly and simmer. Remove with rack, drain, and proceed as in No. 1.

2nd Method:
Place fish, whole or cut into serving pieces, directly in bottom of pan, adding (per pound):

1 tbs. butter	½ cup white wine
2–3 tbs. broth	salt and pepper to taste

Simmer very slowly, tightly covered, until done.

In both boiling and steaming, care should be taken not to let fish fall apart.

3. FRYING:

Small fish may be fried whole, with or without the heads, according to preference. Large fish are cut into serving pieces for frying.

Wash and drain the fish, dust with seasoned flour, and fry either in deep fat or in a skillet. Use butter, olive oil, a combination of both, or vegetable oil, according to personal taste. Fish may also be fried seasoned but without being dredged in flour. Another method is to dip them in beaten egg and bread crumbs. In all cases frying should be done over medium heat and the fish turned once carefully. Fry until a light, golden brown.

4. BROILING:

Brush whole fish or serving pieces with butter or other fat, and place under preheated broiler for about 10 minutes. Large fish takes longer. It is important to preheat the broiler and have temperature high, since turning is awkward. Baste frequently. Larger fish should be split for broiling and done skin-down. Many people prefer the newer method of broiling at medium temperature for a longer time. This results in less shrinkage, but the fish will have a slightly "steamed" taste.

5. BAKING:

For baking, first parboil fish in court bouillon, or dust with flour and fry lightly in butter. Then arrange tightly in a buttered shallow pan. Spread with butter or whatever sauce is recommended, and bake in medium-hot oven (350° or less), allowing 20 minutes per inch of thickness. Fish should be lightly browned on top.

6. PIKE *À LA POLONAISE* WITH HORSERADISH SAUCE
(Szczupak po Polsku)

3- to 4-lb. pike   salt and pepper to taste

I.
Wash, drain, and salt the fish ahead of time if possible. Simmer very slowly in court bouillon (see No. 1), tightly covered, for 15 to 20 minutes. Test for doneness. Drain and serve with Horseradish Sauce (see Index) and lemon slices.

II.
Wrap the fish in a large piece of buttered white paper, and bake in a slow oven for about an hour, basting generously with melted butter. Remove paper and arrange on platter. Serve as in I.

III.
Cut the pike halfway through, into serving pieces. Place carefully in a heavy pan with about a cup of vegetable stock. Cover tightly and steam for about 10 minutes. Spread with Horseradish Sauce (see Index) and continue steaming, covered, over very low heat until thoroughly done. Serves 6 to 8.

7. COOKED PIKE WITH HARD-COOKED EGG SAUCE
(Szczupak Gotowany z Jajami)

3- to 4-lb. pike   3 chopped hard-cooked eggs
    court bouillon (No. 1) to cover   salt and pepper to taste
    for boiling (or steam as in No.   few sprigs of parsley
    2)   lemon slices
¼ lb. butter

Prepare pike as in No. 6, and serve with following sauce: Melt butter to a light, golden brown. Add chopped eggs, season to taste, and cook a minute or two, stirring frequently until egg is thoroughly saturated. Pour over fish. Garnish with parsley sprigs and lemon slices. Serves 6 to 8.

8. SMOTHERED PIKE *(Szczupak Duszony)*

3- to 4-lb. pike, salted ahead of
time
⅓ cup diced carrots
⅓ cup diced celery root
⅓ cup diced parsley root
⅓ cup diced kohlrabi
2–3 stalks celery with leaves, diced
2 diced onions
4 tbs. butter

1 bay leaf (optional)
few peppercorns
dash of thyme or marjoram
(optional)
½ tbs. flour
¼ teaspoon Soy or Maggi extract
salt and pepper to taste
3–4 cups homemade or prepared
cooked noodles

Steam vegetables and onion in half the butter and about a cupful
of water. When vegetables are nearly done, add the previously-
salted fish and another tablespoon of the butter, reserving 1 tbs.
Add spices, cover tightly, and simmer very slowly until done. (More
water may be required, depending on size of fish.) In the meantime
prepare the noodles. Cream remaining butter with ½ tbs. flour.
Dilute with water, stir until smooth, add Maggi extract and seasoning to taste, and add to the fish, together with the noodles. Let
bubble up once and serve on a preheated platter, placing the vegetables over the fish and the noodles along the sides. Pour remaining liquid over this and serve at once. (If sauce is too thin reduce
over high heat.) Serves 6 to 8.

9. STUFFED PIKE JEWISH-STYLE
(Szczupak po Żydowsku)

4-lb. pike
2 hard rolls, moistened with milk
3 med. onions, parboiled and
grated
salt and pepper to taste
dash of nutmeg
2 tbs. butter
1 egg

⅓ cup diced carrots
⅓ cup diced celery root
⅓ cup diced parsley root
⅓ cup diced parsnip
⅓ cup green beans or peas (optional)
2 tsp. flour for thickening

Scale, wash, and dry the fish. Cut off head. Then carefully skin the
body down to the tail. Remove all the meat from the bones and
chop fine. Add rolls, onion, and seasoning, and continue chopping
until all ingredients are thoroughly mixed. Cream 1 tbs. butter with
the egg, add to chopped fish, and mix. Stuff the fish skin with this
mixture. Sew together with cotton thread or secure with toothpicks.
Return the head to the body and arrange the whole fish on a bed of
diced vegetables in a heavy oblong dish. Add the remaining butter
and ½ to 1 cup of water—just enough so that the fish and vegetables
will cook without burning. Cover tightly and steam over very low
heat for at least an hour. Serve with the steamed vegetables and
the sauce in which it cooked, thickening the sauce by adding ½ to

1 tbs. of flour. If the fish is served with Horseradish Sauce, omit the flour. Serves 8.

10. BAKED PIKE *(Szczupak z Pieca)*

3- to 4-lb. pike   ½ tbs. flour
½ lb. butter   2 cups sour cream
1 lemon   salt and pepper

Parboil fish in court bouillon. Place belly-down in an oblong baking dish, spreading with butter. Bake in a moderate oven until it begins to brown. Sprinkle with juice of a whole lemon. Beat the flour into the sour cream until smooth, and spread over the fish. Continue baking, basting frequently with the cream, for another 30 minutes. Serves 6 to 8.

11. PIKE OR CARP STUFFED WITH ANCHOVIES
(Szczupak lub Karp Nadziewany Sardelami)

3-lb. pike (male) with milts and   2 eggs, separated
  liver   salt and pepper to taste
¼ lb. dried anchovies or 1 can an-   butter for rubbing
  chovy fillets   2 cups sour cream
1 tbs. butter   ½ tbs. flour
1 hard roll, moistened with milk

Soak the dried anchovies in water for a few hours, then bone. Cut half the anchovies in thin strips and lard the fish with them. Chop the other half fine, and cream with a tablespoon of butter. Divide this in half. Use one half to make a stuffing with the rolls, slightly-beaten egg yolks, and the chopped liver and milts from the fish. Season with salt and pepper, mix thoroughly, and fold in the beaten egg whites. Stuff the fish, sew up with cotton thread, rub with butter, and bake in a moderate oven for about an hour. When fish begins to brown, spread with the remaining anchovy-butter paste. Ten minutes later pour over it the sour cream to which ½ tbs. flour has been added. Baste occasionally and allow to brown. Serves 6 to 7.

12. PIKE HUNGARIAN-STYLE *(Szczupak po Węgiersku)*

3-lb. pike   ½ tsp. paprika
1 large onion, cut fine   3–4 tbs. bread crumbs
1 tbs. butter   3–4 tbs. sour cream (optional) *or*
1 cup white wine   ½ tsp. Maggi extract
1 cup vegetable broth

Salt the fish an hour in advance. Cut into serving pieces, cutting halfway through the bone so that fish will hold together. Simmer onion and butter until transparent but not brown. Arrange fish on top of the onion, add wine and broth, sprinkle with paprika and bread crumbs. Simmer, tightly covered, until soft. (Fish should be half-immersed in liquid—if necessary use less, in the same proportion of 1 to 1.) Sauce may be thickened with a few spoonfuls of sour cream or flavored with Maggi extract. Serves 6.

13. CARP IN BUTTER *(Karp z Masłem)*

2- to 3-lb. carp	parsley to garnish
court bouillon to half-cover (see	¼ lb. melted butter
No. 1)	

Cook carp according to directions for boiling or steaming (No. 1 or No. 2). Drain. Arrange on platter, belly down, garnish with fresh parsley, and serve with hot melted butter and parsley potatoes. Serves 4 to 6.

14. CARP IN GRAY SAUCE *(Karp na Szaro)*

2- to 3-lb. carp	Polish Gray Sauce (see Index)
court bouillon to half-cover (see	
No. 1)	

Boil or steam carp in the bouillon until half-done. Make Polish Gray Sauce with raisins and almonds, using the fish stock. Return fish to sauce and continue simmering 15 to 20 minutes or until tender. Serve with buttered noodles or macaroni. Serves 4 to 6.

15. FRIED CARP *(Karp Smażony)*

2- to 3-lb. carp	1 beaten egg
flour for dredging	½ cup bread crumbs
salt and pepper to taste	butter for frying

Cut carp into serving pieces or, if it is to be served whole, cut halfway through the bone at intervals equivalent to serving-piece size. Dredge with flour, season, dip in egg, and roll in bread crumbs. Fry in hot butter, taking care not to burn. Serve with Horseradish Sauce (see Index) and fried potatoes, or with cabbage and mushrooms. Serves 4 to 6.

16. SMOTHERED CARP JEWISH-STYLE
(Karp po Żydowsku)

3-lb. carp (with head)	1 diced kohlrabi
½ cup diced carrots	6 onions, chopped fine
1 diced celery root	3–4 stalks celery with leaves,
1 diced parsley root	chopped

1 bay leaf   2 tbs. butter
  a few peppercorns
2 cloves (optional)
  salt and pepper to taste

Simmer the onions and vegetables, tightly covered, in 4 cups salted
water, together with butter and spices. When vegetables are nearly
done, add the fish cut into serving pieces, and let it steam over low
heat at least 30 minutes. Serve fish and vegetables together with
the broth, of which not much should be left. Serves 6.

17. ASPIC OF CARP JEWISH-STYLE

(Karp w Galarecie po Żydowsku)

Prepare the same as No. 16, using a couple of additional fish heads
if available. When done, arrange fish and vegetables in mold or
serving dish (discarding heads and spices). Strain broth and pour
over fish. Chill until the sauce sets. Serve with oil and vinegar.
Serves 6.

18. STUFFED CARP (Karp Nadiewany)

3- to 4-lb. carp (male)   1 tbs. butter
2 truffles   2 eggs, separated
4–6 fresh mushrooms (depending   1 hard roll, moistened in milk
   on size)   (or equivalent in bread
1 heaping tbs. chopped fresh   crumbs)
   parsley   butter for cooking
   salt and pepper to taste

Salt the fish ahead of time. Chop milts and liver, truffles, mushrooms, and parsley. Season to taste. Cream 1 tbs. butter with 2 egg
yolks, add chopped roll (or bread crumbs) and milt mixture, and
mix thoroughly. Then fold in beaten egg whites. Stuff the fish, sew
up with cotton thread, roll in a sheet of buttered white paper, and
bake in medium-hot óven, basting frequently with pan drippings.
Garnish with vegetables and serve with Caper or Lemon Sauce
(see Index). Serves 6 to 8.

19. CARP STUFFED WITH ANCHOVIES
(Karp Nadziewany z Sardelami)

Follow recipe for Pike Stuffed with Anchovies (see Index).

20. CARP ROYALE (Karp po Królewsku)

3- to 4-lb carp (male)   4 cups strong vegetable broth
2 tbs. salt   2 cups white wine
1 tbs. butter   melted butter for basting

Clean and salt the fish a day in advance if possible. Wash salt off before cooking. Put into fish kettle, belly down, and add butter, broth, and wine. Cover with greased paper and steam, tightly covered, over low heat for 30 to 45 minutes, basting occasionally with more butter. (The liquid should half-cover the fish—the proportion of broth to wine is 2 to 1.) While fish cooks, prepare sauce.

Sauce:

fish liver and milt	dash of paprika
12 small mushrooms, sliced	½ tsp. Soy sauce
2–3 truffles, thinly sliced	salt and pepper to taste
½ tbs. butter	3 egg yolks
1 tbs. flour	

Parboil fish liver and milt in water and vinegar (2 parts water to 1 part vinegar), and continue simmering for about 10 minutes. Drain and dice. Simmer mushrooms, truffles, and diced liver and milt in a few tablespoons of the broth in which the fish has been cooking. When mushrooms are transparent, add butter and flour and blend thoroughly, adding more stock if necessary for a medium-thick sauce. Season with paprika, Soy sauce, salt, and pepper. When fish is done, beat egg yolks slightly and stir slowly into sauce, taking care yolks do not curdle. Drain fish, arrange on hot platter, and pour sauce over it. Serve with Fish Quenelles (see Index). Serves 6 to 8.

21. CARP WITH MUSHROOMS *(Karp z Grzybami)*

3-lb. carp	Fresh Mushroom Sauce (see
3–4 tbs. butter	Index)
salt and pepper to taste	

Have carp cleaned, leaving head and tail intact. Wash, drain, rub with salt and pepper, and bake in shallow buttered pan in medium-hot oven, allowing 15 to 20 minutes per inch of thickness. Baste frequently with butter. After half an hour cover generously with Fresh Mushroom Sauce and continue baking another 20 minutes or until sauce browns on top. Serve with parsley potatoes. Serves 6

22. FRIED TENCH * *(Lin Smażony)*

3-lb. tench	salt and pepper
flour for dusting (optional)	3 tbs. butter

Clean tench and cut part way into serving pieces, leaving spine intact. Season lightly and fry in hot butter, turning once. (Follow

* Carp may be substituted in all tench recipes.

general rules for frying fish.) Serve with sauerkraut and mushrooms, fresh horseradish, and salad. Serves 6.

23. SMOTHERED TENCH OR CARP *(Lin Duszony)*

2- to 3-lb. tench	juice ½ lemon
salt and pepper to taste	2–3 tbs. butter

Clean and salt fish, dust with flour, and brown lightly on both sides in hot butter. Sprinkle with lemon juice. Reduce heat very low and simmer, tightly covered, basting frequently with butter. Serve with boiled parsley potatoes. Serves 4 to 6.

24. TENCH OR CARP SMOTHERED IN RED CABBAGE
(Lin Duszony w Kapuście Czerwonej)

3-lb. tench, cut as in No. 22	½ tbs. flour
1 med. head red cabbage,	1 cup red wine
shredded	salt and pepper to taste
1 med. onion, minced	juice ½ lemon
1 tbs. butter	1 tsp. sugar

Clean, cut, and wash fish, and blanch with boiling water. **Drain.** Blanch the shredded cabbage and drain. Brown onion in butter, add flour, and slowly add wine, stirring to dissolve lumps. Season cabbage, sprinkle with lemon juice, and add to sauce. Add sugar, cover tightly, and steam until almost done—about 30 minutes. Add tench, making sure it is covered over with the cabbage. Replace lid and continue steaming another 30 minutes. Serves 6.

25. BAKED STUFFED TENCH OR CARP
(Lin Pieczony z Farszem)

3- to 4-lb. tench (male)	salt and pepper to taste
1 tbs. anchovy paste	juice ½ lemon
2 egg yolks, slightly beaten	3 tbs. butter for basting
1 stale hard roll, moistened	1 cup sour cream (optional)
with milk (or equivalent	2–3 tbs. grated Parmesan (optional)
amount of bread crumbs)	tional)

Clean, wash, and salt the tench, which should be split halfway so that it will hold the stuffing. Make stuffing as follows: Chop milt and liver, mix with anchovy paste and beaten egg yolks, add roll or bread crumbs, and season to taste. Fill the cavity with the mixture and sew together. Arrange fish in buttered shallow baking pan, sprinkle with lemon juice, and bake in medium-slow oven about 45 minutes, basting frequently. When almost done, fish may be spread with sour cream, sprinkled with Parmesan, and browned on top. Serves 6 to 8.

26. PERCH WITH HARD-COOKED EGG SAUCE
(Sandacz z Jajami)

2-lb. perch	2 hard-cooked eggs
court bouillon (No. 1) to half-	2 tbs. butter
cover	salt and pepper to taste

Clean and salt perch, leaving head and tail intact. Steam, tightly covered, in court bouillon until done (20 to 30 minutes). Chop the eggs and brown lightly in butter. Season to taste. When fish is done, drain and arrange on platter. Moisten with 2 tbs. of the stock it has cooked in and pour egg mixture over it. Serve with boiled parsley potatoes. Serves 4.

27. BOILED OR STEAMED PERCH (Sandacz z Wody)
Basic Recipe for Serving with Hot or Cold Sauces

1 large or 2 small perch	salt and pepper to taste
court bouillon (No. 1) to cover	
(or 1 tbs. butter and 1 cup vege-	
table broth)	

Clean, wash, and salt the fish, and either boil slowly in court bouillon or steam, tightly covered, in butter and a small amount of broth. (The second method is preferable, since it conserves juices and makes the fish more tasty.) If fish is steamed, it must be basted frequently. Small fish should steam for not more than 20 minutes. Drain, and use remaining broth for whatever sauce is desired, such as White Caper Sauce, Lemon Sauce, Mushroom Sauce (see Index), if fish is to be served hot; for serving cold, use Tartare Sauce, mayonnaise, etc.

28. PERCH WITH DRIED MUSHROOM SAUCE
(Sandacz z Pieca z Grzybami)

1 large perch (2 to 3 lbs.)	2 tbs. butter
salt and pepper to taste	

Clean, wash, and season fish, and bake in buttered shallow pan, covered with a sheet of greased paper, basting frequently with pan drippings, for about 20 minutes. In the meantime, make following sauce:

6 dried mushrooms, cooked until	½ tsp. Maggi extract
soft and chopped	1 tsp. flour
2 cups sour cream	2 egg yolks
liquid in which mushrooms	salt and pepper to taste
cooked (reduce to 2 tbs.)	

Blend all the ingredients thoroughly.

Remove paper, spread fish with the sauce, and continue baking until slightly brown on top. Serves 5 to 6.

29. PERCH À LA RADZIWILL (Sandacz à la Radziwill)

1 large or 2 smaller perch	1 cup white wine
salt and pepper to taste	2 tbs. melted butter

Fillet the fish and cut into square pieces. (Reserve head, bones, and skin.) Season. Arrange in saucepan, add wine and melted butter, and cover with sheet of greased paper. Cover tightly and steam over low heat for 10 minutes, taking care fillets do not fall apart.

Prepare as many pieces of toast as there are serving pieces of fish, making the toast out of buttered bread and using oven rather than toaster. Keep hot.

Sauce:

1 large onion, diced	¼ lb. calf's milt, diced
2–3 carrots, diced	salt and pepper to taste
½ celery root	½ cup white wine
2–3 celery stalks with leaves	1 tbs. butter
1 parsley root	1½ tsp. flour
6 peppercorns	¼ tsp. Soy sauce or Maggi extract
1 bay leaf	
3 cups water	10 crayfish tails or small shrimp, cooked
6 fresh mushrooms, sliced	
2 truffles, sliced	4 egg yolks, well beaten

Cook fish head and bones with onion, vegetables, and seasonings in the water. Allow liquid to boil down to 2 cups. Add mushrooms, truffles, milt, seasoning, and wine, and simmer until mushrooms and meat are done, about 15 to 20 minutes. Blend butter and flour, dissolve with some of the sauce, stirring until smooth, and then combine with other ingredients. Season with Soy or Maggi extract. Add cooked crayfish or shrimp, and when sauce has bubbled up slowly, stir in the egg yolks, taking care not to curdle. Fish Quenelles may be added to sauce if desired (see Index).

Arrange pieces of fish on toast on a large platter, and pour sauce on top. Serves 6 to 7.

30. PERCH IN WINE SAUCE (Sandacz na Winie)

1 med. or 2 small perch	salt and pepper to taste
1 cup white wine	2 egg yolks
2 tbs. butter	lemon juice to taste
1½ tsp. flour	

Clean and salt the perch, either whole or cut into serving pieces. Steam in wine with 1 tbs. butter, covering dish with sheet of greased paper. (Time will depend on whether fish is cooked whole or in pieces.) Keep fish hot over steam, and strain liquid in which it cooked, adding a little more wine if necessary. Blend 1 tbs. butter with the flour, dissolve with wine sauce, and stir until smooth. Boil up once, season, and at the very last, stir in beaten egg yolks and add lemon juice to taste. Serve very hot. Serves 4 to 5.

31. STUFFED PERCH JEWISH-STYLE
(Sandacz Faszerowany po Żydowsku)

Perch may be stuffed in the same manner as carp. Follow recipe for Stuffed Carp (No. 18).

32. PERCH OR TENCH WITH RICE
(Sandacz lub Lin Duszony z Ryżem)

1 med. perch or tench (2½–3 lbs.)	2 cups rice
salt and pepper to taste	2 tbs. tomato purée
2 cups vegetable broth	2 tbs. melted butter
2 tbs. butter	½ cup Madeira wine

Fillet the fish and cut into small pieces. Season and simmer with butter and vegetable broth (head and bones may be added for stronger taste) until half done. Start with a little broth and keep adding as liquid boils down.

Cook 2 cups of rice so that the grains separate. Add the tomato purée and mix thoroughly. Place alternate layers of rice and fish in buttered casserole, beginning and ending with rice. Sprinkle with melted butter and Madeira. Cover tightly, and simmer another 15 minutes. Serves 5 to 6.

33. MARINATED TROUT (Pstrągi Marynowane)

5 or 6 ½-lb. trout	2 qts. water
1 large onion	1 cup very dry white wine
2 carrots	2 tbs. vinegar or juice 1 lemon
1 celery root	1–2 bay leaves
1 parsley root	6 peppercorns
few sprigs parsley	salt to taste

Dice the onion and vegetables, and cook in water alone until half done, about 10 minutes. Add wine, vinegar, salt, and spices. Cut fish into slices, add to pot, and cook at a slow boil for another 10 to 15 minutes, or until fish and vegetables are done. Allow to cool, put into jars together with vegetables and liquid, cover tightly, and store in refrigerator. Marinated fish may be preserved for a considerable time. Serves 5 to 6.

Note: This recipe may be used for marinating carp, pike, etc.

34. BAKED SALMON WITH MADEIRA
(*Łosós Pieczony z Maderą*)

1 med. salmon, whole, or 3- to 4-lb. piece cut from larger fish	3 tbs. butter for basting
salt and pepper to taste	juice ½ lemon
few strips bacon or salt pork, cut thin	½ cup Madeira wine
1 truffle (optional)	1 tbs. butter
	1½ tsp. flour

Season fish and lard with the bacon strips and, for added delicacy, thin strips of truffle. Arrange in buttered shallow baking dish, cover with sheet of greased paper, and bake in moderate oven, basting frequently. When half done, sprinkle with lemon juice, add wine, and continue baking until slightly brown. Thicken sauce with butter and flour stirred to a paste and thoroughly blended in. Garnish with sprigs of parsley and slices of lemon. Allow a half-pound per serving.

35. SALMON IN RED WINE (*Łosós w Czerwonem Winie*)

1 med. salmon, whole, or 3- to 4-lb. piece cut from larger fish	½ tsp. marjoram
2 onions, diced	½ tsp. thyme
½ cup diced carrots	2 bay leaves
½ cup diced celery root	6 peppercorns
½ cup diced parsley root	2½ cups dry red wine
small bunch fresh parsley	½ tsp. Worcestershire sauce
1 leek	1–2 tsp. flour
3 tbs. butter	salt to taste

Sauté the onions and vegetables in 2 tbs. butter until almost done. Add spices, herbs, the well-salted fish, and 2 cups of the wine. Simmer, tightly covered, until fish is tender. Discard bay leaves. Put vegetables through a sieve, return to pan with liquid, and add remaining half-cup of wine and Worcestershire sauce. Brown remaining butter, add flour, and mix to a paste. Add to sauce. Blend thoroughly, season to taste, and allow to boil up once. Serve fish on a hot platter garnished with salad greens. Serve the sauce separately. Serves 6 to 8.

36. BAKED EEL (*Węgorz Pieczony*)

1 med. eel	1 clove garlic (optional)
salt and pepper to taste	2–3 tbs. butter

Clean and skin the fish and dip in boiling water. Let dry, season with salt and pepper, add garlic if desired, and bake in shallow baking dish in a hot oven for 25 minutes, basting frequently with butter. Cut in serving pieces and arrange on hot platter. Since eel is a very fat fish, it is best served with a sharp sauce. Allow a half-pound per serving.

37. SMOTHERED EEL *(Węgorz Duszony)*

1 med. eel	¼ tsp. fresh-ground pepper
1 cup vinegar	salt to taste
1 small onion, sliced	½ tbs. shrimp or lobster paste
6 peppercorns	½ tbs. butter
1 bay leaf	3 egg yolks, slightly beaten
¼ tsp. thyme	1 doz. cooked crayfish or shrimp
1 cup white wine	(optional)
1 cup bouillon	1 doz. Fish Quenelles (see In-
4–6 mushrooms, sliced	dex) (optional)
1 clove garlic (optional)	

Skin the eel, and roll compactly to fit into as small a saucepan as possible. Boil the vinegar with onion and spices and pour over eel. Let stand a minute or two. Discard vinegar and spices. Add wine, bouillon, sliced mushrooms, garlic, and seasoning, and simmer, tightly covered, for half an hour. Add shrimp paste and butter and remove from heat. Add liquid from the pan, a spoonful at a time, to the egg yolks until they are sufficiently dissolved not to curdle. Return mixture to the pan. Serve on hot platter. Garnish with cooked shrimp (crayfish if available) and Fish Quenelles. Allow a half-pound of fish per serving.

38. ROULADE OF EEL *(Rolada z Węgorza)*

1 med. eel	1 raw egg
5 hard-cooked eggs	4 cups strong vegetable broth
2–3 pickled gherkins	2 tbs. vinegar
4–6 med. mushrooms, sliced and	1 lemon
sautéed in butter	marinated mushrooms for gar-
salt and pepper to taste	nish

Skin and clean the eel, and split lengthwise along the spine for easy boning. Bone. Salt inside and out and fill with following stuffing: Chop 3 hard-cooked eggs, the gherkins, and mushrooms, season with salt and pepper, and add the raw egg. Mix thoroughly.

Wrap stuffed eel in cheesecloth and roll tightly together so that it will fit into as small a saucepan as possible. Add broth and vinegar and simmer, covered, for half an hour. Let eel stand in broth until it cools. Then remove cheesecloth and chill. Garnish with remaining hard-cooked eggs cut into slices, lemon slices, and marinated mushrooms. Serve with Mustard Sauce or mayonnaise. (Remaining broth may be used for fish sauce or aspic.) Allow a half-pound of eel per serving.

39. EEL IN ASPIC *(Węgorz w Galarecie)*

1 med. eel, with head	1 bay leaf
1 onion, sliced	few sprigs parsley
1–2 carrots, diced	1 raw egg
1 celery root, diced	2–3 hard-cooked eggs, sliced
1 parsley root, diced	1 lemon, sliced thin
1 stalk celery and celery leaves	12–16 cooked crayfish or shrimp
6 peppercorns	1 envelope gelatin

Clean and skin eel. Cook diced vegetables and spices in enough water to make stock for aspic—4 to 6 cups. When vegetables are nearly done, add fish and simmer, tightly covered, for 30 minutes. Remove fish from broth, add the raw egg with crushed shell and let broth boil up once. Allow to stand until broth clears, then strain. Cut fish into serving pieces. Arrange in mold, together with slices of egg and lemon and the cooked shrimp. Dissolve gelatin in a little cold water, add to broth, season to taste, and fill the mold. Chill thoroughly. Allow a half-pound of fish per serving.

40. FISH CUTLETS *(Kotlety z Ryb)*

1 lb. boned fish meat (carp, perch, or any fish with few bones)	2 egg yolks
	salt and pepper to taste
½ med. onion, minced and lightly browned in butter	bread crumbs for rolling
	butter or vegetable fat for frying
1 stale white roll, moistened with milk, *or* equivalent in bread crumbs	

I.

Chop raw fish, add onion, roll, egg yolks, and seasoning, and mix thoroughly. Shape into oblong cutlets, roll in bread crumbs, and fry in hot butter or vegetable fat. Garnish with parsley and lemon slices. Separately, serve Tomato, Anchovy, Caper, Brown Butter, or Hollandaise Sauce (see Index). Serves 3 to 4.

II.

Prepare the same as *I*, adding 2 tbs. sweet cream, and 2 egg whites, beaten stiff and folded in after remaining ingredients have been mixed.

III.

Prepare the same as I, but instead of rolling in bread crumbs and frying, roll in flour and cook 10 minutes in boiling water, covered. Drain, allow to dry, dip in beaten egg and in bread crumbs, and fry in butter until golden brown.

41. FISH SOUFFLÉ *(Soufflé z Ryb)*

2 lbs. boned fish	salt to taste
1 tbs. butter	6 egg whites, beaten stiff
dash of pepper	4–6 tbs. grated Parmesan
dash of nutmeg	

Chop fish fine or put through meat grinder. Add creamed butter and seasoning, combine with beaten egg whites, and continue beating until thoroughly mixed and stiff. Pour into well-greased baking dish, leaving mixture in a mound rather than spreading evenly. Sprinkle thickly with grated Parmesan and bake in medium-hot oven for 25 minutes. Test with straw for doneness. Serve with melted brown butter or Anchovy Sauce (see Index). Serves 7 to 8. (A good way to utilize leftover egg whites.)

42. BAKED LEFTOVER FISH *(Potrawa Zapiekana)*

2 lbs. potatoes, peeled and sliced	4–5 tbs. grated Parmesan
2 cups leftover fish, boned and skinned (proportion may be varied)	salt and pepper to taste
	1 cup sour cream
	2–3 tbs. butter
2–3 hard-cooked eggs, sliced	2 tbs. bread crumbs

Cook sliced potatoes in boiling salted water, taking care not to overcook. Drain. In a well-greased casserole arrange alternate layers of potato, fish, and egg, sprinkling each with Parmesan. Potatoes should form the first and last layers. Pour sour cream over top, sprinkle with bread crumbs lightly browned in butter, and bake in medium-hot oven for 30 minutes, or until crisp on top. Serves 4 to 5.

43. FISH CROQUETTES *(Krokiety z Ryb)*

1 tbs. butter	1 tsp. chopped fresh dill
2 eggs, separated	salt and pepper to taste
1 lb. boned cooked fish	1 beaten egg
1 lb. mushrooms, sliced and sautéed in butter	flour, butter, and bread crumbs for frying
1 tbs. chopped fresh parsley	

Cream butter and 2 egg yolks. Combine with fish, mushrooms, and chopped herbs, and season to taste. Beat 2 egg whites until stiff

and fold in. Shape into croquettes, roll in flour, then in the third
egg, slightly beaten, and bread crumbs. Fry in butter to a golden
brown. Serve with a sharp sauce and salad. Serves 3.

44. SOLE IN WHITE WINE *(Sola na Białem Winie)*

1 tbs. butter	¼ tsp. tarragon (optional)
1 cup strong vegetable broth	2 lbs. sole (or flounder)
1 cup dry white wine	2 tsp. butter ⎱ for thickening
4–5 mushrooms, sliced	1½ tsp. flour ⎰
salt and pepper to taste	2 egg yolks, lightly beaten

**Combine 1 tbs. butter, broth, wine, mushrooms and seasonings in
heavy saucepan.** Add fish and simmer, tightly covered, for 20 to 30
minutes. Melt remaining butter without browning, stir in flour,
and dilute with enough of the cooking liquid to blend thoroughly.
Slowly add egg yolks, taking care not to curdle sauce. Add more
broth, until sauce is the desired thickness. Pour over fish arranged
on a hot platter. Serves 6.

45. SOLE BAKED IN SOUR CREAM *(Sola Zapiekana)*

2 lbs. sole (or flounder)	4 tbs. grated Parmesan
flour	1 cup sour cream
salt and pepper to taste	bread crumbs and butter for
3 tbs. butter	topping

**Season fish, dust with flour, and brown lightly in butter. Arrange in
shallow baking dish.** Sprinkle thickly with Parmesan. Pour in the
sour cream to which ½ tsp. flour has been added, sprinkle with bread
crumbs, and top with bits of butter. Bake in hot oven for 20 minutes. Serve with lemon slices. Serves 6 to 7.

46. BAKED SOLE WITH TOMATO SAUCE
(Sola Zapiekana z Pomidorami)

3 lbs. sole (or flounder)	½ parsley root, sliced
3 tbs. butter	1 leek
flour	1 tsp. Worcestershire sauce
5–6 med. tomatoes	few tbs. bouillon
1 onion, minced	salt and pepper to taste
1 carrot, diced	bread crumbs and butter for
1 celery stalk, sliced	topping
¼ celery root, sliced	

Prepare fish as in No. 45, and arrange in baking dish. In separate
pan sauté in butter the tomatoes, onion, and other vegetables. When
quite soft put through a sieve, add Worcestershire, seasoning, and,
if not liquid enough, a little bouillon. Pour sauce over fish, sprinkle
with bread crumbs, and top with bits of butter. Bake in hot oven

for 20 minutes or until brown on top. Serves 6 to 7. (Small flounders may be prepared in similar manner, without, however, skinning and boning. Allow 1 fish per portion.)

47. HERRING *(Śledzie)*

Salt herring should be soaked for 24 hours in water, and the water changed several times. They should subsequently be soaked in milk for 3 to 4 hours. After soaking, dry off, skin, cut open, and clean, reserving milts and roe. Prepare according to any of the following recipes.

48. FRIED HERRING *(Śledzie Smażone)*

8 salt herring	salt and pepper to taste
juice ½ lemon	bread crumbs for rolling
flour	3–4 tbs. butter
1 egg, slightly beaten	

Prepare herring as indicated in No. 47. Drain, sprinkle with lemon juice, dust with flour, and season lightly. Dip in egg and roll in bread crumbs. Fry in hot butter, turning once, until nicely brown. Serves 4.

49. STUFFED HERRING *(Śledzie Nadziewane)*

6 large, fat herring	1 cup bread crumbs
juice ½ lemon	salt and pepper
½ med. onion, minced and browned in a little butter	flour for rolling
2 eggs	3–4 tbs. butter

Prepare herring as in No. 47. Chop milts and roe, combine with onion, 1 whole egg, and about half the bread crumbs (less, if stuffing seems too dry). Season and mix thoroughly. Stuff herring with mixture and secure with toothpicks. Sprinkle with lemon juice, dust with flour, dip in second egg, slightly beaten, and roll in bread crumbs. Fry in butter, turning once, until golden brown. Serves 6.

50. HERRING PATTIES WITH EGGS
(Kotlety ze Śledzi z Jajkami)

6 fat herring	salt and pepper to taste
2 rolls, moistened with milk	bread crumbs
1 small onion, minced and browned in a little butter	3–4 tbs. butter
1–2 eggs, according to taste preference	

Prepare herring as in No. 47. Bone and put through meat grinder, together with rolls. Add onion, the slightly beaten egg, and season to taste. Mix well and shape into patties. Roll in bread crumbs and fry in hot butter until brown on both sides. Keep hot. In the meantime, using the butter in the pan, fry as many eggs as there are patties. (Use a cover so that whites will steam and become firm quickly.) Arrange eggs on top of patties and serve with a sharp sauce. Serve with mashed potatoes. Makes 6 to 8 servings.

51. HERRING CREAM (*Krem ze Śledzi*)

4 large herring	1 onion, grated
2 rolls, moistened with milk	3 tbs. Parmesan cheese
2 tbs. butter	salt and pepper to taste
2 eggs	dash of nutmeg
3 tbs. sour cream	bread crumbs

Soak, clean, and bone herring as directed in No. 47. Put through meat grinder with the rolls. Cream the milts and roe with 1 tbs. butter and 2 egg yolks. Add sour cream, onion, and Parmesan, and combine with chopped fish and rolls. Season to taste and mix thoroughly. Beat egg whites until stiff and fold in last. Pour into greased shallow baking dish, leaving the mixture in pyramid shape. Do not flatten. Sprinkle liberally with bread crumbs, dot with remaining butter, and bake in medium-hot oven for 30 minutes. Serve with melted butter. Serves 5 to 6.

52. BOILED CRAYFISH (*Raki z Wody*)—*Basic Recipe*

live crayfish, 5 or 6 per portion	boiling salted water to cover
large bunch of fresh dill	

Crayfish must be bought live. Pick large ones for entrees, leaving smaller ones for soup or sauce. Scrub well with brush and throw into vigorously boiling, well-salted water to which a large bunch of fresh dill has been added. Cook for 15 to 20 minutes, counting from time when water again comes to a boil. Drain, and serve very hot with drawn butter. (Shrimp may be substituted for crayfish in most recipes.)

53. CRAYFISH POLISH-STYLE
(*Raki po Polsku w Śmietanie*)

30 large crayfish	2 cups sour cream
1 tbs. butter	1 heaping tbs. bread crumbs
salt to taste	1 heaping tbs. chopped fresh dill

Scrub the crayfish thoroughly and throw into boiling unsalted water for a minute or two. Drain and rinse. Put into saucepan with melted butter and simmer for 10 minutes, until crayfish turn red. Salt lightly, add sour cream, bread crumbs, and dill. Simmer, tightly covered, for another 15 minutes. (Overcooking kills the taste.) Serve at once. Serves 5 to 6.

54. CRAYFISH SMOTHERED IN WINE *(Raki na Winie)*

30 large crayfish	½ cup water
boiling milk to cover	1 tbs. vinegar
salt	salt to taste
1 cup white wine	1 heaping tbs. chopped dill

Scrub and rinse the crayfish. Arrange tightly in saucepan and cover with boiling well-salted milk. Allow to stand 4 hours. Rinse again in tepid water, return to saucepan, and cover with combined wine, water, and vinegar, which have been brought to a boil. Add dill, cover tightly, and cook over high heat for 15 minutes. Serve at once, very hot. Serves 5 to 6.

55. RAGOUT OF CRAYFISH WITH BARLEY
(Potrawa z Raków z Kaszą)

30 large crayfish	salt to taste
bunch of dill	1 cup pearl barley
2 tbs. bread crumbs	¼ lb. mushrooms, sliced and
1 tbs. butter	sautéed in butter
2 eggs, separated	

Scrub crayfish and cook in boiling salted water with dill, as in No. 52. Allow to cool, and pick meat from tails and claws, cleaning out black thread on back of tail. Carefully lift out fat and coral from belly; discard eyes and bile. Chop half the tails and combine with bread crumbs, butter, egg yolks, salt, and a heaping tablespoon of chopped dill. Fold in stiffly-beaten egg whites, mix lightly, and use mixture to fill crayfish shells. Cook these in boiling salted water for about 10 minutes.

Separately cook the pearl barley mixed with raw egg and 1 tbs. dill (see Index).

Arrange the cooked, drained crayfish shells on a mound of barley. Make sauce from remaining shells, feet, etc. (see Crayfish Sauce). Combine with remaining half of the cooked tails and with the mushrooms and pour over stuffed shells. Serves 6.

56. CRAYFISH PUDDING WITH GREEN PEAS
(Budyń z Raków z Zielonym Groszkiem)

30 crayfish	2 cups peas
6 tbs. butter	2 tbs. butter
bunch of fresh dill	1 cup rice
salt to taste	2 cups bouillon

Scrub crayfish and cook in salted water with dill as in No. 52. Pick out meat from tail, body, and large claws, discarding only bile and eyes. Remove black thread from undertails. Pound shells, small legs, and bits of meat, and use these to make Crayfish Butter (see Index), using half the butter.

Separately cook 2 cups green peas by steaming in 2 tbs. butter and ¼ cup salted water for 15 to 20 minutes.

Cook 1 cup rice with 1 heaping tbs. of the Crayfish Butter and 2 cups bouillon, until rice is fluffy and dry (see Index).

In a well-buttered casserole arrange alternately layers of rice, crayfish meat, and peas, ending with layer of rice. Melt remaining butter and pour over rice. Bake in medium-hot oven for 30 minutes.

Make Crayfish Sauce, using the liquid in which shells simmered for the Crayfish Butter, and a tablespoon of the Crayfish Butter (see Index). Pour over pudding. Serves 6.

57. FRIED FROG LEGS (Żabki Smażone)

16 pairs frog legs	1–2 eggs, slightly beaten
salt and pepper to taste	bread crumbs for rolling
flour for dusting	4 tbs. butter

Wash, drain, and salt the frog legs an hour ahead of time. Dust with flour, dip in egg, and roll in bread crumbs. Fry in hot butter, turning once, until golden brown. Garnish with lemon slices and parsley. Serves 4.

58. RAGOUT OF FROG LEGS (Żabki w Potrawce)

16 pairs frog legs	½ cup white wine
flour for dusting	¼ cup bouillon
3 tbs. butter	salt and pepper to taste
4 med. mushrooms, sliced thin	3 egg yolks, lightly beaten
¼ lb. sweetbreads	lemon slices

Wash, dry, and salt the frog legs. Dust with flour and fry in half the butter to a light, golden brown. Arrange tightly in saucepan, add sliced mushrooms, the sweetbreads cut in small pieces, the rest of the butter, the wine, and bouillon. Season to taste and simmer, tightly covered, for 30 minutes. Arrange frog legs on a hot platter. Combine pan liquid with egg yolks, stirring in a little at a time and taking care not to curdle. Pour this sauce over the frog legs and garnish with lemon slices. Serves 4.

59. STUFFED SNAILS (*Ślimaki Nadziewane*)

4 doz. snails	2 eggs
½ onion, minced	salt and pepper to taste
6 mushrooms, sliced	dash of fresh-ground nutmeg
4 tbs. butter	2 tbs. bread crumbs
1 white roll, moistened with milk	clove of garlic (optional)

Rinse snails in several waters. Then put into enough hot salted water to cover, and bring to a boil. When snails come out of their shells, drain; rinse shells again and let dry. Combine snails, onion, and mushrooms with 1 tbs. butter and simmer, tightly covered, for half an hour. Add roll and chop fine. Combine with slightly-beaten eggs, another tablespoon of butter, and seasoning. Mix thoroughly and fill snail shells with the mixture. Arrange in shallow baking dish, and over each shell pour melted butter and bread crumbs which may be flavored with garlic. Put into hot oven or under broiler for 10 minutes to allow to brown. Serves 4 to 6.

60. FRIED SNAILS (*Ślimaki Smażone*)

4 doz. snails	butter
salted water to cover	clove of garlic (optional)
2 eggs, slightly beaten	lemon slices
bread crumbs	small bunch parsley
deep fat for frying or ¼ lb.	

Soak and wash snails as directed in No. 59, and start in boiling salted water. When snails come out of their shells, boil up once, drain, and allow to dry. Dip in egg, roll in bread crumbs, and fry in deep fat or in hot butter. (Butter will give them a more delicate flavor.) The fat may be flavored with garlic, which should be later discarded. Garnish with lemon slices and sprigs of parsley fried in the butter. Serves 4 to 5.

Poultry and Poultry Stuffings

Poultry is best fresh-killed and young. Young birds are easily recognizable by their fat necks and well-filled feet and knee-joints. Old birds have skinny feet and stringy, bluish necks. The beak and breastbone (which is cartilege) should be resilient to the touch. Old birds will also have long single hairs on the skin.

The advantage of fresh-killed poultry is that it is eviscerated at once, whereas frozen birds get an ad-taste of whatever feed is left in the gizzards. Oven-ready poultry, on the other hand, is cleaned before it is frozen and so has a fresh taste.

For tenderness it is advisable, though not strictly necessary, to soak poultry in *cold* water for a couple of hours before using.

All poultry should be salted 1 to 3 hours ahead of time, depending on size.

Stuff birds by filling both neck and body cavities lightly. Sew openings together or secure with skewers. Truss birds.

When using a spit or an electric rotisserie, poultry should be done at high temperature and brushed frequently with fat so that it will brown evenly and crisply. For oven roasting, start in slow oven, then turn heat up for last half-hour. Large birds may be roasted in a brown-paper bag rubbed with butter or bacon fat. Remove paper after half an hour.

Small birds, like roasting chickens and squabs, should be done in a hot oven throughout, in order to brown them fast without drying out. Frequent basting is important.

Stuffings

1. WHOLE CHESTNUT STUFFING
(Nadzienie z Całych Kasztanów)

1 lb. fresh chestnuts	2–3 tbs. butter

Make incisions in the nuts with a sharp knife, cover with cold water, and boil up several times. When cool enough to handle, remove shells and inner dark skin. Simmer, tightly covered, with the butter for about 20 minutes, using a heavy skillet so the nuts will not stick. When tender, stuff neck and body cavity of the bird, sew up, and roast as directed.

2. SWEET CHESTNUT STUFFING
(Farsz Słodki z Kasztanów)

1 lb. chestnuts	1 tsp. sugar
2 tbs. butter	4 tbs. heavy cream
3 eggs, separated	dash of salt
3 heaping tbs. bread crumbs	

Slit the chestnuts and boil for about 20 minutes. Shell and remove dark skin. Mash or put through a sieve. Cream butter and egg yolks, add bread crumbs, sugar, dash of salt, the chestnuts, and cream, and mix thoroughly. Beat egg whites stiff and fold in last. Stuff neck and body cavity, sew up bird, and roast as directed.

3. MEAT AND CHESTNUT STUFFING
(Farsz z Mięsa z Kasztanami)

½ lb. pork	dash of nutmeg
¼ lb. veal	2 onions, grated and smothered in
¼ lb. salt pork or fat bacon	butter until transparent but not
1 hard roll, moistened in milk and	brown
mashed (or ½ cup bread crumbs)	½ lb. chestnuts, boiled for 20 min-
1 whole egg	utes and shelled
dash of pepper and salt	

Put meat and salt pork through meat grinder. Combine with other ingredients, season, and mix thoroughly. Boil chestnuts as in No. 1, shell, and leave whole. Add to rest of stuffing and mix. Fill neck and body cavities of bird with stuffing. Sew up and roast according to directions.

4. RAISIN STUFFING *(Farsz z Rodzynkami)*

turkey or capon liver
3 eggs, separated
1 tbs. sweet butter
2 heaping tbs. bread crumbs
salt and pepper to taste
dash of nutmeg

2 cloves
1 tsp. sugar
1 heaping tbs. chopped fresh parsley (or dill and parsley combined)
½ cup raisins

Chop the liver (add an extra liver if available) and combine with egg yolks creamed with butter. Then add other ingredients. Season and mix thoroughly. Beat egg whites stiff and fold in last. Stuff breast and body cavity, sew up, and roast as directed.

5. LIVER PÂTÉ STUFFING *(Farsz Pasztetowy z Wątróbki)*

1 lb. calf's liver
2 tbs. bread crumbs
¼ lb. fat bacon or salt pork, chopped
salt and pepper to taste

dash of nutmeg
dash of grated ginger
3 eggs, separated
1 tbs. butter

Chop liver and put through sieve. Add bread crumbs, chopped bacon, spices, and seasoning. Cream egg yolks with butter, combine with rest of stuffing, and mix thoroughly. Beat egg whites stiff and fold in last. Stuff bird and roast as directed.

6. CRAYFISH OR SHRIMP STUFFING *(Farsz z Rakami)*

1 turkey or capon liver, smothered in butter for about 5 minutes
12 cooked crayfish or shrimp (see Index)
1 tbs. Crayfish Butter (see Index) if available

2 eggs, separated
1 hard roll, moistened in milk and mashed, or ¼ cup bread crumbs
4–6 mushrooms, sliced and smothered in butter for 5 minutes
salt and pepper to taste

Chop liver and press through sieve. Chop crayfish or shrimp meat. Cream Crayfish Butter with egg yolks (if unavailable, use plain butter). Combine everything with roll or bread crumbs and with the smothered mushrooms, and season to taste. Beat egg whites stiff and fold in last. Stuff the bird and roast as directed.

Turkey, Capon, and Chicken

7. ROAST TURKEY OR CAPON
(Indyk lub Kaplon Pieczony)

turkey or capon (6–8 lbs.)	stuffing according to prefer-
salt and pepper to taste	ence
few strips bacon or salt pork	3–4 tbs. melted butter
for larding (optional)	

Prepare bird according to directions at beginning of chapter. Carefully separate the skin from the neck and breast to make a pocket for stuffing. Season inside and out and let stand 3 hours. Stuff both breast and body cavities, sew together, rub with butter, and roast on spit or in oven according to basic directions at beginning of chapter. Baste frequently. A large bird needs about 2½ to 3 hours. A smaller bird should be done in 2 hours. Test by inserting fork in thick part of thigh. If juice is pink, the bird is not done. If fat runs out, it is ready. Add a very little water to pan drippings, let bubble up, and serve separately. Serves 6 to 8.

8. TURKEY IN MADEIRA SAUCE
(Indyk w Sosie Maderowym)

The original recipe calls for 1 lb. of truffles smothered in white wine, half of them for larding the bird and half to be added to a meat and liver stuffing. However, this recipe is still a good one when modified for modern cooking.

Make a stuffing following Recipe No. 3, omitting chestnuts and increasing the quantity of ground meat. Or use Recipe No. 5, or a combination of both (meat, liver, and bacon in any proportion to make up 4 cups, not counting the turkey liver). Use mushrooms instead of truffles in stuffing, allowing about a half-pound. Use dash of thyme.

Madeira Sauce:

½ bottle Madeira wine	2 tbs. butter
1 cup strong bouillon or beef broth	1 tbs. flour

Roast stuffed turkey in oven according to directions at beginning of chapter until half-done. Add wine and bouillon and continue roasting, basting constantly. When meat is tender, make thickening by browning the butter, blending in flour, and then stirring in enough liquid so there are no lumps. Add to pan and allow to bubble up once or twice. Carve the bird, arrange on platter, moisten with a little gravy and serve the rest in separate dish. Serve with broiled mushrooms, asparagus, new parsley potatoes, or with Potato Croquettes and Chicken Quenelles. (See Index.)

9. TURKEY CASSEROLE WITH LEFTOVER MEAT
(Potrawa z Pieczonego Indyka)

2–3 cups leftover turkey, diced	1 tsp. grated lemon rind
Brown Sauce (see Index)	1 bouillon cube
salt and pepper to taste	1 sweetbread or ½ calf's brain
lemon juice to taste	(optional)
dash of ground ginger (grated	½ tsp. Maggi extract
fresh ginger if available)	

Make enough Brown Sauce for generous helpings, 2 to 3 cups. Add seasoning and spices. Dilute bouillon cube with enough water to dissolve and add to sauce. Allow to simmer a few minutes. Add meat and heat through. If sweetbread or brain is used, cook this separately (see Index), then dice and add. Serves 5 to 7.

10. TURKEY PATTIES *(Kotlety z Indyka)*

2 lbs. raw meat from turkey breast	chopped and smothered in but-
3 egg yolks	ter for 5 minutes, may be sub-
1 tbs. butter	stituted)
salt and pepper to taste	¼ cup melted butter
dash of grated or ground ginger	juice ½ lemon
2 truffles (4 small mushrooms,	

Bone the meat, chop fine, and pound or put through a sieve. Cream egg yolks and butter, add seasoning and truffles or mushrooms, and mix thoroughly. Shape into small oval patties, dip each in melted butter, and fry until golden brown. Then arrange in shallow baking dish, and cover with greased paper. Fifteen minutes before serving, put into very hot oven. When done, remove paper and sprinkle with lemon juice. Serve with Chestnut or Mushroom Purée (see Index) or with green peas. Separately serve Mushroom or Madeira Sauce (see Index).

11. ROAST CAPON OR CHICKEN WITH ANCHOVIES
(Kapłon lub Pularda Pieczone z Sardelami)

capon or chicken (5–6 lbs.)	butter for roasting
salt and pepper	

Soak bird for a couple of hours in cold water if possible. Wipe, rub well with salt inside and out, and allow to stand an hour.

Stuffing:

¼ lb. bacon
1 lb. veal
    chicken liver
1–2 tbs. butter
1 med. onion, minced
6 peppercorns
6 allspice
    few sprigs parsley

1 hard roll, moistened with milk and mashed (or equivalent amount of bread crumbs)
8–10 anchovies
3 eggs, separated
½ tsp. lemon rind
    dash of grated ginger
    salt and pepper to taste

Combine bacon, veal cut in pieces, and liver with onion and spices. Smother in butter, tightly covered, for about half an hour or until tender, taking care that mixture does not brown or stick. (It is best to add liver only during the last 10 minutes.) Then put mixture through meat grinder, along with the roll. Chop anchovies very fine, cream with egg yolks, add lemon rind, ginger, and salt and pepper to taste. Combine with meat mixture. Beat egg whites stiff and fold in last. Stuff bird and roast as directed, first in slow, then hot oven, for 1½ to 2 hours. Serves 6.

12. MOCK PHEASANT MADE WITH CAPON
(*Kapłon na Sposób Bażanta*)

  capon (5–6 lbs.)
1 tbs. ground juniper berries

¼ lb. salt pork for larding
  salt and pepper to taste

Rub capon inside and out with ground juniper berries, and refrigerate for 2 to 3 days. When ready to use, allow to stand at room temperature for several hours. Lard generously and rub with salt about an hour before stuffing.

Stuffing:

1 tbs. butter
2 eggs, separated
1 white roll, moistened in milk and mashed (or equivalent amount bread crumbs)

pinch of ground juniper
dash of ground ginger
salt and pepper to taste

Cream butter and egg yolks, combine with roll or bread crumbs, juniper, ginger, and seasoning to taste. Beat egg whites stiff and fold in last. Stuff bird, sew together, and roast on spit or in oven, brushing frequently with melted butter. Cover with greased brown paper during first half-hour. Serves 5 to 6.

13. CAPON OR CHICKEN STUFFED WITH HAM
(*Kapłon Nadziewany Szynką*)

capon or large roasting chicken (5–6 lbs.)

salt and pepper

Soak bird in cold water for a few hours, wipe, rub with salt, and allow to stand an hour before stuffing.

Stuffing:

½ lb. boneless veal (uncooked)
½ lb. boiled ham
¼ lb. (or less) bacon or salt pork
3 tbs. sour cream
½ white roll moistened in milk and
1 hard roll moistened in milk and mashed, or ½ cup moistened

2 whole eggs, lightly beaten
salt and pepper to taste
4 med. mushrooms (or 2 truffles, if available)

Chop meat and bacon fine, then pound in mortar or put through a sieve. Add sour cream in the process. Add mashed roll or bread crumbs, the eggs, seasoning, and chopped mushrooms. Mix thoroughly and stuff neck and body cavities of bird. Sew up, brush with butter, and roast according to basic directions (about 1½ to 2 hours).

14. CAPON OR CHICKEN IN CREAM
(Kapłon lub Kura z Kremem z Pieca)

capon (5–6 lbs.)
court bouillon to cover (see Index)
4 egg yolks
1 heaping tbs. butter

1 tbs. flour
2 cups sour cream
salt and pepper to taste
½–1 cup very strong bouillon

Rub bird with salt an hour beforehand. Simmer for an hour in court bouillon, taking care not to overcook. Allow to cool. In the meantime, cream egg yolks and butter, add flour, blend thoroughly, and combine with sour cream. Season lightly and whip until stiff. Allow to thicken in top of a double boiler, stirring constantly to keep from curdling or sticking (handle like Hollandaise Sauce). Cool. Make incisions in capon as for carving, without cutting through. Fill these with cream, and then spread rest over the whole surface of the bird. Roast in shallow baking pan in very hot oven for 20 minutes, allowing cream to brown. When done, pour hot bouillon over it. Serve with Potato Croquettes and cauliflower, or with salad. Serves 6 to 7.

15. CAPON OR CHICKEN AND RICE CASSEROLE
(Potrawa z Kapłona z Ryżem)

capon or chicken (4–5 lbs.)
1 large onion
2 carrots
½ celery root
1 parsley root
1 leek
1 parsnip
few sprigs parsley

salt and pepper to taste
2 tbs. butter
1 tbs. flour
juice ½ lemon
1 tsp. lemon rind (optional)
2 egg yolks
1 cup uncooked rice

Clean capon and rub with salt one hour ahead of time if possible. Start in just enough cold water to cover, and simmer with giblets, onion, soup greens, and a little pepper until tender—about 1½ hours. (Do not overcook or meat will fall apart and lose its taste.) Carve into serving pieces. Cream 1 tablespoon of butter with the flour, adding enough of the stock to make 1 to 1½ cups sauce, according to thickness desired. In the meantime, use 2 cups of the stock for cooking rice (see Index). Return fowl to sauce, add lemon juice and rind to taste, and allow to simmer about 10 minutes. Cream egg yolks with remaining butter and add to sauce directly before serving, blending thoroughly a little at a time so that egg will not curdle. Arrange on top of rice. The vegetables may be strained out of the broth or not, according to personal preference. Serves 6.

16. CAPON OR CHICKEN CASSEROLE WITH MUSHROOMS *(Pularda z Pieczarkami)*

chicken or capon (4–5 lbs.)	1 cup sweet cream
soup greens as in No. 15	½ tsp. Maggi extract
6–12 mushrooms, depending on size	1 tbs. chopped fresh dill
	salt and pepper to taste
1 tbs. butter	2 egg yolks
1 tbs. flour	

Cook bird the same as in No. 15, but use no more than 2 cups of water to start. Simmer covered. After 1 hour add the mushrooms. When bird is done—about 1½ hours—carve into serving pieces, slice mushrooms, heart, liver, and gizzard, and strain the stock. Cream butter and flour until smooth, blend in soup stock and stir until smooth. Add cream, Maggi extract, dill, and salt and pepper to taste. Return meat to sauce and simmer another 10 to 15 minutes. Just before serving add lightly-beaten egg yolks, taking care not to curdle. Serve with Marrow Balls. Serves 6.

17. CAPON CASSEROLE WITH SOUR CREAM *(Potrawa z Pulardy ze Śmietaną)*

Prepare the same as No. 16, but omit mushrooms and egg yolks. Substitute sour cream for sweet cream.

18. CAPON OR CHICKEN CASSEROLE WITH CURRANTS *(Potrawa z Pulardy z Agrestem)*

chicken or capon (4–5 lbs.)	1 tbs. butter
soup greens as in No. 15	1 tbs. flour
salt and pepper to taste	pinch of sugar (optional)
1 pt. white currants	1 cup sour cream (optional)

Season and prepare chicken as in No. 15. Start with boiling liquid and simmer until done, about 1½ hours. Simmer currants in 1 cup of soup stock for about 5 minutes. Melt butter but do not brown. Blend in flour, dissolve with a little broth, stirring until smooth. Add remaining broth and currant mixture. Cut bird into serving pieces and return to sauce. Let bubble up. For a sweet-sour sauce, add sour cream and sugar to taste. Serves 6.

19. EMPEROR CASSEROLE OF CAPON
(Potrawa z Pulardy po Cesarsku)

capon or chicken (4–5 lbs.)	salt and pepper to taste
butter for browning	1 cup bouillon
12 shallots or small white onions	1 cup red wine
6 med. mushrooms, sliced or quartered	2 tsp. butter
	2 tsp. flour
1–2 truffles, sliced thin	½ tsp. Maggi extract

Clean and salt capon 1 hour ahead of time. Cut in serving pieces and brown lightly in butter in casserole in which it is to cook. Add peeled onions, mushrooms, and truffles. Season to taste and simmer, tightly covered, for about ½ hour. Add bouillon and wine and continue simmering until done—20 to 30 minutes. Melt butter to a light-brown color, blend in flour, add enough of the liquid to blend thoroughly, and use to thicken sauce. Add Maggi extract, allow to bubble up, and pour over meat. If time permits, this dish may be made without cutting the capon until after it is tender; the taste will be more delicate. If cooked whole, allow 1½ hours. Serves 6.

20. CAPON À LA NEVA (Pularda à la Newa)

Capon, prepared as in No. 15.

Stuffing:

¼ lb. chicken or goose livers	1 cup heavy cream, whipped
bacon for wrapping them	2 cups White Sauce made with
1½ ozs. cognac (or brandy)	the chicken stock (see Index)
1½ ozs. Madeira wine	seasoning to taste
¼ lb. butter	1 envelope gelatin
¼ lb. Parmesan cheese, grated	
salt, pepper, and cayenne to taste	

Simmer the capon in water to cover for about 1½ hours, taking care not to overcook—meat must not separate from the bones. Carefully cut skin and carve away meat from breast to make room for stuffing. Make stuffing as follows:

Wrap each liver in a piece of bacon, secure with toothpicks, and bake in slow oven for about 10 minutes. Allow to cool. Pound to a mass or put through ricer together with brandy and wine. Cream butter, add to liver mixture. Add Parmesan, season to taste, and press through a sieve. Fold in whipped cream last. Fill the bird with the stuffing, replace the breast meat, and secure with toothpicks.

Make White Sauce and season rather highly. Dissolve gelatin in ¼ cup water and add to sauce. Allow to cool and pour over chicken, making sure that breast meat is covered quite thickly. Let stand in refrigerator until sauce jells. Garnish with thin slices of truffle or with carrot slices in fancy shapes. Serve on a bed of cold cooked rice, with cooked vegetables in French dressing. Serves 6.

21. CAPON SMOTHERED WITH HAM
(Pularda Duszona Z Szynką)

capon or chicken (4-5 lbs.)	salt and pepper to taste
butter for browning	2 cups chicken broth or bouillon
¼ lb. ham, cut in small strips	3 ozs. alcohol
6-12 mushrooms, depending on size, chopped	1 tbs. butter
1 onion, grated	1 tbs. flour
1 heaping tbs. chopped dill	½ tsp. Maggi extract

Cut capon into serving pieces and salt 1 hour before cooking. Brown the capon lightly on all sides; add ham, mushrooms, onion, and dill, and season to taste. Add a few tablespoons of the broth and simmer, tightly covered. Continue adding broth and alcohol. Simmer until tender, about 1 hour, longer if necessary. When tender, make a thickening of butter and flour, browning butter lightly and diluting with enough broth to blend thoroughly. Add to sauce. Add Maggi extract, and allow to simmer another 5 to 10 minutes or until sauce thickens. Serves 6.

22. VOL-AU-VENT OF CAPON OR CHICKEN
(Vol-au-Vent z Pulardy)

capon or chicken (4-5 lbs.)	1 tbs. butter
court bouillon to cover (see Index)	1 tbs. flour
6 whole and 6 sliced mushrooms	½ cup heavy sweet cream
¼ cup green peas	2-3 egg yolks
½ package frozen asparagus tips (or equivalent in fresh asparagus)	12 cooked crayfish (or shrimp)
	lemon juice to taste
1 calf sweetbread, sliced	pastry shell made of French Pastry Dough (see Index) or a
salt and pepper to taste	prepared mix

Simmer the capon and the giblets in court bouillon, tightly covered, until tender but not falling apart. When meat is done (about 1½ hours) allow to cool enough for handling. In the meantime, cook mushrooms, peas, asparagus, and sweetbreads in the cooking liquid until everything is done—about 20 minutes. While the vegetables cook, skin the chicken, cut the meat into small pieces, and cut gizzard, heart, and liver into thin strips. Cream butter and flour and then make a white sauce, using the cream and about 1 cup of the broth. Stir constantly to blend well. The sauce should have a thick consistency. Add chicken meat, giblets, sweetbreads, vegetables, and the crayfish or shrimp. Season with lemon juice, salt, and pepper, mix thoroughly, and heat in top of double boiler, taking care sauce does not boil. Have pastry shell ready—heat it in oven if necessary. Pour mixture into shell immediately before serving so that dough does not become soggy. Arrange whole mushrooms over the top. Garnish with fresh parsley sprigs. Serves 6 to 7.

23. POUNDED CAPON CUTLETS *(Kotlety Bite z Pulardy)*

3 capon breasts or 3 large chicken breasts, preferably with wings attached	1 egg, lightly beaten bread crumbs and flour in equal parts, mixed, for rolling
6 thick pats butter salt and pepper	butter for frying

Have butcher split each breast along breastbone and bone it, leaving the wing bone in. Skin, season with salt and pepper, and pound thin, as one would veal cutlet for scaloppine. Place a pat of butter on each piece, then fold meat over, pressing edges together and securing with toothpicks if necessary, so that butter will not ooze out. Dip each cutlet in egg, roll in the flour and bread crumb mixture, and fry in hot butter until nicely brown on both sides. When done, allow to stand in medium-hot oven for a few minutes so they will be thoroughly cooked throughout. Serve with peas, spinach, or Chestnut or Mushroom Purée. Serves 6.

24. POZARSKI CUTLETS *(Kotlety Pożarskie)*

3 capon breasts or 3 large chicken breasts	1 whole egg, lightly beaten bread crumbs and flour in equal
½ lb. chopped veal with some marrow added	parts, mixed, for rolling butter for frying
1 egg yolk salt and pepper to taste	juice ½ lemon ½ cup strong bouillon

Prepare cutlets the same as in No. 23. Instead of butter, use a filling made of chopped veal, marrow, and egg yolk, seasoned well and mixed thoroughly. Proceed as in No. 23. After taking cutlets out of the oven, sprinkle with lemon juice. Make a sauce of the pan drippings and bouillon, allow to bubble up, and pour over meat. Serve with green peas, cauliflower, or Chestnut or Mushroom Purée. Serves 6.

25. CHICKEN CROQUETTES *(Bitki z Pulardy)*

2 chicken breasts, skinned and boned	salt and pepper to taste
1 tbs. butter	6–8 chopped mushrooms (add truffle if available), sautéed in butter
2 eggs, separated	
1 stale roll, moistened in milk and mashed, or equivalent amount of bread crumbs	1 whole egg
	bread crumbs for rolling
	butter for frying

Put meat through grinder. Cream butter with egg yolks, add ground chicken, the roll or bread crumbs, and season to taste. Work with a fork or wooden spoon until mixed to a mush. Fold in beaten egg whites. Use a heaping tablespoon of the mixture for each croquette. Flatten each and place a little of the sautéed mushroom in the center. Roll into ball-shape, dip in beaten egg, roll in flour and bread crumb mixture, and fry in butter until golden-brown on all sides. Put croquettes into hot oven for 5 minutes so they will be well done throughout. Serve garnished with fried parsley sprigs. Separately, serve Madeira Sauce (see Index) or any preferred sharp sauce. Serves 4.

26. POULTRY LIVERS SMOTHERED IN MADEIRA *(Wątróbki z Drobiu Duszone w Maderze)*

½ lb. chicken, turkey, or goose livers	salt and pepper to taste
milk for soaking	flour for dredging
2 tbs. butter	¼ cup bouillon
1 small or ½ med. onion, minced	¼ cup Madeira (or sherry or Marsala)

Soak livers in milk for several hours. Drain, and cut large ones in half. Cook onion in butter until transparent, increase heat, and add livers. Brown quickly on both sides. Season, dredge with flour, and when this too browns, reduce heat. Add bouillon and wine and allow to boil up a couple of times. (Livers should never cook longer than 6 to 8 minutes and should be faintly pink inside; otherwise they will be tough.) Serves 2 to 3.

27. LIVER MOUNDS *(Babki z Wątróbek)*

6 turkey or large capon livers, soaked in milk for a couple of hours

1 stale white roll, moistened in milk and mashed, or equivalent in bread crumbs

3 eggs, separated

1 tbs. butter

salt and pepper to taste

½ med. onion, grated and sautéed in butter

Chop livers, press through a sieve, and then combine with roll or bread crumbs. Cream butter and egg yolks, add to liver mixture, season to taste, and mix thoroughly. Fold in stiffly-beaten egg whites, and spoon the mixture into well-greased muffin tins. Cover with white paper greased with butter, and bake in medium oven for about 30 minutes. Serve as a side dish with a sharp sauce. Serves 6.

28. ROAST YOUNG CHICKEN *(Kurczęta Pieczone)*

Young fryers are excellent roasted either in the oven or on a spit. The birds should be fairly large, 3 to 3½ pounds—2½ to 3 months old. Small ones dry out too much. Follow roasting instructions given at the beginning of chapter. The essential thing to remember is that young birds must be roasted at high heat for a short time in order to brown them quickly and not allow juices to escape. They should also be frequently basted with butter. After the skin is crisp and brown, reduce heat but continue basting. When nearly done, dredge with bread crumbs and baste again with butter. Length of time should not exceed 45 minutes—50 minutes at most for oven roasting. Dredging with bread crumbs may be omitted. Carve chickens by cutting in quarters.

29. ROAST YOUNG CHICKENS POLISH-STYLE
(Kurczęta Pieczone po Polsku)

2 young chickens, about 3½ lbs. each

1½ cups bread crumbs

2 heaping tbs. chopped dill

2 heaping tbs. chopped parsley

½ lb. butter

salt and pepper to taste

To prepare chickens, soak in cold water and rub with salt an hour ahead of time, according to basic directions given at the beginning of chapter. Roast as in No. 28, but first fill the body cavity with stuffing made as follows: Combine bread crumbs with chopped dill and parsley, and add as much butter as needed to hold stuffing together without crumbling. Season. Stuff chickens and sew with cotton thread or secure with toothpicks or skewers. Rub outside with a little butter. Roast as directed, about 45 to 50 minutes.

Serves 6 to 7. Serve with Cucumber and Sour Cream Salad.

Note: An excellent variation is to chop the chicken livers and add them to the stuffing.

30. YOUNG CHICKENS PARTRIDGE-STYLE
(Kurczęta na Sposób Kuropatw)

2 small, fat young chickens, 2½ to 3 lbs. each
1 tbs. crushed juniper berries
salt and pepper to taste
4 ozs. salt pork or bacon for larding

6–8 bacon slices
3–4 tbs. strong bouillon
1 heaping tsp. bread crumbs

Clean and prepare chickens according to basic directions at the beginning of chapter. Rub inside and out with juniper and refrigerate overnight. Rub with salt and pepper an hour before cooking. Lard generously. Line heavy casserole with bacon strips, arrange birds over these, cover casserole tightly, and simmer until nicely brown. *Do not add water.* Add bouillon and bread crumbs and continue simmering until tender—in all, not more than 50 minutes to an hour. Cut each bird in half. Pour sauce over them, and serve with new potatoes and Cucumber and Sour Cream Salad. Serves 4.

31. CHICKEN HUNTER-STYLE *(Kurczęta po Myśliwsku)*

2 young chickens, prepared and larded as in No. 30
¼ lb. boiled ham, chopped
1 whole onion, chopped fine
6 allspice
2 bay leaves
salt and pepper to taste

¼ cup dry white wine
flour for dredging
½ tsp. Soy or Maggi sauce
lemon juice to taste
1 tbs. chopped parsley
½ cup (about) bouillon or chicken broth

Prepare chickens and rub with crushed juniper berries the day before using. Rub with salt, and lard an hour before cooking. Arrange in a heavy pot over the chopped ham and onion. Add allspice, bay leaves, seasoning, and wine, and simmer, tightly covered, until quite soft—about an hour. Dredge lightly with flour and continue simmering another few minutes until sauce thickens. Cut each bird in half. Strain sauce and return to pot, adding Soy sauce, lemon juice, parsley, and bouillon and taking care not to make sauce too thin. Allow to bubble up and then pour over chickens. Separately serve pearl barley with drawn butter and chopped dill, or any form of noodles. Serves 4.

Other Poultry

32. ROAST GUINEA HEN *(Perliczki Pieczone)*

2–3 young guinea hens
olive oil and lemon juice for
rubbing
salt and pepper to taste

4–6 ozs. salt pork for larding (optional)
butter for basting

Guinea hens are best purchased two or three days ahead of time; they should be rubbed with olive oil and lemon juice and allowed to stand in the refrigerator, but not frozen. An hour before using, rinse in lukewarm water, dry, and rub with salt inside and out. Lard if desired. Roast in oven or on spit, following directions for Roast Capon (see Index), for about an hour, basting frequently with butter. Serves 6 to 8. Guinea hen may be prepared according to any of the recipes for capon.

33. GUINEA HEN WITH GINGER *(Perliczki z Imbirem)*

2–3 young guinea hens
1 tsp. grated ginger (fresh or
dried) per bird

salt and pepper to taste
4–6 ozs. salt pork for larding
butter for basting

Prepare birds as in No. 32. After rinsing and drying, rub with ginger as well as salt inside and out. Lard generously. Roast the same as Roast Capon (see Index), allowing about 1 hour. Serves 6 to 8.

34. ROAST PIGEON-SQUAB *(Gołębie Pieczone)*

Squab is good only if young—older birds are tough. Their meat is easily recognized by its purplish-blue tinge. Young squab meat is white and plump. Squab should be fresh-killed, and it should be soaked in cold water for 2 hours before using. Wipe off, rub with salt inside and out, cover with strips of bacon, and roast in hot oven for 30 to 35 minutes, basting frequently with butter. Allow 1 squab per serving.

35. ROAST STUFFED SQUAB
(Gołębie Pieczone Nadziewane)

4 young squabs, prepared for cooking as in No. 34

butter for rubbing

Stuffing:

2 tbs. butter
2 eggs, separated
1 stale white roll, moistened in milk and mashed (or bread crumbs)

salt and pepper to taste
1 heaping tbs. chopped parsley, or parsley and dill combined

Cream butter and egg yolks, add mashed roll or bread crumbs, and season to taste. Then add chopped parsley and mix thoroughly. Finally, fold in stiffly-beaten egg whites. Carefully separate skin around neck and breast and stuff the birds, securing the opening with toothpicks or sewing with cotton thread. Truss, rub with butter, and roast in hot oven for 30 to 35 minutes, basting frequently. Cut in halves. Use pan drippings for sauce. Serve with green salad and cranberries or other fruit preserve. Serves 4.

36. SQUAB AS GAME BIRDS
(*Gołębie na Sposób Dzikich Ptaków*)

4 squabs
1 tbs. crushed juniper berries
salt pork for larding
salt
2-3 strips bacon, diced
1 onion, sliced
1 carrot
1 leek
1-2 celery stalks

½ celery root
½ parsley root
10 peppercorns
1 bay leaf (optional)
pinch of thyme
pinch of marjoram
1 cup dry wine, preferably red
1 tbs. bread crumbs
3-4 tbs. sour cream

Prepare squabs a day ahead of time; rub with juniper inside and out. One hour before cooking lard generously and rub with salt. Arrange in heavy pot or casserole, together with diced bacon, onion, and diced vegetables. Add spices and a little of the wine, cover tightly, and simmer about 15 minutes. Add bread crumbs and continue simmering, adding wine a little at a time, until done—30 to 35 minutes. Press sauce and vegetables through sieve, return to pot to heat, add sour cream, and let bubble up once. Pour over squabs. Serves 4.

37. ROAST DUCK OR GOOSE (*Gęś lub Kaczka Pieczona*)

6-lb. duck or small goose
1 tbs. marjoram
salt and pepper
sour apples for stuffing (4 to 6,

according to size)
sugar to taste
1 clove garlic (optional)
1 med. onion (optional)

Clean and prepare bird according to basic directions at beginning of chapter. Rub with salt and marjoram 2 hours before roasting. Stuff with peeled, cored apples cut into pieces. Secure with toothpicks, rub with minced garlic if desired, and roast in hot oven until bird begins to brown, basting frequently with the pan juice. If bird is very fat, pour off some of the grease. (Save goose fat, which is excellent for cooking.) Reduce heat and continue basting, allowing about 1¼ hours for average duck, 1½ to 1¾ hours for goose. When nearly done, add sliced onion and brown it in pan juice for added flavor. Pour pan drippings into sauceboat; carve the bird; remove apple stuffing, sweeten with sugar to taste, and serve with the duck. Average duck serves 5. Average young goose serves 8.

Note: For a sharper sauce, add 2 tbs. French mustard and 1 tsp. Maggi extract to pan drippings when roasting goose. Continue basting. When goose is done, add 3 tbs. bouillon to pan, allow sauce to boil up, and pour into sauceboat. If no stuffing is used, serve Red Cabbage Cooked with Apples (see Index).

38. ROAST GOOSE WITH CHESTNUT STUFFING
(Gęś Pieczona Nadziewana Kasztanami)

1 small goose

Stuffing:

½ lb. chestnuts, blanched, cooked, and pressed through sieve (see Index, Turkey Stuffing)
½ lb. ground fresh pork
6 shallots or white onions, smothered in butter and minced

salt and pepper to taste
dash of nutmeg
1 tsp. marjoram (or less)

Clean and prepare bird according to basic directions at the beginning of chapter. Combine the stuffing ingredients, mix thoroughly, and stuff goose, starting with the breast and neck cavity; use any remaining stuffing for body cavity. Secure with toothpicks or sew with cotton thread. Truss and roast according to directions in No. 37.

39. ROAST GOOSE WITH PÂTÉ STUFFING
(Gęś Pieczona Nadziewana Pasztetem)

1 small goose

Stuffing:

1 goose liver
¼ lb. boneless veal
3–4 strips bacon or 2 ozs. salt pork
1 stale hard roll or equivalent bread crumbs, moistened in milk and mashed

1 egg yolk
salt and pepper to taste
½–1 tsp. thyme
2 truffles, sliced thin (optional)

Clean and prepare bird according to basic directions at beginning
of chapter. To make pâté stuffing, put liver, veal, and bacon
through the meat grinder. Combine with remaining stuffing ingredients and mix thoroughly. Stuff breast and body cavity of bird; secure with toothpicks or sew with cotton thread. Truss and roast
according to directions in No. 37.

40. COLD STUFFED GOOSE NECK
(Gęsia Szyja Nadziewana na Zimno)

skin from large, fat goose neck, carefully removed so as not to tear	½ stale white roll or equivalent amount bread crumbs, mois- tened in milk and mashed
1 goose liver or equivalent amount of calf's liver	salt and pepper to taste dash of nutmeg
½ lb. tender boneless veal, ground	2 truffles or 4 cooked mush- rooms, sliced thin
2–3 ozs. salt pork, ground	2 slices bacon or equivalent amount salt pork, cut fine
1 tbs. butter	
2 egg yolks	

Put liver through a fine sieve. Combine with ground meat, butter,
egg yolks, roll, and seasoning. Add sliced truffles or mushrooms and
the chopped bacon, and mix thoroughly. Stuff the goose neck with
this mixture, taking care to stuff loosely; sew both ends, and prick
here and there with a sharp needle. Simmer tightly covered for one
hour in court bouillon. When done, roll in cheesecloth and place
between boards with a weight on top to flatten it while it cools.
Slice thin. Serve cold, with Tartare Sauce (see Index) or any other
sharp sauce desired.

41. GOOSE LIVER STRASBOURG-STYLE
(Wątróbka Gęsia po Strasbursku)

1 large or 2 small goose livers, soaked in milk for 2 to 3 hours	4–6 mushrooms, sliced and sautéed in butter
salt pork for larding	1 cup sour cream
salt and pepper to taste	1 tsp. flour
flour for dredging	1 level tbs. capers
2 tbs. butter	
1 cup shallots or small white onions, sautéed in butter	

Remove membranes from liver. Lard, season, dredge lightly with
flour, and brown quickly in butter. Add sautéed shallots and mushrooms and simmer, tightly covered, for 10 minutes. Add sour
cream combined with flour, add capers, and boil up once. Slice the
liver, pour sauce over it, and serve with boiled or parsley potatoes.
Serves 2 to 3.

42. STUFFED DUCK (*Kaczka Faszerowana*)

I.

2 young 5-lb. ducks	pinch of paprika
1 clove garlic (optional)	1 onion, chopped
½ cup dry red wine for basting	flour for dredging

Stuffing:

livers from the ducks	3 heaping tbs. bread crumbs
½ lb. bacon or salt pork	1 egg, lightly beaten
½ lb. boneless veal	salt and pepper to taste
1 med. onion, grated	dash of nutmeg

Prepare ducks according to directions in No. 37, salting 2 hours ahead of time. Rub skin with mashed garlic, if desired. Prepare stuffing as follows: Put livers, bacon, and veal through a meat grinder twice. Sauté onion in a little butter until transparent. Add to the meat mixture with bread crumbs, beaten egg, and seasoning, and mix thoroughly. Carefully pull away skin from breast of ducks and fill the neck and breast cavities rather loosely with stuffing. Use any leftover stuffing to fill body cavities. Sew openings with cotton thread or secure with toothpicks. Truss and roast according to directions for goose, first in hot oven until skin is brown and crisp, then in slower oven. Baste frequently, using the wine. Sprinkle with paprika and add chopped onion. Continue basting with pan drippings about 1¼ hours. A few minutes before ducks are done, dredge lightly with flour and baste a few more times. Serve with a green salad and beets or red cabbage. Serves 8 to 9.

II.

Prepare ducks as in *I*, using the following stuffing:

Stuffing:

livers and gizzards from the ducks	4–5 anchovy fillets, chopped
½ lb. fat boneless pork	2 heaping tbs. bread crumbs
1 med. onion, grated or chopped fine	lemon rind to taste
butter for cooking	salt and pepper to taste
few spoonfuls of bouillon for basting	dash of nutmeg
	1 whole egg
	2 truffles or 4–6 mushrooms, sliced

Sauté livers, gizzards, and pork with onion in a little butter until lightly brown, basting frequently with bouillon to prevent sticking and drying out. Put meat through grinder twice. Sauté truffles or mushrooms in a little butter until transparent, and add to meat mixture, along with chopped anchovies, bread crumbs, and other ingredients. Season to taste, mix thoroughly, and fill breast and body cavities of ducks as directed in *I*.

While roasting, baste with butter until enough of the birds' own

fat melts down into pan. Then baste with pan drippings. Allow
1¼ to 1½ hours. Serve with Truffle, Mushroom, or Madeira Sauce
(see Index). Serves 8 to 9.

43. DUCK SMOTHERED WITH OLIVES
(Kaczka Duszona z Oliwkami)

6-lb. duck, prepared and salted ahead of time	2 bay leaves
bacon strips for lining pan (about 6)	1 cup dry red wine
	1 cup strong bouillon
12 shallots or small white onions, peeled but uncut	2 tsp. flour
	1 cup black or green olives (according to preference)
6 peppercorns	

Clean and salt duck 2 hours ahead of time. Line heavy pan or
casserole with bacon strips, add shallots, peppercorns, and bay
leaves. Place duck, breast side up, over these and cover tightly.
Simmer in its own juice until it begins to brown. Then baste frequently with the wine and bouillon until all of it has been used up.
After about 1¼ hours, add olives and continue simmering another
15 to 20 minutes. Serves 5 to 6.

44. SMOTHERED DUCK IN CAPER SAUCE
(Kaczka Duszona w Sosie Kaparowym)

1 duckling (5–6 lbs.)	2 tsp. flour
salt and pepper to taste	2 tbs. capers
1 clove garlic (optional)	pinch of brown or caramelized sugar
3 tbs. butter	
bouillon for basting (about 1 cup)	lemon juice to taste

Clean and season duck 2 hours ahead of time, and rub with mashed
garlic if desired. Brown quickly in butter, reserving 2 tsp. butter.
Then reduce heat and cover tightly. Allow to simmer, basting frequently with bouillon, until well-brown and tender—about 1½ hours.
Blend the reserved butter with the flour, add enough pan juice to
dissolve lumps, and add to duck. Add capers, a pinch of brown
sugar for coloring, and lemon juice to taste. Stir well and baste
duck. Continue braising another 10 to 15 minutes. Serve with
macaroni or noodles. Serves 5 to 6.

45. DUCK BRAISED IN RED WINE
(Kaczka Duszona na Czerwonym Winie)

1 duckling (about 5 lbs.)	1 cup dry red wine
salt	lemon juice to taste
garlic (optional)	1 tsp. lemon rind
2 tbs. butter	pinch of sugar
2 tsp. flour	

Rub duck with salt and garlic 2 hours before cooking. Brown duck quickly in very hot butter. Separately, brown the flour lightly in a dry pan, stirring to prevent sticking or burning. Remove from heat and add wine, a little at a time, stirring constantly to prevent lumps. Add to duck, cover tightly, and braise over low heat about 1½ hours, or until thoroughly tender. At the end of the first hour add lemon juice and rind and a pinch of sugar. Continue braising. Serve with beet purée or with red cabbage. Serves 5.

46. DUCK AND RICE CASSEROLE
(Potrawa z Kaczki z Ryżem)

1 duckling (about 5 lbs.), cut in serving pieces
1 onion
court bouillon, just enough to cover (see Index)
2 cups uncooked rice
salt and pepper to taste
grated Parmesan
1 cup sour cream

Cook duckling with onion in 4 to 5 cups court bouillon, skimming carefully, simmering until done (about 1½ hours). Strain liquid and use to cook rice as follows: Pour boiling bouillon over rice, cover, and let stand 10 minutes. Season to taste. In a heavy, greased casserole, arrange rice and duck in layers, sprinkling each layer with Parmesan and beginning and ending with a layer of rice. Pour sour cream over the top and put into hot oven for half an hour, allowing to brown on top. Serves 6.

47. DUCK BRAISED IN RED CABBAGE
(Kaczka Duszona z Czerwoną Kapustą)

1 duckling (about 5 lbs.)
butter for basting
1 med. red cabbage
salt and pepper to taste
juice ½ lemon
2–3 ozs. salt pork, diced
½ large onion or 1 small onion
2 tsp. flour
1 cup red wine
1 tsp. sugar
pepper to taste
1 tbs. caraway seed (optional)

Prepare duck and salt 2 hours in advance. Roast in hot oven, basting frequently with butter, until nicely brown—30 to 40 minutes. In the meantime, shred the cabbage, blanch with boiling water, and drain. Season and sprinkle with lemon juice. (Juice helps preserve the bright red color.) In a heavy pot, brown the diced salt pork and onion lightly, add flour, and stir to keep from lumping. Add cabbage, red wine, and sugar. Simmer, tightly covered. When duck is brown, transfer to the pot with the cabbage, adding the butter and duck fat from roasting pan. Let simmer, covered, until thoroughly done—another hour. Serves 5 to 6.

48. MOCK WILD DUCK (*Potrawa z Kaczki na Dziko*)

1 duckling (5–6 lbs.)
  marinade to cover
  salt to taste
  1 clove garlic (optional)
2–3 tbs. butter
1 med. onion, sliced
10 peppercorns
10 juniper berries
1 bay leaf (optional)

1 cup bouillon
1 cup sour cream
1 tsp. flour
1 tbs. wine vinegar
  dash of nutmeg
¼ tsp. grated ginger
¼ tsp. Maggi extract or Kitchen
  Bouquet

The marinade should be rather strong—1 part wine vinegar to 2 parts water, or 1 to 1, depending on personal preference. Allow duck to marinate 24 hours. Reserve a little of the marinade for basting. Drain duck and rub with salt an hour before cooking. Rub with garlic if desired. Heat butter in heavy casserole and brown duck quickly on all sides. Then reduce heat. Add onion, peppercorns, juniper, and bay leaf, and simmer, tightly covered, basting with bouillon, until tender—about 1¼ to 1½ hours. (For a sharper taste combine bouillon with marinade.) When meat is done, strain the sauce, add the sour cream blended with the flour, vinegar, nutmeg, ginger, and Maggi extract. Return duck to sauce and simmer another 10 to 15 minutes. Serve with macaroni and with smothered beets or red cabbage. Serves 5 to 6.

Beef

1. BOILED BEEF (Sztuka Mięsa)

Although boiled beef is traditionally a dish for which the cheaper cuts of meat are used, when made with the more expensive cuts, it becomes a *pièce de résistance* at an informal dinner. When serving it as a main course, care must be taken not to overcook. Since the stock in which the meat cooks is to be used for soup, it is best to add marrow bone and, if economy is not a factor, an additional pound of soup meat, and allow this to cook until it falls apart.

3–4 lbs. beef (rump or bottom round, shank, brisket, or plate) soup stock, 4 cups per pound	of meat (see Index for basic soup recipe) salt and pepper to taste

Prepare stock with onions, soup greens, marrow bone, and a pound of soup meat. Start with cold water and let simmer for 1 to 2 hours; add the piece of meat for boiled beef. Continue simmering very slowly about 2 more hours, or until meat is very tender but not falling apart. Season soup. Slice meat thin and serve with boiled potatoes, green vegetables, and horseradish. Hot Horseradish or White Caper Sauce (see Index) is excellent with boiled beef. Serves 6 to 8. A quicker way to prepare boiled beef is to start the soup stock and add the meat as soon as the water has come to a boil. Use less water —3 cups per pound, at most—and simmer meat until done. The stock will be much lighter, but may still be used as a basis for soup, with the addition of bouillon cubes or meat extract.

2. STEAMED BEEF (Sztuka Mięsa w Parze)

3–4 lbs. rump or eye of round salt and pepper to taste 1–2 onions, sliced and blanched ½ cup each diced carrot, celery root, parsley root, parsnip, green peas	2–3 celery stalks ¼ cup asparagus stems (optional) cauliflower core (optional) 1 tbs. butter

94

Pound the meat to tenderize, and salt a half-hour before cooking. Place in top of double boiler, cover with onions and vegetables, add butter, and steam over briskly-boiling water, tightly covered, for at least 3 hours. Test with fork for doneness. Vegetables may be varied according to what is available, and proportions need not be exact. Lower stems of asparagus may be utilized when tips are to be served as a vegetable; broccoli stems, cauliflower parings, etc., may be similarly used. Serve meat thinly sliced, together with the vegetables which have steamed with it. Serve with parsley potatoes and the juice in which meat has steamed. Serves 6 to 8.

3. BAKED BOILED BEEF (*Sztuka Mięsa z Pieca*)

3–4 lbs. rump, round, or eye of round
2 cups Horseradish Sauce with Egg Yolks (see Index)

soup stock, 4 cups per pound of meat
salt and pepper to taste
2–3 lbs. boiled potatoes

Prepare boiled beef according to directions in No. 1. Slice medium-thin and arrange in shallow baking dish, together with the boiled potatoes. Cover with Horseradish Sauce and bake in medium-hot oven for 20 to 30 minutes, or until golden brown. Serves 6 to 8.

4. BAKED BEEF WITH TOMATO SAUCE (*Sztuka Mięsa z Pomidorami*)

Prepare as in No. 3, substituting Tomato Sauce (see Index) for Horseradish Sauce. Over Tomato Sauce pour:

2 tbs. melted butter, combined with
2 tbs. bread crumbs

Allow to brown in hot oven for 20 to 30 minutes. Serves 6 to 8.

5. POT ROAST (*Pieczeń Wołowa Duszona*)

3 lbs. eye of round, bottom round, or top round
salt and pepper to taste
2–3 tbs. butter
1 large or 2 small onions, sliced

3–4 dried mushrooms
6 peppercorns
1 bay leaf (optional)
1½ tsp. flour
few tbs. bouillon

Pound the meat with a mallet, wipe (never wash), and salt a half-hour beforehand. Brown quickly on all sides in butter in heavy skillet. Transfer to casserole, add the butter in which meat has browned, the onions, mushrooms, and other ingredients. Cover lightly and cook over low heat, basting occasionally with cold water, for 2 to 3 hours or until tender. Half an hour before the meat is done, dust with flour. If there is too little sauce, add a few table-spoons of bouillon. When done, slice meat thin and serve with potatoes or noodles. Serves 6.

6. POT ROAST WITH SOUR CREAM
(Pieczeń ze Śmietaną)

Prepare like No. 5. Half an hour before serving, add 1 cup sour cream. Blend the flour into the sour cream, pour over meat, and continue cooking. Serves 6.

7. POT ROAST WITH SMOTHERED PICKLES
(Pieczeń z Duszonymi Ogórkami)

Prepare meat the same as No. 5. When seared and brown, add 2 to 3 dill pickles, pared and diced. At the end of 2 hours, add 1 cup sour cream blended with 1½ tsp. flour. Simmer another half-hour, slice, and serve. Serves 6.

8. POT ROAST WITH MUSHROOMS
(Pieczeń Duszona z Grzybami)

Prepare the same as No. 7. Instead of dill pickles, add ½ oz. dried mushrooms. When meat is almost done, slice mushrooms into thin strips, return to pot, add the sour cream blended with flour, and continue simmering for half an hour. Serves 6.

9. MOCK VENISON POT ROAST
(Pieczeń Wołowa na Dziko)

3 lbs. rump, round, or eye of round

Marinade to cover:

1 qt. water	20 peppercorns
1½ to 2 cups wine vinegar	10 juniper berries
1 carrot	1 bay leaf
½ parsley root	dash of thyme or marjoram
½ celery root	salt to taste
1 onion	

Slice vegetables, add spices, and cook in water and vinegar for 30 minutes. Season. Allow to cool. Add meat and let stand at least 24 hours, turning occasionally. If a more seasoned taste is preferred, meat may marinate under refrigeration for as long as eight days.

When ready to use, wipe meat dry and salt a half-hour before cooking.

To *pot-roast:*

2–3 tbs. butter
1 large or 2 small onions, diced
3–4 dried mushrooms
½ celery root, diced
½ parsley root, diced

few sprigs parsley
dash of thyme and marjoram
(optional)
1 cup sour cream
1½ tsp. flour

Brown meat on all sides in hot butter, using heavy skillet. Transfer to casserole. Add onions, vegetables, butter in which meat browned, spices, and seasoning. Simmer tightly covered, basting occasionally with cold water. When tender—after about 2 hours—add sour cream blended with flour and simmer another 30 minutes. Slice thin, strain the sauce, and serve with pan-fried potatoes, buttered noodles or spaghetti. Serves 6.

10. BEEF À LA MODE (*Sztufada*)

3 lbs. eye of round or bottom round, cut in a short, thick piece marinade to cover (see Mock Venison, No. 9)
salt and pepper to taste
¼ lb. salt pork, cut in strips for larding

3 tbs. butter
pinch of marjoram
¼ cup white wine
1 tsp. flour or 1 tbs. bread crumbs

Marinate meat for 2 or 3 days. Wipe dry, rub with pepper and salt a half-hour before starting to cook, and lard thickly. Brown quickly on all sides in very hot butter in heavy skillet. Transfer to casserole, season, add wine (marinade may be substituted), and cook tightly covered over low heat until tender, at least 2 hours. A half-hour before serving dust with flour, or else sprinkle with bread crumbs directly before serving. Slice thin and pour sauce over the meat. If sauce is too thin, reduce by boiling. Serve with red cabbage cooked in wine, savoy cabbage, or potatoes. Serves 6.

11. POT ROAST BAKED WITH TOMATOES
(*Pieczeń Zapiekana z Pomidorami*)

Follow basic recipe for Pot Roast (No. 5). When done, slice medium-thin and arrange in shallow baking pan.

Sauce:

1 large onion, finely chopped
10–12 mushrooms, sliced thin
2–3 tbs. butter
2 tbs. bread crumbs

salt and pepper to taste
1 cup Tomato Sauce (see Index) or commercially prepared sauce

Brown the onion and mushrooms lightly in the butter. Add bread crumbs, and spread mixture over meat. Season to taste and cover

with Tomato Sauce. Surround with freshly boiled, peeled potatoes.
Bake in hot oven for 20 minutes. Serves 6 to 8.

12. ROLLED BEEF WITH ANCHOVIES
(Pieczeń Wołowa z Sardelami)

3 lbs. top or bottom round, cut in   salt and pepper to taste
  a long thin slice and pounded   ½ lb. fat pork meat, ground twice
  thin   butter for frying
4 large anchovies, soaked and   1 med. onion, chopped
  boned, or 8 anchovy fillets   1 tbs. flour
1 egg   1 cup soup stock or prepared
2 heaping tbs. sour cream   bouillon
1 white roll or ⅓ cup bread crumbs,
  moistened in milk

Chop anchovies fine and combine with egg, sour cream, roll or
bread crumbs, and seasoning. Then mix thoroughly with ground
pork. Spread meat with this stuffing, roll tightly, and secure with
string. Brown on all sides in very hot butter. Transfer to casserole,
add onion and the butter in which meat has browned. Simmer,
tightly covered, occasionally sprinkling with cold water, until tender
(about 1½ hours). Dust with flour and add soup stock. Allow to
simmer another 15 minutes. Serves 8.

13. HUSSAR POT ROAST (Pieczeń Husarska)

3 lbs. rump or eye of round, cut   2–3 tbs. butter
  in a short, thick piece   2 med. onions, sliced
2 cups marinade (see No. 9) or   salt and pepper to taste
  2 jiggers vodka

Blanch the meat with boiling marinade; for a slightly blander taste,
omit marinade and sprinkle meat with the vodka, having first
browned it on all sides in hot butter. Transfer to casserole and
simmer, tightly covered, together with the onions and butter in
which meat has browned. Sprinkle occasionally with cold water.
When meat is nearly tender—about 1½ to 2 hours—make the following stuffing:

Stuffing:

2 med. onions, blanched and   2 tsp. butter
  grated   salt and pepper to taste
2 tbs. bread crumbs

Mix thoroughly. Slice the meat thin, taking care to make every
second incision only part way. Fill these pockets with stuffing, reassemble into original shape, and return to casserole.

Add:

1 tbs. flour, dusted on top of meat   ½ cup soup stock (more if desired)

Allow to simmer another 30 minutes. Serves 6 to 7.

14. HORSERADISH POT ROAST
(Pieczeń Zakrawana z Chrzanem)

Follow directions in No. 13. For a filling, use:

4 tbs. freshly grated horseradish   juice ½ lemon
1 tbs. butter

Fill pockets as in Hussar Pot Roast. Return to casserole, dust with flour, and add soup stock. Allow to simmer 30 minutes longer. Serves 6 to 7.

15. POT ROAST STUFFED WITH MUSHROOMS
(Pieczeń Zakrawana z Grzybami)

Prepare the same as No. 13. Separately, prepare mushrooms as follows:

1 oz. dried mushrooms   salt and pepper to taste
2-3 tbs. bread crumbs   1 egg
2-3 tbs. butter

Simmer mushrooms in 2 cups of water until tender, at least 30 minutes. Drain and chop, reserving liquid, which should be cooked down to not more than 1 cup. Brown the mushrooms lightly in butter, adding bread crumbs and seasoning. Allow to cool. When cool, break in the whole egg, blend thoroughly, and use mixture for stuffing.

In the meantime, use the mushroom liquid for basting the meat. Continue basting after stuffed roast has been returned to pot. Cook 30 minutes longer. Serves 6 to 7.

16. BRIGANDS' POT ROAST (Pieczeń Zbójecka)

3 lbs. boneless sirloin   flour for rolling, plus ½ tsp.
2 tbs. olive oil   3-4 tbs. stock or bouillon
3-4 onions, sliced   2 tsp. caramelized sugar (see
3-4 tbs. butter   Index)
   salt and pepper to taste

Rub the meat thoroughly with olive oil and cover all over with onion slices. Let stand at least 2 hours. Half an hour before serving, heat the butter until brown, season the meat, roll in flour, and sear quickly on both sides. Add a few slices of the onion and allow them to brown. Add ½ tsp. flour, soup stock, and caramelized sugar. When sauce is blended, put pot roast into hot oven for ten minutes, taking care not to overcook. Meat must be red inside. Slice thin and pour sauce over meat. Serve with parsley potatoes, mushrooms, etc. Serves 6 to 7.

17. ROAST DONE ON A SPIT (Pieczeń z Rożna)

3–4 lbs. sirloin roast	salt and pepper to taste
2–3 tbs. olive oil	melted butter for basting
juice ½ lemon	1 tbs. flour
3–4 onions, sliced	

Rub meat with olive oil, sprinkle with lemon juice, and cover top and bottom with onion slices. Let stand 3 hours. An hour before cooking season the meat. Preheat rotisserie and cook on spit at very high temperature, brushing frequently with melted butter. (Be sure to catch all the dripping in a gravy pan.) When meat is well browned, dust with flour, allow to dry out, and again brush with butter. The roast should be ready in not less than 35 or 40 minutes, not more than 40 or 50 minutes, depending on size and how well done one prefers it. Slice thin and serve with potatoes or vegetables. Thicken sauce with flour if desired, or serve plain. Serves 6 to 8.

18. TENDERLOIN COOKED ON A SPIT
(Polędwicz z Rożna)

3-lb. tenderloin	salt and pepper to taste
½ lb. salt pork for larding (optional)	melted butter for basting
	flour for dusting
2 tbs. olive oil	

Lard the tenderloin with thin strips of salt pork, rub well with olive oil, but do not salt until ready to broil. Preheat rotisserie, and broil at very high temperature, brushing frequently with butter (40 to 50 minutes, less if desired). When well browned, dust with flour, allow to dry, then continue brushing with butter. Slice at an angle. Serve with pan drippings. Serves 6.

19. TENDERLOIN ENGLISH-STYLE
(Polędwica Naturalna po Angielsku)

Prepare the same as No. 18. If a spit is not available, pan-broil in very hot, buttered skillet. Dust with flour, add butter in which meat has broiled, and finish by roasting in very hot oven for 10 or 15 minutes, taking care not to overcook. Serves 6.

20. TENDERLOIN WITH TRUFFLES AND MADEIRA SAUCE *(Polędwica z Maderą i Truflami)*

3-lb. tenderloin
¼ lb. salt pork for larding
2–3 tbs. olive oil
melted butter for basting
flour for dusting

salt and pepper to taste
1 cup Madeira Sauce (see Index) with 1–2 truffles (optional)

This dish may be prepared in two ways:

1. Follow directions for Tenderloin English-Style (No. 19), and serve with Madeira Sauce on the side, to which truffles may be added for extra delicacy.
2. The tenderloin may also be pot-roasted. In this case, brown on all sides as in Brigands' Pot Roast (No. 16), transfer to casserole, and simmer, tightly covered, in Madeira Sauce for 20 to 25 minutes.

Serves 6.

21. TENDERLOIN *À LA KREJCIK (Polędwica)*

3-lb. tenderloin
salt and pepper to taste
2 tbs. French mustard
¼ stick of butter
1 lb. roast veal or pork
6 mushrooms, coarsely chopped

1 small onion, chopped
2 small or 1 med. head savoy cabbage
1 tbs. chopped fresh parsley
1 egg
6 slices bacon

Rub meat with salt, pepper, and mustard and return to refrigerator for 2 hours. Brown in very hot butter, and allow to cool. In the meantime, chop roast meat fine or put through meat grinder. Sauté mushrooms and onion in butter; reserve outside leaves of the savoy cabbage and shred the centers. Combine roast meat, mushrooms, onions, and chopped cabbage, add chopped parsley and whole raw egg, season, and mix thoroughly. Spread mixture over the meat, wrap in cabbage leaves, and cover with bacon slices. Secure with cotton string. Add any remaining butter drippings and bake in hot oven for 30 to 35 minutes. Remove string, slice with very sharp knife, and serve with its own juice. Serves 8.

22. TENDERLOIN SMOTHERED IN SOUR CREAM *(Polędwica Duszona ze Śmietaną)*

Prepare meat as directed in No. 18. Brown quickly in butter as in No. 19. Transfer to casserole.

Sauce:

2 cups sour cream, blended with 1 tsp. flour

Cover meat with the sauce, adding whatever butter is left in skillet. Bake, tightly covered, in hot oven or simmer over direct heat for about 35 minutes. Cooked longer, meat will be tough. Serves 6.

23. TENDERLOIN VENISON-STYLE *(Polędwica na Dziko)*

3-lb. tenderloin
  cold marinade to cover (see No. 9)
¼ lb. salt pork for larding

salt and pepper to taste
butter for frying
2 cups sour cream
1 tsp. flour

Marinate the meat for 12 hours. Dry, lard, season at the last moment, and sear in very hot butter. Transfer to casserole, add sour cream and flour, and proceed as in No. 22, adding a few tablespoons of the marinade to the sauce for added piquancy. Serves 6.

24. TENDERLOIN *À LA STROGANOFF*
(Polędwica à la Stroganow)

3-lb. tenderloin
  marinade to cover (see No. 9)
3 tbs. butter
½ large or 1 small onion, blanched and grated
2-3 bacon slices, chopped fine
3 large anchovies, soaked and boned, or 6 anchovy fillets,

chopped fine
½ cup bouillon (more if desired)
2 cups sour cream
1 tsp. flour
1 heaping tbs. capers
1 tsp. Maggi extract
salt and pepper

Marinate the meat for 12 hours. Wipe off, brown quickly in very hot butter, and transfer to casserole. Add butter in which meat has browned, the grated onion, chopped bacon, anchovies, and bouillon. Simmer, tightly covered, for 30 or 35 minutes. Add sour cream blended with flour, the capers, and seasoning, and let cook for 5 more minutes after sauce bubbles up. Serve with new potatoes, Potato Croquettes, cauliflower, or spaghetti. Serves 6 to 8.

25. STEAKS WITH ONIONS *(Befsztyki z Cebulą)*

4-6 tenderloin fillets 1″ thick, one per person
1-2 onions, sliced fine

3 tbs. butter
salt and pepper to taste
1 tsp. flour

Brown onion lightly in butter, push to one side, and increase heat. Salt and pepper the fillets, dust with flour, and pan-broil quickly, turning so they will be seared on the outside and red inside. Top the meat slices with the onions, and pour butter from the pan over the top. Serve with mashed or pan-fried potatoes. Serves 4 to 6.

26. FILLET STEAK FRENCH-STYLE
(Befsztyk po Francusku)

4 tenderloin fillets, 1" thick
2 tbs. olive oil
    salt and pepper to taste

4 tbs. Butter *Maître d'Hôtel* or
    Chive Butter (see Index)

Brush the fillets with olive oil, pile one on top of the other, and allow to stand 2 to 3 hours. Preheat broiler. Salt and pepper the steaks, and broil under very high heat 5 minutes or less per side. Serve at once, garnishing each with a tablespoon of the flavored butter. Serves 4.

27. SMOTHERED ROAST BEEF (Roastbeef Duszony)

3–4 lbs. rib roast, boned
2 tbs. butter
½ cup soup stock or prepared
    bouillon (scant)

¼ cup Madeira or ½ cup red wine
salt and pepper to taste
pinch of marjoram (optional)
1 tbs. flour

Sear the meat on all sides in hot butter and transfer to casserole. Add soup stock, wine, and seasoning, and simmer, tightly covered, for at least 2 hours or until tender. Dust with flour and baste, allowing a few minutes for the flour to cook and sauce to thicken. Slice thin and serve with potatoes and vegetables. Serves 6 to 8.

28. SLICED BEEF WITH ONIONS (Rozbratlę z Cebulą)

2 lbs. rib steak, boned and cut into
    ¼-lb. slices
2 tbs. butter

1 large onion, sliced
salt and pepper to taste

Pound the meat thin. Season just before cooking. Pan-broil in very hot butter, turning once (2¼ to 3 minutes on each side). Brown onion in the same pan, top meat slices with it, and serve at once. (Use two pans if necessary.) Serves 4.

29. SMOTHERED BEEF SLICES (Rozbratle Duszone)

2 lbs. rib steak, cut into ¼-lb. slices
1 tbs. flour
1 tbs. butter
1 large onion, blanched and sliced
    thin

salt and pepper to taste
½ cup soup stock or bouillon
¼ cup red wine (optional)
½ tsp. Maggi extract

Prepare meat the same as in No. 28, pounding flour into the meat. Brown the butter in a heavy casserole, and arrange the meat in it, alternating with onion slices. Season and simmer, tightly covered, until brown and tender (about 1 hour). Add soup stock, wine, and

extract, and continue simmering for at least another half-hour. If
sauce is not sufficiently thick, add more flour. Serves 4.

30. BEEF SLICES WITH ANCHOVIES
(Rozbratle Duszone z Sardelami)

Prepare the same as Smothered Beef Slices (No. 29), adding 4
anchovies, chopped fine. During the last 15 minutes of cooking,
add 1 cup sour cream. Omit wine.

31. BEEF SLICES PEASANT-STYLE
(Rozbratle po Chłopsku)

2¼ lbs. rib steak, boned and cut into 6 slices	1 leek
	1 parsnip
1 cup ham, coarsely chopped	few sprigs parsley
2 cups raw potatoes, diced or sliced thin	10 peppercorns
	1 bay leaf (optional)
1 tbs. butter	10 allspice
1 med. onion, coarsely chopped	salt to taste
1 carrot	1 cup beef stock for basting
1 parsley root	3–4 tbs. sour cream
1 celery root	1 tsp. flour

Pound the meat until very thin. Combine raw potatoes and ham,
season to taste, and spread over meat slices. Roll up meat slices and
secure each with cotton thread, tying tight. Brown the butter and
onion in a heavy casserole. Brown the meat on all sides and push
aside. Arrange the vegetables, which have been thinly sliced, in
bottom of casserole. Arrange the meat on top, and add the spices,
which are best tied in a piece of cheesecloth so that they can be
easily discarded. Season, and simmer tightly covered for 2 hours,
basting occasionally with beef stock. When meat is done, remove
the thread. Discard the spices. Press the vegetables through a sieve,
thicken sauce with sour cream and flour, and return the meat to
casserole. Simmer 10 minutes more. Serve with noodles. Serves 6.

32. POLISH ROLLED STUFFED MEAT BIRDS
(Zrazy Polskie Zawijane)

3 lbs. eye of round or top round steak	¼ lb. butter (2 tbs. of this is for the stuffing)
salt and pepper to taste	2 tbs. bread crumbs
1 large onion, baked and grated, or chopped fine	1 tbs. flour
	1–2 cups soup stock

Have the meat cut into thin slices. Pound very thin, and, if necessary, cut meat into smaller pieces (about 4 by 5 inches). Season,
and spread with stuffing made of the grated onion, bread crumbs,

and butter. Roll each piece tightly and tie securely with cotton thread. Brown quickly on all sides in a heavy skillet in very hot butter, using the butter a little at a time and adding as necessary. When all the rolls have been browned, arrange tightly in one or two layers in a heavy casserole. Dust with flour, add just enough soup stock to cover, and simmer tightly covered for 1 to 1½ hours; never longer. Serve with buckwheat or barley groats. Serves 8. Part may be stored for future use.

Note: If thicker stuffing is desired, double the ingredients.

33. STEAMED BEEF SLICES *(Zrazy na Parze)*

2 lbs. eye of round or top round	1 lemon, peeled, seeded, and sliced
salt and pepper	thin
¼ lb. bacon or salt pork	1 tbs. butter
1 large onion, minced	1 cup beer
2 tbs. flour	½ cup water

Have butcher slice meat thin. Pound even thinner and season. Line a heavy casserole with bacon or salt pork slices, and arrange the meat over these, alternating with minced onion, a little flour, and lemon slices. Add the butter, beer, and water. Cover tightly and bake in medium-hot oven for 1½ hours. Serve with pan-fried potatoes or groats. Serves 6.

34. BEEF SLICES WITH SOUR CREAM AND MUSHROOMS *(Zrazy z Grzybami i ze Śmietaną)*

2 lbs. eye of round or top round	6–8 med. potatoes, peeled and
salt and pepper	sliced
2 tbs. flour	1 cup sour cream
2 tbs. butter	½ tsp. flour
1 oz. dried mushrooms, cooked until soft in 1 (scant) cup of water	

Have butcher slice the meat thin. Cut it into squares (3 or 4 inches), pound thin, season, and dust with flour. Brown quickly on both sides in very hot butter. Separately, simmer the mushrooms in water until soft—20 to 30 minutes—and cut into thin strips. Reserve the liquid. Arrange meat and mushrooms in heavy casserole and simmer, tightly covered, basting occasionally with liquid in which mushrooms have cooked, for about 30 minutes. Parboil potatoes and add to meat. Let cook another 30 minutes, or until meat and potatoes are tender. Add sour cream and flour, blend well, and let bubble up. Simmer another 5 minutes and serve in the casserole. Serves 6 to 7.

35. BEEF SLICES WITH SAUERKRAUT
(Zrazy z Kapustą)

2 lbs. eye of round or top round
salt and pepper to taste
1 large onion, minced
2 tbs. butter

2 lbs. sauerkraut
6 bacon slices
1 cup bouillon or soup stock
½ cup white wine (optional)

Prepare meat as for Beef Slices with Sour Cream and Mushrooms (No. 34), browning the onion along with it. Arrange in heavy casserole, topping each slice thickly with sauerkraut. Put pieces of bacon over the kraut. Add soup stock, cover tightly, and bake in medium-hot oven for 1 hour. If wine is used, reduce the amount of stock. The proportion of sauerkraut to meat may be varied according to taste. Serves 6 to 7.

36. CHOPPED BEEF (Zrazy Siekane)

2 lbs. lean chuck, chopped
2 white rolls (or equivalent amount of bread crumbs), moistened with milk
4 slices bacon, salt pork, or equivalent amount of marrow
1 egg

1 med. onion, minced and browned lightly in butter
salt and pepper to taste
dash of marjoram (optional)
flour for rolling
butter for frying
1 cup bouillon or mushroom liquor

Put meat, bacon, and rolls through meat grinder twice. Add egg, onion, and seasoning. Mix thoroughly and shape into oblong patties. Roll in flour and brown quickly on all sides in hot butter. Arrange in heavy casserole, dust with another teaspoon of flour, and add a little of the bouillon or mushroom liquor. Simmer, tightly covered, for an hour, basting occasionally with more liquid. Serves 6.

37. BEEF BIRDS RADECKI (Zrazy Zawijane à la Radecki)

2 lbs. tenderloin or sirloin
½ lb. mushrooms
2 large onions
2 tbs. butter
2 tbs. chopped dill
2 tbs. bread crumbs

salt and pepper to taste
butter for frying
1 scant tbs. flour
1 cup soup stock or bouillon
½ cup Madeira or 1 cup red wine

Slice meat thin and flatten further by pounding. If sirloin is used, cut pieces about 4 inches square. Season and spread with the following stuffing: Chop fine about two-thirds of the mushrooms and the onions and brown lightly in butter. Add chopped dill and bread crumbs, season, and mix thoroughly. After spreading each piece of meat with a little of the stuffing, roll tightly and tie securely with cotton thread, which should be removed before serving. Brown the birds in hot butter, searing quickly on all sides. Arrange tightly in casserole, add the butter in which they browned, and dust with flour. Slice and add the remaining mushrooms, the soup stock, and wine, and simmer slowly until soft, 45 minutes to 1 hour, depending on cut of meat. Serves 6 to 7.

38. MEAT BALLS IN SOUR CREAM *(Bitki w Smietanie)*

2 lbs. lean chuck, ground	pinch of marjoram (optional)
2 white rolls or equivalent amount of bread crumbs, moistened in milk	pinch of oregano or thyme (optional)
	flour for rolling
1 small or ½ large onion, chopped and browned in butter	butter for frying
	1½ cups soup stock
2 eggs	1½ cups sour cream
salt and pepper to taste	1 tsp. flour

Put the meat and rolls through meat grinder twice. Add chopped onion, egg, and seasoning. Mix thoroughly. Shape into small patties, roll in flour, and brown quickly on all sides in hot butter. Arrange tightly in heavy pan, add soup stock, sour cream, and 1 tsp. flour, taking care to blend well. Simmer, tightly covered, for 30 to 40 minutes. Serve with potatoes or buckwheat groats. Serves 6 to 8.

Note: May also be made of 1½ lbs. ground beef with addition of ¼ lb. each of ground veal and pork.

39. ROYAL MEAT BALLS *(Bitki Królewskie)*

Prepare meat the same as in No. 38. Separately, boil 2 lbs. potatoes, cut into serving pieces. Arrange meat in center of shallow pan with the potatoes around it, and top with sauce.

Sauce:

2 cups sour cream	1 tbs. capers
1 tsp. flour	2 tbs. grated Parmesan cheese

Blend in flour, add capers, and stir thoroughly. Sprinkle with grated Parmesan, and bake in medium-hot oven for 30 minutes or until brown on top. Serves 6 to 8.

40. MEAT BALLS WITH HERRING OR ANCHOVIES *(Bitki ze Śledziem lub Sardelami)*

2 lbs. lean chuck, ground	salt and pepper to taste
1 matjes herring, skinned and boned, or 6 anchovy fillets	flour for rolling
	butter for frying
2 white rolls or equivalent amount of bread crumbs, moistened in milk	1 cup sour cream
	1 tsp. flour
	1 cup bouillon or meat stock
½ med. onion, chopped and browned in butter	½ tsp. grated orange rind
	1 tbs. capers
2 eggs	

Wash, skin, and bone herring, and cut into pieces. Put through
meat grinder twice, together with rolls and meat. Add onion, egg,
and seasoning, shape into patties, and roll in flour. Brown quickly
on all sides in butter and arrange in heavy pan. Add the butter in
which meat has browned, the sour cream with a teaspoon of flour
blended into it, the bouillon, orange rind, and capers. Simmer,
tightly covered, for half an hour. Serves 6 to 8.

41. CHOPPED BEEF PATTIES *(Kotlety Wołowe Siekane)*

Prepare meat as in No. 40, omitting the fish. Instead of flour, use
bread crumbs for rolling. Fry in moderately hot butter a few minutes on each side, taking care not to sear or let too thick a crust
form on the outside, so that the meat will get done throughout.
These patties should be prepared immediately before a meal in
order to serve them light and tender. Excellent with Calf's Brain
Sauce (see Index) or any sharp meat sauce. Serves 6 to 7.

42. MEAT LOAF, OR MOCK HARE
(Klops Czyli Fałszywy Zając)

2 lbs. chuck or round steak	2–3 hard-cooked eggs, sliced
½ lb. fat pork meat	4 slices bacon
2 rolls or equivalent in bread	flour for rolling
crumbs, moistened in milk	butter for frying
⅓ onion, grated and browned in	1 scant cup bouillon or mush-
butter	room broth
2 raw eggs	1 cup sour cream
salt and pepper to taste	

Put meat and rolls through meat grinder twice. Add onion, raw
eggs, and seasoning and mix thoroughly. Flatten out and fill with
slices of hard-cooked egg and bacon cut into strips. Roll and shape
into loaf. Roll in flour and brown quickly on all sides in butter.
Add broth and bake in moderate oven for 1 hour, basting occasionally. Add sour cream and ½ tsp. flour, and return to oven until
sauce bubbles. Serves 6.

43. BEEF TONGUE *À LA POLONAISE*, IN GRAY SAUCE
(Ozór po Polsku w Szarym Sosie)

1 beef tongue, about 3 lbs.	10 peppercorns
1 large carrot	1 bay leaf (optional)
2 med. onions	few sprigs parsley
3 stalks celery with leaves	salt to taste (about 1 tsp.)

The recipe is for a fresh tongue, but corned or smoked tongue may
be substituted. The basic recipe remains the same, with slight

variations. A corned tongue should be soaked in cold water for about 2 hours before cooking. Average cooking time for a fresh tongue is about 3 hours; a smoked tongue may need from 2 to 4 hours, depending on how tender the meat is.

Place tongue in an open kettle together with vegetables and spices. Add just enough boiling water to cover. Simmer until tender, allow to cool enough in the water to handle and skin. Reserve the liquid for soup and/or sauce. Slice the tongue and serve with Gray Sauce (see Index). Serves 6 to 7. Serve with potatoes or spaghetti.

44. BOILED TONGUE *(Ozór Szpikowany w Potrawie)*

A 3-lb. fresh tongue, prepared as in No. 43 and cooked until nearly tender. Tongue should be skinned at the earliest possible moment, at the end of 2 or 2½ hours.

¼ lb. salt pork, cut in strips for larding	½ parsley root, diced
	few sprigs parsley
3 strips lean bacon, diced	2–3 bay leaves
1 large or 2 small onions, diced	salt and pepper to taste
2 carrots, diced	1 cup strong beef stock or commercial bouillon
2 stalks celery, cut into small pieces	1 cup white wine
1 celery root, diced	1 tbs. flour, if necessary

Lard tongue. Combine all the ingredients in a heavy pan, including the partially-cooked tongue, and simmer, tightly covered, until the meat and vegetables are tender (30 to 45 minutes). Slice the tongue. Discard bay leaves and pour sauce over the meat. (Vegetables may be puréed or not, as desired.) If sauce is too thin, stir in enough flour to thicken. Serves 6 to 8.

45. OXTAIL RAGOUT *(Potrawa z Ogona)*

2 oxtails	few sprigs parsley
3 tbs. butter	2–3 dried mushrooms
2 med. onions, sliced	salt and pepper to taste
2 carrots, sliced	1 bay leaf (optional)
1 celery root, diced	water or beef bouillon merely to cover (about 3 cups)
1 parsnip, diced	
3 stalks celery, cut in pieces	1 tsp. Maggi sauce
1 leek	lemon juice to taste

Wash oxtails, dip in boiling water, and cut at each joint to separate into pieces. Brown quickly in very hot butter, add vegetables, and cover with water or soup stock. Season, and simmer, tightly covered, until thoroughly done (about 3 hours). Remove meat, discard bay leaf, and purée vegetables by mashing or putting through sieve. Return to liquid in which they cooked, add the Maggi sauce and lemon juice to taste, stir thoroughly, and pour over meat.

For a more subtle flavor, prepare as above, substituting 1 cup of dry red wine for equivalent amount of bouillon. When sauce is ready, add 2 tbs. sliced Smothered Mushrooms (see Index) and 1 heaping tbs. chopped fresh dill. Serve with boiled potatoes or with potato croquettes. Serves 6.

46. HUNTERS' STEW (Bigos Myśliwski)—Traditional

One of the oldest traditional Polish dishes. Famous in poetry and in novels, this stew was served at royal banquets and hunts, and still is the *pièce de résistance* after a hunting party. Since this dish cannot be prepared in small quantities because of the numerous ingredients required, it is wisest to plan to serve it at a large party; even then a considerable amount will probably have to be refrigerated for future use. It is a good way to utilize leftovers after a holiday meal or large reception. The proportions given here are approximate: they may be varied according to individual taste and availability.

At least ½ lb. of each of the following cooked meats, diced

roast beef or pot roast	chicken or duck
roast lamb	ham
roast pork	sausage
venison or hare	roast veal

6–8 lbs. sauerkraut	browned
1½ oz. dried mushrooms, cooked until soft enough to cut into thin strips	2 onions, minced
	2 tbs. flour
liquid in which mushrooms have cooked	salt, pepper, and sugar to taste
¼ lb. salt pork, diced and	1 cup Madeira wine (or more)

Combine sauerkraut and cooked dried mushrooms, together with the liquid in which they cooked. Brown the diced salt pork, cook the onion in this fat until limp, add flour, and stir until blended. Add to the sauerkraut. Add all the diced meats, season to taste, and simmer, tightly covered, for half an hour. Add the wine, boil up once, and keep covered until ready to serve. *Bigos* is even better reheated, so it may be prepared in the morning for use at dinnertime. Will keep in the refrigerator a full week.

If the meats must be prepared fresh, each piece should be potroasted separately, together with the following:

1 tbs. (or less) butter
1 onion
1 carrot
1 stalk celery
  piece of celery root
  piece of parsley root
6 peppercorns

bay leaf (optional)—Use no
more than half a leaf per meat;
never use with poultry or pork.
½ cup soup stock (approx.)—
enough to keep meat from sticking
salt to taste

Cook each meat until tender (refer to Index for detailed instructions on each). Dice and combine with sauerkraut as directed above. The vegetables with which meats have cooked may be used separately. Traditionally they are not added to the main dish. Either recipe will make 12 generous servings.

47. *BIGOS* FROM LEFTOVER ROAST *(Bigos z Pieczeni)*

2 cups diced leftover meat—
  beef, veal, pork, lamb, or a
  combination
2 lbs. sauerkraut
3–4 dried mushrooms
  liquid in which mushrooms
  cooked

1 onion, minced
4 ozs. salt pork or bacon, diced
1 tbs. flour (less if desired)
1 tsp. Maggi sauce
  salt, pepper, and dash of sugar
  to taste
¼ cup Madeira (optional)

Cook the mushrooms until soft, cut into strips, and combine with sauerkraut and liquid in which the mushrooms cooked. Render the diced salt pork or bacon, add onion, and cook until transparent. Add flour and blend until smooth. Combine with sauerkraut, season, and simmer about 45 minutes longer. Dice the meat and add to the kraut. Meat and sauerkraut should simmer together, tightly covered, for 30 minutes. Serves 4 to 5.

Bigos may also be made with fresh cabbage, as follows:

Cut up 1 med. head of cabbage and prepare as for Cooked Cabbage (see Index).

Add:

2–3 sour apples, sliced and cored
2–3 med. tomatoes or small can
  tomatoes or tomato purée

1 cup sour cream
  salt and pepper to taste
1–2 tsp. vinegar (optional)

Proceed the same as when using sauerkraut.

48. MEAT POCKETS *(Pierogi z Mięsem)*

2 cups chopped leftover roast or
  boiled beef
1 slice stale bread, moistened in
  milk
  salt and pepper to taste

1 tbs. butter
1 med. onion, minced
1–2 tbs. soup stock (optional)
½ stick butter, melted
  Parmesan cheese for sprinkling

Chop the meat very fine, combine with bread, and season. Cook minced onion in butter until light golden-brown and add to meat mixture. If meat is lean, add a little meat stock so that stuffing will not be too dry.

Make dough for Meat Pockets (see No. 16 under Soup Garnishes). Fill each pocket with a little of the stuffing, taking care to pinch edges securely together. Cook in boiling salted water until pockets swim to the surface. Drain, arrange in dish for serving, add the melted butter, and sprinkle generously with Parmesan cheese. Excellent as luncheon dish or with clear soups. Serves 4 as main dish.

49. BAKED MEAT POCKETS (Pierożki Zapiekane)

Prepare the same as No. 48. When done, drain and arrange pockets in casserole.

Sauce:

1 scant cup strong soup stock or commercial bouillon	2 tbs. butter
2–3 tbs. Parmesan cheese	2 tbs. bread crumbs

Pour soup stock over the meat pockets. Sprinkle generously with Parmesan. Melt butter, add bread crumbs, and allow to brown. Dot surface with this mixture. Bake in hot oven about 30 minutes. Serves 4 as a main dish.

50. LITHUANIAN MEAT POCKETS (Kołduny Litewskie)

½ lb. fillet or top sirloin	salt and pepper to taste
½ lb. lean boneless lamb	½ tsp. marjoram
¼ lb. bone marrow or fat from veal kidney	1 tbs. bouillon
1 med. onion, blanched and grated	dough for Meat Pockets (see No. 16 under Soup Garnishes)
1 tbs. butter	

Chop meat fine, but do not grind since too much juice is lost in meat grinder. Mash marrow to consistency of a purée. (Pockets made with marrow are much tastier than those made with kidney fat.) Simmer onion in butter to a light, golden brown, add seasoning and marjoram, combine with marrow, and moisten with bouillon. Blend thoroughly. Combine with chopped meat. Make dough according to directions, cutting out individual pockets with pastry cutter or a glass. Fill with meat stuffing, fold over, and pinch edges securely together. Cook in a large pot of boiling salted water until the pockets come to the surface. Serve in clear bouillon, allowing about 3 per soup plate. These pockets may also be served dry as a luncheon dish. They should then be garnished with bread crumbs browned in melted butter.

51. MUSHROOM AND BEEF POCKETS
(Kołduny z Grzybów i Mięsem)

½ lb. cooked chopped beef	1 whole egg
½ lb. mushrooms sautéed in butter *or* 1½ ozs. dried mushrooms cooked until soft	salt and pepper to taste dough for Meat Pockets (see No. 16 under Soup Garnishes)
1 med. onion, grated and browned in butter	

Dried mushrooms make a tastier dish than the fresh. When using dried mushrooms, cook in just enough water to allow mushrooms to swell. Leftover liquid may be used in the stuffing or reserved for other use. Fresh mushrooms should be sautéed until transparent (about 5 minutes). Combine cooked mushrooms and meat and chop fine. Add cooked minced onion, seasoning, and raw egg, and mix thoroughly. Roll out the dough quite thin and make small pockets. Stuff and pinch together well. Cook in boiling salted water until pockets swim to the surface. Since these should not cook as long as pockets made of raw meat, it is important to keep the size small and the dough thin so that it, too, will be done. (Can also be made with ham.)

52. TRIPE WARSAW-STYLE *(Flaki po Warszawsku)*

2 lbs. tripe (preferably honeycomb tripe)	1 leek, cut fine
soup stock or bouillon to cover (about 2 cups)	2 tbs. butter 1 tbs. flour
2 carrots, diced	dash of nutmeg
1 large onion, minced	dash of marjoram
1 celery root, diced	1 tsp. grated ginger
1 parsnip, diced	salt and pepper to taste
1 parsley root, diced	1 tsp. Maggi extract
	½ cup milk (optional)

Honeycomb tripe, the lining of the stomach, is the most tender and tasty. All tripe should be soaked in cold water for several hours before using. Using fresh water, cover tripe, bring to a boil, drain, then start again in cold water. When water begins to boil, cover and allow to simmer at least 2 hours. (Tripe cut into serving pieces does not need more than 2 hours over-all cooking time; in one piece, it may take as long as 4 hours before it is tender.) Simmer vegetables in soup stock for 15 to 20 minutes. Drain tripe and add to vegetables—the liquid should barely cover them. Melt butter, combine with flour, stir until smooth, and add to the pot. Simmer another half-hour. The seasoning—especially the salt—should never be added earlier than the last half-hour of the cooking; otherwise the tripe will be tough and dark in color. Once the various seasonings have been added, tripe should be simmered very slowly, tightly covered. For a light appearance add milk. Serve with Suet or Marrow Balls (see Index) to which a lot of fresh dill has been added. Serves 4 to 6.

53. TRIPE FRENCH-STYLE *(Flaki po Francusku)*

2 lbs. honeycomb tripe	½ tsp. tarragon
2 med. onions	1 tbs. butter
2 carrots	bouillon to cover (1–2 cups)
1 celery root	2 tbs. tomato purée
1 parsnip	½ cup dry white wine
1 parsley root	1 tsp. Maggi extract
10 peppercorns	salt to taste
dash of nutmeg	1 tsp. flour
½ tsp. ginger	

Follow basic directions in No. 52 for cooking tripe. When nearly done, cut into serving pieces. Arrange a layer of the diced vegetables in a casserole, then a layer of tripe and a sprinkling of spices. Repeat layers. Add butter, bouillon, tomato purée, and white wine. Season with Maggi extract and simmer, tightly covered, until tender. Season with salt and thicken lightly with flour. Allow to bubble up once. The sauce should be fairly thick and a light golden-brown. Serves 4 to 6.

54. BEEF BRAINS IN WHITE SAUCE
(Mózgi Wołowe w Białym Sosie)

2 sets beef brains	1 bay leaf
1 large onion	dash of ginger
½ lemon	dash of nutmeg
10 peppercorns	salt

Cook onion, lemon (including rind), and spices for a few minutes in well-salted water. Add brains, and when the water has again come to a boil, reduce heat, and simmer 5 to 10 minutes, depending on size. Drain, remove veins, and cut into slices. Make enough (about 2 cups) Caper Sauce or Poulette Sauce to cover (see Index). Boil up once; then let stand about half an hour while flavors blend. Keep hot. Serve with parsley potatoes. Serves 4.

55. BRAIN CUTLETS *(Kotlety z Mózgów)*

2 sets brains, prepared as in No. 54	1 or 2 lightly-beaten eggs
flour for rolling	bread crumbs for rolling
	butter for frying (about 4 tbs.)

Parboil brains as for No. 54. Drain, remove veins, cut into thick slices, and shape into patties. Roll in flour, dip in egg, and roll in bread crumbs. Fry in hot butter to a golden brown, turning once. Serve with any sharp sauce or with lemon slices. As a side dish use green peas, cauliflower or new potatoes. Serves 4 to 6.

Veal

1. VEAL ROASTED ON A SPIT
(Pieczeń Cielęca z Rożna)

leg or shoulder of veal (4–5 lbs.)   ¼ lb. butter
juice ½ lemon   flour for dusting
salt and pepper to taste

To make meat most tender, first dip quickly in boiling water. This will seal all the meat juices inside. Since veal is a fairly dry meat, the less juice that escapes, the better. Wipe meat, rub with salt, sprinkle with lemon juice, and let stand for about 2 hours. Roast on a spit (the modern rotisserie is ideal) at high temperature until well browned. Reduce heat and continue roasting for 2 to 2½ hours, brushing frequently with melted butter. Catch all drippings in a pan placed below the roast. When nearly done, dust skin with flour and continue brushing with butter for a brown, crackly skin. Slice thin. Serve with vegetables, roast potatoes, and a green salad. Serves 8 to 10.

2. VEAL ROASTED IN OVEN (Pieczeń Cielęca z Pieca)

leg or shoulder of veal (4–5 lbs.)   2 tbs. butter
salt and pepper   flour for dusting
juice ½ lemon

Dip meat in boiling water for a minute or two. This will make it more tender and also seal the juices inside. Wipe dry, rub with salt, and sprinkle with lemon juice. Let stand for 2 hours. Place in shallow roasting pan, preferably on a rack. Rub with butter, and roast in hot oven (at least 400°), basting frequently, until skin begins to crisp and brown. Reduce heat to 300° and continue roasting for 2 to 2½ hours, still basting. When nearly done, dust with flour and baste again. This kind of roast is excellent with potatoes roasted in the same pan (see Index). Serves 8 to 10.

3. LEMON ROAST VEAL
(Pieczeń Cielęca Zakrawana z Cytryną)

leg or shoulder of veal (4 lbs.)	6 tbs. bread crumbs
juice of 1 lemon	3 tbs. butter
lemon slices	2 tbs. chopped fresh parsley (or
salt and pepper	parsley and dill combined)

Roast the veal as in No. 2. Brown 3 tbs. of the bread crumbs in the butter, add the lemon juice, and mix with chopped parsley. Slice the veal thin. (The meat can be left on the bone or sliced to within about ½ inch of edge so that it can be more easily reshaped.) Spread the stuffing thinly on each slice, reshape into original form, secure with skewer if necessary, and sprinkle with remaining bread crumbs. Baste with pan gravy and return to oven for 10 minutes. Garnish with lemon slices. Serves 8.

4. VEAL ROAST WITH SOUR CREAM
(Pieczeń Cielęca ze Śmietaną)

leg or shoulder of veal (4 lbs.)	2 tbs. butter
salt and pepper	1 cup sour cream
juice ½ lemon	1 tbs. flour
¼ lb. salt pork cut in thin strips for larding	

Prepare veal as in No. 2, except that meat should be larded as soon as blanched. Allow to stand 1 hour instead of 2. Roast according to directions in No. 2, using hot oven until nicely brown, then reducing heat. Combine sour cream with flour, and spread it over the roast for the last half-hour of cooking. Serve with tossed green salad and vegetables or potatoes. Serves 8.

5. MOCK VENISON ROAST
(Pieczeń Cielęca na Sposób Sarniej)

leg or shoulder roast of veal (4 lbs.)	*Marinade:*
20 juniper berries	3 parts water
salt and pepper to taste	1 part wine vinegar
4 ozs. salt pork for larding	10 peppercorns
2 tbs. butter	3–4 cloves
1 cup sour cream	1 large onion, sliced
1 tsp. flour	1 bay leaf (optional)

Crush juniper berries and rub onto meat. Boil water, vinegar, onion, and spices for about 10 minutes. Pour hot marinade over the veal, weight the meat down with a piece of board or inverted plate, and let stand in a cool place for 2 or 3 days. Wipe dry and rub with salt. Cut salt pork into thin strips and lard the meat. Brush with butter and roast in hot oven (400°), uncovered, until skin browns, using a little of the cold marinade for basting. Reduce heat and continue occasional basting, allowing about 2 hours in all. When nearly done, spread meat with the sour cream blended with the flour. For milder taste, baste with cold water or pan drippings, instead of marinade. Serves 6 to 8.

6. ROLLED VEAL ROAST
(Pieczeń Cielęca Zawijana ze Słoniną)

3–4 lbs. rolled veal shoulder	flour for dusting
4–6 ozs., salt pork	salt and pepper to taste
juice ½ lemon	1 cup sour cream (optional)
4 tbs. butter	1 tsp. flour (optional)

Cut salt pork into thin strips. Unroll the veal and lard it; then sprinkle with lemon juice, roll up tightly again, and tie with cotton thread. Refrigerate for 3 to 4 hours. Brush with melted butter and roast in very hot oven (450°) until well browned, basting frequently with pan drippings. Reduce heat to 300° and continue roasting, basting frequently, for 1½ to 2 hours. When nearly done dust with flour, baste once again, and allow sauce to thicken (another 10 minutes). Slice thin and serve with a variety of vegetables. Add sour cream and flour to sauce if desired. Serves 6 to 8.

7. ROLLED VEAL ROAST WITH ANCHOVIES
(Pieczeń Cielęca Zawijana z Sardelami)

3–4 lbs. rolled veal shoulder	6–8 anchovies
4–6 ozs. salt pork	2 tbs. anchovy paste
juice ½ lemon	1 cup sour cream
salt and pepper to taste	1 tsp. flour
4 tbs. butter	

Prepare the same as Rolled Veal Roast (No. 6), but in addition to larding the meat with salt pork, lard it with the anchovies cut into thin strips. Spread inside and out with anchovy paste, roll up again, and tie. Roast in a hot oven, basting frequently, until brown. Follow directions in No. 6, using sour cream blended with a teaspoon of flour for the gravy. Serves 6 to 8.

8. LITHUANIAN VEAL ROAST
(Pieczeń Cielęca po Litewsku)

4 lbs. rump or shoulder of veal, boned	1 parsley root
	½ celery root
1 carrot	3 tbs. dry mustard

salt and pepper to taste
¼ lb. salt pork for larding
2 tbs. butter

3–4 tbs. sour cream
flour for dusting

Grate the vegetables fine and mix with dry mustard. Rub thoroughly or pound into meat until completely absorbed. Refrigerate, weighted with a piece of board or a saucer and tightly covered, for 4 to 5 days (2 days in the summer). Remove from refrigerator several hours before cooking so that meat is at room temperature when ready to go into the oven. Reserve meat juice for basting. Roast in a hot oven (400°) for 1½ to 2 hours, basting frequently with butter and the meat juice. When nearly done add sour cream, dust lightly with flour and baste until sauce browns. Slice thin and serve with vegetables and potatoes. Serves 8.

9. COLD ROAST VEAL IN TARTARE SAUCE
(Pieczeń Cielęca w Sosie Tatarskim)

2 lbs. cold roast veal
1 cup Tartare Sauce (see Index)

made with hard-cooked egg
yolks

Slice leftover cold veal roast thin, and arrange in refrigerator dish, spreading each slice with Tartare Sauce. Spread any remaining sauce over the top, cover tightly, and store until ready to use. Cold roast veal will keep under refrigeration for a full week, and the taste of the sauce will come through best after several days. Serves 4.

10. COLD MARINATED ROAST VEAL
(Pieczeń Cielęca Marynowana na Zimno)

3–4 lbs. rump or rolled veal
    shoulder
    milk to cover
    marinade to cover (see No. 5)
2 carrots
1 large onion

1 leek
1 parsley root
½ celery root
    few sprigs fresh parsley
    salt and pepper to taste

Have butcher bone the meat. Soak for 2 days in just enough milk to cover. Wipe meat off and cover with boiling marinade. Allow to stand 3 to 4 days. Clean and dice vegetables, add to marinade, season, and bring to a boil. Roll meat tight, secure with cotton thread, and simmer in the marinade until tender (about 1½ to 2 hours). Remove from broth, chill, and cut thin for serving. Garnish with gherkins, sliced hard-cooked egg, and tart jelly. Serve with oil and vinegar or with Tartare Sauce (see Index). Serves 6 to 8.

11. FRICANDEAU OF VEAL *(Fricandeau z Cielęciny)*

4 lbs. rump or shoulder veal, boned
¼ lb. salt pork for larding
juice ½ lemon
salt and pepper to taste
1 celery root
2 carrots
1 parsley root
1 kohlrabi or parsnip

2 stalks celery with leaves
½ cup snap beans
¼ to ½ cup peas
1 onion (optional)
1 tbs. butter
1 cup soup stock or commercial bouillon
flour for dusting
few sprigs fresh parsley

Lard meat with the salt pork, sprinkle with lemon juice, season, roll tight, and secure with cotton string. Dice vegetables. Arrange meat in a heavy casserole and cover with vegetables. Add butter and simmer, tightly covered, basting frequently with bouillon, until meat is nicely brown and vegetables soft. Dust lightly with flour and continue basting until sauce thickens. Slice thin and serve with the vegetables. Serves 8.

12. VEAL FRICANDEAU WITH SHARP SAUCE
(Fricandeau z Ostrym Sosem)

4 lbs. rump or shoulder of veal, boned
¼ lb. salt pork for larding
juice ½ lemon
salt and pepper to taste
¼ lb. boiled ham, sliced thin
vegetables as in No. 11

1 onion, blanched, chopped fine, and smothered in butter
bouillon for basting (1 cup)
¼ tsp. dry mustard
1 tsp. Maggi extract
1 cup sour cream
flour for thickening (optional)

Have meat boned and prepare as for Fricandeau of Veal, No. 11, larding, seasoning, and sprinkling with lemon juice. Spread the entire surface with ham slices, then roll tightly, and tie with cotton string. Dice vegetables. Arrange meat in heavy casserole, cover with vegetables and onion, and simmer tightly covered, basting sparingly with bouillon. When meat is done (about 2 hours) add mustard, Maggi extract, and sour cream, and continue simmering until sauce bubbles up. If too thin, thicken with a little flour. Slice meat thin and pour sauce over it. Serve with the vegetables with which the meat has cooked. Serves 8. If desired, the vegetables may be puréed and put through a sieve, together with the sour cream sauce. If sharper taste is desired, add more mustard and seasoning.

13. ROAST LOIN OF VEAL *(Nerkówka Cielęca Pieczona)*

loin of veal with kidney left in (3–4 lbs.)

salt and pepper to taste
2 tbs. butter

Rub meat with salt a half-hour before cooking. Roast with the butter in open pan in a hot oven (400°) until nicely browned. Season lightly with pepper, reduce heat, and continue roasting, basting frequently with pan drippings alternating with cold water. The roasting time should be about 1½ hours. Slice so that the kidney is evenly distributed. Serves 6 to 8.

14. ROAST STUFFED LOIN OF VEAL
(Nerkówka Cielęca Nadiewana)

4 lbs. loin of veal with or without kidney	salt and pepper to taste
	2 tbs. butter

A stuffed roast will stretch the meat by several servings. Have butcher separate meat from bone underneath the ribs and prepare a pocket for stuffing. Season a half-hour before putting into oven, or before starting to prepare the stuffing.

Stuffing:

4 tbs. butter	1 tbs. chopped fresh parsley
1 cup bread crumbs, moistened with milk	1 tbs. chopped fresh dill
	salt and pepper to taste
2 eggs, separated	dash of nutmeg (optional)

Cream butter, combine with bread crumbs and lightly-beaten egg yolks, add the chopped herbs, and season to taste. If fresh dill is unavailable, substitute more parsley. Beat egg whites until stiff and fold in. Fill meat pocket with stuffing, and secure with toothpicks or sew with white cotton thread. Rub meat with butter and roast in open pan, starting at 400° and reducing heat to 300° when meat begins to brown. Baste frequently with pan drippings, alternating with cold water. Cook about 1½ hours. Serves 8 to 10.

15. ROAST RACK OF VEAL (Comber Cielęcy)

6-lb. rack of veal (with kidneys)	juice 1 lemon
salt and pepper to taste	¼ cup butter

Season meat and sprinkle with lemon juice. Allow to stand 2 hours. Spread with butter. Roast in hot oven (400°) for 1½ to 1¾ hours, basting frequently with pan drippings alternating with cold water. For gravy, add a little water or soup stock to pan after meat is done —no more than ½ cup—and allow to boil up. Slice meat thin, and garnish with lemon slices and sprigs of parsley. Serve sauce separately. Serve with green peas, cauliflower, mushrooms, or asparagus, and tart jelly and a salad. Serves 8 to 10.

16. RACK OF VEAL *À LA DUCHESSE*
(Comber Cielęcy à la Duchesse)

6-lb. rack of veal (with kidneys)	2 cups sour cream
4–6 ozs. salt pork for larding	1 tsp. flour

Prepare meat the same as in No. 15. Cut salt pork into thin strips and lard meat generously. Allow to stand 2 hours. Roast as directed in No. 15. When meat begins to brown, add the sour cream blended with flour. Continue basting, omitting water. Slice and serve, with the sauce separate. Traditionally, this roast is garnished with crayfish (shrimps may be substituted) and slices of truffles. Serves 8 to 10.

17. VEAL SCHNITZELS *AU NATUREL*
(Sznycle Cielęce Naturalne)

2 lbs. boneless veal (leg or shoulder)	flour for dredging
	4 tbs. butter
salt and pepper to taste	2 tbs. soup stock

Have butcher cut the meat into serving pieces, and pound well so that meat is not more than ¼ inch thick. Season and dredge in flour. Brown quickly in hot butter. Reduce heat and fry slowly until tender, turning occasionally—about 20 minutes. Arrange on hot platter and garnish each piece of meat with a lemon slice and either Anchovy or Chive Butter. Add soup stock to the butter in the frying pan, allow to boil up, and pour over meat. Serves 5 to 6.

18. SCHNITZELS WITH ANCHOVIES
(Sznycle Cielęce z Sardelami)

Prepare like No. 17. Garnish each with a strip of anchovy. Add 2 or 3 tablespoons of strong soup stock to the butter in the frying pan. Boil up once and pour over the meat.

19. EMPEROR SCHNITZELS *(Sznycle po Cesarsku)*

2 lbs. boneless shoulder or leg of veal	4 tbs. butter
	1 cup sour cream
¼ lb. salt pork for larding	lemon juice and grated rind to
salt and pepper to taste	taste
flour for dredging	1 heaping tbs. capers

Lard the meat, slice, and pound as in No. 17. Season with salt and pepper, dust with flour, and brown in very hot butter, turning once. Transfer to heavy casserole, add sour cream blended with ½ tsp. flour, and a little grated lemon rind and lemon juice. Take care not to make the sauce too sour. Add capers. Cover tightly and simmer for 25 minutes. Serves 5 to 6.

20. BREADED VEAL CHOPS
(Kotlety Cielęce Panierowane)

6 veal loin or shoulder chops	1 egg, lightly beaten
½ lb. chopped veal	bread crumbs for breading
salt and pepper to taste	3–4 tbs. butter
flour for dusting	

Have chops cut about ¾ inch thick. Pound them well, then spread chopped veal thinly on both sides. Season to taste, dust with flour, dip in egg, then in bread crumbs, and fry in hot butter, turning heat down once the chops are brown on both sides. Continue frying over low heat for about 20 minutes or until thoroughly done inside. Serve with lemon slices or sharp sauce, according to preference. Serves 6.

21. VEAL CHOPS IMPERIAL (Kotlety Cielęce "Imperial")

Prepare Breaded Veal Chops, No. 20. Beat up as many eggs as there are chops. For each chop, pour two spoonfuls of beaten egg on a hot buttered griddle as for small pancakes. Place cooked breaded chop in the egg and cook until egg is done. Remove with spatula. Keep hot in a warm oven until all the chops are ready. Serve with Tomato Sauce (see Index). Serves 6.

22. VEAL CHOPS ITALIAN-STYLE
(Kotlety Cielęce po Włosku)

Prepare the same as No. 20, but instead of spreading the chops with ground meat, use the following:

½ cup rice, cooked in water or milk (see Index)	3 tbs. grated Parmesan

Mix rice with Parmesan cheese and spread on chops. Dip in egg and bread crumbs and fry to a golden brown, 20 to 25 minutes. Serve with Tomato Sauce (see Index). Serves 6.

23. VEAL CUTLETS À LA PÉRIGUEUX
(Kotlety Cielęce à la Périgueux)

2 lbs. veal cutlet cut from leg	1–2 eggs, lightly beaten
salt and pepper to taste	¼ cup flour
¼ lb. liver or poultry pâté (see Index) or equivalent amount canned liver pâté	¾ cup bread crumbs
	butter for frying

Have veal cut in thin pieces about 3 by 6 inches, and pound very thin. Season, and spread half of each piece with pâté. Fold over, secure with toothpicks, dip in egg, then in flour and bread crumbs mixed, and fry slowly in hot brown butter, turning occasionally so the meat browns evenly. Allow about 25 minutes cooking time. Serve with purée of chestnuts, green peas, cauliflower, or whole broiled or smothered mushrooms (see Index). Serves 6.

24. VEAL CUTLET ZINGARA
(Kotlety Cielęce à la Zingara)

6 loin veal chops about ¾" thick piece of salt pork	1 parsley root ½ celery root
6 slices boiled ham, the same size as chops and about ¼" thick	1–2 stalks celery ¼ cup snap beans 1 cup strong bouillon
2–3 tbs. butter	1 cup dry white wine
1 med. onion	salt and pepper to taste
1 carrot	

Bone the chops and pound lightly. Season and lard heavily with strips of salt pork and ham (use scraps of ham cut from edges). Brown the meat lightly in hot butter. Dice vegetables and onion and braise in the butter until half done. Arrange veal and ham slices alternately in a heavy casserole and cover with vegetables, using all the butter in the pan. Add bouillon and wine and cover tightly. Place the casserole in another, larger dish half-filled with boiling water, and simmer for half an hour. Purée the vegetables, return to sauce, and boil up once. Serve with Potato Croquettes (see Index). Serves 6 generously.

25. VEAL CHOPS SMOTHERED WITH MUSHROOMS
(Kotlety Cielęce Duszone z Pieczarkami)

6 loin or shoulder veal chops salt and pepper to taste flour for dusting	1 cup strong bouillon ½ med. onion, blanched and grated
4 tbs. butter ½ lb. tiny fresh mushrooms	Madeira Sauce (see Index)

Have the chops cut rather thin. Bone, season, dust with flour and brown lightly in butter. Parboil the mushrooms in bouillon, drain, and reserve the liquid. Season, and sauté with onion in the butter in which meat has cooked for about 10 minutes. In the meantime simmer the chops tightly covered for about 10 minutes in Madeira Sauce made with the bouillon in which mushrooms have cooked. To serve, make a mound of the mushrooms in center of platter and arrange the chops around them. Serve sauce separately. Serves 6.

26. VEAL PATTIES *(Kotlety Cielęce Siekane)*

Prepare the same as Chopped Beef Patties (see Index), adding a tablespoon of melted butter per pound of chopped veal and cooking more slowly than beef because veal must be thoroughly done without being dry. Serve with lemon slices or with any of the following sauces: Caper, Sorrel, Tomato, Calf's Brain, or Crayfish (see Index).

27. STUFFED BREAST OR SHOULDER OF VEAL
(Mostek Nadziewany)

Prepare the same as Stuffed Loin of Veal (No. 14), and roast in a hot oven, basting frequently, for about 1½ hours. Stale white rolls moistened in milk may be substituted for bread crumbs. About 3 servings per pound of meat.

28. BREAST OF VEAL WITH LIVER STUFFING
(Mostek Nadziewany Wątróbką)

Prepare the same as No. 14. Use half the amount of bread crumbs or rolls for stuffing, adding ¼ lb. raw calf's liver, chopped and mashed. Chopped parsley may be used whenever dill is unavailable.

29. BRAISED VEAL WITH RICE
(Potrawka z Cielęciny z Ryżem)

3–4 lbs. breast or shoulder of veal	salt and pepper to taste
1 large onion	1 tbs. butter
1–2 carrots	1 tbs. flour
2 stalks celery with leaves	lemon juice to taste
½ celery root	1 tsp. grated lemon rind
½ parsley root	½ tsp. brown sugar
1 leek	

Have butcher cut meat into serving pieces. (Meat should be boned, but the bones should be added to the cooking and discarded later; they add body to the stock.) Add diced vegetables and onion and just enough cold water to cover. Skim a few times, add seasoning, and simmer tightly covered until meat is done, about 1½ hours. In a heavy skillet melt the butter without browning, add flour, and blend thoroughly with about 1 cup of strained stock. Add lemon juice and rind, and sugar to taste (omit sugar if preferred). Remove bones from the meat pot and add the sauce. Allow to simmer another 30 minutes. Separately cook rice or pearl barley (see Index) and serve. Serves 6 to 8.

30. BRAISED VEAL WITH CRAYFISH OR
SHRIMP SAUCE *(Potrawka Cielęca z Rakami)*

Prepare veal as in No. 29. Using the soup stock and crayfish or
shrimp, make Crayfish Sauce (see Index), add ½ lb. cooked or
canned shrimp, and simmer 10 to 15 minutes. At the last moment
add 2 lightly-beaten egg yolks, taking care not to curdle. Sprinkle
with 2 tsp. chopped fresh dill.

31. RAGOUT OF VEAL *(Ragout z Bruściku Cielęcego)*

2–3 lbs. shoulder or breast of veal	salt and pepper to taste
1 small calf's brain or 1 sweet-bread	¼ lb. mushrooms, sliced thin
onion and soup greens as in No. 29	½ cup green peas
	2 tbs. butter
1 small or ½ med. cauliflower	2–3 egg yolks

Have butcher bone the meat and cut into serving pieces, and chop
the bones for cooking. Add onion, soup greens, and seasoning, and
cook the same as No. 29. After 1 hour add sweetbread or calf's brain
and cauliflower and simmer until done (30 to 40 minutes). Remove
cauliflower and cut into small pieces. Dice sweetbread. Separately,
simmer mushrooms and peas in butter, tightly covered, for about
5 minutes. Add flour a little at a time, stirring to blend well. Dilute
with soup stock and add cauliflower and sweetbread. Discard
bones. Strain remaining soup stock and blend into sauce. (Soup
greens may be mashed through a sieve or discarded, according to
preference.) Combine sauce with meat and simmer another 15
minutes. At the last minute add lightly-beaten egg yolks, taking
care not to curdle. Serve with Marrow Balls (see Index). Serves 6
to 8. The ragout may also be served in a pie or in individual pastry
shells.

32. LEFTOVER VEAL DISH
(Potrawka z Pozostałej Cielęciny)

I.

3 cups leftover veal roast, or 6 veal slices	1 cup sour cream
	1 tsp. flour
1 cup strong soup stock or commercial bouillon	2 egg yolks

Heat the sliced meat in bouillon. Allow to simmer about 10 minutes.
Add sour cream blended with the flour and simmer another 5 to 10
minutes. At the last moment add lightly-beaten egg yolks, taking
care not to curdle. Serves 6.

II.

2 cups leftover veal roast or 4 veal slices	⅛ tsp. Maggi or Soy Sauce
1 tbs. butter	juice ⅛ lemon
1½ tsp. flour	3–4 tsp. sugar (brown sugar or honey may be substituted)
1 cup strong bouillon	1 tsp. grated lemon rind
salt and pepper to taste	

Melt butter but do not brown. Blend in flour, then bouillon, and add all other ingredients except meat. These may be varied according to taste, since preferences vary as to amounts of lemon and sugar as well as seasoning. Let sauce bubble up, add meat, and allow to simmer tightly covered for about 15 minutes. Serves 4.

33. VEAL *BIGOS (Bigos z Cielęciny)*

3 cups diced cooked veal	½ cup strong soup stock or commercial bouillon
3 green apples	
2 tbs. butter	sugar and salt to taste
1 tbs. flour	

Core and pare apples and just cover with water. Allow to boil up once. Blend butter and flour without browning, dilute with ½ cup soup stock, and combine with apples and water. Salt lightly, add sugar to taste, and add meat to sauce. Simmer tightly covered for about 10 minutes. Serves 6.

34. STUFFED VEAL BIRDS *(Zrazy Cielęce Zawijane)*

2 lbs. veal cutlet	flour for dredging
salt and pepper to taste	2–3 tbs. butter
½ lb. meat or liver pâté, *or* stuffing made of	1 cup soup stock or commercial bouillon
½ lb. fresh mushrooms, chopped	¼ cup dry white wine (optional)
1 small or ½ med. onion, chopped	⅛ tsp. Maggi extract (optional)
2 tbs. bread crumbs	

Have veal cut thin as for scaloppine, pound well, and cut into 3-inch squares. Season and spread with stuffing, or canned pâté. The fresh mushroom stuffing is prepared as follows: Simmer chopped onion and mushrooms in a little butter for about 5 minutes and season to taste. Add bread crumbs and mix thoroughly. Spread evenly on the meat. Roll each piece and tie with white thread. Dust lightly with flour and brown quickly on all sides in hot butter. Arrange tightly in a heavy casserole and simmer, covered, basting frequently with bouillon. Meat should not simmer longer than 45 minutes. For a more delicate taste, add white wine and Maggi extract. If sauce is not thick enough, dust in a bit more flour. Serves 6. Serve with parsley potatoes or pearl barley sprinkled with fresh dill.

35. VEAL IN TOMATO SAUCE
(Zrazy w Sosie Pomidorowym)

2 lbs. veal cutlet or other bone-	1–2 carrots
less cut, sliced thin	½ celery root
3 tbs. butter	½ parsley root
flour for dusting	1 leek
salt and pepper to taste	few sprigs parsley
2 cups bouillon	1–2 celery stalks
1 large onion, diced	2 tomatoes or 2 tbs. tomato paste

Have meat cut thin as for scaloppine. Simmer vegetables and onion in bouillon until soft, about 30 minutes. In the meantime, pound meat, season, dust with flour, and brown quickly in as much butter as needed. Allow bouillon to simmer down to about 1 cup. Add tomatoes and remaining butter. Add meat and simmer, covered, for about 30 minutes. Press sauce through a sieve. Serves 6.

36. VEAL BRAISED WITH PÂTÉ
(Zrazy Przekładane Pasztetem)

2 lbs. boneless veal, cut thin	salt and pepper to taste
½ lb. (approx.) leftover meat pâté	3 tbs. butter
or commercial liver sausage	2 tbs. strong bouillon

Have butcher prepare meat as for scaloppine. Pound thin, season, and cut into serving pieces. Brown quickly in part of the butter. Slice pâté (this may be liver, poultry,-meat, or venison pâté, or commercially prepared liver paste) as thin as possible. Alternately arrange veal and pâté slices in a heavy buttered casserole, add soup stock, top with remaining butter, cover tightly, and bake in hot oven for 45 minutes. Add more stock if needed. Cover with Truffle Sauce or Madeira Sauce with Mushrooms (see Index) and allow to cook another 10 minutes. Serves 6.

37. CALF'S LIVER SMOTHERED IN SOUR CREAM
(Watróbka Duszona ze Śmietaną)

1 whole liver	1 small or ½ med. onion,
milk or buttermilk to cover	chopped
4 ozs. salt pork for larding	3–4 tbs. cold bouillon or water
salt and pepper to taste	1 cup sour cream
2–3 tbs. butter	1 tsp. flour

Soak liver in milk or buttermilk for 3 to 4 hours. Wipe, lard with thin strips of salt pork, and season just before putting into skillet. Brown quickly on both sides in hot butter, adding the onion and taking care not to scorch either meat or onion. Reduce heat, cover, and simmer for 15 minutes, basting with cold water or bouillon. Blend sour cream and flour and add to meat. Allow to bubble up. Slice liver and serve on hot platter, covered with the sauce. The cooking process should not take more than 30 minutes. Serve with potatoes. Serves 6.

Note: Sliced liver may be prepared the same way, but the over-all cooking time should be no more than 10 to 15 minutes; otherwise the meat will be dry. Larding may be omitted. Liver, like steak, should never be salted until the last minute, or meat will be tough.

38. FRIED CALF'S LIVER *AU NATUREL*
(*Watróbka Smażona Naturalna*)

2 lbs. calf's liver, sliced	flour for dredging
milk or buttermilk to cover	butter for frying
salt and pepper to taste	

Soak liver slices in milk or buttermilk for 3 to 4 hours, remove membranes, season, dust with flour and fry at once in hot butter, browning quickly on both sides. Liver should be pink inside: cooking time should be 5 to 10 minutes, depending on thickness of slices. Makes 6 servings.

39. FRIED CALF'S LIVER VIENNESE-STYLE
(*Watróbka Smażona po Wiedeńsku*)

Prepare the same as No. 38, but after dredging with flour, dip in beaten egg. (Use 1 egg per pound of meat.) Roll in bread crumbs and fry. Serve with any sharp sauce, potatoes, and a salad.

40. CALF'S LIVER SMOTHERED IN MADEIRA SAUCE
(*Watróbka Duszona z Maderą*)

1 whole calf's liver (about 2 lbs.)	2 tbs. butter
milk or buttermilk to cover	½ med. onion, diced
4 ozs. salt pork for larding	

Prepare as for No. 37, but instead of sour cream, cover with Madeira Sauce with Mushrooms (see Index) and simmer, covered, for about 20 minutes. If liver slices are used, larding may be omitted and the meat dusted with flour, browned quickly in butter on both sides, then simmered in the sauce for 3 to 4 minutes. Serves 6.

41. CALF'S LIVER À LA NELSON
(Wątróbka à la Nelson)

1 whole calf's liver (about 2 lbs.)
milk or buttermilk to cover
6–8 portion-size potatoes, par-boiled and cut in thick slices
12 med. mushrooms, smothered in butter

1 med. onion, chopped
2 tbs. butter
salt and pepper to taste
flour for dredging
1 cup strong bouillon
½ cup Madeira or Sherry

Soak liver in milk for 3 to 4 hours. Wipe dry, remove membranes, and slice. Have mushrooms and potatoes ready before starting to cook liver. Brown onion to a light golden color, season liver, dust with flour, and sear in the same pan in which onion is cooking. Liver should be quite raw inside. Arrange layers of liver and potatoes alternately in a heavy casserole, adding a small amount of onion and mushrooms after each layer. Add 1 tsp. flour to the butter in which onion and liver have cooked, stir to a paste, add bouillon, and blend well. Add wine. Allow to bubble up and pour over the meat. Simmer another 2 minutes. This dish must be prepared quickly or the liver will be tough. Serves 6 to 7.

42. CALF'S LIVER WITH JUNIPER
(Wątróbka Cielęca z Jałowcem)

1 whole calf's liver (about 2 lbs.) prepared as for No. 37
buttermilk or milk to cover
¼ lb. salt pork for larding
salt and pepper to taste
2 tbs. butter
½–1 cup bouillon

2 heaping tbs. bread crumbs browned in 2 tbs. butter
6 juniper berries, pounded
flour for dusting
¼ cup sour cream

Follow directions in No. 37, cooking about 15 minutes over very low heat. Baste frequently with bouillon. Melt butter, add bread crumbs, brown, and combine with crushed juniper. Slice the liver without quite cutting through the meat at the bottom, and spread the stuffing between the slices. Secure with skewers, return to pot, dust with flour, and add sour cream. Allow sauce to bubble up once. If too little sauce remains, add a little more bouillon. Serve with potatoes and mushrooms. Serves 6 to 7.

43. LIVER PUDDING (Budyń z Duszonej Wątróbki)

I.

1 whole liver (about 2 lbs.)
milk or buttermilk to soak
4 ozs. salt pork for larding

salt and pepper to taste
butter for browning
½ onion, chopped

3–4 tbs. cold bouillon or water	salt and pepper to taste
2–3 tbs. butter	dash of nutmeg
6 eggs, separated	1 tsp. grated lemon rind
1 white roll moistened with milk and mashed	bread crumbs

Prepare and cook liver as in No. 37. When liver is done, allow to cool. Strain liquid in which it cooked. Reserve. Cut meat into small pieces, then put through sieve or fine meat grinder. Cream butter and egg yolks, add strained meat sauce, mashed roll (bread crumbs may be substituted), salt, pepper, nutmeg, and lemon rind. Add liver and mix thoroughly. Fold in beaten egg whites last. Pour into buttered mold which has been lined with bread crumbs. Cover tightly and steam for 2 hours. Unmold and serve hot with Mushroom Sauce (see Index) or any sharp sauce. Serves 8.

II.

1 whole liver (about 2 lbs.)	dash of nutmeg
4 eggs, separated	1 white roll, moistened in milk and
2 tbs. butter	mashed (or equivalent amount
1 med. onion, grated	bread crumbs)
salt and pepper to taste	flour for dredging

Remove membranes from liver and cut into pieces. Chop fine or press through a sieve. Cream 1 tbs. butter with the egg yolks. Sauté grated onion in butter until golden brown. Combine onion, roll or bread crumbs, egg yolks, butter, and seasoning. Blend well with chopped liver. Beat egg whites stiff and fold in. Pour into buttered mold lined with bread crumbs and steam for 2 hours. Unmold and serve hot with Mushroom Sauce (see Index) or any sharp sauce.

44. LIVER PATTIES *(Kluseczki z Wątróbki)*

Prepare as for No. 43-*II*, but use 2 eggs and 2 tbs. bread crumbs together with the mashed roll. Shape small patties or croquettes, roll in flour, and cook in boiling salted water. When croquettes come to the surface, allow to cook in steam a few minutes longer. Drain and serve with drawn butter and minced browned onion. Serves 6 to 8.

45. SKEWERED CALF'S LIVER AND KIDNEYS *(Wątróbka z Cynaderką na Szpadce)*

¼–¾ lb. calf's liver	2–3 tbs. butter
1 or 2 veal kidneys, depending on size	2–3 tbs. bread crumbs
milk or buttermilk to cover	salt and pepper to taste
piece of salt pork or several slices of bacon, cut thick	Anchovy or Chive Butter (see Index)

Soak liver and kidney for a couple of hours in milk. Dry and cut in
small slices for skewering. Cut an equal number of small slices of
salt pork or bacon. Skewer liver, kidneys, and bacon alternately.
Season, and fry quickly in hot butter, turning so that meat will
brown on all sides. Arrange on oven-proof platter and put into hot
oven for a few minutes, topping each piece of meat with a pat of
Anchovy or Chive Butter. When butter melts, serve sizzling hot
with parsley potatoes. Serves 4 or 5.

46. FRIED VEAL KIDNEYS (Cynaderki Cielęce Smażone)

2 veal kidneys with most of the fat removed	flour and bread crumbs in equal amounts, for rolling
salt and pepper to taste	butter for frying
1 egg, lightly beaten	

Cut kidneys into diagonal slices. Season, dip in egg, then in combined flour and bread crumbs, and fry in hot butter, browning evenly
on all sides. Serve with a sharp sauce or with lemon slices. Serves 3.

47. SMOTHERED VEAL KIDNEYS (Cynaderki Duszone)

2 veal kidneys with most of the fat removed	½ cup bouillon
flour for dredging	¼ cup sour cream
salt and pepper to taste	¼ tsp. paprika
2–3 tbs. butter	½ tsp. marjoram
	lemon juice to taste

Slice the kidney diagonally, season, and dust with flour. Brown
quickly on both sides in hot butter. Using the butter in which kidneys browned, make a sauce as follows: Add ½ tbs. flour to the butter
and stir to a paste. Blend in bouillon, and add sour cream, paprika,
and marjoram. Season with lemon juice, salt, and pepper. Return
kidneys to sauce, cover tightly, and allow to simmer for about 10
minutes. Serves 3.

48. KIDNEYS STEWED IN MADEIRA
(Cynaderki Duszone z Maderą)

Prepare 2 veal kidneys as in No. 47. Put in a casserole and keep
hot in oven. Make Madeira Sauce as follows:

½ tsp. flour	salt and pepper to taste
½ cup strong soup stock	4 slices of toast
¼ to ½ cup Madeira (or sherry)	1 tbs. chopped fresh parsley
6 med. mushrooms, sliced	
12 shallots, peeled and smothered in butter	

Using pan with butter in which kidneys fried, make a thin paste with the flour, add soup stock, wine, mushrooms, and cooked shallots. Season and allow to simmer for about 10 minutes. Arrange half a kidney on each piece of toast, pour sauce over the kidneys, and sprinkle with chopped fresh parsley. Serve at once. Serves 4.

49. FRIED SWEETBREADS *(Mleczko Cielęce Smażone)*

2 pairs sweetbreads	flour for dusting
milk to cover	1 egg, lightly beaten
court bouillon to cover (see	bread crumbs (about ¾ cup)
Index)	3–4 tbs. butter or lard for frying
salt and pepper to taste	lemon slices

Soak sweetbreads in milk for 2 to 3 hours (water may be substituted). Drop into boiling court bouillon and parboil for 10 to 15 minutes. Allow to cool for convenient handling; then remove membranes and slice. Season with salt and pepper, dust with flour, dip in egg, roll in bread crumbs, and fry in hot fat to a golden brown, taking care to brown evenly on all sides. Decorate each slice with sliver of lemon, and serve with green peas, spinach, or cauliflower. Serves 4.

50. BRAISED SWEETBREADS
(Mleczko Cielęce w Potrawie)

2 pairs sweetbreads	White Lemon Sauce (see
bouillon to cover	Index)

Dip sweetbreads in boiling water for 2 to 3 minutes. Remove membranes, and simmer in just enough strong bouillon to cover for about 20 minutes. Drain, reserving bouillon. Make a White Lemon Sauce, using the bouillon in which meat has cooked. Garnish with Veal Croquettes, whole broiled mushrooms, and croutons. Serves 4.

51. CALF'S BRAINS—PARBOILING *(Móżdżek Cielęcy)*

All recipes for cooking calf's brains require that they be parboiled in salted boiling water which has first cooked a few minutes with an onion, a few celery stalks, a carrot, a bay leaf, half a lemon, and 6 to 10 peppercorns. Parboil the brains for about 10 minutes. Remove membranes, and continue cooking according to any preferred recipe.

52. FRIED CALF'S BRAINS WITH EGG
(Móżdżek Smażony z Jajkami)

1 set of calf brains, parboiled as in
No. 51
1 tbs. butter
1 small or ½ med. onion, chopped
fine

salt and pepper to taste
2 egg yolks

Chop brains coarsely. Brown onion lightly in butter, add brains, season, and fry over moderate heat for 10 minutes, turning frequently. Put into two serving dishes. In center of each make a depression with a spoon, and drop a whole raw egg yolk into the depression. Serves 2.

53. CALF'S BRAIN PATTIES *(Kotlety z Mózgów)*

2 sets of calf brains, parboiled as
in No. 51
salt and pepper to taste
flour for dusting

1 egg, lightly beaten
bread crumbs
3 tbs. butter

Cut brains into thick slices and shape into patties. Season, dust with flour, dip in egg, and roll in bread crumbs. Fry in hot butter to a golden brown, evenly on all sides. Serve with lemon slices. Side dishes: peas, carrots, or spinach. Serves 4.

54. CALF'S BRAIN CROQUETTES *(Krokiety z Mózgu)*

2 sets of calf brains, parboiled
as in No. 51
4 tbs. butter
1 tbs. flour
2–3 tbs. bouillon

2 eggs, separated
salt and pepper to taste
dash of nutmeg (optional)
bread crumbs for rolling

Remove membranes and cut brains into pieces. Melt 1 tbs. butter without browning and stir in flour and bouillon until well blended. Remove from heat; add slightly-beaten egg yolks, season, add brains, and stir thoroughly to a smooth consistency. Make small croquettes and roll them in bread crumbs. Beat the egg whites until stiff, dip the croquettes in them, and then roll again in bread crumbs, allowing for a thick crust. Fry evenly in butter or in deep fat until a golden brown. Drain. Garnish with sprigs of parsley and lemon slices. Serves 4.

55. CALF'S BRAIN PUDDING *(Budyń Cielęcy)*

2–3 sets of calf brains, parboiled
as in No. 51
½ cup heavy sweet cream

4 eggs, separated
salt and pepper to taste
butter and bread crumbs

Using a whisk or blender, beat the brains to a smooth mass the consistency of sour cream. Add sweet cream, egg yolks, salt and pepper to taste, and the stiffly-beaten egg whites. Continue beating with whisk another 5 to 10 minutes. Pour into well-buttered mold which has been lined with bread crumbs. Cover tightly and cook in boiling water for 1 hour. Unmold and serve hot with melted butter. Separately serve Mushroom or Caper Sauce (see Index). Serves 4 to 6.

56. CALF'S HEAD (*Główka Cielęca*)

1 calf's head, parboiled (brain and tongue removed for separate preparation)	4 cloves
	10 peppercorns
	1 leek
2 qts. boiling water	½ celery root
1 carrot	2 stalks celery with leaves
1 onion	1 parsley root
½ lemon, sliced	small bunch parsley
1 bay leaf	salt and pepper to taste

Have butcher split bones at base of head in several places without cutting into meat and skin. Rinse well several times. Parboil. Boil vegetables and spices in water for a few minutes. Add parboiled head. Simmer, covered, until meat is tender, about 2 hours. Add tongue for last hour of cooking. Add brains for the last 15 minutes. Remove bones from head and from base of tongue. Skin tongue. Cut head and tongue into slices lengthwise and serve in any desired way.

57. FRIED CALF'S HEAD WITH TARTARE SAUCE
(*Główka Smażona z Sosem Tatarskim*)

sliced calf's head, prepared as in No. 56	bread crumbs
	butter or deep fat for frying
flour for dredging	bunch of parsley
2 eggs, slightly beaten	lemon slices
salt and pepper to taste	

Dredge slices in flour, dip in seasoned beaten egg, roll in bread crumbs, and fry in hot butter or deep fat to a golden brown. Serve garnished with lemon slices and sprigs of parsley fried quickly in the hot fat. Separately serve Tartare Sauce (see Index).

58. CALF'S HEAD IN TOMATO SAUCE
(*Główka Cielęca w Sosie Pomidorowym*)

Prepare head as in No. 56. Make Tomato Sauce (see Index) or use commercially prepared sauce and simmer head and tongue slices in it for about half an hour. Serve hot.

59. CALF'S HEAD À LA TITUS
(Główka Cielęca à la Titus)

Prepare head as in No. 56. Simmer for 10 minutes in White Lemon Sauce (see Index). Serve garnished with lemon slices and thin wedges of toast. Sprinkle buttered croutons over the top.

60. MOCK TURTLE HEAD *(Główka Cielęca en Tortue)*

Prepare calf's head as in No. 56. Arrange head, tongue, and brain slices in center of platter. Around the edges of the platter arrange mounds of broiled or smothered mushrooms, hard-cooked eggs and sliced gherkins. Serve with Dill Pickle Sauce (see Index) to which ⅛ tsp. Maggi extract has been added.

61. CALF'S HEAD VINAIGRETTE
(Główka Cielęca Vinegrette)

Prepare head as in No. 56. Chill. Slice head, tongue, and brain and arrange on platter. Serve garnished with chopped raw onion, marinated mushrooms, gherkins, and capers. Separately serve olive oil and vinegar and French mustard. May also be served with mayonnaise.

62. CALF'S FEET *(Nóżki Cielęce)*

Have butcher skin and split 2 pairs calf's feet. Dip in boiling water and remove membranes. Cook in court bouillon (see Index) to cover, starting cold, until meat begins to fall away from the bones. Bone. Season meat and simmer in any sharp sauce (see Index) for 10 to 15 minutes, or chill and serve with olive oil, vinegar, and mustard. Serves 4.

63. FRIED CALF'S FEET *(Nóżki Cielęce Smażone)*

2 pairs calf's feet	1 egg, slightly beaten
court bouillon to cover (see Index)	salt and pepper to taste
	bread crumbs
flour for dredging	butter or deep fat for frying

Prepare feet as in No. 62. Allow to cool enough to handle. Bone and cut into pieces. Dip in flour and in seasoned egg, roll in bread crumbs, and fry in butter or deep fat to a golden brown. Serve with pan-fried potatoes and Horseradish Sauce (see Index) or any other sharp sauce, according to preference. Serves 4.

64. CALVES' FOOT JELLY (*Nóżki Cielęce w Galarecie*)

2 pairs calf's feet	1 bay leaf
1 pair pig's feet	10 peppercorns
2 onions	dash of marjoram, thyme,
2–3 carrots	nutmeg
1 parsley root	salt and pepper to taste
½ celery root	2 egg whites
1 leek	lemon slices (optional)

Have butcher prepare the feet as in No. 62 and split the bones. Blanch calf's and pig's feet. Dice vegetables. Start the meat and vegetables in several quarts of cold water, and simmer without salt, skimming carefully, for 3 to 4 hours. Allow enough water so that it will still cover the meat after boiling down, since no water should be added afterwards. When meat has fallen away from the bones, discard them, dice the meat, and strain the soup stock. Clear the stock by pouring in slightly-beaten egg whites and boiling up once. Allow to stand until liquid clears. Put meat into a mold and pour liquid over it, straining again. Chill. Unmold and serve with a green salad, olive oil, and vinegar.

Note: Lemon wedges and some of the diced carrots, parsley, and celery root may be added to the meat in the mold. Also slices of hard-cooked egg.

65. FRESH CALF'S TONGUE (*Ozorki Cielęce*)

Start tongues in cold water, adding vegetables and spices indicated in recipe for Court Bouillon (see Index). Simmer until the tongues can be skinned, 40 to 50 minutes. Reserve liquid. Prepare as follows:

I.

2–3 calf's tongues, cut diagonally into slices	salt and pepper to taste
	bread crumbs for rolling
2 eggs, slightly beaten	4–5 tbs. butter

Dip tongue slices in slightly-beaten, seasoned egg and roll in bread crumbs. Fry in hot butter to a golden brown. Use stock for any sharp sauce, according to preference (see Index). Serves 5 to 8.

II.

2–3 calf's tongues	Index or use commercially
4 ozs. salt pork for larding	prepared sauce)
Tomato Sauce to cover (see	

Remove tongues from stock as soon as they can be skinned—when not quite done. Lard, arrange in heavy casserole, cover with Tomato Sauce, and simmer covered for another 20 minutes. If sauce evaporates, add a few spoonfuls of the broth in which meat has cooked. Slice diagonally and serve with noodles or spaghetti. Serves 5 to 8.

66. CALF'S LUNGS *(Płucka Cielęce)*

1 pair lungs and a heart	1 bay leaf (optional)
1 onion	dash of marjoram and thyme
1 leek	salt and pepper to taste
1 parsley root	1 tbs. butter
½ celery root	1 tbs. flour
1 stalk celery	1 tbs. vinegar
1 carrot	dash of nutmeg
10 peppercorns	

Rinse lungs and heart well and start in cold water to cover, together with diced onion, vegetables, and spices. Add salt last, when water boils. Let simmer about 1½ hours. When tender, drain and chop coarsely or cut into small pieces. Melt and brown a tablespoon of butter, stir in flour, and add about one cup of strained stock, blending carefully until smooth. Add vinegar and nutmeg. Season to taste and allow to bubble up. For more body add a bouillon cube. Return meat to sauce and allow to simmer another half-hour. Serve with noodles or with potatoes. Serves 6.

67. CALF'S LUNGS IN WINE SAUCE
   (Płucka Cielęce z Winem)

Prepare lungs as in No. 66. Instead of using the stock, make sauce with

½ cup bouillon	1 tsp. Maggi extract
½ cup dry white wine	½ tsp. Soy sauce
lemon juice to taste	

Return meat to sauce and allow to simmer for a half-hour. Serves 6.

Lamb and Mutton

1. LAMB ROAST (*Pieczeń Barania*)

A leg of lamb may be roasted in the oven or on a spit; the spit is the ideal way. Do not remove the fell (thin membrane covering) because this will help keep the juices in. Marinate for 24 hours and remove an hour before starting to roast. If meat is to be done in the oven, blanch (pour boiling water over it) after taking it out of the refrigerator.

1 leg of lamb	thyme or ginger (optional)
vinegar	butter for basting
salt and pepper to taste	flour for dredging
1 med. clove of garlic	

Wrap meat in a cloth moistened with vinegar and allow to marinate overnight. Wipe dry and allow to stand at room temperature for an hour. Season with salt and pepper and rub with mashed garlic. Sprinkle with thyme or with ginger if desired. Roast in hot oven, fat side up, or on a spit, brushing frequently with butter. When skin begins to brown, dredge with flour and continue basting. Europeans prefer lamb rare inside like roast beef. This means a roasting time of 1 to 1½ hours, depending on size. American preference is for well-done meat, in which case the oven should be medium-hot and the roasting time longer. A meat thermometer will assure the right degree of doneness. Serves 6 to 8.

2. BRAISED LAMB WITH GARLIC
(*Pieczeń Duszona z Czosnkiem*)

4-lb. piece leg of lamb	10 juniper berries
salt and pepper	pinch of thyme
1 clove garlic, mashed	½ med. onion
2 tbs. butter	flour for dredging
10 peppercorns	1 cup soup stock or bouillon

Rub meat with salt and garlic and let stand an hour. Sear in butter, and when brown on all sides, add spices and onion. Simmer, tightly covered, for about 2 hours, sprinkling frequently with cold water. When nearly done dredge with flour, baste with soup stock, and allow gravy to thicken. Slice thin. Strain gravy. Serves 6.

3. BRAISED LAMB WITH SOUR CREAM SAUCE
(Pieczeń Duszona ze Śmietaną)

Prepare the same as No. 2. Instead of bouillon, make sauce with 2 cups sour cream and 1 tsp. flour. Allow to simmer another 15 minutes.

4. MOCK VENISON ROAST
(Pieczeń Barania na Sposób Sarny)

leg of lamb or crown roast	*Marinade:*
4 ozs. salt pork for larding	1 cup vinegar
salt and pepper to taste	2 cups beer
2 tbs. butter	1 cup water
1–2 cups sour cream	1 onion diced
1 tsp. flour	10 peppercorns
	20 juniper berries
	piece of ginger
	(optional)
	1 bay leaf
	6 cloves
	¼ tsp. nutmeg

Boil all the ingredients for the marinade. Allow to cool completely, pour over meat, and let stand 4 days to a week. (A cool place is better than the refrigerator; if meat stands in refrigerator, have the temperature fairly high.) When ready to use, rinse meat off and reserve some of the marinade for basting. Proceed as follows: Lard meat well and rub with salt and pepper an hour before roasting. For crown roast omit larding. Sear in butter and roast in shallow pan in hot oven for ½ hour, basting frequently with pan drippings alternating with the cold marinade. Reduce heat to 300° and roast 1½ hours longer. When nearly done, cover with sour cream blended with flour and continue basting for another 15 minutes. Serves 8.

Note: This recipe may also be used for pot-roasting lamb. If the meat is fatty, remove excess fat.

5. ROAST LAMB HUNTER-STYLE
(Pieczeń Barania po Myśliwsku)

leg of lamb with bone left in	1 large onion, sliced (optional)
(5–6 lbs.)	¼ lb. salt pork for larding
2 cups vinegar	salt and pepper to taste
20 juniper berries, pounded or	1 tsp. butter
ground	flour for dredging
1 large clove garlic, mashed	¼ cup sour cream

Remove excess fat from meat, pound well, and pour boiling vinegar over it. Rub well with juniper and garlic and surround with onion slices. Wrap in a cloth dipped in the vinegar and allow to stand 4 to 5 days. Discard onion, wipe off meat, lard generously, rub with salt and pepper, and roast in hot oven, basting frequently for about 1¼ hours. When nearly done add sour cream. Also excellent with any sharp sauce, in which case omit the sour cream. Serves 6 to 8.

6. ROAST LAMB MUSCOVITE
(Pieczeń Barania à la Moscovite)

leg of lamb (4-lb. piece or whole small leg)	4 cups marinade, made with
	2 cups water
2 tbs. butter	2 cups vinegar
salt and pepper to taste	1 onion
3 onions, diced	1 bay leaf
3 carrots, diced	10 peppercorns
2 stalks celery	6 cloves
1 celery root	1 stalk celery with leaves
1 tsp. Maggi extract	

Remove excess fat from meat, pound well, and blanch with boiling marinade. Reserve marinade. Wipe off meat, rub well with salt, and sear in hot butter. Roast in hot oven, basting frequently with pan drippings. Cook the vegetables in marinade, allowing liquid to simmer down so that there will be no more than 2 cups of sauce. When vegetables are thoroughly done (about ½ hour), add Maggi extract and pour everything over meat. Reduce heat to 300° and continue basting. Meat should be pink inside when ready to serve. Put vegetables through sieve and add to pan drippings. Slice meat, arrange back on the bone, and pour sauce over it.

7. STUFFED ROAST LAMB *(Pieczeń Barania Faszerowana)*

1 leg of lamb, boned	10 juniper berries
2 cups vinegar	1 cup strong bouillon
salt and pepper	flour for dredging
1 large clove garlic, mashed	
2–3 tbs. butter	*Stuffing:*
1 jigger pure alcohol or gin (optional)	½ lb. pork
	½ lb. veal
1–2 carrots	1 roll, moistened in milk and mashed
1 onion	
½ celery root	2 onions, grated and browned lightly in butter
1 parsley root	
2 celery stalks with leaves	2 egg yolks
1 leek	dash of nutmeg
10 peppercorns	1 tsp. Maggi or Soy sauce
1 bay leaf (optional)	salt and pepper to taste

Pound meat well, remove excess fat, and blanch with boiling vinegar. Wipe off and then rub with salt and garlic. Make the stuffing as follows: Put pork, veal, and roll through meat grinder, add other ingredients, and mix thoroughly. Spread over inside of meat, roll tight, and tie securely. Sear in very hot butter. Sprinkle with alcohol. Add diced vegetables, onion, and spices. Add bouillon, and simmer, tightly covered, for 2½ hours. When done, dust with flour, baste and let bubble up once or twice. If necessary, add more stock as meat cooks, taking care not to make sauce too watery.

8. LAMB BIRDS (Zrazy Baranie)

2 lbs. lean boneless lamb, preferably from leg (loin or boned shoulder may be used)	12 shallots
	12 small or 6 larger mushrooms
	1 tbs. tomato purée
salt and pepper to taste	½ cup dry red wine
flour for dusting	½ tsp. Maggi or Soy sauce
1 tbs. butter	

Have butcher cut meat into thin slices as for scaloppine. Pound well, season, and dredge with flour. Brown quickly in very hot butter, and then arrange in casserole with shallots and sliced mushrooms. Simmer 15 minutes, add tomato purée, wine, and Maggi sauce and continue simmering until done—1 hour in all. Serve with potatoes or Potato Croquettes. Serves 6.

9. SHASHLIK (Szaszłyk Barani)

2 lbs. lean boneless lamb cut into serving pieces (loin, leg, or shoulder)	mushroom caps and/or green pepper slices
	salt and pepper to taste
marinade to cover (optional)	olive oil or butter
bacon or salt pork slices	Rice Pilau (see Index)

Have the rice ready before broiling the meat. Meat may be used fresh, or marinated overnight. For marinating, use ⅔ water and ⅓ wine vinegar. Another method is to rub meat with olive oil, cover with onion slices, and let stand overnight.

Using as many pieces of bacon or salt pork (cut the same size as the meat) as there are pieces of lamb, arrange meat and bacon alternately on skewers, allowing about 10 pieces per skewer. Mushroom caps and green peppers may also be added, as well as slices of tomato. In all cases alternate these, one piece of vegetable per piece of meat and bacon. Season, brush with butter or oil, and broil under high heat or pan-broil in hot butter enough to sear and brown quickly. The cooking should not take more than 5 to 8 minutes. Serve with rice and salad. Serves 5 to 6.

10. BRAISED LAMB WITH SAVOY CABBAGE
(Baranina Duszona z Włoską Kapustą)

3 lbs. breast of lamb
salt
1 clove garlic, mashed
2 small heads savoy cabbage, parboiled and cut in quarters
salt and pepper to taste
1 tbs. butter
1 tbs. flour

court bouillon, made with
1 large onion
2 carrots
  celery root
2 stalks celery with leaves
1 leek
½ parsley root
1 bay leaf

Rub meat with salt and garlic and let stand 1 hour. Dice vegetables for the bouillon. Put meat and vegetables in just enough water to cover, and simmer, skimming occasionally, for about 1 hour. Strain broth, cut meat into serving pieces, and return to broth together with the cabbage. Season to taste and continue simmering, tightly covered, until meat and cabbage are thoroughly done. Melt butter without browning, blend in flour, and dissolve with some of the broth. Add to the pot. Allow to simmer until sauce thickens, another 15 minutes. Serves 6.

Note: Instead of savoy cabbage, turnips may be used. The turnips should be peeled, diced, and handled like the cabbage. For Braised Lamb with Green Peas, cook peas separately (see Index) and add when meat is thoroughly done, together with 1 tbs. chopped dill. Still another variation is to make a macédoine of several vegetables, such as carrots, peas, green beans, Brussels sprouts, etc., as well as new potatoes.

11. BRAISED LAMB WITH CARAWAY SEED
(Baranina Duszona z Kminkiem)

3 lbs. breast of lamb, rubbed
  with salt and mashed garlic
court bouillon (see No. 10)

1 cup sour cream
1 tsp. flour
1–2 tsp. caraway seed

Prepare meat the same as in No. 10. When done, cut into serving pieces, strain broth, and combine with sour cream blended with flour. Add caraway seed. Simmer another 15 minutes. Serves 6.

12. BRAISED LAMB WITH PICKLES
(Potrawka Barania z Ogórkami)

Prepare the same as No. 10. When half done, cut meat in serving pieces, strain broth, and discard vegetables. Add 2 or 3 dill or sour pickles, peeled and diced. Continue simmering, tightly covered, until done. Add to sauce:

1 cup sour cream
1 tsp. flour

sugar to taste
1 tbs. chopped fresh dill

Allow to simmer a few minutes longer and serve with rice or potatoes. Serves 6.

13. BRAISED LAMB WITH TOMATOES
(Potrawka Barania z Pomidorami)

3–4 lbs. lean breast or shoulder
  lamb, boned
1 clove garlic (optional)
2 tbs. butter
  soup stock as needed, no more
  than 1 cup
  salt and pepper to taste
12 shallots
2–3 tomatoes or 2 tbs. tomato
  purée

10 peppercorns
1 bay leaf (optional)
10 juniper berries
  dash of allspice
1 cup red wine
1 tbs. flour
½ tsp. each of Maggi and Soy
  sauce
  sugar to taste

Sear meat in butter with or without garlic. Add a couple of tablespoons of soup stock and simmer, tightly covered, until meat is nicely brown and half done. Cut into serving pieces, return to pot, add peeled shallots, the tomatoes or tomato paste, spices, and red wine. Continue simmering until thoroughly done. Dredge with flour, add more soup stock, and allow another 15 minutes so that sauce will thicken. Add Maggi and Soy sauce and a dash of sugar. Let bubble up and serve with potatoes. Total cooking time should not be more than 2 hours. Serves 6 to 8.

14. LAMB RAGOUT (Ragoût z Baraniny)

3–4 lbs. breast and shoulder of
  lamb, boned and cut into serving pieces
  salt and pepper to taste
1 clove garlic, mashed
2 tbs. butter
1 med. onion, minced
2 cups cold broth or soup stock
½ celery root
1 carrot
1 parsley root

12 shallots, peeled
¼ cup snap beans
¼ cup peas
1 tbs. tomato purée
¼ tsp. paprika
4 med. potatoes, parboiled and
  diced
½ tbs. butter
½ cup dry red wine
½ tsp. each of Maggi and Soy
  sauce

Remove excess fat from meat, rub with salt and garlic, and sear in hot butter. When all the meat is brown, add minced onion. Reduce heat and continue cooking until onion is a light, golden brown. Sprinkle with a few tablespoons of cold broth and simmer, tightly covered, for an hour, basting occasionally with cold broth. Dice vegetables, peel shallots, and add to meat. Season with paprika, add tomato purée and remaining broth. Simmer until vegetables are nearly done. Add parboiled potatoes. Make brown paste of the butter and flour, adding a few spoonfuls of sauce to dissolve lumps. Return to pot. Add wine, Maggi and Soy extract, and simmer another 10 minutes. Over-all cooking time should be about 2 hours. Serves 6 to 8.

15. FRICASSEE OF LAMB *(Fricassée z Baraniny)*

3–4 lbs. lean shoulder or breast of lamb, boned	6 med. mushrooms, sliced
boiling water	3 anchovies, chopped
salt and pepper to taste	1 tsp. grated lemon rind
1 clove garlic, mashed	lemon juice to taste
2 tbs. butter	2 cups soup stock
½ med. onion, minced	2 tsp. butter
1 heaping tbs. chopped fresh parsley	2 tsp. flour
	1 tsp. Worcestershire sauce

Blanch meat, cut into serving pieces, and rub with salt and garlic. Season with pepper. Sear in hot butter. When all the meat is brown, add onion, parsley, and other ingredients, and about ½ cup soup stock. Simmer, tightly covered, until tender (about 1½ to 2 hours), adding stock as needed. When meat is done, cream butter and flour, add to meat, and allow to melt. Add Worcestershire sauce, boil up once, and serve with cauliflower and Suet or Marrow Balls (see Index). Serves 6 to 8.

16. TURKISH PILAU *(Pilaw Turecki)*

3 lbs. breast of lamb, boned and cut into serving pieces	30 shallots or small white onions, peeled (or 2–3 onions, sliced)
boiling water	1 tbs. butter
1 clove garlic (optional)	2 tbs. tomato purée
salt and pepper to taste	1 cup soup stock with bouillon cube added
2 cups rice, cooked for 10 minutes	¼ tsp. paprika

Blanch meat with boiling water, rub with salt (garlic if desired), and season with pepper. Cook rice according to directions (see Index) and drain well when half done. In a greased casserole, arrange alternate layers of rice and meat, adding several shallots after each layer. Start and end with layers of rice. Dissolve butter and tomato purée in hot broth, add paprika, and pour over rice. Cover tightly and bake in moderate oven for a good 2 hours. Do not stir. Serve very hot. Serves 6 to 8 as a full meal.

17. STUFFED BREAST OF LAMB
(Mostek Barani Faszerowany)

3–4 lbs. breast of lamb
1 clove garlic, mashed
  salt and pepper to taste
2 cups court bouillon (see
  Index)

Stuffing:
½ lb. chopped veal or lean
  pork
6 small or 4 large mush-
  rooms, chopped
1 med. onion, minced and
  cooked in butter until
  limp but not brown
1 white roll, moistened in
  milk and mashed
  salt and pepper to taste
1 tbs. chopped parsley
1 whole egg

Have butcher make pocket in the meat for stuffing. Remove excess
fat and rub with garlic, salt, and pepper. Make the stuffing by mixing all the ingredients thoroughly. Fill pocket and sew with cotton
thread or secure with toothpicks. Simmer in court bouillon until
tender, about 2 hours. Serve with Mustard Sauce (see Index).
Serves 6 to 8.

18. BREAST OF LAMB IN WINE
(Mostek Barani Duszony na Winie)

3–4 lbs. breast of lamb
2 tbs. butter
1 onion, sliced
2 carrots, diced
½ celery root, diced
½ parsley root, diced
1 leek

1–2 stalks celery with leaves
  salt and pepper to taste
2 cups soup stock or bouillon
1½ cups dry white wine
1 tbs. flour
3 egg yolks

Sear meat in half the butter, add onion and vegetables, and braise,
tightly covered, adding soup stock a little at a time. After 1 hour
add wine and simmer another hour. Cut the meat into pieces. Melt
the rest of the butter and combine with flour, adding a little of the
sauce and stirring to dissolve lumps. Return to meat. Lightly beat
the egg yolks, dissolve with a little of the hot sauce, a spoonful at a
time so that eggs will not curdle. Add to sauce, stir, and serve at
once. (It may not be necessary to use the full amount of meat
stock—the sauce should be thick and have a distinct winey flavor.)
Serves 6 to 8.

19. *BIGOS* MADE WITH LEFTOVER LAMB
(Bigos z Resztek Baraniny)

2 cups leftover lamb roast
3–4 cups sauerkraut
½ med. onion, minced
2 strips bacon, diced (or a few

tablespoons bacon drippings)
salt and pepper to taste
¼ lb. sausage, diced (optional)

Lightly brown minced onion in bacon fat and add to sauerkraut. Heat thoroughly. Add diced lamb, salt, and quite a bit of pepper. Heat and serve. Other leftover meats may be added as well (bits of beef, pork, or veal), and diced sausage (*kiełbasa*) will add flavor. Serves 4.

Pork

The best fresh pork comes from young animals, and can be identified by its light-pink color. The fat should be white and firm. Even though trichinosis in pork has been largely eliminated, it must still be guarded against. Trichinae in raw meat are easily distinguishable to the naked eye: the meat appears to be larded with tiny white specks. However, it is always a good precaution to cook all pork thoroughly; never serve it rare.

1. ROAST FRESH HAM *(Pieczeń Wieprzowa z Szynki)*

1 whole fresh ham (7–8 lbs.)	caraway seeds (optional)
light marinade to half-cover	salt and pepper to taste
⅙ stick butter	1 large onion, sliced

Make a marinade of water, wine vinegar, onion, bay leaf, spices to taste, taking care not to have it too sour (⅓ vinegar to ⅔ water, at most), and bring it to a boil. Pour the boiling liquid over meat and let stand for 24 hours, turning occasionally. Wipe meat dry. Rub well with salt, sprinkle with pepper and caraway seed, and roast in 500° oven, basting first with butter. When meat fat begins to melt, baste with the pan drippings. Once meat begins to brown on top, add onion, reduce heat to 300°, and continue to roast until thoroughly done, basting occasionally. Allow 25 to 30 minutes per pound or use an oven thermometer. Serve with red cabbage, beets, or puréed split peas. Serves 8 to 10. Leftover meat may be served cold or used in a casserole dish.

Note: If time does not permit marinating for 24 hours, meat may be prepared in the morning for use the same night. Unmarinated meat will give good results, although it will be less tender. A smaller piece may be used for roasting if using a whole ham is not practical, but anything less than 3 to 4 pounds will produce a dry roast and would be better braised or pot-roasted.

2. PORK POT ROAST *(Pieczeń Wieprzowa Duszona)*

3–4 lbs. fresh ham or boned loin
   salt and pepper
1 tbs. butter
1 med. onion
1 carrot
½ celery root
½ parsley root
1–2 stalks celery
   few sprigs parsley

2 fresh tomatoes or 2 tbs. tomato
   paste (optional)
spices to taste: peppercorns,
   allspice, pinch of marjoram,
   caraway seed
flour for dusting
½ cup bouillon
½ tsp. Maggi extract

Pound meat and rub well with salt an hour before using. Sear in hot butter in the pan in which it will cook (preferably heavy cast-aluminum or cast-iron). Add diced vegetables and onion, spices, and seasoning to taste, and simmer, tightly covered, until brown and tender. Do not add water. Allow about 30 minutes per pound. When done, dust with flour, baste with a little bouillon, add Maggi extract, and allow sauce to thicken. Slice thin, strain sauce, and pour over meat. Serves 6 to 8.

3. PORK POT ROAST IN WINE
(Pieczeń Wieprzowa Duszona na Czerwonem Winie)

Prepare as in No. 2. When meat begins to brown, add ½ cup red wine and the tomatoes, which must *not* be omitted in this recipe. When done, dust with flour, and add a little bouillon to taste. Add Maggi extract, allow to bubble up, and simmer another 10 minutes. Strain sauce before pouring over meat.

4. STUFFED ROAST PORK
(Pieczeń Wieprzowa Faszerowana)

3–4 lbs. boned fresh ham or loin
   roast
   salt
vegetables and onion as for
   No. 2
bouillon for basting
2 tbs. melted butter
   grated Parmesan cheese
1 tbs. tomato purée
1 tsp. Maggi extract
1 tsp. Soy sauce

Stuffing:
1 can anchovies
2 tbs. capers
8 shallots or 1 onion
1 stale white roll, moistened in
   milk and mashed (or equivalent amount bread crumbs)
   pepper to taste
   dash of nutmeg
1 whole egg, lightly beaten

Have butcher bone the meat. Rub well with salt. Remove a little meat from the center, preferably ragged bits and pieces with membranes and tendons, and use these pieces for stuffing, as follows: Chop meat or put through meat grinder together with anchovies, capers, and shallots. Add mashed roll, beaten egg, pepper to taste (anchovies and capers will provide sufficient salt), and a dash of nutmeg. Mix well. Spread meat with the stuffing, roll tight, and tie with string. Sear, then simmer for an hour, tightly covered, together with the diced vegetables, onion, and spices as in No. 2, basting occasionally with bouillon. Remove from sauce, take off string, moisten with melted butter, and sprinkle generously with Parmesan. Roast for an hour in hot oven (375° to 400°), basting frequently with butter. Add tomato purée, Maggi extract, and Soy sauce to the sauce and vegetables in which the meat has cooked. Heat and strain. Slice meat, arrange on platter, and pour sauce over it. Separately serve rice, potatoes, or noodles. Serves 6 to 8.

5. ROAST LOIN OF PORK *(Schab)*

3 lbs. loin of pork with fillet left in	1 med. or ½ large onion, minced
salt and pepper to taste	2 tsp. caraway seed (optional)
2 tbs. butter	flour for dusting

Season meat and sear in very hot butter, browning quickly. Add minced onion and caraway seed. Reduce heat and either roast in slow oven or pot-roast, tightly covered, over low direct heat until thoroughly done, basting frequently with cold water. Allow 30 to 35 minutes per pound. (For best results, use meat thermometer.) Dust with flour and continue basting until sauce thickens. If necessary, add a few spoonfuls of water to the pan drippings after the meat has been removed. Scrape pan and allow to bubble up. Serve with potatoes and red cabbage. Serves 6.

6. ROAST LOIN OF PORK VIENNESE-STYLE
(Schab po Wiedeńsku)

loin of pork (about 3 lbs.)	other ingredients as in No. 5
1 cup vinegar	

Pour boiling vinegar over meat 2 hours before cooking. Allow to stand in vinegar, turning occasionally. Wipe dry, rub well with salt, and sprinkle with caraway seed. Roast in hot oven, basting frequently with melted butter. When fat begins to melt, use pan drippings for basting. Add minced onion when meat begins to brown on top, dredge lightly with flour, and continue basting until done, about 1½ hours. Serves 6.

7. PORK TENDERLOIN IN SOUR CREAM
(Polędwica Wieprzowa ze Śmietaną)

2 pork tenderloins	flour for dusting
salt and pepper to taste	4 tbs. sour cream
1 lemon, sliced thin	2 tsp. capers
3 tbs. butter	

The tenderloin, or fillet, must be specially ordered since butchers seldom carry it. Or when purchasing a large loin of pork, ask that the tenderloin be cut out to cook separately. Rub the meat well with salt, season with pepper, and cover with lemon slices. Roast in hot oven, basting frequently with butter, then with pan drippings. When meat begins to brown, dust with flour, add the sour cream mixed with the capers, and continue basting until thoroughly brown and tender, 45 minutes to 1 hour, depending on size and thickness of meat. Care should be taken, however, not to overcook, or meat will be too dry. Serves 4 to 6.

8. PORK SCHNITZELS (Karmonadle)

6 loin pork chops

Prepare like Breaded Veal Cutlets (see Index). Serve with cabbage, creamed turnips, or green beans; also with Mustard or Caper Sauce. Serves 6.

9. PORK CHOPS AU NATUREL
(Kotlety Wieprzowe Naturalne)

6 loin pork chops	flour
juice ½ lemon	butter or fat for frying
salt and pepper	

Pound chops lightly, sprinkle with lemon juice, and allow to stand about an hour. Season, dust with flour, and fry in hot butter or fat until brown and well done. Garnish each chop with a pat of Chive or Anchovy Butter (see Index), and serve with potatoes and vegetables. Serves 6.

10. SMOTHERED PORK CHOPS
(Kotlety Wieprzowe Duszone)

6 loin chops	¼ cup soup stock
juice ½ lemon	flour for dusting
salt and pepper to taste	½ cup white wine (optional)
2 tsp. caraway seed	1 tbs. butter

Sprinkle chops with lemon juice and let stand 2 hours. Season, sprinkle with caraway seed, and simmer with soup stock, tightly covered, until fat on the meat has melted and most of the stock is gone. Remove cover and brown lightly on both sides. Dust with flour, cover again, and continue cooking until tender, about 45 minutes in all. Add butter after taking pot off the heat and let stand, covered, until butter melts. For a more subtle flavor, add white wine to sauce after browning chops. Serves 6.

11. PORK AND RICE PATTIES
(Zrazy Wieprzowe z Ryżem)

2 lbs. fresh pork shoulder or butt, chopped	1 whole egg
	flour for rolling
1 med. onion, grated and lightly browned in butter	butter for frying
	1 cup soup stock
salt and pepper to taste	2 cups sour cream
1 cup rice half-cooked in 2 cups soup stock	1 tsp. flour
	½ tsp. Maggi extract

Combine meat, onion, seasoning, cooked rice (see Index), and egg. (If Minute Rice is used, use proportions suggested on package, and allow to stand only long enough for liquid to be absorbed.) Shape into patties, roll in flour, and brown quickly on both sides in hot butter. Arrange tightly in heavy casserole and add the butter in which patties browned. Add the half-cup of soup stock and simmer, covered, for half an hour. Add sour cream blended with the flour, and the Maggi extract, and let bubble up once. Serve with pan-fried potatoes. (Recipe may be varied by adding herbs to taste, such as marjoram, oregano, or thyme.) Serves 6 to 7.

12. PORK GOULASH *(Gulasz Wieprzowy)*

I.

2 lbs. fresh pork butt or shoulder, cut in pieces	flour for dusting
	1½ cup soup stock
4–6 med. onions, chopped	1–2 tbs. tomato purée
2 tsp. paprika	6 large or 12 small potatoes, peeled, cut, and parboiled
salt and pepper	

Use cheaper cuts of meat. Have butcher bone and cut meat into serving pieces. Combine in heavy casserole the meat, onions, seasoning, and paprika, and simmer, tightly covered, turning occasionally, until meat browns. Dust with flour, add soup stock, tomato purée, and the parboiled potatoes. Cover and continue to simmer until meat and potatoes are done, about 1 hour. Serves 6.

II.

Prepare the same as *I*, but instead of potatoes, add the following:

2 lbs. sauerkraut	½ parsley root, sliced
½ celery root, sliced	

This Goulash, known in Hungary as *Székely Gulyas*, is especially good with beer.

13. SPARERIBS AND CABBAGE
(Boczek Duszony z Kapustą)

3 lbs. spareribs	1 parsley root, diced
2 small heads cabbage or savoy cabbage	salt and pepper to taste
	1 tbs. butter
1 onion, diced	2 tsp. flour
1 carrot, diced	½ bouillon cube (optional)
¼ celery root, diced	

Start meat in enough cold water to cover. When water begins to simmer, remove scum. Simmer, uncovered, for a half-hour. Cut cabbage into quarters and parboil in salted water. Drain, add to meat, and add diced onion and vegetables. Season to taste and continue simmering, tightly covered, until meat is tender—about 1 hour. Discard vegetables. Melt butter, blend in flour, and dilute with a little of the stock in which meat has cooked. If stock has not cooked down enough and seems too thin, enrich with bouillon cube. Pour over meat and cabbage and simmer another half-hour. Serves 4 to 5.

14. HAM IN WINE
(Szynka Duszona na Czerwonym Winie)

The original recipe was for a whole smoked ham. A thick slice of ham steak may be substituted, or the more economical smoked shoulder butt or picnic shoulder. In either case, the meat need not be pre-boiled nor soaked unless directions specify.

½ smoked ham, boned and rolled tight	10 peppercorns
	10 juniper berries
1 large or 2 med. onions	6–8 cloves
1 leek	½ bottle red wine
¼ celery root	broth made with soup bones
½ parsley root	1 tsp. Maggi or Soy sauce
2 carrots	¼ cup Madeira, Marsala, or sherry
2 stalks celery with leaves	
1 bay leaf (optional)	1 tsp. flour (optional)

Dice vegetables and onion. Combine meat, vegetables, and spices in heavy casserole. (Tie spices in a piece of cheesecloth so that they can be easily discarded later.) Add wine and soup stock in equal proportions, and simmer until meat is tender—about 3 hours for half a ham, proportionately less time for smaller pieces. Remove and slice. Discard spices, put vegetables through a sieve, add Maggi sauce and Madeira, and return to liquid in which meat has cooked. If sauce is too thin, thicken with flour. Allow to bubble up once.

15. BAKED HAM AND RICE—LEFTOVER HAM DISH
(Szynka z Ryżem Zapiekana)

1 lb. boiled or baked ham, cut in medium-thin slices
½ cup strong bouillon
1 cup uncooked rice, steamed in soup stock (see Index)

3 tbs. grated Parmesan cheese
2 egg yolks
1 cup Fresh Mushroom Sauce (see Index)

Arrange the ham slices in a greased *gratin* dish, and pour bouillon over the meat. Combine rice, cheese, and egg yolks, season to taste, and spread over ham. Top with Fresh Mushroom Sauce and bake in medium oven for half an hour. Serves 3 to 4.

16. BAKED SMOKED BACON
(Boczek Wędzony Wypiekany)

I.

1 lb. lean bacon, unsliced
2 lbs. potatoes, parboiled

4 tbs. sour cream

Boil bacon until transparent in just enough water to cover, about ½ hour. Parboil potatoes. When cool enough to handle, cut bacon in strips and potatoes into slices. Line a buttered casserole with potatoes, arrange a layer of bacon on top, then more potatoes, and continue in layers, ending with potatoes. Cover with sour cream and bake in moderately hot oven for about half an hour, or until potatoes are done. Serves 4.

II.

1 lb. lean bacon, unsliced
2 cups split peas

1 cup pearl barley
hot bacon fat

Prepare meat as in *I*. Cook peas and barley separately (see Index) until half done. Drain, combine, add enough of the water in which bacon has been cooking to prevent sticking, and steam, tightly covered, in the oven until done, taking care not to cook to a mush. Arrange the barley and beans on a platter, top with hot bacon fat, and arrange the slices of bacon around the edge. Serves 6 to 7.

Polish Sausage (Kiełbasa Polska)

Kiełbasa is the general word for sausage in Polish, but in the United States it has come to mean a particular type of sausage known even in chain stores as Polish Sausage. This sausage is sold in rings about an inch and a quarter in diameter and has a mild taste slightly flavored with garlic. Although excellent served cold as a variety meat or in sandwiches, it is also used in many other ways, of which we quote a few. Some of these recipes may also be used for frankfurters or knockwurst.

17. FRIED SAUSAGE (Kiełbasa Smażona)

1 Polish sausage ring (about 1½ lbs.)	1–2 tbs. butter or bacon fat 1 onion, minced

Perforate the sausage casing with a pin to prevent its bursting in cooking. Half-cover with water, bring to a boil, and simmer, covered, for 20 minutes. Drain, allow to cool slightly, and fry slowly in butter or bacon fat until lightly brown on both sides. Add onion and continue frying until onion browns lightly. Slice the meat and serve with cooked cabbage or potatoes, using butter and onion·as garnish. Serves 4.

18. SAUSAGE IN POLISH SAUCE
(Kiełbasa w Polskim Sosie)

1 Polish sausage ring (about 1½ lbs.)	1 tbs. flour
2 cups beer	½ tsp. Maggi extract
2 cups water	2 tbs. vinegar
2 onions, sliced	1 tsp. to 1 tbs. sugar (according
1 tbs. butter	to taste)

Simmer sausage and onion in combined water and beer for 20 minutes. Brown the butter and blend in flour, then slowly add 1 cup of liquid strained from the meat. Stir until thoroughly blended. If sauce is too thick, add more liquid. Add Maggi extract, vinegar, and sugar to taste (brown sugar may be substituted). Slice the sausage, pour the sauce over it, and serve with boiled potatoes. Serves 4.

19. SAUSAGE SMOTHERED IN RED CABBAGE
(Kiełbaski Duszone w Czerwonej Kapuście)

1 sausage ring or 6 frankfurters or knockwurst	1½ tsp. flour
1 small head red cabbage	1 cup red wine (or strong broth)
vinegar or lemon juice	salt and pepper
1 tbs. butter	1½ tsp. Maggi extract
	sugar and lemon juice to taste

Shred cabbage, blanch, and sprinkle with lemon juice or vinegar to restore color. Brown the butter, blend in flour, and slowly add the wine, stirring until smooth. Add cabbage, season with salt, pepper, Maggi extract, sugar and lemon juice to taste, and simmer tightly covered for about half an hour. When nearly done add the sausage, cover, and continue simmering for another 15 minutes. Serves 4. (Meat may be added in greater proportion to cabbage, if desired.)

20. KNOCKWURST IN MUSTARD SAUCE
(Sosiski à la Sierzputowski)

4–6 frankfurters or knockwurst, boiled or pan-broiled in butter	⅓ cup red wine
1 tbs. butter	1 tbs. (or less) dry mustard
1 tbs. flour	salt and pepper to taste
	⅓ tsp. Maggi or meat extract

Heat sausages in boiling water or pan-broil in a little butter. Make sauce as follows: Melt butter and allow to brown lightly. Blend in flour, stirring constantly, add wine and stir until smooth. Add other ingredients and allow to boil up once. Pour over frankfurters. Serve with pan-fried potatoes. Serves 2 to 3.

21. ROAST STUFFED SUCKLING PIG
(Prosię Pieczone Nadziewane)

1 whole suckling pig (10–12 lbs.)	piece of salt pork or bacon
salt and pepper	⅓ cup beer
1 stick butter	

A suckling pig must generally be ordered in advance, except in holiday season. Wash well in cold water, dry, and rub with salt inside and out an hour before stuffing. Stuff according to preference, and sew together or secure with skewers. Arrange on its stomach in roasting pan, rub well with butter, and roast in hot oven at first; then reduce heat. Roast pig will taste best if the skin is browned fast. It should crackle when done. To that end the roast should be basted very frequently, first with the pan drippings, which will be mostly butter, then (after it has begun to brown) with beer. Alternate the basting with beer with rubbing the skin with a piece of salt pork or bacon on a stick. The roasting time is 2½ to 3 hours. To test doneness, try meat with a fork where it is thickest; if watery liquid comes out, the meat is still raw; if fat, the meat is done. The skin should by then be a good orange color, but care must be taken not to burn it. Serves 12 or more.

Stuffings for Roast Pig

22. LIVER PÂTÉ STUFFING (Farsz Pasztetowy)

pork liver
pork lungs
1 lb. boneless veal, ground
2 tbs. butter
1 large onion
1 carrot
1–2 stalks celery
½ celery root
½ parsley root
few sprigs parsley

1 parsnip
10 peppercorns
salt and pepper to taste
2 stale rolls moistened in milk and mashed, or equivalent in moistened bread crumbs
dash of nutmeg
2 whole eggs
¼ lb. salt pork or bacon

Peel and cut vegetables. Combine with all the meats. (Be sure that when the butcher dresses the pig the liver, lungs, and heart are given to you.) Season and simmer, tightly covered, with butter and a very small amount of water. The liver will be done in 15 to 20 minutes. Lungs and veal will take longer. When done, put everything through a meat grinder, combine with mashed rolls, seasoning, and two whole eggs. (For a lighter stuffing eggs may be separated, the egg whites beaten stiff and folded in last.) Add the liquid in which meat has simmered, and the bacon or salt pork, diced fine. Mix well and stuff.

23. BUCKWHEAT GROATS STUFFING (Farsz z Kaszy)

1 cup buckwheat groats or pearl barley, cooked so that it separates (see Index)
liver, lungs, and kidney from the pig
¼ lb. bacon or salt pork
2 med. onions, chopped fine and

smothered in butter but not browned
1 whole egg
salt and pepper to taste
dash of nutmeg
¼ tsp. marjoram
½ cup strong bouillon

Chop meat and bacon fine, combine with smothered onions, egg, seasoning, and spices. Add to groats and mix thoroughly. Moisten with bouillon, and stuff the pig.

24. RAISIN STUFFING *(Farsz z Rodzynkami)*

lungs and liver from the pig, smothered with vegetables as in No. 22
¼ lb. bacon or salt pork
1 stale roll, moistened in milk
2 tbs. butter

3 eggs, separated
2 heaping tbs. bread crumbs
salt and pepper to taste
dash of nutmeg
½ tsp. sugar
¼ lb. raisins

Cook liver, lungs, and bacon according to directions in No. 22. Put through meat grinder, together with the roll. Cream butter and egg yolks, add bread crumbs, salt, pepper, nutmeg, sugar, and raisins. Combine with meat mixture and mix thoroughly. Finally fold in the stiffly-beaten egg whites and mix lightly. Stuff the pig, sew up or secure with skewers, and roast as in No. 21.

Venison, Game, and Game Birds

Since Poland is a country of vast, ancient forests, and hunting is a traditional sport as well as a practical pastime, the Polish tradition of venison, game, and wild bird cookery is extremely varied. Polish poets have written of the preparation of *Bigos* after a wild boar hunt, and the trapping of wild birds is constantly referred to in folk songs. Game also frequently stretches the poor man's meat supply.

The following chapter, while much more extensive than is customary in cookbooks meant for the American home, is nevertheless only a sampling. The recipes have been adapted to the exigencies of our kitchens and time schedules. Such dishes as Wild Boar's Head and Roast Peacock, while colorful, have been omitted, for obvious reasons. Nor have we included directions for the preparation of ortolans, or of other tiny birds whose very names must be hunted down in dictionaries. But we have tried to give enough varied recipes so that the cook who is interested in the preparation of game can get a good grounding in the principles of this type of cookery; too many people consider game either difficult or a mystery, and so never venture to try it at all.

1. GAME MARINADE

Venison and hare are best if marinated for 2 to 4 days. If this is not practical, allow at least 24 hours. Marinade should boil for 30 minutes, then be allowed to cool before meat is immersed. There should be enough marinade to cover meat. The proportion of vinegar to water varies according to individual taste; cider vinegar is much more tart and less tasty than wine vinegar, which is recommended for this recipe. With wine vinegar, the proportion may be 1 cup vinegar to 2 cups water, or even less.

Marinade:

1 large onion	20 peppercorns
1 bay leaf	10 whole allspice
1 large carrot	dash of thyme
½ celery root	2–3 cups vinegar
⅛ parsley root	6 cups water

2. SADDLE OR LOIN OF VENISON
(Comber Jeleni ze Śmietaną)

saddle of venison (about 4 lbs.)	4 tbs. butter
marinade to cover (see No. 1)	1 cup sour cream
salt and pepper to taste	1 tbs. flour
6 ozs. salt pork for larding	

Marinate meat according to directions in No. 1. Rinse, wipe, rub with salt, and sprinkle sparingly with pepper. Cut salt pork into thin strips and lard meat generously. Roast on spit or in a hot oven, basting frequently with butter. After butter has been used up, baste with sour cream. Reduce heat after first 20 minutes. Roast about 1 hour in all. If roasting is done on a spit, catch drippings in a pan. Thicken sauce with flour, blending in to avoid lumps. Slice fairly thin. Serve with salad and a tart compote or jelly. Serves 6 to 8.

3. BRAISED SHOULDER OR BREAST OF VENISON
(Potrawka z Jelenia)

4 lbs. shoulder or breast of veni-son	6 strips bacon, cut small
	1 cup dry red wine
marinade to cover (see No. 1)	20 prunes
salt and pepper to taste	1 sour apple, pared, cored, and diced
10 peppercorns, ground	
20 juniper berries, ground	10 shelled walnuts
1 tsp. thyme	2 tbs. bread crumbs made from pumpernickel
1 med. onion, sliced	

Marinate meat according to directions, at least 24 hours. Drain, reserving some of the marinade. Season, rub with ground pepper, juniper, and thyme, and sauté with onion and bacon. When meat has browned slightly, add ¼ cup marinade, and the wine, prunes, diced apple, walnuts, and bread crumbs. Simmer, tightly covered, until meat is tender and sauce thickened, about 1½ to 2 hours. Serve with noodles. Serves 6 to 7.

4. VENISON CUTLETS (Zrazy z Jelenia)

2 lbs. cutlets from loin or rump (no more than ½" thick)	2–3 tbs. butter
	1 med. onion, chopped
3–4 ozs. salt pork for larding	6 med. mushrooms, sliced
salt and pepper	1 cup dry red wine
flour for dredging	2 bay leaves

Pound the cutlets, lard generously, season, and brown quickly on both sides in hot butter, adding the onion. Add mushrooms, wine, bay leaves, and simmer, tightly covered, for 1½ hours. Discard bay leaves. Serves 5 to 6.

Note: Another way of preparing these is with sour cream, in which case substitute bouillon for wine and add ½ cup sour cream.

5. VENISON FILLET *(Filet z Jelenia)*

I.

2 lbs. fillet of venison	3–4 tbs. butter
3–4 ozs. salt pork for larding	Anchovy or Chive Butter, 1
pepper to taste	pat per portion (see Index)
juice ½ lemon	

Cut well-seasoned venison into individual portions about ¾ inch thick. Pound well, and lard generously, using larding needle. Sprinkle with pepper and lemon juice, pile one on top of the other, and refrigerate for a couple of hours. (For convenience and speed, larding may be done before meat is sliced.) Fifteen minutes before serving, heat butter in shallow pan, arrange the steaks in it, cover with buttered paper, and bake in very hot oven for 10 minutes. Transfer to hot platter and garnish each piece with a pat of Anchovy or Chive Butter. Serve with White or Brown Caper Sauce or Venison Sauce (see Index). Serves 6.

II.

Prepare meat as in *I.* Prepare as many oblong pieces of toast as there are portions of meat and keep hot. Prepare Purée of Beets (see Index). Pan-fry meat like Fillet Steaks French-Style (see Index). Arrange beets in center of platter and fillets and slices of toast alternately around it. Add ½ cup strong bouillon and 2 or 3 tbs. Madeira or sherry to pan drippings. Let bubble up and pour over meat. Serves 6.

6. ROAST VENISON *AU NATUREL*
(Pieczeń Sarnia z Naturalnym Sosem)

3–5 lbs. leg of venison	4–6 ozs. salt pork for larding
2 ozs. pure alcohol	3–4 tbs. butter
salt and pepper	flour for dredging
10 juniper berries, pounded	½ cup dry white wine (optional)
(optional)	

For roasting venison without marinating, pound the meat well, sprinkle with alcohol (gin may be substituted), and wrap in cloth saturated with alcohol. Allow to refrigerate for 2 to 3 days. Rinse, rub with salt and a little pepper (juniper berries if desired), lard generously, and roast in 400° oven 15 minutes; then reduce temperature to 300°. Dredge lightly with flour. Baste frequently with butter. If white wine is also used for basting, the roast will be more delicate and tender. Allow about 20 to 25 minutes per pound—venison needs longer than beef, but should be pink inside. For well-done meat allow 30 minutes per pound. Slice thin and serve with pan gravy. Serve with salad and a tart jelly or compote. Allow ⅛ to ¼ lb. per serving.

7. LOIN OF VENISON *AU NATUREL*
(Comber Sarni Naturalny)

3–5 lbs. loin of venison	ground pepper, thyme, and
olive oil	juniper (optional)
juice 1 lemon	2 cups red wine
2–3 onions, sliced	salt to taste
1 celery root, sliced	4–6 ozs. salt pork for larding
1 parsley root, sliced	4 tbs. butter

Rub the meat with olive oil, sprinkle with lemon juice, and cover with slices of onion and vegetables. Season with pepper, thyme, and juniper, if desired. Wrap in cheesecloth, pour red wine over it, and allow to refrigerate 2 days. Turn occasionally. When ready to use, discard vegetables but do not rinse. Rub with salt, lard generously, and roast in 300° oven for about 2 hours, basting frequently with butter. Serve with pan drippings or Venison Sauce (see Index) and a green salad and vegetables. Serves 5 to 8.

8. VENISON STEAKS *À LA GODARD* *(Kotlety z Sarny)*

6 individual steaks about ¾″ thick,	salt and pepper
cut from loin or leg	12 thin slices salt pork
juice ½ lemon	2 tbs. butter
olive oil	6 pieces toast, preferably spread
sliced onion, celery root, and	with Liver or Venison Pâté
parsley root	1 cup strong bouillon
2 cups dry red wine	

Pound meat lightly and rub with lemon and olive oil. Pile one on top of the other in a small container, cover with wine, and let stand 2 days in refrigerator. Drain and dry off with paper towel. Season, put each between two thin slices of salt pork, and pan-broil in hot butter for 10 minutes. Serve, together with the salt pork, on slices of toast. Make gravy of pan drippings and bouillon and pour over meat. Serves 6.

9. VENISON STEAKS À LA NORMANDE
(Kotlety z Sarny)

6 individual steaks about ¾"
thick, cut from loin or leg
3–4 ozs. salt pork for larding

salt and pepper to taste
flour for dredging
3–4 tbs. butter

Pound meat lightly, lard, and rub with salt and pepper. Dredge with flour and pan-fry quickly in hot butter about 10 minutes. Serve with green peas or purée of chestnuts and a sharp sauce. Serves 6.

10. VENISON STEAKS SMOTHERED IN WINE
(Kotlety z Sarny Duszone w Winie)

6 individual steaks about ¾" thick,
cut from loin or leg
3 tbs. butter
1 med. onion, sliced

ground pepper, juniper berries,
and thyme
½ cup dry white wine

Brown steaks in hot butter quickly on both sides as in Steaks à la Normande, No. 9. Transfer to heavy casserole, arranging meat and onion in layers. Add ground spices, butter in which meat fried, and the white wine. Simmer tightly covered for half an hour. Serve with purée of chestnuts or with mushrooms. Separately serve Truffle Sauce (see Index) or any sharp sauce desired. Serves 6.

11. VENISON BIRDS (Zrazy Zawijane z Sarny)

2 lbs. boneless venison meat, cut
in thin pieces 3" by 4"
salt and pepper to taste
thin strips of salt pork or bacon
for rolling
flour for dredging
½ cup dry red wine
1 cup bouillon
¼ tsp. Maggi extract
¼ tsp. Kitchen Bouquet

Stuffing:
¼ lb. ground venison (use odds and
ends of discarded meat—veal
may be substituted)
2 tbs. bread crumbs
¼ lb. chopped mushrooms
1 onion, minced and browned
lightly in a little butter
salt and pepper to taste

Mix stuffing ingredients thoroughly. Pound meat thin, season, and spread with stuffing. Roll. Then wrap each roll in a thin strip of salt pork or bacon and tie securely with cotton thread, which should be discarded when meat is done. Arrange tightly in heavy casserole and simmer, covered, until meat begins to brown. Dredge with flour, add wine and bouillon (use half the bouillon, then add more if necessary), and when tender—in about 1 hour—add Maggi extract and Kitchen Bouquet. Allow to bubble up. Serve with potatoes or rice. Serves 6 to 7.

12. HARE OR RABBIT (*Zając z Naturalnym Sosem*)

Hare is a gamier meat than rabbit and more of a delicacy. If it is to be prepared unmarinated, it should be well-seasoned as well as young. Have the butcher dress and clean the carcass, then cut off neck, shoulders, and front legs, all of which may be used for pâté dishes (see Index). For roasting and stewing, the best meat is the lower two-thirds of the animal, behind the shoulders. Hare should be washed thoroughly in running water but never soaked. Remove membranes and tendons as much as possible.

2 hares	root, and parsley root (about 2
6 ozs. salt pork for larding	cups in all)
juice 1 lemon	salt to taste
ground pepper, thyme, and juni-	3 tbs. butter
per berries	flour for dredging
slices of onion, carrot, celery	

Prepare hares as directed above. Lard generously, sprinkle with lemon juice, rub with spices, and cover with sliced vegetables. Allow to refrigerate for several hours, overnight if possible. Season with salt a half-hour before roasting. Discard vegetables. Arrange meat in shallow baking dish; cover with dabs of butter. Roast in hot oven for 1 to 1½ hours, depending on size, basting frequently with pan drippings. When nearly done, dredge lightly with flour and baste again. Serves 6 to 8. Serve with a tart jelly or preserves and a salad.

13. HARE À LA POLONAISE, WITH SOUR CREAM
(*Zając po Polsku ze Śmietaną*)

2 hares, dressed as in No. 12	ground pepper, thyme, and juni-
2 cups sour cream	per berries
marinade to cover (No.1)	salt to taste
6 ozs. salt pork for larding	3 tbs. butter
2 cups sliced vegetables: onion,	2 cups sour cream
carrot, celery root, parsley root	⅛ tsp. flour
1 bay leaf (optional)	

Marinate about 2 days. Wipe off and proceed as in No. 12. When nearly done, add 1 cup sour cream blended with flour. Blend this well into pan drippings, basting meat again several times. Serves 8.

14. PÂTÉ OF HARE FOR GARNISH OR HORS D'OEUVRES *(Grzanki Faszerowane Zającem)*

shoulders, neck, and forepaws of hare, together with liver and heart
3–4 slices bacon or salt pork
1 cup vegetables discarded from cooking hare
pinch of marjoram, thyme, and ground juniper

1 cup bouillon
2 tbs. sweet cream
2 egg yolks
salt and pepper to taste
2–3 tbs. butter
2 tbs. bread crumbs
thin oblongs of toast, buttered and heated in oven

Combine meat, bacon, vegetables, spices, and bouillon, and simmer together until meat falls away from the bones. Pick all the meat from the bones, put it through meat grinder twice, together with liver and bacon. Add cream, egg yolks, salt and pepper to taste, and mix thoroughly. Spread toast rather thickly with this mixture. Directly before serving, brown butter and bread crumbs and pour over pâté.

15. FRENCH SAUCE FOR HARE *(Sos do Zająca po Francusku)*

Serve roast hares with following sauce:

1 onion, minced fine
10 shallots or small white onions
2 tbs. butter
¼ cup white or red wine, according to preference
2 tsp. wine vinegar
pinch of thyme and marjoram

pinch of fresh-ground pepper and juniper
1 bay leaf (optional)
2–3 cloves
hare liver
2–3 tbs. fresh blood from hare, chicken, or beef

Simmer minced onion and shallots in butter until transparent. Add wine, vinegar, and spices and simmer a few minutes longer. Chop the hare liver, press through sieve, then add to sauce. Add the blood if available (otherwise, substitute strong bouillon). Season to taste, allow to boil up, and press everything through sieve. Heat and pour over hare.

16. HARE HUNTER-STYLE *(Zając Duszony po Myśliwsku)*

2 hares, marinated for 2 days and cut into serving pieces
6 ozs. sliced salt pork or bacon
bread crumbs
10–12 shallots or small white onions, chopped

2 tsp. paprika
ground juniper and thyme (optional)
2 cups dry red wine
salt and pepper to taste

Line heavy casserole with slices of pork or bacon, sprinkle with bread crumbs, then with a layer of chopped shallots. Add paprika. Arrange meat over this and cover with more chopped onion, bacon slices, and red wine. Season to taste. Cover tightly and bake in hot oven for 3 hours. Serve with red cabbage. Serves 8.

17. COLD STUFFED HARE (Zając do Zimnej Zastawy)

2 hares, marinated and roasted according to directions in No. 12

Stuffing:
    shoulders, neck, and forepaws of hares
    hare liver
4 ozs. salt pork
1 cup diced soup greens: carrot, celery root, parsley root, celery, leek
1 med. onion, diced
10 peppercorns

10 juniper berries
    pinch of thyme
1 bay leaf
    salt to taste
4–5 anchovy fillets
4 hard-cooked egg yolks
4 tbs. olive oil
2 tbs. (level) French mustard
    lemon juice and pepper to taste

2 cups very strong bouillon with ½ to 1 envelope gelatin added

Simmer meat, liver, and salt pork with soup greens, onion, spices, and seasoning until meat falls away from the bones. Clean all the meat from bones and put meat, liver, and pork through meat grinder twice, together with anchovy fillets. Press through sieve. Blend egg yolks and olive oil. Add French mustard, combine with meat pâté, and season to taste with pepper and lemon juice. Carve the cold roast hares, reassemble, and spread with stuffing. Pour bouillon with gelatin dissolved in it over the meat and allow to stand a few hours. The amount of gelatin depends on personal preference— whether a consistency of aspic is desired or merely a coating heavy enough to stick. Serve with a mayonnaise salad. An impressive dish for buffet suppers. Serves 8.

18. STEWED HARE (Potrawka z Zająca)

shoulders, neck, and forepaws of 3 hares, chopped into small pieces
hearts, livers, and lungs of the hares
    salt and pepper to taste
3 tbs. butter
¼ lb. bacon, diced

8–10 shallots or small white onions
    salt, pepper, and paprika to taste
2 bay leaves
2 tsp. flour
1 cup red wine
6 mushrooms (optional)
¼ tsp. Maggi extract

This is an excellent way to utilize the less desirable parts of hare after the rest of the meat has been used for roasting. Meat may be marinated or fresh, although the original recipe calls for unmarinated hare.

Brown meat quickly in butter on all sides, starting it in the pot in which it will stew. Add bacon and onions, salt, pepper, paprika, bay leaves (which are to be discarded later), flour, and wine; also mushrooms, if available. Cover tightly and simmer until meat is quite soft, about 2 hours. If sauce is too thick, add a few tablespoons of bouillon. Add Maggi extract. Serve with rice. Serves 6.

19. WILD GEESE OR DUCKS, ROASTED
(Dzikie Gęsi lub Kaczki Pieczone)

Wild geese or ducks should be cleaned immediately upon killing, then allowed to hang for a week; otherwise they are likely to be tough. Feathers may be plucked later, when birds are ready for use. Pour boiling marinade over the birds, wrap in cheesecloth moistened with the marinade, and refrigerate 2 more days. Prepare as follows:

1 large wild goose or several small ducks	1 tbs. marjoram
	salt and pepper to taste
marinade—about 2 cups (see No. 1)	1 onion
	½ apple
salt pork for larding	3 tbs. butter

Lard generously. Salt 1 hour before cooking and rub with marjoram. Stuff with one large onion and half an apple (for small birds, reduce proportions), and discard these when serving. Roast in 300° oven, basting very frequently with butter and cold water, allowing 18 to 20 minutes per pound for large goose, 15 to 20 minutes per pound for ducks, depending on the ducks and one's preference in degree of doneness. Increase heat toward the end so that skin will be brown and crackling. Allow ½ hour for smallest birds, up to 2 hours for large geese. Allow about 1 lb. per serving. Serve with salad and a tart jelly.

20. BRAISED WILD DUCK OR GOOSE
(Dzikie Gęsi i Kaczki Duszone)

1 large wild goose or several small ducks	3 tbs. butter
	1 cup bouillon
marinade—2–3 cups, approx. (see No. 1)	1 heaping tbs. capers
	6 mushrooms, sliced
1 tbs. crushed juniper berries	1 cup sour cream
salt and pepper to taste	1 tsp. flour

I.

Marinate birds for 2 days. Wipe off, and rub with ground juniper and salt an hour before using. Brown quickly in hot butter, cut into serving pieces, and arrange in heavy casserole with the butter in which the birds browned. Add bouillon and about 1 cup of the marinade, capers, sliced mushrooms, and seasoning to taste. Simmer, tightly covered, for 1 to 1½ hours. Add sour cream blended with flour and let bubble up. Serve with macaroni, rice, or wild rice. Allow about 1 lb. meat per serving.

II.

A second method of preparation is to add the following to the cooking:

dash of thyme and nutmeg	12–16 pitted olives
1 bay leaf	3 ozs. Madeira or sherry
1 tbs. butter blended with 2 tsp. flour	(Omit sour cream.)

Cook as in *I*. Discard bay leaf. Brown the butter lightly, blend in flour, and dissolve with a few tablespoons bouillon. Add to sauce. Add olives and wine, allow to bubble up, and then simmer another 20 minutes.

21. ROAST PHEASANT *(Bażant Pieczony)*

2 pheasants	3 tbs. butter
salt and pepper to taste	
6 ozs. salt pork for larding and covering	

Singe and wash pheasants. Wipe dry, and salt inside and out an hour before using. Lard breast and drumsticks generously. Use remaining salt pork or bacon in slices to cover bird while roasting. Baste frequently with butter. Roast in medium-hot oven for 1 to 1½ hours, depending on size. During the final 15 minutes, discard bacon slices and continue basting with pan drippings so that skin will be brown and crisp. Carve like chicken and serve with pan drippings, a salad, and tart jelly or preserves. Serves 6.

Note: The traditional way to serve pheasant is to reassemble bird after it has been carved and decorate it with its own colorful feathers to simulate a live pheasant.

22. PHEASANT WITH TRUFFLE STUFFING
(Bażant z Truflami)

Prepare pheasants as in No. 21. Use stuffing as in Turkey with Madeira Sauce (see Index), substituting mushrooms if truffles are unavailable. Prepare about the same amount of stuffing as for 2 young chickens. Use 1 or 2 truffles cut in thin strips for larding bird. Roast as in No. 21. Serve with Truffle or Mushroom Sauce (see Index). Serves 6.

23. HEATH COCK OR GROUSE *(Cietrzew lub Głuszec)*

Both these birds, though small, are likely to be tough unless young birds are used. They must also be well cured—kept for at least a week after killing. After the birds are cleaned they should be thoroughly rinsed several times, then marinated (see marinade recipe following) for 2 days. Two hours before using, take out of the marinade, wipe off, rub inside and out with salt and crushed juniper berries, lard generously, and sprinkle with lemon juice.

Marinade:

2 cups water	20 juniper berries
2 cups white wine	10 peppercorns
2 tbs. vinegar	4–5 cloves
1 onion	2 bay leaves

Boil all the ingredients together for half an hour. Pour boiling-hot marinade over birds and let stand for 2 days.

24. ROAST GROUSE OR HEATH COCK
(Cietrzew lub Głuszec Pieczony)

Prepare as in No. 23. Roast on spit or in moderately hot oven for 50 to 60 minutes, basting frequently with butter. Serve with pan drippings, and with green salad, cucumbers in sour cream, and tart fruit preserve. Allow 1 grouse per person.

25. HEATH COCK OR GROUSE IN SOUR CREAM
(Cietrzew lub Głuszec ze Śmietaną)

Prepare like Roast Grouse (No. 24). When almost done—after 40 to 45 minutes—baste birds with 2 cups sour cream blended with 1 tsp. flour. This amount is for 6 birds. Makes 6 servings.

26. HEATH COCK OR GROUSE SMOTHERED IN
MADEIRA *(Cietrzew lub Głuszec Duszony w Maderze)*

6 grouse or heath cock	½ cup Madeira (or sherry)
marinade to cover	6 med. mushrooms cut in quar-
1 tbs. crushed juniper berries	ters (optional)
salt to taste	12 shallots (optional)
bacon strips for lining casserole	
flour for dredging	

Marinate according to basic directions in No. 23. Cut birds in quarters, rub with crushed juniper berries and salt, and arrange in casserole lined with bacon strips. Simmer, tightly covered, until birds begin to brown. Dredge lightly with flour and add Madeira (or sherry). Continue to simmer until tender, about 1 hour. Add mushrooms and shallots at the same time as the wine. Allow 1 bird per portion.

27. HEATH COCK OR GROUSE SMOTHERED IN RED CABBAGE
(Głuszec lub Cietrzew Duszony w Czerwonej Kapuście)

Prepare birds as directed in No. 23. Prepare red cabbage as for Duck Braised in Cabbage (see Index), and follow that recipe. Allow a good hour and a half for braising. This recipe may also be used for any of the smaller game birds.

28. PARTRIDGES AND HAZEL HENS
(Kuropatwy i Jarząbki)

Partridges and hazel hens are the most delicate in taste of the game birds. They do not need marinating. Neither should they be soaked as is recommended for other fowl, since they will lose their taste. Wash them quickly under running water. For roasting they should be either larded generously or wrapped in bacon or salt pork strips, and basted frequently with butter. They are even more tasty if pot-roasted under cover, in which case they should cook about 30 minutes—40, at most. Before serving, make several incisions in the breast and fill with fresh butter creamed with a little lemon juice. Let stand a few minutes, covered, to give butter a chance to melt. They are also excellent with Anchovy Butter.

29. PARTRIDGES OR HAZEL HENS IN POLISH SAUCE
(Kuropatwy i Jarząbki w Polskim Sosie)

6 partridges or hazel hens	1 cup strong bouillon
salt and pepper to taste	2 tbs. bread crumbs
6 slices bacon or salt pork for	lemon juice to taste
larding	

Clean birds, rub with salt and a little pepper, and either lard with salt pork or wrap in bacon slices. Arrange tightly in heavy casserole and simmer, tightly covered, basting frequently with cold bouillon. When brown, sprinkle with bread crumbs and lemon juice, and allow to simmer another ten minutes—about 45 minutes in all. Add a few more spoonfuls of bouillon to pan drippings to make gravy. Serves 6.

30. PARTRIDGES OR HAZEL HENS SMOTHERED IN SOUR CREAM
(Kuropatwy lub Jarząbki Duszone w Śmietanie)

6 partridges or hazel hens	2–3 tbs. butter
salt	flour for dredging
salt pork for larding	1 cup sour cream

Clean birds, rub with salt, and lard generously. Brown in butter, cut into halves, dredge lightly with flour, and add the sour cream. Cover tightly and let simmer half an hour. Serve on toast. Serves 6.

31. PARTRIDGES OR HAZEL HENS SMOTHERED IN MADEIRA
(Kuropatwy lub Jarząbki Duszone w Maderze)

Prepare the same as in No. 30. Instead of sour cream, add ½ cup strong bouillon and ¼ to ½ cup Madeira (depending on personal preference). Simmer in this sauce for 30 minutes. Serves 6.

32. STUFFED PARTRIDGES (Kuropatwy Faszerowane)

6 partridges, including livers and hearts	salt and pepper to taste
2 good-sized goose livers (or equivalent amount of calf's liver) soaked in milk	3–4 tbs. Madeira
	3–4 tbs. strong bouillon
	salt pork for larding (about 6 ozs.)
4 bacon slices	4 tbs. butter
2 truffles or 4 small mushrooms, chopped	

Clean and salt the partridges and fill with stuffing made as follows: Soak goose livers in milk for a couple of hours, wrap in bacon slices, and braise, tightly covered, until just beginning to brown. Chop and put through a sieve, together with the bacon and the raw partridge livers and hearts. Add truffles or mushrooms, season to taste, and moisten with Madeira and bouillon. Mix thoroughly. Stuff birds and secure with toothpicks or small skewers. Lard breast generously and roast in fairly hot oven or on a spit, brushing frequently with melted butter, for about 45 minutes. Serve on buttered toast. Separately serve Truffle or Mushroom Sauce and a green salad. Serves 6.

33. SNIPE AND FIELD THRUSHES (Bekasy i Kwiczoły)

These little birds feed on juniper berries and hence have a special taste much prized by gourmets. They are prepared with heads and feet intact. Of the entrails, only the small intestine is carefully removed, but the gizzard and everything else is left in. To remove the intestine, make an incision close to the tail and carefully pull the intestine out with two fingers. Make another incision under the left wing and remove liver together with the bile sack, taking care not to crush the latter. The liver may then be put back in after rinsing, or tucked in under the wing. Truss the birds, tucking head under one wing. Wrap each in a strip of bacon or salt pork and secure with string. Sprinkle with salt—no other condiments are necessary. Roast in shallow pan or on a spit at high heat for 20 to 25 minutes, basting frequently with butter. Serve on individual pieces of toast, with pan drippings in a sauce boat. Allow 1 or 2 birds per serving.

34. SNIPE OR FIELD THRUSHES SMOTHERED IN WINE
(Bekasy lub Kwiczoły Duszone)

Prepare 6 to 8 snipe or thrushes as in No. 33. Instead of roasting, arrange tightly in heavy casserole and simmer, tightly covered, until bacon begins to brown. Add

½ cup strong bouillon   6 juniper berries
½ cup dry white wine

Continue simmering until tender, about half an hour. Allow one to two birds per serving.

35. QUAIL OR COOT (Przepiórki i Kurki Wodne)

Quail and coot should hang several days before being plucked and dressed. They should be salted and roasted on a spit or in a hot oven like partridge (see No. 28). Wrap each bird in a strip of bacon or salt pork and secure with string or toothpick. Baste frequently with butter. When birds begin to brown, discard the bacon and continue basting. Do not roast longer than 30 minutes from the time birds begin to brown. Serve on pieces of toast. Allow 1 quail or coot per person.

Sauces for Meat, Fish, and Vegetables

GENERAL DIRECTIONS: Even with standardization of measures, sauce recipes are difficult to give exactly because such intangibles as the size of eggs, the quality of flour, and even atmospheric conditions have to be considered. A little practice and even a few failures will teach the cook what no book can, since experience must be the final gauge. When flour and butter are used for the basis of a sauce, care must be taken not to cook over too hot a fire (medium for brown sauce, slow for white), and the ingredients must be thoroughly blended before any liquid is added. The liquid, whether soup stock, water, or milk, should be hot for best results (unless otherwise indicated), and it should be added a little at a time and stirred constantly. Adding a lot of liquid at one time will result in lumps which are difficult to dissolve. The use of meat extracts or bouillon cubes is often indicated, as well as the use of wine. As a rule use red wine for meat sauces and white wine for fish or poultry. In soups, the heavier wines like Madeira, Marsala, and vermouth are most satisfactory. For added delicacy, after the sauce is ready, melt in half a tablespoon of butter creamed with one or two egg yolks.

Thickenings

1. WHITE THICKENING OR SAUCE *(Zaprażka Biała)*

1 tbs. butter	1 tbs. flour

Melt the butter in heavy skillet and heat until it bubbles. Add the flour, a little at a time, stirring constantly and taking care not to brown. Add water or stock a little at a time, and continue to stir to the consistency of a loose paste. Stir out all lumps. Use as thickening for soups and stews, or season as necessary and use as a sauce.

2. DARK THICKENING *(Zaprażka Rumiana)*

1 tbs. butter   1 tbs. flour

Proceed as in No. 1, except that the butter should be browned before adding flour. Let the flour brown light or dark, depending on whether the sauce is to be light or dark. The darker the color, the tangier the taste. For a very dark brown sauce, add a teaspoon of caramelized sugar.

3. CARAMELIZED SUGAR *(Karmel)*

1 cup sugar   ½ cup water

Moisten sugar with a teaspoon of water and melt in heavy pan over moderate heat, stirring constantly. Allow to darken to a rich brown, but take care not to scorch. Dissolve with ½ cup of water (less for very thick syrup) and allow to bubble up. Simmer 10 minutes. Use as needed. May be stored in refrigerator almost indefinitely.

4. BUTTER *MANIE (Zaprażka na Surowo)*

1 tbs. flour   ½ cup soup stock
1 tbs. butter

Cream butter and flour, dilute with cold soup stock, and then simmer over low heat for 10 to 15 minutes, adding a little stock if necessary. For fish, veal, or ragout of poultry.

5. BROWN SAUCE THICKENING FOR STORING
(Zaprażka Rumiana do Przechowania)

½ lb. unsalted butter   1 cup flour

Melt the butter, stir in the flour, and brown lightly. Store, tightly covered, in refrigerator. Heat and use in sauces as necessary. If dark sauce is called for, brown further.

6. USE OF RAW EGG YOLKS IN SOUPS OR SAUCES

Separate eggs, reserving egg whites for future use. Beat the yolks lightly with a few spoonfuls of soup stock or cold water, in proportion of one to one. Slowly add the hot liquid, a spoonful at a time, stirring constantly. When enough liquid has been added to heat the mixture, stir it into the remaining sauce or soup. Let stand over very low heat a few more minutes to thicken, taking care not to boil; otherwise the eggs will curdle. Raw egg should always be added just before serving.

7. USE OF BOUILLON AND MEAT CONCENTRATES

Commercial bouillon as well as bouillon cubes and concentrates may be substituted for soup stock or added for a stronger taste. Canned or frozen consommé may be used according to directions on can. A bouillon cube is always more satisfactory if diluted with water in the amount required and simmered for at least 30 minutes, preferably a full hour. The slightly artificial taste then disappears.

Hot Sauces

8. SAUCE MADEIRA *(Sos Maderowy)*

2 tbs. butter	¼ tsp. sugar
1 tbs. flour	¼ cup Madeira
⅓ cup meat broth	2 tbs. chopped mushrooms, sim-
1 tsp. Soy or Maggi sauce	mered in butter (optional)

Melt and brown the butter, and stir in flour. Blend well, and add broth and sharp sauce extract. Simmer 15 to 20 minutes, or until well thickened. Add Madeira and sugar and simmer another 15 minutes. If too thick, add more broth. Makes 1 scant cup.

9. WHITE CAPER SAUCE *(Sos Kaparowy Biały)*

2 tbs. butter	½ tsp. lemon juice and a little
1 heaping tbs. flour	grated lemon rind
1 cup meat or fish broth, de-	salt to taste
pending on whether sauce is	2 egg yolks
to be served with meat or fish	
1–2 tbs. chopped capers, according	
to taste	

Melt butter and stir in flour, taking care not to brown. Blend well with broth. Chop and add capers, lemon juice, and rind, and season to taste. (Seasoning will depend on amount of capers used, since these are both salty and tangy.) Let simmer for 10 minutes, and if too thick, dilute with more broth. When done, beat up two egg yolks and add slowly, taking care not to let yolks curdle (see No. 6), and serve at once. Used for veal, poultry, and fish.

10. BROWN CAPER SAUCE *(Sos Kaparowy Rumiany)*

1–2 tbs. butter	½ tsp. lemon juice
1 heaping tbs. flour	1 tsp. caramelized sugar (see
1 cup beef broth or bouillon	No. 3)
cube diluted in cup of water	salt, and pepper to taste
1–2 tbs. capers, chopped	sugar to taste

Melt and brown butter, blend in flour and broth, add the chopped capers, lemon juice, caramelized sugar, and seasoning. Let bubble half an hour, and then add sugar to taste. If sauce is too thick, dilute with a little more broth. Serve with veal cutlet, beef patties, or boiled beef.

11. FRESH MUSHROOM SAUCE *(Sos Pieczarkowy)*

8 large fresh mushrooms	1 cup broth
½ med. onion	¼ cup white wine
2 tbs. butter	2–3 tbs. sweet cream
1 tbs. flour	lemon juice to taste
salt and fresh-ground pepper to taste	2 egg yolks (optional)

Chop mushrooms, using both stems and caps. Chop onion fine, and sauté together with mushrooms in butter until onions are a golden brown and mushrooms soft (about 15 minutes). Add flour and seasoning, and continue cooking, stirring constantly and taking care not to brown the flour, until thoroughly blended. Slowly add the broth, and when sauce is smooth, add the wine and cream. Season with lemon juice to taste and let simmer another 5 to 10 minutes. For richer texture add beaten egg yolks, taking care not to curdle. Serve at once. Makes 2 cups of sauce.

12. SOUR CREAM AND MUSHROOM SAUCE
(Sos Grzybowy ze Śmietaną)

¼ lb. fresh mushrooms, coarsely chopped	1½ tsp. flour
½ med. onion, finely chopped	1 cup sour cream
2 tbs. butter	salt and pepper to taste

Sauté the mushrooms and onion in a little butter, tightly covered, until thoroughly done and nearly dry, about 20 minutes. Stir occasionally to prevent sticking. Add the rest of the butter and continue cooking, dusting the mushrooms with flour and stirring frequently. When the mixture again looks dry, add sour cream, season to taste, let bubble up, and serve with boiled or broiled meat, pot roast, or cutlets. Yield is about 2 cups. If too thick, dilute with bouillon.

13. DRIED MUSHROOM SAUCE *(Sos z Suchych Grzybów)*

1½ oz. package dried mushrooms	1½ tsp. flour
1 cup water	1 cup sour cream
1½ tsp. butter	salt and pepper to taste

Simmer mushrooms in the water for 45 minutes to an hour. Brown the butter and blend in flour. Strain the mushrooms, and use the liquid (which should have boiled down to about ¼ cup) to dilute the sauce. Stir until smooth. Cut mushrooms into small bits, add to sauce, and beat in a cup of sour cream. Stir well, season to taste, and allow to simmer another 5 to 10 minutes. Serve with pot roast, beef patties, or over boiled potatoes or buckwheat groats (see Index). About 2 cups.

14. ONION SAUCE *(Sos Cebulowy)*

2 large or 3 med. onions	1 tsp. caramelized sugar (see
2–3 tbs. butter	No. 3)
1 tbs. flour	½ tsp. vinegar
1 cup broth	salt and sugar to taste

Cut up onion and sauté in butter, tightly covered, until soft enough to press through strainer (20 to 30 minutes). Remove onions. Make a brown paste of butter and flour. Put onions through a sieve, using a little of the broth to help them through. Blend sieved onions with the butter-and-flour paste, and continue adding broth until thoroughly blended. Color with caramelized sugar, season with salt, sugar, and vinegar, and simmer another 5 minutes. If sauce is too thick, add more broth; if too thin, simmer another minute. About 2 cups. Serve with boiled beef, roast pork, or fried sausage.

15. HOT HORSERADISH SAUCE *(Sos Chrzanowy Gorący)*

1¼ tbs. butter	1 cup sour cream
2 tbs. freshly-ground horseradish	1½ tsp. sugar (optional)
1½ tsp. flour	¼ tsp. lemon juice
½ cup broth	2 egg yolks (optional)

Melt butter without browning, add the horseradish, and dust in the flour, stirring constantly until smooth and taking care not to brown. Dilute slowly with the broth, and when well blended, add the sour cream and seasonings. Let bubble up once and serve. If sugar is omitted the sauce will be sharper. If egg yolks are used (beat and blend in egg yolks according to directions at beginning of chapter), the sauce will have a richer, subtler taste. About 2 cups.

16. DILL SAUCE *(Sos Koperkowy)*

1 tbs. butter	salt to taste
1½ tsp. flour	2 tbs. chopped fresh dill
¼ cup broth	2 egg yolks (optional)
1 cup sour cream	

Melt butter, stir in flour, blend thoroughly, and dilute with broth. Combine with sour cream, stirring constantly until smooth. Add dill, season to taste, and let bubble up once. For a more delicate

taste add the beaten egg yolks, taking care not to let sauce curdle.
Makes 1¼ to 1½ cups. Excellent for boiled beef, or boiled steak fish
such as sturgeon, salmon, or cod.

17. DILL PICKLE SAUCE *(Sos Ogórkowy)*

2 med. dill pickles	1½ tsp. flour
1 cup broth	½ cup sour cream
1 tbs. butter	sugar to taste

Peel pickles, slice thin, and simmer in broth 15 to 20 minutes. Melt
butter, add flour, and stir until smooth. Combine with sour cream,
and slowly add the cucumbers and broth, stirring constantly until
thoroughly blended. Let bubble up once. If sauce is too sour add
a pinch of sugar. About 2 cups.

18. SORREL SAUCE *(Sos Szczawiowy)*

1 cup fresh sorrel (spinach sea-	½ cup soup stock
soned with 1 tbs. lemon juice	1½ tsp. flour
may be substituted)	1 cup sour cream
3 tbs. butter	salt and pepper to taste

Wash, clean, and chop sorrel fine. Sauté, covered, in 2 tbs. butter
without any water. Add salt at once to preserve color. When done—
about 15 minutes—combine with soup stock, and thicken with flour
stirred to a paste with the rest of the butter. Blend thoroughly and
let simmer about 10 minutes. Blend in sour cream, let bubble up
once, season, and serve with boiled beef, veal cutlet, or poached or
hard-cooked eggs. (The sauce should be rather thick.) About 2
cups.

19. CHIVE SAUCE *(Sos Szczypiorkowy)*

1½ tsp. flour	salt and pepper to taste
1 tbs. butter	lemon juice to taste
¼ cup beef broth	2–3 tbs. chives, chopped fine
1 cup sour cream	

Cream butter and flour, add broth, and stir until smooth. Simmer
5 to 10 minutes. Add sour cream, blend thoroughly over low heat,
season with salt, pepper, and a few drops lemon juice. Add chives
last, and let bubble up once. About 1½ cups.

20. JUNIPER BERRY SAUCE *(Sos Jalowcowy)*

1½ tsp. butter	¼ cup Madeira wine
1½ tsp. flour	salt and pepper to taste
1 cup beef broth	1 tsp. ground juniper berries
1 bouillon cube	

Brown the butter, thicken with flour, and stir until smooth. Add broth in which the bouillon cube has been dissolved, and simmer at least 15 minutes. Add the wine, juniper berries, and seasoning, and simmer another 15 minutes. Sauce should be medium thick. Makes 1 generous cup. Served with venison pâté or *chaud-froid* of game birds.

21. POLISH GRAY SAUCE *(Sos Polski Szary)*

1 tbs. browned flour	1-2 bitter almonds (optional)
1 tbs. butter	juice ½ lemon
1 cup beef or fish broth, depending on whether serving over meat or fish	2 tsp. sugar
	1 tsp. caramelized sugar (see No. 3)
1½ tsp. Maggi extract	salt and pepper to taste
2 tbs. seedless raisins	¼ cup red table wine or half as much Malaga wine
2 tbs. chopped almonds	

Combine flour and butter and stir until smooth. Add broth, stir until thoroughly blended, and let simmer 10 minutes. Blanch, peel, and chop the almonds. Combine all ingredients, stir thoroughly, and let simmer another 5 to 10 minutes. Serve with fresh or smoked tongue or with carp. About 1½ cups.

22. BROWN SAUCE FOR FISH *(Sos Rumiany do Ryb)*

1 carrot	2 cups fish broth
1 celery root	1 med. onion, chopped
1 celery stalk	1 tbs. butter
1 parsley root	¼ cup red wine
1 small turnip	salt and pepper to taste
2 med. potatoes	

Peel and dice all vegetables but onion, and simmer in broth until very soft, about 45 minutes. Simmer onion in butter until golden brown. Press both onion and other vegetables through a sieve and return to broth (potatoes should make the addition of other thickening unnecessary). Add wine and season to taste. If sauce is not thick enough, simmer a little longer. About 3 cups.

23. WHITE LEMON OR POULETTE SAUCE
(Sos Biały Cytrynowy)

2 tbs. butter	4-6 mushrooms, chopped and sautéed in a little butter
1 tbs. flour	1 tbs. chopped fresh parsley
1 cup soup stock	salt and pepper to taste
juice ½ lemon	2 egg yolks
grated lemon rind to taste	

Cream flour and butter without cooking. Blend with soup stock over very low heat. Add lemon juice (less if preferred), lemon rind, and the sautéed mushrooms. Let bubble up, and add the chopped parsley and salt and pepper to taste. Cream egg yolks with remaining butter and add slowly to sauce, taking care not to curdle. About 1½ cups.

24. SAUCE *AUX FINES HERBES* (Sos aux Fines Herbes)

1 tbs. butter	1 tbs. chopped dill
1 tbs. flour	1 tbs. chopped parsley
1 cup beef broth	salt and pepper to taste
¼ cup white wine	2 egg yolks, creamed with 1 tsp.
lemon juice to taste	sweet butter

Melt butter, combine with flour, and stir until smooth. Blend in the broth, add the wine, a few drops of lemon juice, the chopped herbs, and seasoning to taste. Cream egg yolks with butter, and add just before serving, taking care not to let curdle. Makes 1¼ to 1½ cups.

25. STROGANOFF SAUCE (Sos à la Stroganow)

1 tbs. butter	½ cup sour cream
1 tbs. flour	1 tsp. Worcestershire Sauce
½ cup beef broth	½ tsp. tarragon
1 med. onion, chopped or grated	salt and pepper to taste

Melt butter, combine with flour, and stir until smooth. Blend in broth, add onions, and simmer about 5 minutes. Add sour cream and sharp sauce, and season with tarragon, salt, and pepper. Stir thoroughly and let simmer another 10 to 15 minutes. For all broiled meats. About 1 cup.

26. VENETIAN FISH SAUCE (Sos Wenecki do Ryb)

4–6 med. mushrooms	4 tbs. olive oil
12 shallots or 10 small white onions	4 egg yolks
	½ tbs. chopped dill
1 cup fish broth	½ tbs. chopped parsley
¼ cup dry white wine	salt and pepper to taste

Slice mushrooms and stems thin, peel and quarter onions, and simmer both with the broth and wine until thoroughly done, about 45 minutes. Using blender or rotary egg beater, beat egg yolks and olive oil until almost white. Combine the two mixtures and beat together without cooking, preferably using a double boiler. Add herbs, season to taste, and serve at once. For sturgeon, boiled salmon, perch, or pike. About 2½ cups.

27. GENOESE FISH SAUCE (Sos Genewsky do Ryb)

2 strips bacon	4-5 anchovy fillets, chopped fine
1 carrot	spices to taste (6 peppercorns,
1 parsley root	1 bay leaf, ¼ tsp. mustard
1 celery root	seed, pinch of thyme)
1 stalk celery	¼ cup sweet white wine or
3-4 fresh mushrooms	Madeira
1½ cups broth	¼ tsp. Soy sauce
1 tbs. flour	salt and pepper to taste

Cut up bacon, vegetables, and mushrooms, and simmer in a little broth until very soft and broth has been absorbed (about 45 minutes). Brown lightly, dust in the flour, add the chopped anchovies and spices, and simmer a few more minutes. Force through a sieve, using the remaining broth to help it through. If sauce is too thin, cook down to desired consistency. Add wine and Soy sauce, season, and serve. About 2 cups.

28. CRAYFISH SAUCE (Sos Rakowy)

20-25 crayfish (shrimp may be substituted)	3 tbs. broth in which shells have simmered (see Index
1 bunch fresh dill	for Crayfish Soup)
2 tbs. butter	salt and pepper to taste
2 cups sour cream	1 tbs. chopped fresh dill
1½ tsp. flour	3 egg yolks (optional)
1 tbs. Crayfish Butter (see Index)	

Prepare crayfish and cook in salted water with the dill, proceeding as for Crayfish Soup. (Directions are given there for cleaning and handling both meat and shells.) Pound shells and other small bits, and simmer first in butter, then with addition of 3 to 4 tbs. of the water in which the crayfish cooked. Skim butter according to directions. Combine sour cream, flour, Crayfish Butter, and the broth made with the shells. Season and heat thoroughly. Add chopped dill and crayfish meat, and let bubble up once. For a subtler taste, beat egg yolks and stir into sauce without cooking. About 2½ cups. For veal, chicken, or capon.

29. CALF'S BRAIN SAUCE (Sos Mózgowy)

1 set of calf brains	1 lemon (juice and rind)
salted boiling water to cover	1 tbs. butter
1 onion	1 tbs. flour
1 bay leaf	½ cup broth
6 peppercorns	2 cups sour cream
pinch of thyme	2 egg yolks
1 stalk celery	

Start brains in boiling water with onion, bay leaf, peppercorns, thyme, celery, and juice and rind of half a lemon. When water boils again, simmer 10 minutes. Drain, and when cool enough to handle, remove membranes and cut brains up fine. Melt butter, blend in flour, and combine with broth, stirring until smooth. Add sour cream, lemon juice and grated lemon rind to taste, and let bubble up. Cream the egg yolks and add slowly, taking care not to curdle. Add the brains. Makes about 4 cups of sauce. Serve with veal cutlet. Excellent reheated.

30. HOT SAUCE FOR VENISON AND GAME
(Sos Gorący do Dziczyzny)

1 med. onion	6 juniper berries
1 carrot	pinch of thyme
1 leek	pinch of marjoram
1 celery root	2 cups bouillon
1 parsnip	1 tbs. browned flour
1 turnip	salt and pepper to taste
few sprigs parsley	pinch of sugar
1 bay leaf	1 cup sour cream
6 peppercorns	½ tsp. Maggi or Soy sauce

Cut up onion and vegetables, add bay leaf, herbs, and spices, and simmer, tightly covered, in bouillon until very tender (at least 45 minutes). Dust in the flour, blend in, and press all through a sieve, discarding only the bay leaf. Add sour cream, salt, pepper, and sugar, and flavor with Soy or Maggi sauce. If too thin, let simmer a little longer. About 2½ cups.

31. BREAD-CRUMB SAUCE (Masło z Rumianą Bułką)

3 tbs. butter	2 tbs. bread crumbs

Melt butter and brown lightly. Add bread crumbs and cook over medium heat for another 2 to 3 minutes, just long enough to let the crumbs brown to the color of toast. For vegetables and dairy dishes.

32. BÉCHAMEL SAUCE (Sos Béchamel)

I.

1 heaping tbs. butter	3 tbs. grated Parmesan cheese
1 tbs. flour	4 egg yolks, slightly beaten
2 cups milk or sweet cream	salt and pepper to taste

Melt butter but do not brown. Add flour and stir until smooth. Slowly add milk or cream, stirring constantly to dissolve all lumps, and allow to bubble up. Remove from heat, cool a few minutes, and add grated cheese and beaten egg. Season to taste and stir thoroughly. Do not boil or heat after egg yolks have been added. Makes 2½ cups.

II.

1 heaping tbs. butter	dash of sugar
1 tbs. flour	½ tsp. lemon rind
2 tbs. strong bouillon	4 egg yolks, slightly beaten
2 cups sour cream	salt and pepper to taste

Melt butter but do not brown. Add flour and stir until smooth. Dissolve with bouillon, then slowly add sour cream, stirring constantly. Add sugar, lemon rind, and seasoning to taste, and allow to bubble up. Remove from heat, cool a few minutes, and beat in the egg yolks. Heat again over very low heat but do not boil. Pour over fish or meat and let brown in oven or under broiler. Makes 2½ cups.

33. CLEAR TOMATO SAUCE *(Sos Pomidorowy Czysty)*

1 small or ½ large carrot	2 tbs. butter
½ med. onion	1½ cups bouillon or soup stock
½ leek	6–8 fresh tomatoes, sliced
¼ parsley root or celery root	Butter *Manié* ⎰1½ tsp. butter
1 stalk celery	(see Index) ⎱1½ tsp. flour
few sprigs fresh parsley	½ tsp. Maggi extract
6 peppercorns	½ tsp. Kitchen Bouquet or
1 bay leaf	Worcestershire sauce
salt and pepper to taste	

Dice onion and vegetables and simmer with bay leaf and peppercorns in butter and a few spoonfuls of soup stock for about 10 minutes. Add tomatoes, season with salt and pepper, and continue cooking, covered, over very low heat for about 30 minutes. (Add a little stock as necessary during cooking.) Press through sieve, discarding bay leaf and peppercorns. Thicken with Butter *Manié*, stirring until smooth. Add remaining bouillon, Maggi extract, and any other sharp sauce. Simmer another 5 minutes, longer if sauce is too liquid and needs to be reduced. Sauce should be thick in consistency. Excellent for egg dishes, fish, or meat. Makes about 2½ cups.

34. SOUR CREAM AND TOMATO SAUCE
(Sos Pomidorowy ze Śmietaną)

5–6 tomatoes, sliced	1 cup sour cream
1 tbs. butter	1½ tsp. flour
½ cup bouillon or soup stock	sugar to taste
salt and pepper to taste	

Sauté tomatoes in butter until mushy, about 15 minutes. Press through sieve, diluting with bouillon. Season to taste. Combine sour cream and flour, stirring until smooth, and add to tomato and bouillon mixture. Sweeten very sparingly with sugar for a sweet-and-sour taste. Simmer another 5 minutes. Excellent with boiled beef, cutlets, or meat patties. Makes about 2 cups.

35. MUSTARD SAUCE (Sos Musztardowy)

2 med. onions, diced	salt and pepper to taste
2 tbs. butter	2 tbs. dry mustard
1 tbs. flour	½ tsp. Maggi extract
1 cup strong bouillon	½ tsp. Worcestershire sauce
¼ cup dry white wine	

Sauté diced onions in butter until light golden-brown. Add flour and bouillon, a little at a time, stirring constantly until smooth. Add wine, season with salt and pepper, and simmer 5 to 10 minutes. Press through sieve, return to pan, and heat. Remove from heat and add mustard, Maggi extract, and Worcestershire sauce. Mix thoroughly but do not cook. Serve at once. Excellent with fish, venison, game, cutlets, and liver. Makes 1½ cups.

36. HAWTHORNE BERRY SAUCE (Sos Głogowy)

1 tbs. butter	1 cup white wine
1 tbs. flour	sugar if desired
1 cup strong bouillon	
2 heaping tbs. Hawthorne Butter (see Index)	

I.

Cream butter and flour, dissolve with hot bouillon, and blend thoroughly. Add Hawthorne Butter and wine. Sweeten slightly if too tart, mix thoroughly, and bubble up once. Excellent with game or venison.

II.

Proceed as in *I*, using 2 cups sweet cream instead of bouillon and wine, and reducing flour by half. Serve with veal cutlets.

37. TRUFFLE SAUCE (Sos Truflowy)

Prepare the same as Madeira Sauce (No. 8), but instead of mushrooms use truffles which have been simmered in a small amount of bouillon until tender and then sliced thin. Use this bouillon instead of the meat broth in preparing the sauce.

37A. SAUCE *AU BEURRE NOIR* (Sos au Beurre Noir)

6 tbs. wine vinegar	1–2 cloves
10 peppercorns	2 tbs. butter
1 bay leaf	salt and pepper to taste
dash of thyme, marjoram,	1 tbs. chopped parsley
oregano, and tarragon, in any	
combination desired	

Combine vinegar and spices and simmer a few minutes. Separately, melt butter and allow to brown. Strain vinegar into the butter, season to taste, and add chopped parsley. Use for eggs or fish.

Cold Sauces

Homemade mayonnaise can be tricky even with electric appliances to take the place of the three hands one needs for an ordinary rotary beater. The secret is to use eggs and oil at room temperature. If the eggs are taken straight from the refrigerator, let them stand in warm water for a few minutes to remove the chill. Satisfactory mayonnaise can be made with any commercial vegetable oil, but high-grade olive oil gives delicacy of flavor.

The traditional way to proceed is as follows: Separate eggs carefully, removing all egg whites. Start by beating one yolk, slowly adding a trickle of oil, then a few drops of lemon juice. Then beat in the second yolk, and continue adding oil, lemon juice, and so on. The proportion is 2 tbs. of oil to each egg yolk. Do not add second yolk until the first has been thoroughly blended with all the oil it will take.

If the mayonnaise separates, which will happen if there is too much oil in proportion to egg or if the oil is too cold, place the mixing bowl in hot water and continue beating, adding an extra egg yolk. Adding the lemon juice a little at a time after each yolk helps prevent the mayonnaise from separating. Mayonnaise can be made in quantity and stored in the refrigerator, tightly covered, for a considerable time.

38. BASIC MAYONNAISE RECIPE (Majonez Zwykły)

6 egg yolks	salt and white pepper to taste
12 tbs. olive oil	dash of sugar (optional)
lemon juice to taste	

Beat 1 egg yolk and 2 tbs. olive oil with rotary beater or in electric blender, pouring the olive oil in gradually. When thick, add a few drops of lemon juice and blend in thoroughly. Add second yolk and two more spoonfuls of oil, following the same procedure. Continue until all ingredients have been used. Season to taste and chill.

39. MAYONNAISE MADE WITH HARD-COOKED EGGS
(Majonez z Jaj na Twardo)

4 hard-cooked egg yolks	lemon juice to taste
4 raw egg yolks	salt and white pepper to taste
1 cup olive oil	

Mash the hard-cooked egg yolks thoroughly or, still better, put through a sieve. Add the raw egg yolks and beat with whisk or rotary egg beater, adding the oil in a thin trickle. When thick and very light in color, season with lemon juice, salt, and pepper. Chill before serving.

40. TARTARE SAUCE (Sos Tatarski)

6 egg yolks	2 tsp. dry English mustard
¾–1 cup olive oil	2–3 sharp relish pickles, chopped
¼ cup cold water	pinch of sugar

Follow directions given in No. 38. When thickened, place in top of double boiler over low heat and continue beating, adding the cold water and remaining ingredients. If not tart enough, add a few drops of lemon juice. Take care not to let the sauce boil. Chill before serving. If the sauce is too thick, add more cold water while still beating over the heat.

41. TARTARE SAUCE WITH HARD-COOKED EGGS
(Sos Tatarski z Jaj na Twardo)

6 hard-cooked egg yolks	salt, pepper, and sugar to taste
6–8 tbs. olive oil	1 tsp. vinegar
2 tbs. prepared French mustard	½ tsp. Worcestershire sauce

Mash egg yolks thoroughly or press through a sieve. Slowly add the olive oil, beating constantly. When thick and thoroughly blended, add mustard, seasoning, and vinegar. Add sharp sauce. Continue beating a minute or two more. Chill. This sauce is traditional with cold meats at Easter.

42. CHIVE SAUCE *(Sos Szczypiórkowy)*

2 hard-cooked eggs
1 tbs. olive oil
1 tbs. vinegar with equal amount
cold water

1 tbs. chopped chives
salt, pepper, and sugar to taste

Cream the egg yolks and olive oil until very light and thick. Add vinegar and water and blend thoroughly. Add chopped egg whites, chives, and seasoning to taste. Serve with boiled beef.

43. COLD HORSERADISH SAUCE *(Sos Chszanowy Zimny)*

3 tbs. freshly-grated horseradish
1 cup sour cream
1 tsp. vinegar (approx.)

pinch of sugar
salt to taste

Combine all the ingredients, blend well, and chill. The amount of vinegar depends on personal preference.

44. HORSERADISH-VINEGAR SAUCE *(Chszan z Octem)*

6 tbs. freshly-grated horseradish
1 cup wine vinegar (or equivalent
amount of vinegar diluted with
water)

salt and sugar to taste

Combine all ingredients. Store the sauce in refrigerator, tightly covered, and use as needed. Serve cold or heated.

45. COLD SAUCE FOR VENISON AND GAME
(Sos Zimny do Dziczyzny)

2 raw egg yolks
6 tbs. olive oil
2 hard-cooked eggs
6 shallots
grated rind of 1 lemon

4–6 juniper berries, crushed fine
salt, pepper, and sugar to taste
1 tsp. lemon juice
1 tsp. Worcestershire sauce

Beat egg yolks and olive oil to the consistency of mayonnaise. Chop hard-cooked eggs and shallots. Combine all ingredients, mix thoroughly, and season to taste.

46. ANCHOVY SAUCE FOR FISH OR VENISON
(Sos Sardelowy do Ryb i Dziczyzny)

4 chopped anchovy fillets
3 hard-cooked eggs
1 tsp. dry mustard

1 tsp. olive oil (or more)
juice ½ lemon
salt, pepper, and sugar to taste

Press the chopped anchovies and cooked egg yolks through a sieve. Combine with mustard, oil, and lemon juice until blended. Mix and stir thoroughly, season to taste, and sprinkle with chopped egg whites. (Excellent for beef roasts as well.)

47. SAUCE FOR COLD VENISON
(Sos do Zimnej Zwierzyny)

2 tbs. prepared French mustard	3 cloves, ground fine
1 cup strong bouillon	4 peppercorns
1 tbs. olive oil	2 tbs. wine vinegar
4 raw egg yolks	juice ½ lemon
3 lumps of sugar	1½ tsp. flour
dash of lemon rind	salt and pepper to taste

Combine all the ingredients and beat with whisk about 15 minutes. Let thicken in top of double boiler or very low direct heat, stirring constantly. Chill before serving. Excellent with cold pot roast or cold lamb.

48. BUTTER MAÎTRE D'HÔTEL (Masło Maître d'Hôtel)

4 tbs. butter	few drops lemon juice
1 tbs. chopped parsley (dill may be substituted)	salt to taste
	slices of lemon

Cream butter and parsley, season with lemon and salt, and shape into squares. Chill and serve on lemon slices with all broiled or fried meats.

49. CHIVE BUTTER (Masło Szczypiórkowe)

Prepare the same as No. 48, using chopped chives instead of parsley. Omit lemon juice.

50. ANCHOVY BUTTER (Masło Sardelowe)

3–4 anchovies, chopped and pressed through sieve, or	2 tbs. anchovy paste
	1 stick butter

Combine anchovy paste and butter, shape into patties, and chill thoroughly before serving.

51. BEET AND HORSERADISH SAUCE (Ćwikła)

2–3 med. beets	salt and pepper to taste
1 cup grated horseradish	
½ cup vinegar (or less) and water	

The beets for this sauce are best baked in their skins and peeled while hot. If boiled, they should be steamed in about ½ cup water in a tightly-covered saucepan, and the cooking liquid should be used instead of water with the vinegar. Slice the cooked, peeled beets thin, cut into strips, and combine with horseradish and seasoning. Add enough liquid to make a medium-heavy (not runny) sauce. Store, tightly covered, in refrigerator and use as required. For boiled beef and other meats.

Vegetables

Vegetables, unless bought frozen, are best and most economical if used in season. Out of season they are likely to be not only expensive but often tasteless, for they are forced in greenhouses, have the slightly artificial taste of too many chemicals, and in addition are often picked unripe for long-distance shipping. Most vegetables taste best steamed. Otherwise, they should be cooked in very little water, tightly covered, in heavy-gauge aluminum, earthenware, or enamel-coated iron pots. A long-standing rule is to start those vegetables which grow underground in boiling water, those which grow aboveground in cold water. Since valuable vitamins and minerals cook away in the liquid, it is a wise idea to reserve this for use in soups or sauces. Another good way to cook tender vegetables is in a few spoonfuls of water and butter. Salt while cooking, never before. Add a pinch of sugar to the water.

There are several standard ways to serve vegetables which apply to most green and yellow ones as well as to the large cabbage family (including white, savoy, Chinese, Brussels sprouts and cauliflower). One of these is with melted butter. Another is Polish Style, which is traditional. This simply means topped with Bread-Crumb Sauce (see Index). A few drops of lemon juice may be added as a variation.

Time for cooking vegetables varies with quality, the size of pieces into which they are cut, and finally with personal preference. Thus, "until tender" must be taken to mean "until it suits the cook." A little experience will give the average person a good idea of how long to cook each vegetable. The smaller the cooking pieces, the shorter the time.

No attempt is made here to give an exhaustive number of recipes, but rather a sampling for general guidance. Where recipes are given in detail, they have been picked for being either unusual, complicated in some way, or a sample of a general rule.

1. EGGPLANT *(Bałtarzany)*

Eggplant may be peeled, sliced, seasoned, and fried in butter or olive oil until transparent. Or it may be dipped in egg and bread crumbs and then fried. It is also excellent in casserole dishes.

2. EGGPLANT STUFFED WITH MEAT OR RICE
(Bałtarzany Faszerowane Mięsem lub Ryżem)

Follow recipe for Stuffed Tomatoes (see Index).

3. EGGPLANT *À LA PROVENÇALE*
(Bałtarzany à la Provençale)

6 small eggplants	bread crumbs for topping
6 small shallots or 1 small onion, chopped fine	1 heaping tsp. each chopped dill and parsley
olive oil	salt and pepper to taste
1 heaping tbs. bread crumbs for stuffing	2 egg yolks

Cut tops off eggplants and scoop out as much of the meat as possible without injuring skin. Parboil shells in salted water. Drain. Chop eggplant meat. Combine with shallots, bread crumbs, herbs, and olive oil, taking care not to make stuffing too greasy. Season and sauté until transparent and tender. Allow to cool, and then add egg yolks and mix thoroughly. Fill eggplants with stuffing, cover with their own tops, arrange tightly in a shallow baking dish, top with bread crumbs and olive oil, and bake in moderately hot oven for 30 minutes. Serves 6.

4. EGGPLANT SALAD *(Sałata z Bałtarzanów)*

Follow recipe for Tomato Salad (see Index).

5. BABY LIMA BEANS IN PODS
(Bób Zielony w Strączkach)

Prepare like String Beans (see Index) and serve with Bread-Crumb Sauce.

6. TURNIPS *(Brukiew)*

Choose yellow, round turnips and peel like carrots. Dice and cook, covered, in salted water or in light broth. When half-done—after about 15 minutes—add a pinch of sugar. Make *manié* with 1 tbs. each of butter and flour, dissolve with liquid in which turnips have cooked, add to pot, and continue simmering until thoroughly done. Allow 2 pounds for 6 portions. Especially good with ham or lamb.

7. MASHED TURNIP AND POTATOES
(Brukiew Duszona z Kartoflami)

1 lb. turnips, diced	bacon fat
2 cups broth (or less)	salt and pepper to taste
1 lb. potatoes, sliced	
2–3 slices well-done bacon, crumbled	

Simmer turnips until half done (15 to 20 minutes) in broth saved from cooking ham, or made with vegetables and a ham bone. Add potatoes and continue simmering until both are done. Drain, mash, season, and serve topped with crumbled bacon and bacon fat. Serves 6.

8. GLAZED SHALLOTS (Cebulka Glasowana)

1 lb. shallots (or very small white onions)	2 level tbs. sugar
	bouillon to cover (about 1 cup)
2 tbs. butter	salt and pepper to taste

Blanch onions, and when cool enough to handle, peel and brown lightly in butter. In a shallow casserole melt the sugar and allow to brown. Add onions, bouillon, salt and pepper, and more sugar if necessary—for a sweet-salty taste. Simmer, tightly covered, until onions are tender, 25 to 30 minutes. There should be almost no liquid left. If too much liquid remains, remove cover and allow to simmer, open, until sauce has been reduced to consistency of honey. Serves 4.

9. JERUSALEM ARTICHOKES (Czyściec Bulwiasty)

I.

2 lbs. artichokes	Bread-Crumb Sauce (see Index)
salted water, just enough to cover	

Scrub tubers, scrape carefully (these vegetables are difficult to pare because of their knobby skins), blanch, and simmer in salted boiling water like potatoes, until tender. Serve with topping of Bread-Crumb Sauce. Serves 6.

II.

A method that is less trouble is to scrub the Jerusalem artichokes, rub skins with a little butter, and bake like potatoes; serve with fresh butter.

10. PUMPKIN (*Dynia*)

For all pumpkin recipes, begin by scooping out the seeds and paring. Then parboil. Proceed according to any preferred recipe.

11. SMOTHERED PUMPKIN (*Dynia Duszona*)

I.

2 lbs. pumpkin	1 tbs. chopped herbs—fresh dill,
1 tbs. butter	parsley, chives, tarragon
½ tsp. sugar	1 tsp. flour
salt and pepper	

Dice the parboiled pumpkin and simmer with butter and other ingredients, tightly covered, until tender. Use no water. Serves 6.

II.

Prepare as for *I*. Simmer in 2 cups of milk blended with 1 tbs. flour, omitting herbs. When done, blend in 2 egg yolks, taking care not to let eggs curdle.

12. SOUR PUMPKIN (*Dynia na Kwaśno*)

2 lbs. pumpkin	1 cup sour cream
manié made with 1 tbs. butter,	1 tbs. chopped fresh dill and
1 tbs. flour	parsley
1 cup dill pickle liquid or Fermented Rye Soup (see Index)	

Dice parboiled pumpkin, drain, and simmer in a sauce made with the butter *manié*, pickle liquid, sour cream, herbs, and seasoning. Cook until tender, about 30 minutes. Serves 6.

Note: Pumpkin may also be served fried like eggplant or, if young and tender, boiled in salted water with a pinch of sugar and served with Bread-Crumb Sauce.

Squash may be prepared according to the pumpkin recipes. Summer squash, however, being much more tender, need not be parboiled and also takes less time.

13. SNAP BEANS OR WAX BEANS
(*Fasola Zielona lub Żółta*)

Snap beans can be cooked whole or sliced (Frenched). Steam in a little salted water and drain. Then add a lump of butter and allow to stand covered a few minutes while butter melts.

14. FRENCH BEANS *(Fasola po Francusku)*

1 lb. snap or wax beans	1 tbs. chopped fresh dill and
1 small onion, blanched and grated	parsley
1 tbs. butter	dash of nutmeg
salt and pepper to taste	lemon juice to taste

Steam beans 10 minutes in a little salted water. Cook grated onion in butter until golden brown, add drained beans, seasoning, herbs, and lemon juice to taste. Simmer tightly covered 10 minutes longer. Serves 3 to 4.

15. SWEET-SOUR SNAP BEANS *(Fasolka na Kwaśno)*

1 lb. snap beans	sugar to taste
juice ½ lemon or a few spoonfuls	1 heaping tbs. butter
wine vinegar	

Steam beans 10 minutes in a little salted water. Drain. Combine all the ingredients and simmer 10 minutes more. Excellent served with fillet steak or with roast lamb. Serves 3 to 4.

16. SNAP BEANS WITH SOUR CREAM
(Fasolka na Kwaśno ze Śmietaną)

2 lbs. snap beans	1 tsp. flour
1 cup court bouillon (see Index)	lemon juice, salt, and pepper to
1 tbs. butter	taste
1 cup sour cream	

Blanch beans, season, then simmer in court bouillon until tender (about 10 minutes). Add other ingredients and simmer another 5 minutes. Serves 6.

17. DRIED BEANS WITH BUTTER
(Fasola Sucha Z Masłem)

2 cups dried beans—brown, red,	water to cover generously
or white, soaked overnight in	salt
lukewarm water	Bread-Crumb Sauce

Simmer dried beans in water until tender, about 1½ hours. Drain and serve with Bread-Crumb Sauce. Serves 6.

Note: Dried peas or lentils may be cooked in the same manner.

18. BEANS OR LENTILS IN SOUR SAUCE
(Fasola lub Soczewica na Kwaśno)

2 cups beans or lentils	1 tbs. butter
½ med. onion, minced	1 tbs. flour

| 1–1½ cups liquid in which beans cooked | wine vinegar to taste salt and pepper to taste |

Cook beans or lentils the same as in No. 17. Brown onion in the butter, add flour, and blend thoroughly. Dilute with the cooking liquid, stirring until smooth. Add vinegar and seasoning to taste and simmer 10 minutes longer. Sauce should not be too thin; if beans cooked in a lot of liquid, discard some of it. Serves 6.

19. PURÉE OF DRIED BEANS *(Purée Z Fasoli)*

| 2 cups red kidney, brown, or navy beans | 2 tbs. butter or rendered bacon fat |
| 1 med. onion, blanched and grated | 2–3 tbs. bouillon salt and pepper to taste |

Soak beans and cook as for No. 17. Drain. Put cooked beans through a sieve. Brown onion lightly in the fat, add to beans, and moisten with enough bouillon for a purée consistency. Season. Keep hot. Serve with meats, especially pork or grilled bacon. Serves 6 to 7.

Note: Dried peas or lentils may be puréed in the same manner.

20. BEAN—OR LENTIL OR DRIED PEA—PATTIES *(Kotlety z Fasoli)*

2 cups beans, lentils, or dried peas	salt and pepper
2 whole eggs, lightly beaten	bread crumbs for rolling
3 tbs. bread crumbs	butter or bacon fat for frying

Cook beans and purée as for No. 19. Purée for patties should be rather dry, which is the reason for omitting bouillon. When the purée has cooled, add beaten eggs, bread crumbs, and seasoning. Make patties. Roll in crumbs and fry in butter or bacon fat. Done with butter, this is an excellent Lenten dish. Serves 5 to 6.

Note: Split peas may be handled like any of the other dry legumes. They are especially tasty when cooked with ham broth instead of bouillon or with ham scraps added. Serve as a purée with Bread-Crumb Sauce.

21. SPLIT PEA FRITTERS *(Opiekanki z Grochu)*

2 cups green or yellow split peas	salt and pepper
1 onion, minced	1 whole egg, lightly beaten
1 tbs. butter	bread crumbs for rolling
4 tbs. bread crumbs	butter or fat for frying
1 heaping tbs. chopped fresh dill and parsley	

Prepare peas the same as the beans in No. 17. Purée them without diluting with liquid. Brown onion in butter and add to purée, together with bread crumbs, seasoning, herbs, and half the beaten egg. (The proportions should be—accurately—1 egg and 4 tbs. bread crumbs to 2 cups of purée.) Shape into patties or fritters, dip in remaining egg, roll in bread crumbs, and fry to a golden brown on all sides. Serve with a sharp sauce and in combination with other vegetables, such as stewed kohlrabi, spinach, carrots, etc. Serves 6.

22. SMOTHERED GREEN PEAS
(Groszek Zielony Duszony)

2 lbs. peas, shelled	½ tsp. sugar
water to half-cover	1 tsp. flour
salt	2 tsp. chopped fresh dill
1 heaping tbs. butter	(optional)

Simmer peas, tightly covered, with salt and butter for about 10 minutes. Add sugar, dust with flour, and continue simmering until tender—another 10 to 15 minutes. Add chopped dill, mix thoroughly, and serve. Serves 6.

23. PEAS WITH EGG SAUCE
(Groszek Zielony Zaprawiany Żółtkami)

Prepare peas as for No. 22, substituting light bouillon for water in cooking. When done, beat 2 egg yolks lightly with ½ cup sweet cream, and add slowly to sauce, taking care not to curdle. Add more sugar if necessary. Serves 5 to 6.

24. CAULIFLOWER (Kalafjory)

This vegetable is best blanched before cooking. It should then be either cooked in enough water to cover, or steamed; in either case, add a lump of sugar as well as salt. If cooked whole, allow about 25 to 30 minutes cooking time; the time can be shortened if cauliflower is broken up and the core discarded. Serve with a generous topping of Bread-Crumb Sauce.

25. CAULIFLOWER ITALIAN-STYLE
(Kalafjory po Wlosku)

1 large cauliflower	1–2 slices boiled ham or Canadian
6–8 med. mushrooms	bacon, shredded
butter	½ to 1 cup Tomato Sauce
grated Parmesan	

Boil or steam cauliflower. Break into flowerets. Slice mushrooms and cook in butter until limp. Arrange cauliflower in shallow buttered baking dish; sprinkle generously with Parmesan, then with shredded ham and mushrooms. Cover with Tomato Sauce and bake in hot oven (450°) for about 15 minutes, or until brown on top. Serves 4 to 5.

26. CAULIFLOWER FRENCH-STYLE
   (Kalafjory po Francusku)

Prepare as in No. 24. Break into pieces and simmer 10 minutes in following sauce:

2 tsp. butter	2 raw egg yolks
1 tbs. flour	1 tbs. butter
1 cup bouillon	few drops Maggi extract
4 tbs. heavy sweet cream	

Make a *manié* of the butter and flour. Combine with bouillon and cream, stirring until smooth. When ready to serve, remove from heat. Cream egg yolks, butter, and Maggi extract. Add slowly to sauce, so that eggs will not curdle and the taste of fresh butter will come through. Serves 5.

27. KOHLRABI *(Kalarepka)*

6–8 young kohlrabies, pared and diced or sliced thin	sugar to taste
salted water to cover	1 tbs. butter
	2 tsp. flour

Simmer in salted water with a little sugar until tender (45 to 50 minutes). Thicken gravy with *manié* of butter mixed with flour. Serves 6.

28. STUFFED KOHLRABI *(Kalarepa Faszerowana)*

I.

6–8 kohlrabies	lightly browned
½ lb. beef, lamb, or pork small piece suet	1 whole egg, lightly beaten salt and pepper
½ white roll, moistened in milk and mashed	sugar to taste 1 tbs. browned butter
1 small onion, minced and	1 tbs. flour

Peel kohlrabies carefully and cut in halves lengthwise. Scoop out centers with potato scoop. Put meat through meat grinder and mix with roll, onion, egg, and seasoning. Stuff kohlrabies and arrange in shallow water. Add salt and a little sugar to water, and the scooped-out pieces to cook with the rest. Cook tightly covered so that the kohlrabies will steam. When tender (about 30 minutes), brown 1 tbs. butter, add flour, and stir, adding a little of the cooking liquid, until thoroughly blended. Add to sauce and simmer another half-hour. Serves 6 to 8 as side dish, 3 to 4 as main dish.

II.

The stuffing may also be made with:

2 egg yolks, lightly beaten	3 tbs. bread crumbs
1 tbs. Crayfish Butter	1 tbs. chopped dill
½ lb. crayfish or shrimp, peeled and chopped	salt and pepper to taste

Cream eggs and butter, and add chopped shrimp or crayfish. Then add other ingredients, season, mix thoroughly, and proceed as in *I*.

29. CABBAGE IN SOUR SAUCE (*Kapusta na Kwaśno*)

1 head cabbage	1 tbs. flour
salt	lemon juice, wine vinegar, or
boiling water	wine to taste
1 med. onion, minced	sugar to taste
2 tbs. butter or bacon fat	2–3 tart apples (optional)
salt and pepper	2–3 peeled tomatoes (optional)

Shred cabbage, sprinkle liberally with salt, and let stand until juice runs out. Drain, throw into boiling water, and let boil up a few times. Drain again. Brown minced onion lightly in butter or bacon fat, add cabbage, season with salt and pepper, dust with flour, and allow to simmer tightly covered until quite soft. Sprinkle with lemon juice, wine, or vinegar, add sugar to taste, and simmer another 10 to 15 minutes. The amount of sugar and juice will depend on how tart and tangy one likes the cabbage. Serves 6.

For added taste, simmer with cored, peeled, and quartered apples alone, with tomatoes alone, or with a combination of both.

30. SAUERKRAUT IN WINE (*Kapusta Kiszona na Winie*)

2 lbs. sauerkraut	salt and pepper to taste
1 cup dry white wine	2 tsp. flour
1 heaping tbs. butter	½ tsp. Maggi or Kitchen Bouquet
1 med. onion, blanched and grated	sugar to taste

Squeeze kraut as dry as possible. Simmer in a heavy casserole, tightly covered, with wine, butter, onion, and seasoning. Stir frequently. After about 30 minutes, dust with flour, add Maggi extract and sugar to taste, and mix thoroughly. Allow to cook uncovered for about 5 minutes more. Serves 6.

31. SAUERKRAUT WITH DRIED MUSHROOMS
(Kapusta Kiszona z Grzybami)

Prepare as in No. 30, omitting wine. Add 1 to 2 ozs dried mushrooms which have been soaked for a couple of hours in a little water. Add the water also. Simmer until mushrooms are soft, then take them out, and cut into thin strips. Mix thoroughly. Serves 6.

32. SAUERKRAUT WITH PICKLES
(Kapusta Kiszona z Ogórkami)

Prepare as for No. 30, substituting bouillon for wine and adding 3 or 4 peeled, sliced dill pickles. Five minutes before serving, add 2 to 3 tbs. sour cream, mix, and allow to bubble up once or twice. Serves 7 to 8.

33. SMOTHERED RED CABBAGE
(Kapusta Czerwona Duszona)

1 head red cabbage, shredded

Prepare like No. 29. Sprinkle cabbage with lemon juice after blanching, to restore red color. Then simmer, tightly covered, in butter or bacon fat and flour diluted with a few spoonfuls of bouillon. Red cabbage should be fairly dry. When half done, season to taste, add more lemon juice or wine vinegar or red wine, and sugar to taste. Apples may be added, but not tomatoes.

Note: Red cabbage may also be simmered with a tablespoon of caraway or dill seed.

34. SWEET CABBAGE WITH CARAWAY SEED
(Kapusta na Słodko z Kminkiem)

2 small heads white cabbage	3 tbs. bouillon
salted boiling water	salt and pepper to taste
2–3 ozs. salt pork or bacon, minced	2 tsp. flour
1 med. onion, minced	½ tsp. Maggi extract or Kitchen
2–3 tsp. caraway seed	Bouquet

Cut cabbage into small sections, core, and parboil in salted water for 10 minutes. Drain. Heat salt pork until transparent, add onion, and continue cooking until onion is lightly brown. Add cabbage, caraway, bouillon, and seasoning. Simmer, tightly covered, stirring occasionally, until soft—about 1 hour. Dust with flour and add Maggi extract, stir, and let simmer another 5 minutes. Serves 6 to 7.

35. MEATLESS STUFFED CABBAGE BIRDS
(Gołąbki ze Słodkiej Kapusty, Postne)

I.

1 large or 2 small heads white
cabbage
salted boiling water
2 cups cooked-dry rice or pearl
barley
2 med. onions, chopped and
browned lightly in butter
2–3 tbs. cooked dried mushrooms
(see Index), chopped fine

salt and pepper to taste
2 cups fermented rye liquid (see
Index), or bouillon with the
mushroom cooking water
added
1 heaping tbs. butter
2 tsp. flour
sour cream (optional)

Parboil cabbage in salted boiling water for 10 minutes. Separate individual leaves as soon as cabbage is cool enough to handle. Make a stuffing of the rice or barley mixed with onions, mushrooms, and seasoning. Spread leaves with it and roll up, securing with cotton thread. Arrange birds tightly in heavy casserole, add liquid and butter, and simmer tightly covered until tender (about 1 hour). There should be little sauce left. Dust with flour and baste. Add sour cream to pan gravy if desired. Serves 6. Excellent reheated in butter.

II.

Cabbage Birds may be made with sauerkraut if this has been prepared in whole leaves instead of shredded, as is customary. This is a traditional Russian recipe.

III.

Stuffed Cabbage Birds may also be made with meat, in which case substitute 1 cup chopped fresh pork for half of the rice or barley, and use only 1 onion. Omit sour cream. Add a little strong bouillon and ½ tsp. Maggi extract to pan drippings.

36. SAVOY CABBAGE (Kapusta Włoska)

Prepare like ordinary cabbage, but allow only 20 minutes cooking time after parboiling. Excellent with dill, or parboiled and then cooked smothered with butter and seasoned lightly. Serve with a generous topping of Bread-Crumb Sauce. A medium-sized head of savoy cabbage makes 4 servings.

37. STUFFED SAVOY CABBAGE
(Kapusta Włoska Faszerowana)

I.

2 small heads savoy cabbage, quartered
salted boiling water
1 med. onion, minced
1 tbs. butter
1 lb. ground meat (pork or lamb)

1 white roll, moistened in milk and mashed
salt, pepper, and a dash of nutmeg
2 whole eggs, lightly beaten
bacon strips for lining casserole

Parboil cabbage for 5 minutes in salted boiling water. Drain, and when cool enough to handle, spread the leaves with stuffing made as follows: Brown onion lightly in butter. Mix thoroughly with meat, roll, seasoning, and eggs. After spreading the leaves, roll up and secure each roll with cotton thread. Then arrange tightly in a casserole lined with bacon strips. Add ½ cup water and simmer, tightly covered, until almost dry. Bake, still covered, in a 375° oven for 1½ hours, so that cabbage looks baked and brown.

Sauce:

To pan drippings, add:

1 tbs. butter
1½ tsp. flour
1 tsp. Maggi extract or Kitchen Bouquet

water or bouillon to taste (½ to 1 cup)

Place cabbage in sauce and simmer another 10 minutes. Serves 8.

II.

Stuffed Savoy Cabbage may also be made with rice and mushroom stuffing. Follow directions in *I*, but make stuffing as for No. 35 (Meatless Stuffed Cabbage Birds) and use liquid in which the mushrooms cooked instead of bouillon for the sauce.

38. BRUSSELS SPROUTS *(Kapusta Brukselska)*

Prepare like savoy cabbage or like cauliflower. Excellent steamed in a little salted water and served topped generously with Bread-Crumb Sauce.

39. POTATOES *(Kartofle)*

Potatoes may be boiled peeled, or in their skins or jackets. Cook them covered in salted water with a spoonful of butter added. Add a few sprigs of fresh dill or parsley if available. Try with a fork after 20 minutes, If not done enough, boil a few minutes longer. Drain, add butter and chopped parsley or dill (if cooked in jackets, peel first), and let stand, covered, for a few minutes so that the butter melts and the steam gives them a mealy taste. Never cook potatoes ahead of time.

40. MASHED POTATOES *(Purée z Kartofli)*

I.

Mash potatoes that have been boiled as directed in No. 39. For each pound add 1 heaping tablespoon of butter and a few table-spoons of milk or cream. Continue mashing until fluffy. Season with salt, pepper, and a dash of nutmeg.

II.

For a slightly varied taste, omit milk, increase the amount of butter, and brown the butter first with a little minced onion.

III.

Prepare according to *I*. Divide into three equal parts. Color one part with a little chopped spinach, one part with tomato juice, and leave one part white.

41. POTATO CROQUETTES *(Krokiety z Kartofli)*

I.

2 lbs. mashed potatoes (see No. 40)	flour, beaten egg, and bread crumbs for rolling
2–3 whole eggs, lightly beaten	butter, bacon fat, or deep fat for frying
salt and pepper to taste	
1 tbs. chopped fresh dill and parsley (optional)	

Add seasoning and eggs to mashed potatoes; also add herbs if desired. Roll into croquettes, roll in flour, dip in egg and then in bread crumbs, and fry to a golden-brown color. Serve with a sharp sauce as a side dish for meat. Serves 8.

II.

Prepare as in *I*, with the addition of 2 to 3 tbs. chopped mushrooms and half a medium-sized onion grated and browned lightly in butter. Onion is optional. Use either fresh or dry mushrooms cooked in water or broth. Use the mushroom cooking liquid instead of milk in mashing.

III.

Tiny potato balls *à la Dauphine* are croquettes prepared as as in *I*, with eggs, milk, butter, and a dash of nutmeg. Omit herbs. Shape into balls the size of pigeon eggs, roll in flour, and fry in deep fat until golden brown.

42. POTATOES STUFFED WITH MUSHROOMS
(Kartofle Nadziewane Grzybami)

I.

6 baked Idaho potatoes

Stuffing:
2–3 tbs. cooked dried mushrooms, chopped fine
1 small or ½ med. onion, minced
1 tbs. butter
2 whole eggs, lightly beaten
1 tsp. each of chopped fresh dill and parsley
2–3 tbs. of the mushroom cooking liquid

Sauce:
1 cup Mushroom Sauce (see Index) *or* 1 cup sour cream thickened with 1 tsp. flour
grated Parmesan
bread crumbs and melted butter for topping

Bake potatoes until skins are crisp (45 to 60 minutes). Cut each lengthwise in half or cut off a thin top layer to use later as a cover. Scoop out centers and mash. Brown onion lightly in butter, combine with chopped mushrooms, mashed potato, eggs, herbs, mushroom liquid, and seasoning, and refill the shells. Cover with their own tops, arrange in shallow baking dish, and pour Mushroom Sauce or sour cream over them. Sprinkle with grated Parmesan and melted butter, and dot generously with bread crumbs. Bake in hot oven for 5 to 10 minutes. Serves 6. An excellent Lenten dish.

II.

May also be prepared with the addition of 2 tbs. sour cream to the stuffing. Omit Parmesan and Mushroom Sauce. Top only with melted butter and bread crumbs. Bake 5 minutes.

43. POTATOES SMOTHERED IN SOUR CREAM
(Kartofle Duszone ze Śmietaną)

2 lbs. potatoes, peeled and sliced
2 med. onions, chopped
1 tbs. butter

½ cup sour cream
1 heaping tbs. chopped dill
salt and pepper to taste

Parboil potatoes in salted water 5 minutes. Drain. Brown onions lightly in butter and add to potatoes, with sour cream, dill, and seasoning. Cover tightly and simmer until done, about 30 minutes. Serves 6.

Note: These potatoes are also excellent if done with mushrooms. Slice 10 to 12 medium mushrooms and cook with 1 minced onion in butter until onion is lightly brown and mushrooms transparent. (See Index for Smothered Mushrooms.) Add to potatoes, and proceed as directed above, using only 1 onion instead of 2. Omit the dill.

44. POTATO CASSEROLE WITH EGGS AND HERRING
(Kartofle Wypiekane z Jajami i Śledziem)

4 cups peeled, sliced potatoes	butter and flour (or bread
1 large or 2 smaller matjes her- ring	crumbs)
	1 tbs. melted butter
3–4 hard-cooked eggs, sliced	¼–½ cup sour cream

Parboil potatoes about 10 minutes and drain. Rinse, bone, and chop herring and combine with potatoes. Butter a heavy casserole, dust with flour or bread crumbs, and arrange potatoes and sliced eggs in layers, beginning and ending with layer of potatoes. Add the melted butter and sour cream, season lightly, and bake covered in a hot oven for 30 minutes. Serves 6. An excellent Lenten dish.

Note: May also be prepared without herring.

45. SWISS POTATOES *(Kartofle po Szwajcarsku)*

2 med. onions, chopped	1 parsley root, sliced thin
2 tbs. butter	salt and pepper to taste
4 cups peeled, sliced potatoes	1 cup sour cream
1 carrot, sliced thin	1 tsp. lemon rind
1 celery root, sliced thin	lemon juice to taste

Brown onions lightly in butter. Blanch the sliced vegetables, drain, and add to onions. Season, mix thoroughly, add sour cream, lemon rind, and a little lemon juice. Bake uncovered in medium-hot oven for about 1 hour. Top should be crisp. Serves 6.

46. POTATOES HUNTER-STYLE *(Kartofle po Myśliwsku)*

2 lbs. potatoes, cooked in jackets	salt and pepper to taste
butter for frying	½ cup strong bouillon and liquid
4–6 anchovies, chopped	from capers
1 heaping tbs. chopped capers	
1 tbs. chopped fresh dill and parsley	

Peel and slice potatoes. Pan-fry until lightly brown on both sides. Mix other ingredients, add to potatoes, and stir lightly to avoid breaking potato slices. Heat through and serve with dark meat or game or venison. Serves 6.

47. POTATO PUFFS *(Racuszki)*

10 baby Idaho potatoes, cooked in jackets	2–3 tbs. sugar (to taste)
	dash of salt
1 heaping tbs. butter	deep fat for frying
2 tbs. sour cream	sugar and sour cream for gar-
3 eggs, separated	nish

Allow potatoes to cool. Then peel and mash. Add butter, sour cream, egg yolks, and seasoning. Mix thoroughly; then fold in stiffly-beaten egg whites. Spoon into hot fat. Puffs will rise. They are done when nicely brown on all sides. Drain on paper towel. Serve with sugar and sour cream. Serves 6 to 7.

48. ARTICHOKES *(Karczochy)*

Artichokes should be freshly picked; leaves and stems should be green, not brown, and the leaves tight together. The secret of good artichoke cooking is to be sure they are very well done; unlike other vegetables, they should be almost mushy. Trim stems, cut top leaves off with a sharp knife (about 1 inch) since tops are not edible, and if possible scoop out chokes before cooking. This, however, is not essential. Cook in boiling water to cover. Add juice of half a lemon, a teaspoon of sugar, and salt to taste. Stand upside down to drain before serving. Artichokes are also excellent if, in addition to lemon and sugar, the following are added to cooking water: 1 tbs. olive oil, 1 clove garlic, 1 tsp. thyme, marjoram or oregano. Cook 30 to 40 minutes. Serve artichokes hot with drawn butter, butter and lemon, Bread-Crumb Sauce, Mayonnaise or Hollandaise (see Index).

Serve artichokes cold with Mayonnaise or French Dressing.

49. ARTICHOKES IN WINE *(Karczochy na Winie)*

4. med. artichokes	1 cup dry white wine
2 tbs. melted butter	salt and pepper to taste

Cook artichokes 20 minutes according to directions in No. 48. Drain half-cooked artichokes, and when cool enough to handle, cut in quarters, scoop out hairy centers, and arrange tightly in casserole. Add butter and wine, season lightly, and simmer tightly covered another 20 minutes. Serve with olive oil and vinegar, or other sauce according to preference. Serves 4 to 8.

50. STUFFED ARTICHOKES *(Karczochy Faszerowane)*

4 med. artichokes	*Stuffing:*
2 strips bacon	1 onion, blanched and grated
½ cup strong bouillon	6 med.-small mushrooms, chopped
1 cup dry white wine	salt and pepper to taste
clove of garlic (optional)	2–3 strips salt pork or bacon, chopped
2 tsp. butter	1 stale roll (or bread crumbs), moistened in milk and mashed
2 tsp. flour	
½ tsp. Maggi extract	1 whole egg, lightly beaten

Cook artichokes 20 minutes as in No. 48. For stuffing, cook onion in butter until limp. Add chopped mushrooms, season, and simmer a few minutes until mushrooms are transparent. Add chopped bacon, roll or bread crumbs, and lightly-beaten egg. Mix thoroughly. Using potato scoop, scoop out inedible centers of artichokes, or cut in halves and scoop out. Fill centers with stuffing and arrange tightly in casserole so that artichokes stand up. Cover each with half a strip of bacon, add bouillon and wine (garlic if desired), and bake covered in hot oven for 30 minutes. Discard garlic. Brown flour and butter and use to thicken pan gravy. Season with Maggi extract and pour over artichokes. Serves 4.

51. CHARD *(Kardy)*

Discard tops and leave only the stems or ribs. Cut into pieces 2 to 3 inches long. Boil in salted water with 1 tbs. vinegar or juice of half a lemon until fibers may be removed. Drain, rinse in cold water, and remove fibers. Simmer until tender in 1 cup bouillon with a few drops of lemon juice added.

Garnishes:

I.

bouillon in which chard has   2 tsp. each butter and flour
cooked

Thicken bouillon with brown butter and flour, and pour over vegetable.

II.

Serve with Bread-Crumb Sauce (see Index).

III.

Serve sprinkled with Parmesan. Cover with 1 cup sour cream to which 1 tsp. flour and ½ tsp. Maggi extract have been added. Sprinkle with buttered bread crumbs and bake in hot oven for 10 to 15 minutes.

Note: In Garnishes *II* and *III*, 3 tbs. butter and ½ cup white wine may be substituted for the bouillon. Allow ½ cup vegetable per portion.

52. CHESTNUTS *(Kasztany)*

Make incisions in shells and parboil for 10 to 15 minutes so that the nuts will peel easily. Peel off the shells and the dark-brown skin inside. Continue cooking until tender in milk to cover. Use for stuffings, purée, or pastry.

53. CHESTNUTS FRIED IN SUGAR
(Kasztany Osmażane w Cukrze)

½ lb. chestnuts	½ lb. sugar

Prepare chestnuts as in No. 52, but do not mash. Make a thick syrup of sugar and very little water. When syrup begins to bubble and brown, stick toothpicks in the chestnuts and dip each so that it becomes well glazed. Allow to cool on well-buttered dish. Then use as garnish for spinach, green peas, carrots, etc.

54. CHESTNUT PURÉE (Purée z Kasztanów)

1 lb. chestnuts	sugar to taste
1–2 tbs. butter	dash of salt

Cook chestnuts as directed in No. 52. Mash with butter and sugar, adding a very little salt. Reheat in top of double boiler. Serves 3 to 4. For creamier purée, add a few tablespoons of sweet cream.

55. SMOTHERED CARROTS (Marchew Duszona)

2 bunches very young carrots, washed and blanched	dash of sugar
2 tbs. butter	½ cup bouillon
salt and pepper to taste	flour for dusting

Very young carrots (3 inches long) need not be peeled or scraped. Wash carefully and cut off tops and tips. Blanch in salted water and simmer, tightly covered, with butter, bouillon, and seasoning until tender. When done, dust with flour and stir. Let cook a few minutes uncovered to reduce liquid. Older carrots should be scraped, sliced, and parboiled; then they may be prepared the same way. Allow ½ cup per portion.

56. FRIED CARROTS (Marchew Smażona)

2 bunches carrots, blanched	¼ cup bouillon or water
1–2 tbs. butter	sugar to taste (lemon juice
salt and pepper to taste	optional)

Very young carrots may be used whole, unpeeled; older ones should be scraped and cut in halves or quarters. Blanch, then simmer tightly covered with butter, seasoning, and bouillon. When steamed through, add sugar for a sweetish taste, lemon if desired, and cook uncovered, stirring constantly, until sauce thickens and carrots begin to brown. Serves 6.

57. CARROTS WITH PEAS OR ASPARAGUS
(Marchew Krajana z Groszkiem lub ze Szparagami)

1 bunch carrots, scraped and diced	2 tsp. flour
1 lb. peas or 12 asparagus tips (see Index for directions)	1 tbs. chopped fresh dill and parsley
salt, pepper, and sugar to taste	2 egg yolks, slightly beaten (optional)
1 tbs. butter	

Cook each vegetable separately until done. Drain, reserving liquid for sauce. Combine vegetables and simmer another 10 minutes in white sauce made with the flour, butter, and ¾ cup vegetable water. Add herbs, season to taste, and bubble up once. When ready to serve, beat egg yolks into the sauce for added flavor. Serves 6.

58. CARROTS MAZUR-STYLE *(Marchew po Mazursku)*

4 cups diced carrots	3 tbs. sugar
2 cups water	1 heaping tbs. butter
2 cups milk	1 heaping tbs. flour
1 tbs. butter	1 cup heavy sweet cream
salt and pepper to taste	2 tsp. chopped fresh dill

Simmer carrots in milk and water, adding butter, salt, and sugar. When tender, drain and reserve the liquid. Mix butter and flour and use to thicken the cream and 1 cup of the carrot cooking liquid. (Remainder may be used for a cream soup base.) Return carrots to sauce, add dill, and heat until sauce bubbles. Serves 8.

59. STUFFED CUCUMBERS *(Ogórki Faszerowane)*

6–8 cucumbers	½ lb. ground veal, raw or leftover roast, *or*
thin bacon strips to cover	½ lb. raw boned fish
1 cup strong bouillon	1 stale white roll, mois-
2 tsp. flour	tened in milk and
½ tsp. Maggi extract	mashed (or bread
3 ozs. Madeira or sherry	crumbs)
Stuffing:	salt and pepper to taste
½ onion, grated	1 egg, lightly beaten
1½ tsp. butter	

Pick out medium, even-sized cucumbers. Peel, cut in half lengthwise, and scoop out seeds. Blanch in boiling salted water. To make stuffing, brown onion lightly in butter. Combine all the stuffing ingredients, mix thoroughly, and fill cucumber halves. Arrange tightly in casserole, cover with bacon strips, and add bouillon. Simmer, tightly covered, until transparent and completely done, about 30 minutes. Brown flour in a dry skillet, taking care not to burn. Dilute with a little of the sauce, add Maggi extract and

Madeira, and pour over cucumbers. Allow to bubble up and serve. Serves 6 to 8 as main dish.

60. FRIED STUFFED CUCUMBERS
(Ogórki Faszerowane Smażone)

Prepare as in No. 59, choosing small cucumbers instead of medium ones. Stuff and put halves together again, securing with toothpicks. Dip in beaten egg, roll in bread crumbs and fry in butter to a golden brown. Omit bacon. Serve with Caper Sauce (see Index). Serves 4 to 6.

Note: Cucumbers may also be breaded and fried without stuffing, and served as a vegetable.

61. BAKED TOMATOES *(Pomidory Pieczone)*

12 small, even-sized tomatoes	salt and pepper to taste
6 lumps butter	1 tbs. chopped dill or chives

Cut tops off tomatoes and scoop out seeds. Fill with butter and herbs, season, and cover again with the tops. Bake in shallow dish, uncovered, in medium-hot oven for about 30 minutes. Serves 6.

62. STUFFED TOMATOES *(Pomidory Faszerowane)*

For stuffing, use medium-sized, evenly matched, firm tomatoes. Blanch, cut off tops, and scoop out seeds. Season with salt and a little pepper, stuff according to preference (see recipes following), and sprinkle generously with bread crumbs. Arrange in shallow baking dish, pour melted butter on top, and bake in hot oven. Meat stuffing requires cooking time of 30 to 40 minutes, depending on size of tomatoes. Mushroom stuffing requires about 25 minutes; rice, 20 minutes. Allow 2 tomatoes per serving as a main course.

63. TOMATOES WITH MEAT STUFFING
(Pomidory Faszerowane Mięsem)

For 6 large or 12 smaller tomatoes, use:

½ med. onion, chopped	salt and pepper to taste
1½ tsp. butter	3 tbs. bread crumbs
½ lb. ground raw pork, lamb, or beef	1 heaping tbs. chopped fresh dill and chives
a little marrow	1 whole egg, lightly beaten

Brown onion lightly in butter. Combine all the ingredients, mix thoroughly, and stuff the tomatoes. Proceed as directed in No. 62.

64. TOMATOES WITH MUSHROOM STUFFING
(Pomidory Faszerowane Pieczarkami)

For 6 large or 12 smaller tomatoes, use:

12 med. mushrooms, chopped	2 tbs. bread crumbs
½ med. onion, chopped	2–3 tbs. sour cream
1 heaping tbs. butter	salt and pepper to taste

Prepare tomatoes as directed in No. 62. Simmer chopped mushrooms and onion in butter until transparent and limp—about 5 minutes. Combine with bread crumbs and sour cream, season to taste, and fill the tomatoes. Cover with tomato tops and arrange in shallow buttered baking dish. Bake in 375° oven 20 to 25 minutes. Serves 6.

65. TOMATOES WITH RICE STUFFING
(Pomidory Faszerowane Ryżem)

1 cup cooked rice	2–3 tbs. sour cream
6 dried mushrooms	salt and pepper

Soak mushrooms (see Index). Simmer in a little water until soft. Drain and chop. Mix all ingredients thoroughly and stuff tomatoes prepared according to directions in No. 62. Sprinkle with grated Parmesan and melted butter. Bake in buttered baking dish, uncovered, for about 20 minutes. Serves 6.

66. RHUBARB (Rzewień)

Combined with potatoes, rhubarb makes an excellent vegetable. Prepare as follows:

10 stalks rhubarb, with leaves cut off	**Broth:**
2 cups new potatoes or potato balls	2 cups water
1 tbs. butter, lightly browned	6 dried mushrooms
1 tbs. flour	1 onion, peeled and sliced
1 heaping tbs. chives	1 bay leaf
1 clove garlic	few sprigs dill
½ tsp. Maggi extract or Kitchen Bouquet	salt and pepper
salt and pepper	

Allow broth to simmer about half an hour so that mushrooms will cook and lend it their special flavor. Clean rhubarb, cut into 1 inch pieces, and cover with boiling broth. Simmer until tender. Then drain, reserving liquid, and rinse in cold water. In the meantime, cook the potatoes separately. Brown the butter, add flour, and blend well. Add about 1 cup of the rhubarb broth. Stir until smooth. If too thick add more broth. Add chives, garlic, and Maggi, and season to taste. Return rhubarb and potatoes to the sauce and simmer together until thoroughly heated. Serves 6.

67. SMOTHERED TURNIPS WITH SAUSAGE
(Rzepa Duszona z Kiełbaskami)

3–4 young turnips
1 cup White Sauce (see Index)
　　made with bouillon

1 tsp. caraway seed
　salt and pepper to taste
1 tbs. chopped fresh parsley
1 sausage ring or 6 frankfurters

Peel, dice, and parboil turnips in salted water for 5 minutes. Simmer in White Sauce with caraway seed and seasoning. When tender, add parsley. Serve with hot frankfurters or with Polish sausage (*kiełbasa*) heated in boiling water or pan-broiled. Serves 3 to 4.

68. SMOTHERED SALAD GREENS (Sałata Duszona)

4 young heads lettuce or esca-
　role or endive
3–4 strips bacon, diced
1 tsp. chopped fresh dill and
　parsley

salt and pepper to taste
2–3 tbs. sour cream
½ tsp. flour

If small heads of salad greens are not available, discard the outside green leaves of larger heads and cut in halves or quarters. Blanch with salted water and drain. Heat diced bacon until transparent, together with a little extra bacon fat. Add salad greens and herbs. Season and simmer, tightly covered, until limp and transparent—about 10 minutes. Blend sour cream with flour. Add to sauce, let bubble up, and serve. Serves 4.

69. SMOTHERED CELERY ROOTS (Selery Duszone)

3–4 celery roots, cleaned and par-
　boiled in salted water
1 cup bouillon
　lemon juice to taste

salt and pepper
1 tbs. butter
2 tsp. flour

Slice parboiled celery roots thin. Cover with bouillon, add a little lemon juice, season, and simmer tightly covered until tender. Combine butter and flour, dilute with the bouillon, and when smooth add to the celery roots. Let bubble up and then serve with croutons. Serves 4.

70. CELERY ROOTS SMOTHERED IN WINE
(Selery Duszone na Winie)

Prepare as for No. 69, adding ¼ cup Madeira to the bouillon. When done, season sauce with a little sugar. The original recipe calls for handling the celery as one would old potatoes—scooping out small balls with a scoop. However, dicing is equally satisfactory, less wasteful, and much less trouble.

71. LEAF CELERY (Selery Liściaste)

2 bunches white or Pascal celery   water or light bouillon for
salt and pepper   cooking

Cut off leaves, clean celery stalks, and cut into serving pieces. Simmer in salted water or bouillon until transparent, about 12 to 15 minutes. Serve like asparagus—with Bread-Crumb Sauce, Hollandaise, or Dill Sauce (see Index). Serves 6 to 8.

72. STUFFED CELERY ROOTS (Selery Faszerowane)

4 even-sized, round, well-shaped   Stuffing:
  celery roots   4–6 mushrooms, chopped
1 cup bouillon   ½ med. onion, minced
½ cup Madeira   1 tbs. butter
2 tsp. butter   2 egg yolks
2 tsp. flour   ½ lb. ground veal
                                      a little marrow
                                      ½ white roll, moistened in
                                        milk and mashed
                                      salt and pepper

Pare celery roots and parboil in salted water. Cook onion and mushrooms in butter until limp. Mix with rest of stuffing ingredients. Scoop out centers of celery roots, fill with stuffing, and arrange in a well-buttered casserole. Add bouillon and Madeira, and simmer tightly covered for 1 hour. Brown the butter and blend with flour. Add a little of the sauce and blend. Then add to the sauce and stir well. Serves 4.

73. ASPARAGUS (Szparagi)

Asparagus should be very fresh—never wrinkled or with dry or soft tops. Wash thoroughly, and scrape lower part of stems. The best cooking method is to tie the spears into a bunch and stand them in the lower half of a double boiler in about 5 inches of water to which 1 tsp. salt and 1 tsp. sugar are added. Reverse upper part of double boiler and use as cover so that the more tender tips will steam while the tougher lower stems cook in water. Allow 20 to 30 minutes, depending on thickness of stems. Serve with Hollandaise Sauce or with Bread-Crumb Sauce (Asparagus à la Polonaise), or cold with Mayonnaise or French Dressing. Allow ½ lb. per portion.

74. ASPARAGUS IN CRAYFISH SAUCE
(Szparagi w Sosie Rakowym)

Prepare as in No. 73. When tender, arrange in shallow dish, sprinkle with Parmesan cheese, and separately serve Crayfish or Shrimp Sauce (see Index), with a few chopped crayfish or shrimp added.

75. SPINACH WITH SWEET CREAM
(Szpinak ze Śmietanką)

3 lbs. spinach, cleaned and parboiled in salted water for 5 minutes	1 tbs. flour
	½ cup sweet cream (milk if preferred)
white sauce, made with:	salt and pepper to taste
1 tbs. butter	dash of sugar

Drain parboiled spinach and rinse under cold water to restore color. Chop fine and press through a sieve. Melt butter, blend in flour, add cream, and stir until smooth. Season, add spinach, and simmer tightly covered for 15 to 20 minutes. Serves 6.

Note: Serve garnished with slices of hard-cooked egg if desired.

76. SPINACH WITH GARLIC (Szpinak z Czosnkiem)

Prepare and chop spinach as for No. 75. Instead of white sauce, simmer in a brown sauce made as follows:

1 tbs. butter	1 clove garlic, mashed
1 tbs. flour	salt and pepper to taste
½ cup strong bouillon	

Brown the butter. Mix in the flour smoothly. Add bouillon and stir over low heat until thickened. Then add garlic and seasoning. Combine chopped spinach with the brown sauce and simmer, tightly covered, for 15 to 20 minutes. Excellent with steak, chopped beef, or roast lamb. Serves 6.

77. SPINACH CROQUETTES (Kotlety ze Szpinaku)

2 rolls or 2 slices bread	1 tbs. creamed or melted butter
1 tbs. butter	salt and pepper to taste
2 cups chopped cooked spinach	bread crumbs for rolling
2 cups bread crumbs	butter for frying
2 eggs, lightly beaten	

Cube the rolls or bread and make croutons by frying cubes in 1 tbs. butter. Combine with the spinach (preferably cooked in bouillon), the bread crumbs, eggs, creamed butter, and seasoning. Shape into oval croquettes, roll in bread crumbs, and fry in butter to a golden brown. Serves 6.

78. SORREL *(Szczaw)*

Prepare like Spinach with Sweet Cream (No. 75). Instead of sweet cream use 1 cup sour cream and a dash of sugar. When done, beat in 2 or 3 egg yolks and let stand for a minute or two, covered, after removing from fire. Garnish with slices of hard-cooked egg if desired. Serve with either dark or light meats. Serves 6.

79. BEETS *(Buraki)*

5–6 med. beets	2–3 tbs. sour cream
1½ tsp. flour	salt and pepper to taste
1 tbs. bacon fat	sugar to taste
2 strips bacon, fried and crumbled (optional)	vinegar to taste

Wash and dry unpeeled beets and bake in hot oven until soft. (The beets may also be boiled in salted water and then peeled, but baking is the preferred method.) Chop coarsely. Combine flour and bacon fat, stir until smooth, and allow to brown lightly. Add sour cream and bacon, salt and pepper, then the chopped beets. Simmer a few minutes, taking care not to scorch. Season with sugar and vinegar to a sweet-sour taste. Serves 4 to 6. Serve with roast beef, roast lamb, roast duck, hare, or venison.

80. PURÉE OF BEETS AND APPLES
(Purée z Buraków z Jabłkami)

5–6 med. beets	lemon juice to taste
2 sour apples	sugar to taste
1 tbs. bacon fat	2–3 tbs. sour cream
salt and pepper to taste	1½ tsp. flour

Peel beets and apples and grate coarsely, reserving all the juices. Melt bacon fat, add grated beets and apples, together with all their juices. Season with salt and pepper, and add lemon juice and sugar to taste. Simmer, covered, for half an hour. Reduce liquid, add sour cream combined with flour, and let bubble up. Simmer a few more minutes. Excellent with roasts. Serves 5 to 6.

81. VEGETABLE MACÉDOINE *(Macédoine z Jarzyn)*

¼ cup each diced carrots, kohlrabi, celery root, parsnip, and
parsley root
salt and sugar to taste
2 tbs. butter
1 scant cup bouillon

½ cup green peas, cooked separately
½ cup snap beans or asparagus
tips, cooked separately
1½ tsp. flour

Combine carrots, kohlrabi, celery root, parsnip, and parsley root
with 1 tbs. butter, sugar, seasoning, and bouillon. Simmer, tightly
covered, until tender. Combine with peas, snap beans and/or
asparagus tips. Dust in the flour and simmer a few minutes longer
or until sauce thickens. Remove from heat. Add remaining butter
and allow to melt. Serve garnished with croutons as a side dish.
Serves 6.

Note: For use in salads, omit butter and flour in preparing macédoine. Allow to cool and serve with French dressing or Tartare
Sauce (see Index).

Mushrooms

Most of these recipes are adapted from the varied ways of cooking the many wild mushrooms that grow in Poland. Domestic mushrooms, delicate in taste, only approximate the tangier flavor of those found in the woods. Wild mushrooms are, of course, also available in the United States, but here mushroom-picking is a relatively little-known sport, and wild mushrooms are best left alone by amateurs ignorant of which kinds are edible and which poisonous. A person thoroughly familiar with the wild varieties, however, will find that dishes made with them are particularly delicious. Any of the recipes given here can be used interchangeably for either domestic or wild mushrooms.

1. MUSHROOMS SMOTHERED IN BUTTER
(Grzyby Duszone z Masłem)

1 lb. mushrooms	½ med. onion, minced
salt and pepper to taste	2 tbs. flour

Wash mushrooms and slice thin both stems and caps, which do not need to be peeled. Season, add onion, and simmer, tightly covered, in their own juice for a few minutes, stirring to prevent burning. When mushrooms are limp, add butter, and continue cooking until thoroughly limp and dark. Although mushrooms may be served after 8 to 10 minutes, they will have more flavor if allowed to stew longer. Serves 4 to 6 as a side dish.

2. MUSHROOMS IN SOUR CREAM (Grzyby ze Śmietaną)

Prepare the same as in No. 1. After 10 minutes, add 1 cup sour cream blended with 1 tsp. flour, and continue simmering 10 to 15 minutes. Serves 4 to 6.

3. WHOLE FRIED MUSHROOMS
(Grzyby Smażone w Całosci)

1 lb. small white mushrooms (or 2 tbs. butter
   mushroom caps)   salt and pepper to taste
½ med. onion, minced

Wash and clean mushrooms, but do not peel. Lightly brown the onion in butter, add mushrooms, season, and cook about 10 minutes covered. When juice begins to form (mushrooms have a good deal of water in them), uncover and continue to fry until lightly brown. Serves 4.

Note: The same procedure may be used for broiling, in which case broil in a pan so that the juices will not drip away and leave mushrooms too dry. Dot with butter.

4. BREADED MUSHROOMS (Grzyby Panierowane)

15–20 mushrooms of even size   salt and pepper
  ½ minced onion   1 egg, lightly beaten
  4 tbs. butter   bread crumbs

Cook onion in a little butter until limp. Add mushrooms, season, and simmer tightly covered until transparent. Dip in egg, roll in bread crumbs, and fry evenly in hot butter. Serve with another vegetable in lieu of meat during the Lenten season. Serves 3 to 4.

5. MUSHROOMS AU GRATIN (Grzyby au Gratin)

1 lb. mushrooms of even size   1 cup sour cream blended with 1
3 tbs. butter   tsp. flour
½ onion, minced   grated Parmesan
  salt and pepper   bread crumbs for topping

Wash and clean mushrooms. Simmer with a little butter and the onion and seasoning, tightly covered, until transparent—about 10 minutes. Arrange in oven-proof *gratin* dish, cover with sour cream with the flour blended into it, sprinkle generously with grated Parmesan, then with bread crumbs, and top with remaining butter. Brown under broiler or in very hot oven for a few minutes. Serves 4.

6. MUSHROOM PATTIES (Kotlety z Grzybów)

1 lb. mushrooms   2 whole eggs, lightly beaten
1 med. onion, grated   1 tbs. chopped fresh parsley
  butter   bread crumbs for rolling
  salt and pepper to taste butter for frying
2 white rolls, moistened in milk
  and mashed

Wash, clean, and chop mushroom caps and stems. Cook grated onion in a little butter, and when onion begins to brown, add the mushrooms. Season and simmer, covered, for about 5 minutes. Mix thoroughly with the mashed rolls, eggs, and parsley, and shape into patties. Roll in bread crumbs and fry in hot butter to a golden brown. Serves 4. Serve with pan-fried potatoes.

7. CULTIVATED MUSHROOMS SMOTHERED WHOLE
(Pieczarki Duszone w Całości)

15–20 mushrooms of even size	flour for dredging
juice ½ lemon	3–4 tbs. sweet or sour cream,
salt and pepper	according to preference
½ med. onion, minced	1 tbs. chopped fresh parsley
1 tbs. butter (approx.)	2 egg yolks, lightly beaten

Wash and clean mushrooms and cut stems even with caps. (Reserve stems for other use. Sprinkle with a little lemon juice to avoid discoloration.) Season and smother with the onion in a little butter (cover tightly) until tender—about 10 minutes. Dust with flour, add cream and lemon juice to taste, add parsley, and let simmer another 5 minutes. When ready to serve, stir beaten egg yolks into sauce, taking care not to curdle egg. Serves 3 to 4. Excellent with veal cutlet, capon, or venison.

8. STUFFED MUSHROOMS (Pieczarki Faszerowane)

12–16 large mushrooms and 4–6 smaller ones	1 veal kidney with surplus fat removed, or equivalent
½ med. onion, chopped fine	amount roast veal
butter	salt and pepper to taste
1 heaping tbs. chopped fresh dill or parsley, or combination of both	1 egg, lightly beaten
	bread crumbs and butter
	for topping
2 tbs. bread crumbs	½ cup strong bouillon

Clean and wash mushrooms. Cut out stems from the large ones, leaving only caps for stuffing. Simmer mushroom caps in salted boiling water for about 5 minutes. In the meantime, chop stems and remaining small mushrooms and simmer with the onion, tightly covered, until transparent and limp. Add chopped dill, bread crumbs, and slightly-cooked kidney or roast veal, chopped fine. Season, add beaten egg and mix thoroughly. Fill mushroom caps with the mixture, sprinkle with bread crumbs, and dot with butter. Bake in 375° oven for 15 to 20 minutes, taking care not to dry out too much. Bread crumbs should be nicely brown on top. Add bouillon to pan after removing mushrooms. Allow to boil up once and use as gravy.

Serve with meat or on toast as a luncheon dish. Makes 3 to 4 servings.

9. MUSHROOM RAMEKINS *(Pieczarki w Muszelkach)*

12–15 med. mushrooms	2 tbs. grated Parmesan cheese
lemon juice	1 cup sweet cream
½ med. onion, minced	2 egg yolks, lightly beaten
butter	butter and bread crumbs for
salt and pepper to taste	topping
1 heaping tsp. flour	

Wash and clean mushrooms, slice thin, and sprinkle with lemon juice. Simmer, tightly covered, with the onion and a little butter until transparent. Season, dust with flour, add grated Parmesan, cream, and egg yolks. Mix thoroughly. Pour mixture into buttered ramekins, sprinkle with bread crumbs, and dot with butter. Bake in hot oven 5 minutes. Makes 3 to 4 servings.

10. MARINATED MUSHROOMS *(Grzyby Marynowane)*

For marinating, choose only very young, small mushrooms with caps still tight around the stem. Wash thoroughly, then place in an earthenware casserole. If cooked in a metal pot they will discolor.

1 lb. mushrooms	wine vinegar to taste
1 large onion, sliced	10 peppercorns
salt to taste	10 whole allspice
½ cup water	2 bay leaves

Combine mushrooms, onion, salt, and water. Simmer, tightly covered, until mushrooms are done—15 to 20 minutes. Add vinegar to taste (depending on how tart one likes the marinade), spices, and bay leaves. Allow to boil up a few times. When mushrooms have cooled enough to handle, transfer to glass jars and seal tightly. Refrigerate for use as required.

11. TRUFFLES

Truffles are seldom available fresh in the average city market. They are the most delicate of all mushrooms. To prepare, parboil in red wine, peel carefully, reserving peel for sauces, and slice. Add a few spoonfuls of red wine or Madeira and 1 tbs. butter. Simmer, tightly covered, until tender. Serve with the sauce in which the truffles have cooked. Truffles may also be simmered whole in Madeira, and served with melted butter.

12. CANNED TRUFFLES (*Trufle w Konserwach*)

1 can truffles   Madeira or red table wine
    vegetable broth to cover

Cook canned truffles covered with broth for 15 minutes. Measure broth and add equal amount of wine. Put truffles in small jars, 1 or 2 per jar, and divide liquid evenly. Seal tightly, then cook in steam for 30 minutes. Cool and store in refrigerator or in cool storage place, for use as necessary.

Note: Canned truffles ready for use may also be purchased in specialty food stores.

13. DRIED MUSHROOMS (*Suche Grzyby*)

Imported dried mushrooms are tangier than domestic ones. Polish mushrooms, now readily available in the United States, are particularly recommended, since they are wild European mushrooms specially prepared. In Europe, where they are cheaper and more abundant, they are used as a vegetable. Here, however, this would be an impossible luxury, since good imported mushrooms cost about $12.00 a pound. But they are excellent in sauces and soups, for an ounce or even a half-ounce can "make" a dish. Dried mushrooms are best soaked overnight in milk or a little water, then simmered half an hour in the soaking liquid. If a recipe does not call for milk, be sure to soak in water. This water can then take the place of bouillon in sauce.

Mayonnaises and Aspics

Recipes for basic mayonnaise and similar sauces are included elsewhere in the book (see Index). Commercial variants are often substituted as a timesaving device. When time is at a premium this is an inevitable short cut; however, many cooks are deterred from trying their hand at sauces only because these are reputedly so difficult and unpredictable. As a matter of fact, with standardization of food quality, refrigeration, the introduction into most kitchens of electric blenders and, hence, the possibility of exact timing and speed control, the old bugaboo of ruining a dozen good eggs while beating up a batch of bad mayonnaise need no longer haunt us. Electric gadget manufacturers and also the packers and distributors of cooking oils all furnish recipe booklets with directions on how to operate blenders to make mayonnaise, hollandaise, etc. These homemade sauces can be safely stored, tightly covered, in the refrigerator and therefore can be made in quantity. The added gourmet taste makes the effort worth while.

1. MAYONNAISE OF PIKE, SALMON, OR PERCH
(Szczupak, Łosoź lub Sandacz w Majonezie)

The recipe below is a traditional one for serving at large parties and receptions. We give it in its full glory, but the modern hostess can easily reduce it to modern kitchen and table proportions.

1 whole fish, 9–12 lbs., cleaned and salted down the day before	20 peppercorns
4–5 onions	3–4 carrots
2 leeks	2 celery roots
1 bunch parsley	3 parsley roots
3 bay leaves	2 lemons
	3–4 stalks celery
	water

Make a court bouillon of all the vegetables with enough water to cover the fish. When vegetables are soft, immerse the fish (complete with head and tail) in the boiling water, belly down. Reduce the heat. Let simmer 10 minutes, counting from the time the water

221

begins to boil again. Remove from heat and let stand, covered, in the water for another 30 minutes. Remove carefully (using a rack facilitates this), drain, and place on a platter when cool, belly down. Spread thickly with mayonnaise.

Garnish:

10 sweet and sour pickles, sliced colored aspic made with beet juice, tomato juice, etc.
¼ lb. each of red and black caviar
30 crayfish tails or shrimp

1 can lobster meat salad greens (watercress, romaine, Boston lettuce, iceberg lettuce, endive, etc.)
4–6 cups Vegetable Macédoine oil and vinegar

Garnish as follows: Put a sprig of watercress in the mouth, decorate the back with thin slices of pickle, slices of colored aspic, capers, dabs of red and black caviar, crayfish tails (or shrimp), and canned lobster meat. Along the edges of the platter arrange various kinds of green salad leaves and mounds of Vegetable Macédoine (see Index) marinated in vinegar and oil. Refrigerate until thoroughly chilled. Serves 18 to 24.

2. PULLET OR CAPON IN MAYONNAISE
(Pularda lub Kaplon w Majonezie)

2 pullets or 1 capon
1 lemon
2 large onions
3 carrots
1 leek

1 celery root
1 parsley root
2 celery stalks
salt and pepper to taste
2 cups mayonnaise

Clean and wash capon, rub with salt inside and out, and sprinkle with lemon juice. Let stand 2 hours. Peel and cut up onions and vegetables. Place bird in a pan on top of vegetables, add salt and pepper, and cover with cold water. Bring to a boil, then let simmer as for chicken soup, skimming carefully, until meat comes away easily from the bones (2 hours for capon, 1 hour for pullets). Drain, reserving chicken stock for the basis of soup. Skin, remove meat from large bones, and cut up into small serving pieces. Dip each piece in mayonnaise and arrange on platter. Spread with remaining mayonnaise, and garnish. Serves 6.

Garnish:

4–6 sweet and sour pickles, sliced
4 hard-cooked eggs, sliced or quartered
1 cup cooked cauliflower, separated into individual flowerets
12 marinated mushrooms (canned)

2 tbs. capers
green salad leaves
mounds of aspic or jellied consommé
1½ cups marinated macédoine of vegetables (see Index)

3. VEAL MAYONNAISE (*Cielęcina w Majonezie*)

3 lbs. boneless veal for roasting	1 leek
salt	1 celery root
1 lemon	1 parsley root
4 cups cold water	2 celery stalks
1 onion	salt and pepper to taste
3 carrots	mayonnaise

Prepare the meat like the capon in previous recipe. Then simmer, covered, with vegetables until thoroughly done, about 1½ hours, taking care not to overcook to the point where it falls apart. Drain and cut in small pieces. Reduce liquid to 1 cup and strain. Combine with cut-up meat and chill thoroughly. Spread with mayonnaise and garnish as in No. 2. Serves 6 to 8.

4. MOCK SALMON MADE WITH VEAL (*Fałszywy Łosoś*)

3 lbs. boned veal, rolled as for roasting	1 parsley root
	few sprigs fresh parsley
veal bones, split in several pieces	10 peppercorns
	1 bay leaf
1 large onion	1–2 cloves
1–2 carrots	salt and pepper to taste
1 celery root	3 cups water
2 celery stalks	1 cup vinegar

Peel and cut up onion and vegetables, and boil with veal bones, spices, and salt and pepper in water and vinegar. (Proportions of water and vinegar may be varied according to taste. There should be just enough liquid to cover meat.) When water comes to a boil, put in the meat and simmer for 3 hours. Cool and leave in the liquid until the following day. Drain, slice, and arrange on platter. Pour the following sauce over the meat.

Sauce:

3 hard-cooked egg yolks	1 tin anchovy fillets, chopped fine
1 cup olive oil	salt and pepper to taste
juice of 2–3 lemons	dash of sugar
1 tbs. capers	

Mash the egg yolks and beat in one cup olive oil, a spoonful at a time, beating constantly until all the oil has been absorbed. Add the lemon juice, continuing to beat. Add capers and anchovies. Season to taste and mix thoroughly. Serves 6 to 8.

5. TONGUE IN MAYONNAISE (*Majonez Z Ozora*)

1 corned beef tongue, cooked and skinned (see Index)	bination of both, ground twice
	1 roll, moistened with milk
2 lbs. veal or lean pork, or com-	5 dried anchovies, soaked over-

night in water and chopped fine
2 egg yolks
2 tbs. chopped fresh parsley
2 tbs. sour cream

salt and pepper to taste
dash of nutmeg
butter for cloth
vegetable stock for cooking

In a large bowl mix thoroughly the ground meat, roll, chopped anchovies, egg yolks, parsley, and sour cream. Season to taste. Spread on a piece of well-buttered white cloth and wrap around the tongue. Secure tightly with string, making sure to tie both ends. Immerse in boiling vegetable stock and cook for an hour and a half, leaving to cool in the liquid. Drain, press down with a weighted board, and store overnight. Slice thin, and serve with same sauce used for Mock Salmon (No. 4). Serves 8.

6. CALF'S BRAIN MAYONNAISE
(Majonez z Mózgów Cielęcych)

3 sets of calf brains
¼ lb. sweetbreads
6 med. mushrooms
2 tbs. vinegar
1 onion
1 bay leaf
6 peppercorns

2 cloves
water to cover
salt to taste
3 tbs. gelatin (3 envelopes)
6 scant cups bouillon
1 cup mayonnaise
1½ tsp. dry mustard

Immerse brains, sweetbreads, and mushrooms in boiling salted water to which vinegar, onion, and the spices have been added. Simmer 10 minutes after water boils again. Allow to cool; then strain, reserving liquid. Remove membranes from brains and sweetbreads, and cut meat into small slices. Dissolve gelatin in a little cold water and add to reserved liquid. Add meat, pour into mold, and chill. Unmold just before serving. Serve with mayonnaise to which a little dry mustard has been added, or with Tartare Sauce (see Index). Serves 6 to 8.

Aspics

The basis of a good aspic is the jelly with which it is made. Prepared jellied consommé, or bouillon made with bouillon cubes and gelatin, serves the modern cook nicely and is a good timesaving device. But homemade jellied soup and meat drippings, as well as fish stock, add an extra taste fillip. When these are available, they should be thickened with gelatin for use in aspics, the proportion of gelatin being about one-half of what is ordinarily necessary when starting from scratch. If, on the other hand, the stock is completely liquid, the proportions are approximately 1 envelope of gelatin to 2 cups of liquid, including the cold water used to dissolve the gelatin powder at the start. Homemade soups should be strained through cheesecloth before using for aspic.

Calves' foot jelly, the old stand-by for aspics, is easy to prepare and well worth the trouble. It can be made in quantity and stored in a couple of square molds in the refrigerator. To vary the color without introducing much extra taste, a little saffron, caramelized sugar, or beet juice may be used.

7. CALVES' FOOT JELLY *(Galareta)*

4 calves' feet, scalded	1 bay leaf
2–3 onions	1 bunch parsley
4 carrots	salt
1 leek	1 cup white wine
1 celery root	juice ½ lemon
2 celery stalks	2 egg whites and egg shells
1 parsley root	1 tbs. gelatin to 4 cups liquid
10 peppercorns	

Clean and scald calves' feet. If other calf bones are available, have butcher split them and use in addition to the feet. Peel and slice onions and vegetables. Add these and the spices and salt to the meat and bones, and cover with water. Simmer until meat separates easily from the bone, 1½ to 2 hours. Strain. Add wine and lemon juice to taste; add egg whites beaten with a little cold water, and egg shells. Bring to a boil, take off the heat, and let stand a half-hour. Strain carefully through cheesecloth. Add dissolved gelatin powder, pour into molds, and chill. The meat may be used in any recipe for boiled or leftover veal; or both meat and vegetables may be cut in small pieces and returned to gelatin to make headcheese. Thin slices of lemon may also be added.

8. PULLET OR CAPON ASPIC
(Pularda lub Kapłon w Auszpiku)

1 capon or 2 pullets	1 parsley root
salt	1 celery root
juice of 1 lemon	2 stalks celery
2 onions	few sprigs parsley
3 carrots	6 peppercorns
1 leek	salt

Wash and dry the capon, rub with salt inside and out, and sprinkle with lemon juice. Let stand 2 hours. Add all the giblets from the bird and place in enough salted *boiling* water to cover, together with vegetables and spices. Reduce to a simmer when the water begins to boil again. Cook until meat separates easily from the bones, about 1½ hours. Drain, reserving liquid and carrot. Skin, bone, and cut into small pieces.

Gelatin:

3 cups broth in which capon was cooked
1 cup white wine
2 egg whites and shells

lemon juice to taste
½ tsp. Maggi extract
2 tbs. (2 envelopes) gelatin to 4 cups liquid

Strain soup stock, add white wine, beaten egg whites and shells, lemon to taste, and Maggi extract. Bring to a boil and let stand half an hour. Strain, and then add dissolved gelatin and pour over chicken in individual molds, lined as follows:

slices of lemon
slices of hard-cooked egg
slices of gherkin

slices of marinated mushrooms
slices of cooked carrot (from broth)

Arrange lemon and egg slices, augmented with any of the other ingredients, according to taste, in bottom and on sides of molds. Follow with pieces of chicken, using best pieces for the top. Pour in liquid, filling molds full. Chill. Unmold just before serving and garnish with lemon slices and parsley sprigs. Serve with oil and vinegar or with Tartare Sauce (see Index). Serves 8.

9. FISH ASPIC (Galareta z Ryby)

1 whole pike, perch, or carp (3–4 lbs.)
broth to cover, made according to recipe for Capon Aspic (No. 8)

2 egg whites and egg shells
juice of ½ lemon
1 whole lemon, peeled and sliced
2 hard-cooked eggs, sliced
salt and pepper

Cook the broth until vegetables are tender. Have the fish cleaned and split, and the head cut off. Simmer very slowly in broth until fish is done (about 20 minutes). Remove from broth and drain Continue cooking fish head until broth thickens. Then add slightly. beaten egg whites, shells, and lemon juice. Boil up once and let cool for half an hour. Strain through cheesecloth, reserving carrot. Line mold with slices of hard-cooked egg, peeled lemon, and carrot from the broth. Arrange the fish on top of these, fill mold with broth, and chill. If there is any leftover broth, this may be colored with saffron or beet juice, chilled separately, and used for garnish.

Garnish:

salad leaves
2–3 hard-cooked eggs, sliced or quartered

6 cooked crayfish (shrimp or scampies)
1 truffle, sliced

Unmold the aspic on a bed of salad leaves, garnish, and serve with Tartare Sauce or with oil and vinegar. Serves 6 to 8.

10. SUCKLING PIG IN ASPIC *(Auszpik z Prosięcia)*

1 whole suckling pig, including liver and lungs (about 12 lbs.)	2 eggs dash of nutmeg
1 lb. boneless pork	salt and pepper to taste
1 roll, moistened with milk	vegetable stock to cover (see
¼ lb. salt pork or bacon	Capon Aspic, No. 8)
1 med. or ½ large onion, grated and browned, in ½ tbs. butter	

Put pork, the liver and lungs from the pig, and the roll through a meat grinder. Add diced salt pork, the whole eggs, onion, nutmeg, and seasoning, and mix well. Stuff the pig, sew up or secure with toothpicks, wrap tightly in cheesecloth, and simmer for at least 2½ hours, counting from the time when stock begins to boil again. Drain and let cool. Continue boiling the stock until it is reduced to no more than 2½ quarts. Slice the pig, and arrange in molds lined with the following:

6 hard-cooked eggs, sliced	sliced vegetables from the broth
2 lemons, peeled and sliced	

Strain the broth, and then add:

1 glass white wine	juice ½ lemon
2 egg whites and egg shells	

Let boil up once, allow to settle, and strain again. Fill the molds and chill. Unmold and serve with green salad and olive oil and vinegar, or with Tartare Sauce (see Index). Serves 12 to 16. (May be refrigerated and served on several different nights.)

11. GOOSE OR CALF'S LIVER ASPIC
(Auszpik z Gęsich lub Cielęcych Wątróbek)

1 whole calf's liver, about 2 lbs., or equivalent in goose livers milk to cover	12 cooked crayfish tails (or shrimp or scampies) butter for cooking
1 truffle, cut in thin strips	calves' foot jelly to cover
½ cup soup stock	(canned jellied consommé
½ lb. smoked beef tongue, sliced	may be substituted)
2–3 hard-cooked eggs	
1 whole lemon, peeled and sliced	

Soak the liver in milk for 24 hours. Skin and remove veins. Lard with strips of truffle, salt slightly, wrap in heavily-buttered paper, and simmer tightly covered for about 20 minutes, basting with soup stock to keep from browning. Allow liver to cool, remove from paper, and slice. Cut the tongue in thin slices. Line a mold with the lemon and egg slices and the crayfish. Arrange alternate layers of liver and tongue, and fill the mold with liquid calves' foot jelly. Chill, unmold on a bed of green salad leaves, and serve with Tartare Sauce (see Index) or with vinegar and oil. Serves 6.

Note: Slices of cold pâté may be substituted for tongue.

12. LIVER AND CALF'S BRAIN ASPIC
(*Auszpik z Wątróbek i Mózgów Cielęcych*)

1 calf's liver	other ingredients as in Goose
2 sets calf brains, parboiled in court bouillon (see Index)	Liver Aspic (No. 11)

Prepare the same as Goose Liver Aspic, substituting calf's brain for the tongue. Serves 8 to 10.

13. DUCK IN ASPIC (*Auszpik z Kaczek*)

2 ducks, cleaned and salted 2 hours ahead of time	10 allspice
	1 clove garlic
2–3 onions	small piece fresh ginger root
1 leek	3–4 dried mushrooms
3–4 carrots	½ tbs. butter
1 celery root	Calves' Foot Jelly to cover
3 celery stalks	(see Index) or equivalent in
1 parsley root	canned consommé
10 peppercorns	

Simmer ducks, giblets, and livers together with vegetables, spices, and butter in a tightly-covered pan in just enough water so that the ducks cook in steam (about half-covered) for 2 to 3 hours. Allow to cool. Cut meat in small pieces, remove large bones, and cut livers and gizzards into thin slices. Arrange in molds and fill with liquid calves' foot jelly, or with canned consommé to which has been added the strained broth in which the ducks were cooked. If broth seems thin, reduce by cooking down. Chill, unmold, and garnish with lemon slices and hard-cooked eggs, sliced or quartered. Serve with oil and vinegar or any sharp sauce. Serves 10. (Recipe may easily be halved for ordinary household purposes.)

14. TURKEY OR CAPON GALANTINE
(*Galantyna z Indyka lub Kapłona*)

1 small turkey or capon (5–6 lbs.) with liver and giblets	2 eggs
salt	salt and pepper to taste
juice ½ lemon	dash of nutmeg
½ lb. boneless veal	3–4 hard-cooked eggs, sliced or
½ lb. salt pork or bacon	quartered
1 white roll or ½ cup bread crumbs, soaked in milk	1 truffle, thinly sliced

Have the butcher split the bird along the back only. Rinse turkey, rub with salt inside and out, sprinkle with lemon juice, and let stand 2 hours. Cut off wings. Carefully remove the skin without tearing. Remove the bones. Cut the meat into small slices and spread flat on the skin. Spread with the following stuffing: Grind the veal, turkey liver (½ lb. calf's liver may be substituted), and half the salt pork twice. Add the moistened roll, the slightly-beaten eggs, salt and pepper, and a dash of nutmeg. Mix thoroughly. Spread about an inch thick over the meat. Spread the rest of the salt pork, thinly sliced, the eggs, and truffle slices. Cover with a second layer of stuffing. Fold over edges of skin, roll tightly, and tie securely with cotton. Roll in a piece of white cloth, tie tightly, and cook for 2 hours, covered, in a broth made as follows:

turkey carcass, wings, feet, giblets	3 carrots
2 onions	1 leek
1 parsley root	1 bay leaf (optional)
1 celery root	10 peppercorns
2–3 stalks celery	6 juniper berries (optional)
few sprigs parsley	salt and pepper to taste
	water to cover

Let the galantine cool in the stock. Remove from the cloth, rewrap in another piece of dry cloth, tie again, and cover with a flat board weighted down enough to flatten the galantine. Chill, slice, arrange on a bed of salad leaves and garnish with bits of colored jelly (see Index). Serve with a sharp, cold sauce.

15. PARTRIDGE OR WOOD-HEN GALANTINE
(Galantyna z Kuropatw lub Jarząbków)

6 partridges

Stuffing:	*Ingredients for Simmering:*
½ lb. boneless veal	1 large onion, minced
¼ lb. calf's liver	2–3 carrots, cut fine
partridge livers	1 celery root
¼ lb. salt pork	1 parsley root
2 eggs, separated	1 leek
1 tbs. butter	½ cup strong bouillon
1 white roll or ½ cup bread crumbs, moistened with milk salt and pepper to taste dash of nutmeg	1 tbs. butter

Carefully clean and salt the birds. Stuff, beginning at neck, with filling made as follows: Grind veal, livers, and salt pork together twice. Add slightly-beaten egg yolks creamed with 1 tbs. butter. Then add the roll or bread crumbs, salt, pepper, and nutmeg to taste, and mix thoroughly. Beat egg whites until stiff and fold in. Stuff the birds, pulling the skin carefully away from the breast.

Sew up with cotton thread. Place the birds to cook in a heavy casserole, together with ingredients for simmering. Cover and simmer for 1 hour. Allow to cool in the liquid. Drain.

Galantine liquid:

stock in which birds cooked
1 glass red or white wine, according to preference
dash of lemon juice
1 tbs. gelatin dissolved in a little

cold water, for each quart of liquid
calves' foot jelly or jellied consommé to cover
2 egg whites and egg shells

Add wine, lemon juice, and jelly to broth in which birds have cooked. The final proportion should be 1 cup liquid to 1½ cups solid meat. Let boil up once, strain, add egg whites, shells, and gelatin. Split the birds carefully. Arrange in molds garnished with:

2 lemons, peeled and sliced
1 truffle, sliced into thin strips
3–4 gherkins, sliced

2 dozen cooked crayfish tails
(shrimp or scampies)

Strain liquid again; pour in molds and chill. Unmold and serve on a bed of lettuce with oil and vinegar or with any cold sharp sauce.

Note: To estimate portions, allow one small bird or half a larger bird per person. This recipe may be used for any game birds, such as quail, grouse, young pheasant, and pigeon squabs. It will also serve for Rock Cornish hens.

16. MOUSSE OF HARE *(Muss z Zajǫca)*

1 hare or 2 rabbits
½ lb. salt pork or bacon
2 onions
4 carrots
1 celery root
1 parsley root
1 leek
2–3 dried mushrooms (optional)
1 bay leaf (optional)
2–3 cloves
10 juniper berries

10 peppercorns
pinch of thyme and marjoram
1 jigger brandy
1 cup sweet cream, beaten stiff
1 tbs. pistachio nuts, chopped fine
2 tbs. gelatin dissolved in ¼ cup aspic jelly (see beginning of section)
½ lb. cooked tongue or ham, diced
1 cup aspic jelly for spreading

Have butcher clean and cut up the hare. Do not marinate. Simmer, covered with onions, vegetables, and spices in enough water to half-cover, until quite soft but not falling apart (about 1 hour). Remove all meat from bones, and put through meat grinder twice, together with broth in which the meat cooked. (Be sure to remove spices but not vegetables.) Press the mixture through a sieve or whirl in a blender. When cool, add brandy and beat with a whisk in an iced bowl, adding beaten cream toward the end. Continue beating, adding nuts and the gelatin dissolved in liquid aspic. When stiff and fluffy, fold in diced tongue or ham. Spread mold with a little cool aspic. Cover with:

slices of lemon	small marinated or fresh-cooked
strips of tongue	mushrooms

Pour in meat mixture, and chill thoroughly. Unmold and serve with Tartare Sauce (see Index) or any other sharp sauce. Serves 7 to 8.

Salads

Except where marinating is indicated, salad should never be dressed until directly before the meal. This insures freshness. Green salad may be served in various combinations: romaine, lettuce, endive, escarole, chickory, field salad, bib lettuce, watercress—whatever is available. Other additions are cucumbers, tomatoes, raw cauliflower, radishes, carrot, fresh dill, parsley, and many more.

1. SALAD WITH POLISH SOUR CREAM DRESSING
(Sałata po Polsku ze Śmietaną)

> green salad in any combina-
> tion desired—enough for 6
> portions
> 2–3 hard-cooked eggs
> 1 cup sour cream
>
> ⅛ tsp. sugar (optional)
> lemon juice or white vinegar
> to taste
> salt and pepper to taste

Cream 2 egg yolks with sour cream. Add sugar, lemon juice, salt, and pepper to taste and stir thoroughly. Add to salad and toss. Chop remaining egg whites and use for garnish, together with the third egg, cut into thin slices. Omit sugar if desired. Serves 6.

2. SALAD IN OIL DRESSING *(Sałata z Oliwą)*

> green salad, according to prefer-
> ence—enough for 6 portions
> 2 hard-cooked eggs
>
> ¼ cup olive oil
> lemon juice to taste
> salt and pepper

Pour olive oil and lemon juice over salad, season, toss, and garnish with hard-cooked egg slices.

3. SAUERKRAUT SALAD *(Sałata z Kiszonej Kapusty)*

> 1 lb. sauerkraut
> 3–4 tbs. olive oil
> salt and pepper to taste
> 1 tsp. sugar
>
> lemon juice to taste (optional)
> 1 apple, cored, pared, and
> shredded

Mix all the ingredients together, adding sufficient sugar and lemon juice to give sauerkraut a sweet-and-sour taste. Serve chilled. Serves 4 to 6.

4. RED CABBAGE SALAD *(Sałata z Czerwonej Kapusty)*

1 med. head red cabbage, shredded	salt and pepper to taste
salted, boiling water	sugar to taste
juice of 1 lemon	olive oil

Throw shredded cabbage into boiling water. As soon as the water boils again, drain and allow cabbage to dry off. Sprinkle with lemon juice to restore bright red color. Chill. An hour before serving, season with salt and pepper. Add sugar to taste and several tablespoons of olive oil, depending on one's preference. Serves 6.

5. CUCUMBER SALAD *(Sałata Mizerja)*

2–3 large cucumbers	olive oil and vinegar to taste
salt and pepper	1 tbs. dill (optional)

Peel cucumbers and slice very thin. Salt down generously and let stand half an hour. Drain off liquid, press down with weight, and drain again. Season with a little pepper, and add olive oil and vinegar in the proportion of 2 parts oil to 1 of vinegar. Fresh dill is an excellent addition to cucumber salad. Serves 4 to 6.

6. CUCUMBER AND SOUR CREAM SALAD
(Mizerja ze Śmietaną)

Prepare cucumbers as in No. 5. Instead of olive oil and vinegar, add

1 cup sour cream	2 tbs. vinegar

Mix thoroughly. Do not omit the dill. Serves 6.

7. CELERY ROOT SALAD *(Sałata z Selerów)*

3–4 celery roots	1 tbs. chopped fresh dill
salted, boiling water to cover	olive oil and vinegar (prefer-
salt and pepper to taste	ably wine vinegar) to taste
½ med. onion, minced, *or* 1 tbs. chopped chives	

Pare or scrape celery roots, cook in boiling water until tender, drain, and cool in cold water. Slice thin, season with salt and pepper, and mix with chopped chives or minced onion and fresh dill. Add 3 to 4 tbs. olive oil and 2 to 3 tbs. vinegar. Serves 3 to 4.

8. CELERY ROOT AND POTATO SALAD
(Sałata z Selerów z Kartoflami)

2 celery roots   other ingredients as in No. 7
2 med. potatoes

Cook potatoes along with the celery roots until done, but not so soft
that they will not fall apart in slicing. Prepare salad the same as
No. 7. Serves 3 to 4.

9. RAW CELERY ROOT SALAD
(Sałata z Surowych Selerów)

2–3 young celery roots   ¼ cup olive oil
2–3 apples   2–3 tbs. wine vinegar
    salt and pepper to taste

Carefully peel and shred celery roots. Pare, core, and shred apples.
Season with salt and pepper, add olive oil and vinegar, and mix
thoroughly. Let stand in refrigerator for 3 to 4 hours before serving.
Serves 4.

10. CELERY ROOT SALAD WITH MUSTARD DRESSING
(Sałata z Selerów z Musztardą)

Prepare the same as No. 9, but add 2 tsp. French mustard. Garnish
with small marinated mushrooms and gherkins.

11. TOMATO SALAD (Sałata z Pomidorów)

4 med. tomatoes   parsley, or either herb sepa-
    salt and pepper to taste   rately
½ med. onion, blanched and   4 tbs. olive oil
    minced   lemon juice or vinegar (pref-
1–2 tbs. chopped fresh dill and   erably wine vinegar) to taste

Slice tomatoes, season, and sprinkle with minced onion and fresh
herbs. Add olive oil and lemon juice or vinegar—the proportion
should be considerably more oil than lemon juice, not the usual
French dressing. Allow to refrigerate for 1 to 2 hours. Serves 4 to 5.

12. POTATO SALAD (Sałata z Kartofli)

I.

6 med. potatoes   ¼ cup olive oil
    salt and pepper to taste   3 tbs. vinegar
½ med. onion, minced, or equiva-
    lent amount chopped chives

Potatoes for salad should be cooked in their jackets, peeled, and allowed to cool. Avoid Idahos and other mealy potatoes—new potatoes are excellent. Slice thin, season, add minced onion or chives and olive oil and vinegar. Mix and refrigerate for 1 hour. Serves 6.

II.

Prepare potatoes as in *I*.

Dressing:

2–3 hard-cooked egg yolks
¼ cup olive oil
salt and pepper to taste
¼ cup white wine

lemon juice to taste
1 heaping tbs. chopped chives
or chopped dill and parsley

Cream egg yolks and olive oil, season, add wine and lemon juice to taste. Mix with potatoes. Sprinkle with chopped chives or herbs. Refrigerate until cold. Serves 6.

13. POTATO, APPLE, AND CAPER SALAD
(Sałata z Kartofli z Jabłkami i Kaparami)

6 med. potatoes, cooked in salted water in jackets
2 med. apples
1 heaping tbs. capers

¼ cup olive oil
¼ cup dry white wine
lemon juice to taste
salt and pepper

Peel potatoes and allow to cool. Core and peel apples. Slice potatoes and apples very thin, mix with capers, olive oil, wine, and lemon juice to taste. Season with salt and pepper. Refrigerate 1 hour. Serves 6 to 7.

14. POTATO SALAD WITH HERRING OR ANCHOVIES
(Sałata z Kartofli ze Śledziem lub z Sardelami)

6 med. potatoes, cooked in salted water in jackets
1 matjes herring or 6 anchovy fillets
½ med. onion, blanched and chopped fine

1 heaping tsp. each of chopped chives, dill, and parsley
¼ cup olive oil
3 tbs. vinegar
pepper

Peel potatoes and slice thin. Chop herring. Mix with other ingredients, then add olive oil and vinegar and a little pepper. Mix thoroughly and refrigerate for about an hour. Salad will probably not need salt, since herring or anchovies are salty in themselves. Serves 6.

15. HERRING SALAD *(Sałata ze Śledzi)*

2 large matjes herring
2-3 med. potatoes, cooked in
    jackets and peeled
2 apples, peeled and cored
6 marinated mushrooms or a few
    gherkins (optional)

½ med. onion, minced
    salt and pepper to taste
¼ cup olive oil
3 tbs. wine vinegar
    lettuce leaves for garnish

Clean and bone herring and chop coarsely. Dice potatoes and
apples. Add marinated mushrooms or gherkins if available. Add
minced onion, season to taste, and add olive oil and vinegar. Mix
thoroughly, arrange on a bed of lettuce, and refrigerate about 2
hours. Serves 6 to 8 as a side dish.

16. BLACK RADISH SALAD *(Sałata z Rzodkwi)*

3-4 large black radishes (white
    may be substituted)
¼ cup sour cream

lemon juice to taste
salt and pepper to taste

Peel radishes and grate coarsely. Mix with sour cream, and add
lemon juice and seasoning to taste. Serve with cold meats as one
would horseradish.

17. MIXED WINTER SALAD *(Sałata Zimowa Mięszana)*

Prepare each vegetable separately:

1 cup cooked snap beans, mari-
    nated in oil and vinegar, sea-
    soned to taste, with a little
    minced onion added

1 cup cooked brown or black-
    eyed or red kidney beans, cooked
    until tender, marinated in oil and
    vinegar with the addition of 1
    tsp. French mustard

1 cup red cabbage salad (see No.
    4)

2 cups potato and celery root salad
    (see No. 8)

½ cup marinated mushrooms
    (see Index)

Arrange the vegetables separately on a bed of green lettuce leaves,
garnish with sections of hard-cooked egg if desired, chill, and serve.
Any other cold vegetables may be used similarly—cauliflower,
asparagus, peas, beets, etc. Allow about 1 cup of ingredients per
serving.

18. DIPLOMAT SALAD *(Sałata "Diplomate")*

2-3 tomatoes, peeled and diced
2-3 slices fresh or canned pine-
    apple, cut in pieces
1 large or 2 small bananas, sliced

1 large or 2 small apples, cored,
    pared, and diced
3 medium potatoes, cooked in
    jackets, peeled, and sliced thin

2 truffles, cut in thin strips
1 cup mayonnaise (preferably homemade)
¼ cup Rhine wine

Worcestershire sauce to taste (1 tsp. or less)
dash of cayenne pepper

Combine fruits, potatoes, and truffles. Dilute mayonnaise with wine (add according to taste), season with Worcestershire sauce and cayenne pepper, and add to mixture. Toss lightly and refrigerate for 3 to 4 hours. Serves 6.

19. RUSSIAN SALAD *(Sałata Rosyjska)*

½ cup each of cooked, marinated snap beans, kidney, or black-eyed beans; peas, beets, carrots, celery root, potatoes, cauliflower, and red cabbage (or any substitutions desired)
2 truffles, cooked and diced
1 small can lobster, crabmeat, or shrimp
4–6 anchovies, cut in small pieces
1 slice cooked salmon

1 heaping tbs. capers
12 green and 12 black olives
1 cup cooked, diced venison or poultry
salt and pepper to taste
olive oil and vinegar to taste
green lettuce leaves for garnish
¼ lb. red or black caviar
mayonnaise

Combine vegetables, truffles, fish, capers, olives, and meat. Season and sprinkle with oil and vinegar to taste. Place in large salad bowl on a bed of lettuce leaves. In the center arrange the caviar. Refrigerate for a couple of hours. Serve mayonnaise separately. Serves 8 generously.

20. JAPANESE SALAD *(Sałata Japónska)*

4 med. potatoes, cooked in jackets, peeled, and diced
10 mussels or steamer clams, cooked and diced (canned may be used)
1 tsp. each chopped parsley, dill, chives, and tarragon
olive oil to taste (about ¼ cup)

¼ cup white wine
lemon juice to taste
salt and pepper to taste
lettuce leaves
2 hard-cooked eggs, quartered
1–2 cooked truffles, cut in thin strips

Combine potatoes, clams, and herbs with olive oil, wine, and lemon juice. Season to taste. Toss, arrange on a bed of lettuce leaves, and garnish top with strips of truffle and hard-cooked egg sections. Refrigerate about 2 hours. Serves 6.

21. MAYONNAISE SALAD OR ASPIC
(Sałata Majonezowa w Auszpiku)

6 cups Russian Salad or Mixed Winter Salad (see Index), or any variation of cooked vegetables

Or

a combination of carrot, celery root, kohlrabi, beets, potatoes, peas, and 2 apples, cored, pared and diced

2–3 tbs. marinated mushrooms
2–3 cooked fresh mushrooms, sliced
salt and pepper to taste
2 cups mayonnaise
lettuce leaves
2 hard-cooked eggs, sliced
3–4 gherkins, sliced

Combine all the ingredients except eggs and gherkins. Season and mix thoroughly with mayonnaise. Arrange in salad bowl on a bed of lettuce, garnish with egg slices and gherkins, and chill. This salad may also be served on a bed of jellied bouillon or Tomato Aspic (see Index). Serves 6 generously.

Egg Dishes

1. EGGS *AU BEURRE NOIR* (*Jaja au Beurre Noir*)

Prepare Sauce *au Beurre Noir* (see Index). Melt butter in proportion of 1 tsp. per egg, but do not brown. Pan-fry eggs until the whites are just beyond runny stage. Garnish generously with sauce.

2. EGGS CODDLED IN SOUR CREAM
(*Jaja Sadzone na Śmietanie*)

6 eggs	1 cup sour cream
1 tbs. butter	salt and pepper to taste
1 tsp. (scant) flour	

Melt but do not brown the butter. Blend in flour, then add sour cream, and stir until smooth. When mixture is hot and bubbly, carefully drop eggs into it, cover and allow to steam until whites are done. Serves 3 generously as a luncheon dish.

Note: This may be varied by the addition of a little chopped dill or caraway seed sprinkled over the eggs directly before serving. Another variation is to sprinkle with Parmesan cheese.

3. CODDLED EGGS IN BOUILLON
(*Jaja Sadzone na Buljonie*)

1 cup soup stock	6 eggs, coddled or poached
1 bouillon cube	salt and pepper
½ tsp. potato flour	chopped parsley for garnish
1 tbs. butter	

Dissolve bouillon cube in soup stock and simmer while preparing eggs. Poach, coddle or fry eggs until the whites are just done but not crisp. Dissolve potato flour in butter, stirring until smooth, and blend with bouillon. Allow to bubble up. Pour sauce into a platter, arrange eggs carefully on top, and sprinkle with chopped parsley. Season to taste. Allow 1 or 2 eggs per person.

4. EGGS VENICE-STYLE (*Jaja po Wenecku*)

Prepare the same as No. 3. Then serve each egg on a slice of Liver Pâté. (Original recipe calls for Strasbourg Pâté.)

5. FRIED EGGS IN TRUFFLE OR MADEIRA SAUCE
(*Jaja Sadzone z Sosem Maderowym lub Truflowym*)

6 eggs, fried in butter until just done   1 cup Truffle (or Mushroom or Madeira) Sauce (see Index)

Allow sauce to simmer so that it will be quite thick. Serve eggs directly on hot plates or on toast, and pour sauce over them. Serve at once. Allow 2 eggs per portion as a luncheon dish.

6. FRIED OR CODDLED EGG WITH TOMATO SAUCE OR ANCHOVIES
(*Jaja na Pomidorach lub z Sardelami*)

6 eggs, fried lightly in butter, poached, or coddled   1 cup thick Tomato Sauce (see Index) *or* 6 anchovy fillets

Prepare eggs according to personal preference. Serve on a bed of Tomato Sauce. If anchovy fillets are used instead, cut each fillet in half lengthwise, arrange crisscross over eggs, and serve on toast. Serves 3 to 6.

7. BAKED EGGS ON TOAST (*Jaja na Grzankach*)

6 eggs
6 very thin slices of white bread
   butter for frying

2–3 tbs. Parmesan cheese or chopped chives
salt and pepper to taste

Slice bread very thin, scooping slightly in center. Fry in butter, or toast, butter, and dry out in oven. Sprinkle each piece with Parmesan or with chopped chives. Carefully drop an egg on each piece, season with salt and pepper, and bake in 400° oven for 5 minutes, or until whites are just done and not runny. Allow 1 or 2 eggs per person.

8. EGGS WITH SORREL SAUCE
(*Jaja z Sosem Szczawiowym*)

1½ cups thick Sorrel Sauce (see Index)
6 eggs, cooked until either semi-

hard or quite hard, depending on preference

Peel eggs and cut lengthwise. Arrange over the sorrel sauce. Season to taste, and serve garnished with oblong slices of toast. Serves 3 as luncheon dish.

9. DEVILED EGGS *(Jaja Faszerowane)*

6 hard-cooked eggs, cut length- wise in their shells salt and pepper to taste 1 tbs. chopped chives	3 tbs. butter 2–3 tbs. sour cream bread crumbs

Using a very sharp knife, cut the eggs lengthwise through the shells, taking care not to crush shells. Scoop out eggs, chop fine, and mix with the chopped chives, 1 tbs. of the butter, sour cream, and seasoning. Return mixture to shells, cover with bread crumbs, and fry quickly in remaining butter, open side down. Serve at once as side dish or appetizer. The same deviled egg mixture may also be spooned into scallop shells or small ramekins. In that case, brown the butter and bread crumbs and pour over the eggs. Then place in a hot oven for a few minutes to heat through. Duck or goose eggs are excellent for this dish. Allow 1 egg per person.

10. STUFFED EGGS *(Jaja Nadiewane)*

12 hard-cooked eggs, peeled and cut lengthwise 6 anchovy fillets ½ stale white roll, moistened in milk and mashed salt and pepper to taste 2 tbs. butter	1 cup sour cream, blended with ½ tsp. flour 1 tbs. chopped fresh parsley 1 raw egg bread crumbs ½ tsp. Maggi extract or Kitchen Bouquet

Chop anchovies. Put hard-cooked egg yolks, anchovies, and roll through a sieve, mix thoroughly, and season to taste. Add 1 tbs. butter, 1 tbs. of the sour cream, and the chopped parsley. Beat raw egg slightly, add to mixture, and fry lightly in remaining butter. Spoon mixture into the egg whites—there will be enough of it so that each will have the shape of an egg. Sprinkle with bread crumbs, arrange in shallow pan, and add the remaining sour cream blended with flour, and the Maggi extract. Bake in moderate oven for about 15 minutes. Serves 6 generously.

11. STUFFED EGGS WITH CRAYFISH OR SHRIMP SAUCE *(Jaja Nadziewane z Sosem Rakowym)*

12 hard-cooked eggs 12 cooked crayfish (or shrimp) 1 tsp. chopped dill	1 tsp. chopped parsley 2 tsp. butter salt and pepper to taste

Cut peeled eggs so that they can stand on end and so that the egg yolks can be scooped out without damaging the whites. Chop egg yolks, the tip ends of egg whites, and crayfish. Add dill, parsley, butter, and seasoning, and mix thoroughly. Fill the egg whites.

Arrange in shallow dish which may be brought to the table. Cover with the following sauce:

Sauce:

1–1½ cups Crayfish Sauce (see Index)

1 tbs. chopped dill
bread crumbs

Pour Crayfish Sauce over the eggs, top with chopped dill and bread crumbs, and place in hot oven for 5 minutes. Serves 6.

12. EGGS À LA PAYSANNE (*Jaja à la Paysanne*)

2–3 slices bacon
4 eggs
    salt and pepper to taste
¼ cup croutons (or several

pieces of bread, diced and toasted in oven)
½ cup diced ham
1 tbs. chopped fresh parsley

Cook bacon until crisp. Remove from pan and crumble. Break eggs into the hot bacon fat, season with salt and pepper, sprinkle with croutons, ham, crumbled bacon, and parsley. Bake in hot oven for a few minutes, or until egg whites set. Serves 2 to 4.

13. EGGS À LA PRINCESSE (*Jaja à la Princesse*)

8 soft-boiled eggs (about 3½ minutes)
8 pieces of toast
butter

1½ cups Truffle or White Mushroom Sauce (see Index)
chopped parsley for topping

Cook eggs just enough so they can be shelled without breaking. Dip in cold water so that shells will come off more easily. In the meantime, cut 8 rather thick pieces of white bread, scooping the middle slightly. Toast these, butter, and keep hot in oven. Arrange eggs on pieces of toast, season, and top with sauce and chopped parsley. This makes an elegant luncheon dish. Allow 1 or 2 per person.

14. EGGS AND DUCK ASPIC (*Jaja à la Jockey Club*)

12 5-minute eggs, shelled
1 small duckling, smothered with vegetables and bacon or salt pork (see Smothered Duck in Index)
2–3 duck livers
3 ozs. cognac or other brandy
    cayenne to taste
    salt and pepper to taste
2 cooked or canned truffles, cut in thin strips
    few ounces boiled ham or Canadian bacon, cut in strips

Aspic made with
    2 cups broth
    1 envelope gelatin moistened in ¼ cup water
¼–½ cup Madeira, according to taste
    cayenne pepper
    salt and pepper to taste

Cook extra duck livers with the duck for about 15 minutes. Remove livers and allow duck to simmer until very tender (see Index). Pick all the meat from bones, chop meat and livers fine, add cognac and cayenne and enough broth from the duck to make a smooth mass. Make a mound of this in the center of round platter. With a spoon make indentations and arrange eggs in these in a pattern, standing up. Garnish each egg with truffle and boiled ham strips. Dissolve gelatin in broth, add Madeira and seasoning to taste, and pour over the eggs. Chill for several hours. Serve garnished with salad greens. Excellent for a buffet supper.

15. EGYPTIAN EGG CASSEROLE *(Jajka po Egipsku)*

1 cup rice, cooked oriental style (see *Note* in No. 23, Flour and Cereal Dishes)	1 cup white sauce
	1 raw egg yolk
	1 tsp. dry mustard
8–12 mushrooms, chopped and smothered in butter until transparent	few tbs. sweet cream
	cayenne to taste
	salt and pepper to taste
8 eggs, poached or coddled	grated Parmesan

Combined rice, mushrooms, and a little seasoning. Line a buttered baking dish with the mixture, arrange poached eggs over the rice, and top with sauce made as follows: Combine white sauce, slightly beaten egg yolk, dry mustard, cream, and seasoning, and mix thoroughly. Sprinkle with grated Parmesan and bake in 400° oven until cheese begins to brown, 15 to 20 minutes. Serves 4.

16. EGG RAMEKINS WITH ANCHOVIES *(Tębaliki z Jaja)*

8 eggs	½ cup strong bouillon
8 anchovies, sprinkled with olive oil	sliced tomato or smoked salmon
butter or olive oil for rubbing ramekins	slices of toast (optional)

Grease each ramekin with olive oil or butter. Cut anchovies lengthwise and arrange one, crisscross, on the bottom of each dish. Carefully break a raw egg over each anchovy. Place ramekins in a shallow dish of boiling water, taking care not to let water overflow into eggs. Bake in 400° oven or steam, covered, on top of stove until egg whites are done and yolks still soft. Unmold on hot plates or onto pieces of toast. Sprinkle with bouillon and garnish each egg with a tomato slice or piece of smoked salmon. Serves 4 generously.

17. SCRAMBLED EGGS *(Jajecznica)*

There are many variations of this stand-by dish, and recipes for a few of them follow. The basic recipe for scrambled eggs, however, bears repeating: Allow 2 medium eggs per serving. Beat lightly, season, and add 1 tbs. milk or cream. Many people prefer to add water to eggs because this makes them especially light. Heat butter in skillet but do not brown (about 1 tbs. per portion). Do not have skillet so hot that it sizzles. Pour eggs in gently and stir constantly, from the edges and underneath, so that eggs will not stick. Do not cook until dry—eggs will continue hardening for a moment after the heat has been turned off. If eggs are cooked covered, they will rise but will have the consistency of an omelet.

18. SCRAMBLED EGGS WITH CHIVES
(Jajecznica ze Szczypiorkiem)

Follow directions in No. 17, adding 1 heaping tbs. chopped chives for 6 eggs.

19. SCRAMBLED EGGS WITH HAM, SAUSAGE OR BACON *(Jajecznica ze Szynką, Kiełbasą lub Słoniną)*

Follow directions in No. 17, adding ½ cup diced ham, sausage, or cooked and crumbled bacon to eggs before cooking.

20. SCRAMBLED EGGS WITH ANCHOVIES, HERRING, OR SMOKED SALMON
(Jajecznica z Sardelami, Śledziem lub Łososiem)

Follow directions in No. 17. Add 1 chopped matjes herring, 4 anchovies, or a couple of slices of smoked salmon cut into small pieces, to the eggs before cooking.

21. SCRAMBLED EGGS WITH MUSHROOMS
(Jajacznica z Pieczarkami)

Follow directions in No. 17. Add 6 to 8 mushrooms, chopped and smothered with ¼ cup chopped onion.

22. OMELET *AU NATUREL (Omlet Naturalny)*

For best results, use no more than 5 to 6 eggs. If larger quantities are desired, make two small omelets. Add 2 to 3 tbs. of milk or sweet cream. Season and beat with whisk or rotary egg beater—do not beat to a froth. Use a large, heavy skillet or griddle, and just enough butter to grease surface. Pour egg mixture into hot skillet.

Do not stir. When eggs begin to set, carefully lift edges of omelet with a knife and allow some of the runny egg to flow under. This will speed up the process. Omelet should be nicely brown underneath and soft and fluffy inside. When done enough to handle, use a spatula to separate it from skillet in case it sticks. Fold over from both sides, so that omelet will be folded in three. Put a plate over the omelet, and then reverse quickly. If a filling is to be used, fill before folding. An omelet made with 5 or 6 eggs and a filling should serve 3.

23. HAM OMELET *(Omlet z Szynką)*

5–6 eggs, seasoned and with 2 tbs. cream added	1 cup finely-cut cooked ham butter for frying

This may be prepared in two ways. Either add ham to eggs before cooking and follow directions in No. 22, or prepare No. 22, fill center with ham, and then fold over as directed. Serves 3.

Note: Polish sausage or any other type of sausage may be substituted for the ham.

24. OMELET WITH MUSHROOM FILLING
(Omlet z Gzybami)

½ med. onion, minced 2 tbs. butter ½ lb. mushrooms, sliced	5–6 eggs beaten with 2–3 tbs. milk or cream salt and pepper to taste

Sauté onion until transparent in 1 tbs. butter. Add mushrooms, cover, and simmer another 5 to 6 minutes or until mushrooms are done. Prepare omelet like No. 22. Arrange mushrooms in center of omelet, carefully fold over in three, reverse onto platter, and serve. Serves 3.

Note: Creamed spinach or stewed tomatoes may be used similarly as a filling.

25. OMELET WITH VEAL KIDNEY
(Omlet z Cynaderkami)

4–5 eggs, beaten with 2 tbs. milk or cream salt and pepper to taste ½ med. onion (or less), minced butter for frying	1 veal kidney, sliced very thin few tbs. bouillon

Sauté onion in a little butter until limp. Add sliced kidney from which excess fat has been removed, and continue frying gently, basting with a little bouillon, for about 5 minutes. Prepare **omelet** the same as No. 22. Fill with the kidney and onion mixture, **fold** over edges, reverse onto platter, and pour remaining **bouillon over** it. Serves 3.

26. OMELET WITH CRAYFISH OR SHRIMP
(Omlet z Rakami)

4–5 eggs, beaten with 2 tbs. milk or cream salt and pepper to taste 12 cooked crayfish or shrimp	2–3 tbs. Crayfish Butter (see Index) 2 tsp. chopped fresh dill

Prepare omelet as in No. 22. Heat crayfish or shrimp in ½ tbs. Crayfish Butter. Fill omelet, fold over edges, reverse onto platter, and sprinkle with chopped dill. Pour remaining Crayfish Butter (hot) over omelet. Serves 2 or 3.

27. SORREL OMELET *(Omlet ze Szczawiem)*

4–5 eggs beaten with 2 tbs. milk or cream salt and pepper	½ tbs. butter salt, pepper, and sugar to taste 1 tsp. flour 2–3 tbs. sweet cream

Filling:
  ½ cup sorrel leaves

Clean sorrel carefully, blanch, chop, and put through sieve. Melt butter in skillet, add sorrel, season to taste, and cook a few minutes until it just begins to brown. Add flour, season to taste, and dilute with sweet cream. Fill the omelet, fold over edges, and serve with drawn butter. Serves 2 or 3.

28. SERBIAN OMELET *(Omlet po Serbsku)*

4 eggs 2–3 potatoes, cooked in jackets, peeled, and mashed salt, pepper, and nutmeg to taste	2 tbs. sour cream 1 tbs. grated Parmesan butter for frying

Mash potatoes first, add all the other ingredients except butter, and mix thoroughly. Divide into two equal parts and fry each in hot butter on both sides until nicely brown, turning carefully once with spatula. For best results use two roomy frying pans. Use any of the following fillings. Fold over once and serve with drawn drawn butter. Serves 2 or 3.

Fillings—see Index for Omelet with Smothered Veal Kidney or with Smothered Mushrooms.

29. EGG SOUFFLÉ *(Suflet z Jaj Zapiekany)*

5 soft rolls, diced
1 cup heavy cream
15 hard-cooked egg yolks
  salt and pepper to taste
4 whole hard-cooked eggs

3 egg whites
2 tbs. White Lemon Sauce (see
  Index)
4 tbs. melted butter
  grated Parmesan

Combine diced rolls and cream, bring to a boil, and set aside. Mash hard-cooked egg yolks. Add to bread and cream mixture, season, mix thoroughly, and put through a sieve. Arrange in mound in a buttered shallow baking dish, garnish all around with quartered hard-cooked eggs, and cover the whole thing with the stiffly-beaten egg whites, to which 2 tbs. of hot White Lemon Sauce have been added. (This must be done quickly or egg whites will fall.) Sprinkle lightly with Parmesan, then with remaining melted butter, and bake in 400° oven until brown on top, about 15 minutes or less. Serves 6 to 7.

Flour and Cereal Dishes

All noodles, macaroni, and dough pockets that require boiling should be cooked directly before serving. They should be started in furiously boiling, salted water. Never allow them to stand in water; they become soggy. If it is absolutely necessary to reheat them, throw them into boiling salted water for a moment or two when ready to use. In most recipes calling for various kinds of noodles, lasagne, and macaroni, many people will prefer to use a commercially-prepared brand, of which a great many varieties are available, especially in Italian and Jewish groceries. A few basic recipes are given here for those who prefer to experiment with homemade noodles.

1. NOODLES *(Kluski)*

2¼ cups sifted flour
2 eggs, lightly beaten

2–3 tbs. water
¼ tsp. salt

Add eggs and salt to flour and work on a pastry board, adding a little lukewarm water to make elastic dough. Add more flour if necessary. Work until little bubbles begin to form in dough. Divide in two, roll out very thin on floured board, and sprinkle with a little flour to help dry. Let stand a few minutes; then roll up as for jelly roll and cut into strips. Cook in salted boiling water 5 to 10 minutes, according to thickness. Drain and serve at once. Makes about 8 ozs. Serves 6.

2. NOODLES WITH CHEESE *(Kluski Krajane ze Serem)*

Recipe No. 1 for noodles, or
8-oz. package broad noodles
1 lb. farmer cheese, mashed
(more if desired)

3–4 strips bacon, fried until crisp
and then crumbled
hot bacon fat or drawn butter
for garnish

Cook noodles according to directions. Combine with cheese and garnish with crumbled bacon and bacon fat or butter. Serves 6.

248

3. BAKED NOODLES WITH CHEESE *(Kluski Wypiekane)*

Recipe No. 1 for noodles, or	butter and bread crumbs
8-oz. package broad noodles	1 cup sour cream
12-oz. container farmer or	2–3 egg yolks
cottage cheese	salt and pepper to taste

Prepare noodles according to directions. Drain. Mix with cheese and arrange in well-buttered casserole lined with bread crumbs. Combine egg yolks and sour cream and pour over the noodle and cheese mixture. Top with 2 to 3 tablespoons drawn butter and bake in 350° oven for 25 to 30 minutes, or until edges are brown. Serves 6.

4. NOODLES WITH POPPY SEED *(Kluski z Makiem)*

Recipe No. 1 for noodles or	3–4 tbs. sugar
8-oz. package broad noodles	melted butter (optional)
¼ cup poppy seeds	dash of salt

Mash poppy seeds with sugar. Prepare noodles, drain, and mix with the poppy seeds. Top with melted butter and serve at once. Serves 6.

5. POURED NOODLES *(Kluski Kładzione)*

I.

1 tbs. butter	salt to taste
4 eggs, separated	2–3 tbs. milk
1 cup unsifted flour	

Cream butter and egg yolks, sift in the flour and salt, and mix with a fork. Fold in stiffly-beaten egg whites. If dough is too stiff add a little milk—the consistency should be that of dumpling dough. Using soup spoon, spoon into furiously-boiling salted water. Cover so that noodles will rise in the steam. Steam 5 to 10 minutes, according to size. Take out with strainer spoon, drain, and serve with melted butter or bacon fat seasoned with a little minced onion. Serves 3 (approx.).

II.

1 cup milk	1 cup unsifted flour
1 tbs. butter	3 eggs, lightly beaten

Combine milk and butter and scald. Then add flour, a little at a time, stirring constantly until smooth. Allow to cool; then slowly add eggs, stirring until dough is smooth and no longer sticks to the edges of pan. Have large container of furiously-boiling salted water ready. Proceed as in *I*. These noodles are also excellent if served with ¼ lb. goat cheese (*bryndza*), cut into small pieces and heated, but not browned, in a tablespoon of butter. They may also be sprinkled with Parmesan and butter and baked in a 350° oven for 20 minutes.

Note: As a dessert dish, serve with 3 to 4 tablespoons apple butter or other fruit preserves combined with an equal amount of sour cream and a little sugar and cinnamon. Serve hot.

6. SAXON NOODLES *(Kluski Saskie)*

4 cups bread crumbs	1 white roll or 2 slices bread
1 cup scalded milk	2 slices boiled ham, shredded
2 tsp. butter	flour for rolling
3 eggs, separated	few strips bacon fat
salt to taste	

Combine bread crumbs with scalded milk and let stand a few minutes to soften and cool. Add butter and egg yolks and fold in stiffly-beaten egg whites. Cube roll or bread and fry in butter to make croutons. Combine croutons and shredded ham with first mixture and mix lightly. Shape into oblong croquettes, roll in flour and cook in furiously-boiling salted water for about 10 minutes. Cook bacon until crisp, drain, and crumble. Use both bacon and bacon fat for topping. Serves 4 to 6.

7. BOILED POTATO DUMPLINGS
(Kluski Kartoflane Gotowane)

2 lbs. potatoes	salt and pepper to taste
4 eggs, separated	3 tbs. bread crumbs
2 tsp. chopped fresh parsley	drawn butter or bacon fat

Cook potatoes in boiling salted water. Drain and mash. Combine mashed potatoes, egg yolks, parsley, and bread crumbs. Season to taste, and then fold in stiffly-beaten egg whites. Stir lightly. Drop by the spoonful into boiling salted water, cover, and steam until dumplings rise to the top. Remove with a perforated spoon, drain, and serve with butter or bacon fat. Serves 6.

8. RAW POTATO DUMPLINGS
(Kluski z Surowych Kartofli)

2 lbs. potatoes, peeled and grated	salt and pepper to taste
1 cup flour	drawn butter or bacon fat for
2 eggs, lightly beaten	topping

Press grated potatoes in clean white cloth to squeeze out excess moisture. Combine with flour, eggs, and seasoning. Mix thoroughly and proceed as for Boiled Potato Dumplings (No. 7). Serves 6.

9. LASAGNE, OR BROAD NOODLES (*Lazanki*)

An 8-oz. package commercial lasagne, prepared in any of the following ways:

I. With cheese:

½ lb. farmer or cottage or pot cheese	1 cup sour cream
	dash of salt
4 egg yolks	butter and bread crumbs for lin-
2 tbs. sugar	ing casserole

Cook noodles according to directions on box. Drain. Combine cheese, egg yolks, sugar, sour cream, and salt. Mix with the noodles and arrange in well-buttered casserole lined with bread crumbs. Bake in 350° oven for 40 to 45 minutes. Sprinkle with sugar. Serves 6.

II. With minced ham:

½ lb. cooked ham	butter and bread crumbs for lin-
3 tbs. sour cream	ing casserole
1 tbs. melted butter	

Combine ham, sour cream, and melted butter. Prepare noodles according to directions on box. Drain. Combine with ham mixture and arrange in well-buttered casserole lined with bread crumbs. Bake in 350° oven 45 minutes. Serves 6.

III. With fresh-cooked cabbage or sauerkraut:

1 lb. sauerkraut or 1 head shredded cabbage	salt and pepper to taste
	butter and bread crumbs for lin-
1 med. onion, minced	ing casserole
1 tbs. melted butter	

Combine kraut and onion; or cook shredded cabbage according to basic recipe for cabbage (see Index). Simmer until onion is limp. Prepare noodles according to directions on package. Drain. Combine with melted butter and sauerkraut or cabbage. Season to taste. Arrange in casserole lined with butter and bread crumbs and bake in 350° oven for 45 minutes. Serves 6.

IV. With dried mushrooms:

2 oz. dried mushrooms	salt and pepper to taste
1 med. onion, minced	butter and bread crumbs
3 tbs. sour cream	

Soak mushrooms and cook until tender (see Index). Prepare lasagne as directed on package. Drain. Simmer cooked diced mushrooms and minced onion in a little butter until onion is a light golden-brown. Add to noodles and season to taste. Arrange in buttered casserole lined with bread crumbs and bake in 350° oven for 30 minutes, or until lightly browned. Serves 6.

10. MACARONI, HAM, AND TOMATO CASSEROLE
(Makaron z Szynką i Pomidorami)

8 ozs. commercially-prepared macaroni or spaghetti
1 cup Tomato Sauce (see Index) or tomato paste
½ tsp. Maggi extract

salt and pepper to taste
butter and bread crumbs for lining casserole
¼ lb. cooked ham, shredded
drawn butter

Cook macaroni according to package directions. Drain. Combine Tomato Sauce and Maggi extract, and season to taste. Butter casserole and line with bread crumbs. Arrange macaroni and ham in layers, moistening each layer with a little sauce. End with layer of macaroni, sprinkle with drawn butter, and bake in 350° oven about 1 hour. Serves 6.

11. MACARONI AND HAM IN PATTY SHELL
(Makaron z Szynką w Kruchem Cieście)

Pastry Dough made with 2 cups flour (see Index), or prepared piecrust mix
8 ozs. macaroni or spaghetti
½ lb. boiled ham or ham leftovers, cut in chunks

1 heaping tbs. butter
2 tbs. grated Parmesan
salt and pepper to taste

Cook macaroni according to package directions and drain. Combine with ham, butter, and Parmesan cheese, and season if necessary. Line baking dish with pastry dough. Arrange macaroni mixture in dish, cover with a layer of pastry dough, and perforate a few times with a fork. Bake in 350° oven for 30 minutes. Serves 6.

12. SPAGHETTI WITH CRAYFISH OR SHRIMP
(Makaron z Rakami)

1 lb. very thin spaghetti
20 crayfish or shrimp cut into pieces
1 tbs. Crayfish Butter (see Index)

butter for lining casserole
Crayfish (or Shrimp) Sauce (see Index)

Cook spaghetti according to package directions. Drain. Make sauce (see Index) with the 20 crayfish. Combine cut-up crayfish with spaghetti. Add Crayfish Butter and arrange in buttered casserole. Pour Crayfish Sauce over the top, and bake in 350° oven for 30 minutes. Serves 7 to 8.

13. MACARONI OR SPAGHETTI WITH MEAT STUFFING
(Makaron z Farszem Mięsnym)

8 ozs. macaroni or spaghetti	2 tbs. bread crumbs
2 cups chopped leftover cooked meat (beef, veal, pork, or lamb)	3 tbs. sour cream
1 med. onion, chopped	1 tbs. melted butter
salt and pepper to taste	butter and bread crumbs for lining casserole

Cook macaroni according to package directions. Chop or dice meat and brown lightly with the onion in a little butter. Season, add bread crumbs and sour cream and the melted butter. Mix with macaroni. Line casserole with butter and bread crumbs. Put mixture in casserole and bake in 350° oven until brown on top (about 30 minutes). Serves 6.

14. PIROGEN OR DOUGH POCKETS (Pierogi)

Basic Dough:

2 cups flour	few spoonfuls lukewarm water
2 small eggs or 1 large egg	

Mix flour, eggs, and water, and work dough until firm. Divide in 2 parts and roll each piece into a thin sheet on a floured board. Arrange stuffing (*see below*) by the spoonful along one edge of a piece of dough, 2 to 3 inches from edge. Fold over and cut out in shape of semi-circles with a pastry cutter or a glass. Press edges of dough together. Repeat until all the dough and filling have been used up. If necessary, reroll leftover dough and repeat. This is a fast way of making the pockets. Cook in boiling water like noodles, covered, so that they will steam. In a few minutes, when pockets rise to the top, they are done. Serve with drawn butter.

Fillings:

I. Cheese:

2 egg yolks	dash of salt
1 tbs. butter	1 tbs. sugar and
1 lb. pot cheese or farmer cheese, mashed	¼ cup raisins (optional)

Cream egg yolks and butter. Combine with cheese, season, and mix thoroughly. For a sweet filling, add sugar and raisins. Fill pockets as directed above. Serves 4.

II. Potato:

2 lbs. potatoes	2-3 tbs cottage or farmer cheese
½ onion, minced	(optional)
1 heaping tbs. butter	drawn butter and Parmesan
salt and pepper	or bread crumbs for topping

Cook, mash, and season potatoes. Fry onion to a light, golden brown in butter. Combine with mashed potato and season to taste; add cheese if desired. Mix thoroughly and proceed to fill and cook pockets. Serves 6 to 8.

III. Cabbage:

2 small or 1 large head cabbage	topping of drawn butter with
2 tbs. cooked dried mushrooms	bread crumbs or fried minced
salt and pepper	onion

Prepare cabbage as directed for Sweet Cabbage (see Index), omitting caraway and salt pork and substituting a tablespoon of butter. Soak and cook mushrooms (see Index) and chop. Combine with cabbage, season, and use to fill pockets. Cook as directed and serve with drawn butter and bread crumbs or onions. Serves 6 to 7.

IV. Fruit:

Blueberries, blackberries, or cherries are an excellent filling if the *pierogi* are to be used as a summer dish or as dessert. Fill the dough pockets with a spoonful of berries each, or with 3 or 4 pitted cherries. Press edges tightly and cook in boiling water as directed. Serve with sour cream and sugar. If sour cream is omitted, garnish with melted sweet butter.

15. LAZY DUMPLINGS *(Pierogi Leniwe)*

1 tbs. butter	2 tbs. flour
4 eggs, separated	salt to taste
1 lb. dry pot cheese	Bread-Crumb Sauce (see Index)

Cream butter and egg yolks. Press cheese through sieve. Combine butter-egg mixture and cheese with 2 tbs. flour and salt to taste. Mix thoroughly. Fold in stiffly-beaten egg whites. Divide mixture into two parts and roll each half out on a floured board into a long, thin stick. Flatten and cut on the bias into pieces about 2 inches long. Boil in salted water for 10 to 15 minutes, take out with perforated spoon, and drain carefully. Serve garnished with Bread-Crumb Sauce. Serves 3 to 4.

16. BAKED STUFFED POCKETS IN YEAST DOUGH
(Pieroźki Droźdzowe)

1 cake yeast (or 1 envelope) dissolved in a little milk or water	4 eggs, lightly beaten
4 cups unsifted flour	1 tbs. sugar
2 cups lukewarm milk	dash of salt
	½ cup melted butter

Dissolve yeast according to directions on package and let stand 5 minutes. Sift flour. Combine half with the milk, mix until smooth, and add yeast. Cover and let stand at room temperature for 20 to 30 minutes or until dough begins to rise. Add remaining flour, eggs, sugar, melted butter, and a dash of salt. Mix thoroughly, using wooden spoon, until bubbles form. Then work with hands until dough begins to come away from the hands. Cover and let stand in warm place until it rises to double its bulk. Prepare any of the fillings suggested below. Make pockets by flattening dough by the spoonful on buttered wax paper (do not roll). Spread with filling, roll up, and allow to stand another half-hour so that the dough rises again. Bake in 350° oven for 25 to 30 minutes.

Fillings: Use meat, cabbage, cheese, or fruit as for Boiled Pockets (No. 14). If meat or cabbage is used, serve with drawn butter. If fruit or cheese, add more sugar to the dough and serve with sour cream.

17. DUMPLINGS *(Knedle)*

4 stale white rolls	2–3 ozs. salt pork, diced and rendered
¼ cup fat from baked ham	
3 eggs, separated	3 tbs. flour
1 cup milk	

Dice the rolls. Chop ham fat, combine with diced rolls, and put in oven to make croutons. When dry and brown, combine these with egg yolks and milk, and part of the rendered salt pork. Add flour, mix, and then fold in stiffly-beaten egg whites. Dip hands in flour and, using hands, roll mixture into balls the size of walnuts. Throw into salted boiling water and cook, covered, for 10 to 15 minutes. Drain and serve, using the rest of the rendered salt pork as a topping. Serve with steamed sauerkraut. Serves 5.

Note: Leftover *Knedle* may be sliced and baked in a well-buttered dish with the addition of 1 or 2 lightly-beaten eggs (depending on amount left over). Arrange in a flat dish in one layer, and bake in medium-hot oven for 15 minutes.

18. DUMPLINGS WITH PRUNES OR APRICOTS
(Knedle ze Śliwkami lub Morelami)

2 cups flour
1 tbs. melted butter
2 egg yolks
½ tsp. salt

lukewarm milk (about 1 cup)
2 doz. dried prunes or apricots,
   pitted, washed, and drained

Combine flour, melted butter, egg yolks, salt, and enough milk to make a soft dough that pulls. Cover and let stand about half an hour. Then roll out thin on a floured board, cut into small squares, and wrap a prune or an apricot in each (preserves may be substituted). Cook in boiling salted water for about 10 minutes. Drain and serve with sugar and drawn butter.

19. BUCKWHEAT CAKES *(Hreczuszki)*

I.

1 cup sour cream
buckwheat flour (about 1½ cups)

salt to taste
hot melted butter or bacon fat

Beat buckwheat flour into sour cream to form dough the consistency of rather thick griddlecake batter. Season. Drop by spoonfuls into frying pan with hot butter or fat. When brown on one side, turn cakes and brown on the other. Serve with sour cream. Serves 3 to 4.

II. Filled Buckwheat Cakes
Make Buckwheat Cakes as in *I*. For filling, combine

½ lb. pot cheese   2 beaten egg yolks

Spread half the buckwheat cakes with this mixture, cover with the remaining cakes, and arrange on a platter. Heat in oven for 5 minutes.

20. POLISH PANCAKES *(Bliny Polskie)*

3 cups lukewarm milk
1½ cakes or 1½ envelopes yeast
4 cups all-purpose flour
2 cups buckwheat or whole-
   wheat flour

5 eggs, separated
½ cup melted butter
½ tsp. salt
butter for frying

Dissolve yeast in milk, add flours, and mix thoroughly. Add lightly-beaten egg yolks, melted butter, and salt, and finally fold in stiffly-beaten egg whites. Let stand at cool room temperature for 3 to 4 hours. The batter should be about the consistency of waffle or griddlecake batter—not too thin. Use several griddles or skillets. Fry in very hot butter, but be careful not to burn. When browned on

one side, turn. Until ready to serve, keep hot in warming oven.
Serve with sour cream, drawn butter, or red or black caviar. Serves
12, but recipe can be halved or even quartered. For half the quantity, use 2 or 3 eggs, depending on size.

Groats, Cereals, and Rice (Kasza I Ryż)

All rice and cereals should be prepared in heavy earthenware or
enameled-iron casseroles; in thin enamel or aluminum they will
stick and burn. To cook so that grains will remain separate, use
only enough water to cover. Except where otherwise indicated,
always cover with *boiling* salted water and add a piece of butter.
Stir once, simmer a few minutes, cover, and put into hot oven from
45 minutes to 1 hour. To cook over direct heat, use an asbestos
sheet.

21. PEARL BARLEY WITH DRIED MUSHROOMS
(Kaszka Krakowska na Grzybach)

2 ozs. dried mushrooms	1 heaping tbs. butter
1 egg	salt and pepper to taste
2 cups barley	

Soak mushrooms and cook in 4 cups salted water until tender. Beat
egg lightly and mix with barley. Allow to dry. Add butter to the
water in which mushrooms cooked. Let it melt, and then pour the
boiling liquid over the barley. Simmer very slowly for 10 minutes.
Cut mushrooms into thin strips, add to the pot, and mix lightly.
Cover and bake in 350° oven for 1 hour. Serves 6 to 7.

22. BARLEY AND MUSHROOM PIE
(Kaszka z Grzybami w Kruchym Cieście)

Prepare as for No. 21, but do not bake. Make dough as follows:

2 cups flour	2 tbs. sour cream
2 tbs. butter	salt

Mix thoroughly until dough is workable. Line a buttered dish as
if for pie. Fill with the barley and mushroom mixture, cover with
thin layer of dough, perforate with fork, and bake in medium-hot
oven for 1 hour. Serves 6 to 8.

Note: Pearl barley is also excellent cooked according to the basic
directions given at beginning of this section, the kernels first coated
with slightly-beaten egg and allowed to dry out. Add a tablespoon

of butter and a tablespoon of chopped fresh dill before putting into oven.

23. COOKED RICE *(Ryż Gotowany)*

1 cup rice, blanched	1 tbs. butter
2 scant cups salted boiling water or broth	

Dissolve butter in broth and pour over rice. Use heavy pot or casserole. Simmer, covered, over low heat for about 10 minutes; then steam in 350° oven for half an hour. Serves 3 to 4.

Note: To cook rice oriental style, start in cold water, bring to a boil, and proceed as above. Fluff up once with fork, but do not stir.

24. RICE WITH CRAYFISH AND MUSHROOMS *(Ryż z Rakami i Szampinjonami)*

2 cups rice, cooked in broth as in No. 23	1 tbs. Crayfish Butter (see Index)
20–30 crayfish (or shrimp)	1 tbs. chopped dill (optional)
12–15 mushrooms	2 cups sour cream
butter for simmering	salt and pepper to taste

Prepare rice and crayfish as in basic recipes. Slice or quarter mushrooms and simmer in a little butter until transparent. Combine pan liquid from mushrooms, Crayfish Butter, dill (if desired), and sour cream, and let bubble up. Arrange rice in buttered shallow baking dish and put the crayfish and mushrooms on top. Cover with sour cream mixture and bake in moderate oven for 15 minutes. Serves 6. Excellent Lenten dish.

25. RICE WITH HAM *(Ryż z Szynką)*

2 cups rice cooked in water or broth as in No. 23	2 egg yolks, lightly beaten
2 tbs. sour cream	1 cup cooked ham, chopped
	salt and pepper to taste

Prepare rice as in No. 23. Combine sour cream and egg yolks; add rice when it has cooled, and mix together. Add ham. Season. Bake covered in buttered dish in 350° oven until rice begins to brown, 20 to 30 minutes. Serves 6.

26. TURKISH RICE *(Ryż po Turecku)*

2 cups uncooked rice	3–4 cups hot lamb broth with fat unskimmed
salt and pepper	
dash of saffron (enough to color rice)	

Combine rice, seasoning, and broth. Stir once and bake in 350° oven, covered, for about an hour. Uncover and bake a few minutes more, until dry and lightly brown on top. Serves 6.

27. RICE PATTIES (*Kotlety z Ryżu*)

2 cups rice, cooked in milk	1 tbs. chopped fresh dill (or dill
2 tbs. dried mushrooms	and parsley)
1 tbs. butter	bread crumbs
2 whole eggs, lightly beaten	butter for frying
salt and pepper to taste	

Cook rice as in No. 23. Soak and cook mushrooms (see Index). Drain, reserving liquid, and chop. While rice is cooling, cream butter and eggs. Combine with mushrooms. Season, add dill, and mix with rice. Shape into patties, roll in bread crumbs, and fry in butter to a golden brown. Serve with a mushroom sauce made with the mushroom liquid, 2 tsp. butter browned with 1 tbs. flour, and 2 to 3 tbs. sour cream. Blend these well, let bubble up once, and pour over the rice patties. Serves 6.

28. RICE AND PEAS (*Risi-Bisi*)

1 cup rice, cooked in broth	salt and pepper to taste
1 cup green peas	grated Parmesan

Smother peas in butter (see Index). Arrange cooked rice in well-buttered casserole so that bottom and sides are lined with it. Arrange peas in center. Bake in 350° oven for 15 minutes. Sprinkle generously with grated Parmesan, and serve. Serves 4.

29. BUCKWHEAT GROATS (*Kasza Hreczana na Sypko*)

1 cup whole groats	1 tbs. butter
1 egg (optional)	2 cups boiling salted water

Use the whole-kernel groats rather than the so-called "refined" grinds, which cook up to a mush or gruel. Heat dry in a heavy skillet, stirring constantly to avoid scorching. Coat with the butter. Pour boiling water over *kasza*, stir once, cover, and cook in 350° oven for 1 hour. For cooking on top of range, turn heat down as low as possible or cook over asbestos. Serves 3 to 4.

Note: Another way to cook *kasza* is to coat kernels with beaten egg instead of butter, let them dry out, and then proceed as above, adding butter to the water.

30. BUCKWHEAT GROATS WITH CHEESE
(Kasza Hreczana ze Serem)

1 cup whole-kernel groats, blanched	salt and pepper to taste
2 cups sour cream	½ lb. farmer or pot cheese
1 tbs. melted butter	2 egg yolks

Combine blanched groats with sour cream and butter. Season, and put half into the bottom of well-buttered baking dish. Cream farmer cheese with egg yolks, spread over groats in the casserole, and then cover with remainder of the groats. Bake covered in 350° oven for 50 minutes to 1 hour. Serve with sour cream. Serves 4.

31. RUSSIAN KASZA STRUDEL (Knysz)

2 cups buckwheat groats or pearl barley	½ onion, minced
	Strudel Dough (see Index)
2 tbs. goose fat	salt to taste
2 tbs. chopped bacon or salt pork cubes	melted butter and bread crumbs

Cook groats as in No. 29, so that they separate. Render bacon or salt pork with minced onion. Drain off fat. Combine groats, goose fat (bacon fat if goose is not available), cracklings, and onion. Have Strudel Dough ready. Pull out paper-thin, brush with melted butter, and spread with the *kasza* mixture. Roll lightly, arrange in well-buttered baking dish lined with bread crumbs, and bake according to Strudel directions. Serve with Mushroom, Anchovy, or Caper Sauce. May be reheated.

Pastries, Mazurkas, and Tortes

For successful baking, have all the ingredients ready at hand and the oven preheated to the correct temperature. Recipes calling for beaten egg whites mean last-minute preparation, since egg whites will fall and become watery if allowed to stand. All pastry tins should be greased with butter and, where specified, lined with bread crumbs. Since the flour measurements in the original recipes were given by weight instead of volume, the amounts referred to in this chapter are for *unsifted* flour. Always sift before using.

GENERAL INFORMATION:
Using electric mixers: Whip egg whites at high speed; egg yolks, cream, or gelatin mixtures (where called for) at medium speed.

Nuts and Almonds: When recipe calls for ground nuts, this may be done either by putting nuts through grinder or using an electric blender. A blender is especially recommended where nuts are to be ground to a pulp, as for marzipan, a laborious procedure once carried out with a mortar and pestle. Nuts may also be purchased already ground from specialty nut stores.

To Blanch Almonds: Throw into boiling water, remove from fire, and let stand covered for a few minutes. Drain. The skins will slip off easily. Allow almonds to dry before using. Almonds may also be purchased already blanched, in cans.

Bitter Almonds are used for added flavor and should be added sparingly. Three or four of them added to a cup of sweet ones are sufficient, unless a larger amount is specified. If used over-generously, bitter almonds will prove to be too much of a good thing.

Wafer paper, otherwise called rice paper, is a thin, white edible sheet used to line baking sheets before spreading pastry or macaroons on them. It is available only at confectioners' specialty shops. If wafer paper is used, do not grease baking sheet. Otherwise, grease and flour sheet generously.

261

Use of Lemon or Orange Rind in Sugar: The original recipes in the book called for rubbing a piece of sugar loaf with the rind, to flavor sugar before using. For granulated sugar, add a few twists of lemon or orange rind to the sugar and let stand an hour before using.

Vanilla beans may be purchased in specialty stores. The bean has much more flavor than vanilla extract. It may be used two ways: Cut an inch or so of bean and add it to the ingredients according to directions; or split, scrape, and pound the pulp and the seed before using. Vanilla extract may be substituted for the bean by using about 1 tsp. extract to replace 1 inch of bean. When using extract, always add it after other ingredients have cooled, or its alcohol content will cause the flavor to evaporate.

Vanilla Sugar: For baking cakes and flavoring desserts, put 2 vanilla beans into a tightly-covered jar with 1 to 2 pounds of sugar and let stand a few weeks before using. Replenish the vanilla every 3 or 4 months.

To Bake Pastry Shells: After lining pastry tins with dough, fill them with dry split peas or lentils to keep the dough in shape. Remove peas after baking.

Overheated Oven: If oven gets overheated and pastry is in danger of browning too fast, cover with buttered sheet of paper and at the same time reduce the oven temperature. The paper will keep the dough from drying out or burning before right temperature is obtained.

1. WHITE ICING *(Lukier)*

Combine 5 stiffly-beaten egg whites with 2 cups powdered sugar. Mix with a wooden spoon or in a blender at a low speed until bubbles appear. Add lemon juice or orange juice to taste, spread over cake, and let stand 5 minutes in lukewarm oven.

2. TRANSPARENT ICING *(Lukier Przezroczysty)*

Combine 2 cups confectioner's sugar and enough water, added a little at a time, to make a mixture which may be easily spread with a knife. Work in a bowl with wooden spoon until transparent. Add a dash of rum or maraschino for flavoring, and proceed as for White Icing, No. 1.

3. THICK ICING *(Lukier Pomadkowy)*

Make a thick syrup with 1 cup granulated sugar and ¼ cup water. Cook until it looks pearly and spins a thread. Pour into bowl and work in one direction with a wooden spoon (or use blender at low speed) until it becomes thick and white and the mixture coats the spoon. Allow to cool and harden. Dilute with any of the following: lemon juice, maraschino liqueur, orange juice, lemon and rum, rum, strong black coffee, pineapple juice, etc. Spread over cake and allow to set before cutting cake.

4. CHOCOLATE ICING *(Glazura Czekoladowa)*

Melt ½ lb. milk or bitter-sweet chocolate (depending on preference) over very low heat with 1½ tsp. sweet butter. Then simmer with 1 cup water until it forms a thick syrup. Spread this on cake while still hot. For a slightly different taste, add 1 tsp. powdered instant coffee.

5. ALMOND TORTE *(Tort z Migdałów)*

10 egg whites, stiffly beaten	juice 1 lemon
2 cups sugar	2 tbs. flour
1 lb. (4 cups) unpeeled almonds, ground	tart jelly or jam for filling (gooseberry, etc.)

Combine egg whites with sugar and mix with wooden spoon (or in blender set at low speed) until bubbles appear. Combine with ground almonds, lemon juice, and flour, and divide in half. Bake in two well-buttered layer-cake pans in 350° oven until light brown, about 25 to 30 minutes. Cool, spread a layer of jam between cake layers, and decorate top with Thick Icing (see Index) flavored with lemon and rum.

6. ALMOND TORTE IN SHELL
(Tort Migdałowy w Kruchem Cieście)

Pastry:

2 cups unsifted flour	½ lb. sweet butter
1 cup sugar	dash of salt

Sift flour, combine with remaining ingredients, and work until smooth. Let stand in cool place 15 to 30 minutes. Roll out thin on floured pastry board. Line a buttered baking tin with the dough, leaving enough dough for covering.

Filling:

1 lb. (4 cups) blanched, peeled   2 cups sugar
  almonds   6 whole eggs
½ vanilla bean or 1½ tsp. vanilla 6 eggs, separated
  extract

Grind almonds and vanilla bean, combine with sugar, and cream
with the whole eggs, adding the eggs one by one. Then add egg
yolks, also one by one, creaming for half an hour in all, or until
mixture is a light, creamy color. (This may be done in a blender
set at low speed.) Fold in stiffly-beaten egg whites. Turn into
pastry shell, cover with thin layer of dough, press edges together,
and bake in 375° oven for 45 minutes to an hour, or until nicely
brown. Ice if desired.

7. WALNUT TORTE *(Tort z Orzechów Włoskich)*

12 eggs, separated   ¼ cup flour
 2 cups sugar (divided in half)   3 tbs. sweet cream (approx.)
 4 cups shelled walnuts, packed
   tight (1 lb.), ground fine and
   divided in half

Cream egg yolks with 1 cup sugar, add 2 cups walnuts and the
flour, and mix thoroughly. Fold in stiffly-beaten egg whites. Divide
mixture in half and pour into two well-buttered layer-cake pans
lined with bread crumbs. Bake in 300° oven for 25 to 35 minutes,
or until light brown. Cool. In the meantime, make the filling.

Filling: Combine remaining 2 cups ground nuts with remaining 1
cup sugar and add enough sweet cream so that the mixture will hold
together. Spread between layers of the torte, and return to slow
oven for 10 minutes. When cool, garnish with glazed nuts. Use
lemon icing if desired.

8. NUT TORTE WITH FILLING
(Tort Orzechowy Przekładany Masą)

6 eggs, separated   2 tbs. pine nuts (optional), ground
½ cup sugar   fine
¼ cup each of walnuts and al-   ½ vanilla bean *or* 1½ tsp. vanilla
  monds, tightly packed (2 ounces   extract
  each), ground fine   2 heaping tbs. bread crumbs

Cream egg yolks and sugar until light and creamy-colored. Grind
nuts very fine and grind and pound vanilla bean; add to creamed
mixture. Mix thoroughly with bread crumbs and finally fold in
stiffly-beaten egg whites. Divide into halves and pour into two well-
buttered layer-cake tins lined with bread crumbs. Bake in 300°

oven for 25 to 30 minutes or until light brown. Cool, and fill with any of the following:

I. Almond Filling:

1 cup sugar
2 cups ground blanched almonds

3–4 tbs. sweet cream or lemon or orange juice to taste

Combine sugar and ground almonds and add enough liquid to hold together.

II. Coffee Filling:

¼ lb. sweet butter
½ cup sugar

2–3 egg yolks, depending on size
3 tbs. very strong black coffee

Cream butter and sugar. Add egg yolks one by one and continue creaming for a few more minutes. Add coffee a little at a time and blend thoroughly.

III. Chocolate Filling:

½ lb. semi-sweet chocolate, half-melted
½ lb. sweet butter

4 egg yolks
sugar to taste (scant ½ cup)

Melt chocolate by placing in lukewarm oven until just soft. Cream with butter. Add egg yolks one by one, then sugar. Cream until thoroughly blended.

9. UNBAKED CHOCOLATE TORTE
(Tort Czekoladowy Niepieczony)

½ lb. sweet butter
1 cup sugar
½ lb. butter-sweet chocolate, grated

Topping:
2 cups (½ lb.) walnuts or hazelnuts, finely ground
1 cup sugar
3–4 tbs. heavy sweet cream

Cream butter until very light, add sugar and grated chocolate, and continue creaming until thoroughly blended. Chill in a buttered removable-bottom layer pan until mixture sets. Make topping with finely-ground nuts, sugar, and enough cream to hold together. Remove chocolate base from pan and spread with topping. Cover with chocolate icing (see Index) and decorate with large chunks of almonds, candied orange peel, and lemon peel.

10. TORTE WITH COFFEE FILLING
(Tort Kawowy z Kremem)

1¼ cups sweet butter (10 ozs.)
2 whole eggs
1¼ cups sugar
2½ cups (10 ozs.) finely ground almonds

2½ cups flour
dash of salt

Cream butter and eggs until very light. Add sugar and almonds and continue mixing until thoroughly blended. Add flour, a little at a time, and the salt. Work with hands for a few minutes; then divide in three and bake each layer separately in buttered layer-cake pan in 300° oven for 35 to 40 minutes. Cool and spread with following filling.

Filling:

4 egg yolks	1" vanilla bean or 1 tsp. vanilla
4 tbs. sugar	flavoring
1½ tsp. flour	4 tbs. very strong coffee
½ cup heavy sweet cream	

Cream egg yolks and sugar until very light, add flour, and blend thoroughly. Bring cream to a boil with vanilla bean; then discard bean, and slowly add boiling cream to egg and sugar mixture. Stir over low heat in top of double boiler until mixture thickens. Cool, add coffee, mix well, and use as filling for torte layers. Refrigerate. The following day, ice with coffee icing.

11. POPPY SEED TORTE *(Tort Makowy)*

⅔ cup sweet butter (scant)	2 tbs. honey
⅔ cup sugar	1 tbs. flour
5 egg yolks	
1 scant cup poppy seeds (about ½ lb.)	

Cream butter, sugar, and egg yolks until light and cream-colored. Blanch and drain poppy seeds; then pound and mash thoroughly (original recipe gives the time as 45 minutes). Combine all the ingredients, and pour into buttered mold well dusted with flour. Bake 30 minutes in 350° oven.

Note: For variations in flavor, try adding cinnamon and/or ground cloves, and a tablespoon each of citron and candied orange peel. May also be baked with addition of the stiffly-beaten egg whites for fluffier consistency.

12. CHESTNUT TORTE *(Tort Kasztanowy)*

1 cup blanched, peeled almonds, chopped and pounded to a paste	6 egg whites, stiffly beaten
½ cup sugar	dash of salt

Combine almond paste, sugar, and salt, and stir until blended. Fold in stiffly-beaten egg whites. Line two pie tins with butter and bread crumbs, pour half the mixture into each, and bake in 350° oven for 20 to 25 minutes, or until light golden-brown.

Filling:

1 lb. parboiled chestnuts, shelled   vanilla sugar to taste
    and peeled   ¼ lb. butter
    milk to cover

Simmer the chestnuts in milk until very soft. Mash, combine with sugar, and press through fine sieve. Melt butter and then cool. Cream the melted butter until frothy, and blend with chestnut purée. Fill the torte, and ice with No. 3 flavored with lemon or rum.

13. LINC TORTE *(Tort Lincki)*

¼ lb. sweet butter
3 cups flour
1 cup (¼ lb.) blanched, peeled almonds, ground fine
½ cup sugar

grated rind of ½ lemon
cinnamon and nutmeg to taste
¼ tsp. ground cloves
6 hard-cooked egg yolks, mashed
jam or jelly, and icing

Combine butter and flour, using two knives or a pastry cutter. Add ground almonds, sugar, lemon rind, spices, and finally the mashed egg yolks. Stir thoroughly and then leave in a cool place for half an hour. Divide in half. Spread in two layer-cake pans lined with butter and bread crumbs and bake in moderate oven for 40 to 50 minutes, or until nicely brown. Cool. Use any preferred jam or jelly for filling, and ice according to taste.

14. MARZIPAN TORTE *(Tort Marcepanowy)*

½ lb. sweet butter
1 lb. (2 cups) sugar
8 hard-cooked egg yolks
3 whole eggs, lightly beaten
4 cups unpeeled almonds, ground fine

2″ piece vanilla bean, ground, or vanilla extract to taste
2 tbs. flour
sheet of wafer paper (see Index)

Cream butter until frothy. Add sugar, mashed cooked egg yolks, whole raw eggs, and almonds, and stir thoroughly. Add vanilla and flour, and blend. Reserve ¼ of mixture. Line baking tin with wafer paper and pour in ¾ of the mixture. Smooth the top. Roll remainder of mixture into long thin strips and arrange these crisscross over top of torte. Bake in 350° oven until nicely brown. Cool and ice with No. 3 flavored with lemon or orange.

15. SAND CAKE *(Tort Piaskowy)*

6 tbs. melted butter
9 tbs. vanilla sugar
6 whole eggs

6 egg yolks
¾ cup potato flour

Cream butter and sugar in bowl until light and cream-colored. Add eggs and egg yolks one at a time. Add potato flour, blend, and continue mixing for half an hour. Bake in well-buttered tin in 375° oven for 50 to 55 minutes. Cool and ice according to preference.

16. CRACOW TORTE *(Tort Krakowski)*

¼ lb. butter	dash of cinnamon
3 cups flour	½ tsp. ground cloves
3 tbs. sugar	jam, jelly, or marmalade for
4 egg yolks	spreading

Cut butter into the flour. Add sugar, egg yolks, cinnamon, and cloves and mix thoroughly. Refrigerate for 30 minutes. Roll out to a half-inch in thickness and bake in moderate oven to a golden brown (about 20 minutes). Cool and spread with marmalade or jelly, then with following mixture:

4 egg whites, stiffly beaten	juice ½ lemon
3 tbs. sugar	1 cup blanched almonds, chopped

Combine all the ingredients and pour into hot buttered pan. Let simmer a minute or two, turning a few times with spoon. Spread over the layer of jam. Put torte into a very slow oven (200°) for half an hour, until the egg whites set.

17. SACHER TORTE *(Tort Sachera)*

½ lb. butter, melted	¼ cup cocoa (scant)
10 eggs, separated	1 cup flour
1 cup sugar	

Cream butter and egg yolks until very frothy. Add sugar, cocoa, and flour and continue mixing until thoroughly blended. Add stiffly-beaten egg whites. Pour into greased mold and bake in 250° oven for about 1 hour. Test with straw. Cool and spread with chocolate icing.

18. ALMOND MAZUR CAKE *(Mazurek Migdałowy)*

4 cups blanched, peeled almonds, ground fine	2 whole eggs, lightly beaten juice 1 whole lemon
2 cups sugar	wafer paper (see Index)

Combine almonds and sugar and mash together. Add eggs and lemon juice and blend thoroughly. Grease shallow pastry tin, cover with wafer paper, pour mixture over it, and bake in very slow oven (about 200°) until lightly done on top, 20 to 25 minutes. Use a fruit icing.

19. MACAROON MAZUR CAKE *(Mazurek Makaronikowy)*

4 cups unpeeled almonds
2 cups sugar
4 whole eggs, lightly beaten

juice 1 lemon
⅞ cup flour + 1 tbs.
wafer paper (see Index)

Chop almonds fine or put through grinder. Add sugar, eggs, and lemon juice. Combine with flour. Proceed as for No. 18.

20. RAISIN MAZUR CAKE *(Mazurek Rodzynkowy)*

2 cups seedless raisins
1 cup sugar
2 cups unpeeled almonds, grated
   or chopped very fine

grated rind 1 lemon
1 whole egg and 1 egg yolk, lightly
beaten
wafer paper (see Index)

Combine all the ingredients. Pour into shallow cake pan lined with wafer paper and proceed as for No. 18.

21. APPLE MAZUR IN SHORT SHELL
(Mazurek Kruchy z Jabłkami)

Dough:

½ lb. unsalted butter
2 cups blanched, peeled almonds,
   ground
1 cup sugar

4 med. eggs, lightly beaten (8
   ozs.)
2 cups flour

Cream butter, combine with almonds, sugar, eggs, and flour, and work until thoroughly blended. Roll out ¼ inch to ⅜ inch thick. Bake in greased tin in 350° oven until nicely brown.

Topping:
I.

1 cup sugar
¼ cup water
12–13 greenings, peeled, cored,
   and sliced thin

grated lemon or orange rind
for flavoring (about 2 tsp.)

Make a thick syrup of sugar and water, and cook for 5 minutes. Add apples and lemon rind, and simmer until they are transparent and fall apart, stirring to prevent burning. (If too thick, add more water.) When the apple mixture begins to separate from edges of the pan, allow to cool somewhat. Spread over the baked layer of cake and allow to cool again.

II.
Make Apple Topping as in *I*. Add 1½ cups blanched, peeled, and chopped almonds, 2 ozs. citron, chopped, and lemon rind from 2

lemons. Mix thoroughly. Proceed the same as for *I*, or spread about 1 inch thick on wafer paper (see Index) and chill.

22. ORANGE MAZUR *(Mazurek Pomarańczowy)*

2 cups blanched, peeled almonds, ground fine	juice 1 lemon
	wafer paper (see Index)
1 cup sugar	

Combine almonds, sugar, and lemon juice, and blend thoroughly. (There should be just enough juice to moisten so that paste will spread.) Grease baking dish, line bottom and sides about 1½ inches high with wafer paper, put in almond mixture, and bake in very slow oven (about 200°) for 15 to 20 minutes. It should not brown.

Spread:

2 oranges	2 cups sugar
1 lemon	½ cup water

Grate oranges and lemon—both rind and pulp, discarding only pits. Combine with sugar and water and simmer until syrup is very thick. Pour into bowl and rub with wooden spoon until it begins to turn white. Spread over baked base and chill.

23. DATE MAZUR *(Mazurek Daktylowy)*

6 egg whites, beaten stiff	2 cups chopped dates
2 cups sugar	½ lb. bittersweet chocolate, grated
2 cups blanched almonds, peeled and chopped	wafer paper (see Index)

Slowly add sugar to egg whites, beating until all sugar has disappeared. Then cream in bowl for 30 minutes. Add almonds, dates, and chocolate, and mix thoroughly. Oil baking sheet, line with wafer paper, and spread mixture over it. Bake for 20 to 25 minutes in very slow oven (about 200°). Cool and cover with No. 3 flavored with lemon or pineapple.

24. CHOCOLATE MAZUR IN SHORT SHELL
(Mazurek Czekoladowy na Kruchym Spodzie)

Make shell as for Apple Mazur, No. 21. Cool.

Spread:

4 whole eggs, lightly beaten	1 tbs. flour
1 cup sugar	1 cup blanched, peeled almonds,
½ lb. bittersweet chocolate, grated	coarsely chopped

Combine eggs and sugar and cream until thoroughly blended. Add chocolate and continue creaming for a few more minutes. Add flour, mix thoroughly, and then add almonds. Mix again. Spread over the baked shell and bake in very slow oven (about 200°) for 10 minutes.

Note: Where wafer paper is unavailable, line greased pan with thin white paper.

25. CHEESE CAKE IN SHORT SHELL
(Placek Serowy na Kruchym Spodzie)

Make shell as for Apple Mazur, No. 21.

Cheese Mixture I:

4 cups farmer or pot cheese, rather dry
⅔ cup (liberal) butter
10 eggs, separated
⅝ cup sugar

½ vanilla bean, ground and mashed with a little sugar, *or*
¼ lb. candied orange peel, chopped fine

Press cheese through sieve, then mash in bowl with a wooden spoon. Cream butter, adding egg yolks one at a time until mixture is very light. Add sugar, then cheese and vanilla, and continue creaming for a full hour. Fold in stiffly-beaten egg whites and spread evenly over baked pastry shell. Enough for 2 pastries.

Cheese Mixture II:

4 cups cottage or pot cheese
1 whole egg and 3 egg yolks
½ cup melted butter
⅝ cup sugar

½ jigger (about 1 oz.) rum
1½ cups blanched almonds, grated
⅝ cup candied orange peel, chopped fine

Follow directions in *I.*

26. ALMOND PASTRIES IN SHELLS
(Babki Migdałowe w Kruchem Cieśie)

Short Pastry Dough (see Index) to fill 12 well-buttered individual pastry tins.

Filling:

9 eggs, separated
1 cup sugar

2 cups unpeeled almonds, grated
2 tbs. bread crumbs

Cream egg yolks and sugar until light and cream-colored. Combine with grated almonds, fold in stiffly-beaten egg whites, and add bread crumbs. Stir lightly and fill unbaked pastry shells with the mixture. Bake in 350° oven 40 minutes until dough is lightly brown.

27. CREAM PASTRIES *(Babki Śmietankowe)*

Short pastry dough for 6 shells, made with

½ lb. sweet butter	1½ cups flour
½ cup sugar	1 egg, lightly beaten

Cream butter and sugar, adding sugar a spoonful at a time. Sift in flour, add egg, and mix thoroughly. Work a few minutes and then let stand in a cool place for half an hour. Line buttered individual pastry shells with the dough, and fill.

Filling:

2 egg yolks	½ cup heavy cream
½ cup sugar	2–3 blanched bitter almonds,
½ vanilla bean, ground and mashed	chopped and mashed

Cream egg yolks with sugar, add vanilla, sweet cream, and bitter almonds, and place in top of double boiler over boiling water. Beat with whisk until mixture thickens. Allow to cool before pouring into the unbaked shells. After shells are filled, cover with thinly-rolled layer of pastry. Pinch edges together and bake in 375° oven for 30 minutes. Do not unmold until cool.

28. ALMOND AND HONEY STRIPS *(Makagigi)*

4 cups almonds, blanched	½ cup water
2 ozs. bitter almonds, blanched	½ cup honey
½ cup sugar	

Chop almonds coarsely. Make a very thick syrup of sugar and water and simmer chopped almonds in it until syrup begins to brown. Add honey and continue to simmer for half an hour. Pour out on a cold, flat surface—an enamel table top moistened with cold water—and roll out with porcelain rolling pin or a wooden one moistened in cold water. Let cool, and then cut into diagonal strips.

29. WAFERS *(Andruty)*

2 cups milk	1 whole egg
2 cups flour	1 tsp. melted butter
½ cup sugar	

Combine all the ingredients and pour into greased wafer irons. Bake over medium heat until nicely brown (3 to 5 minutes). Roll or leave flat.

30. ALMOND WAFERS (*Andruty Migdałowe*)

I. Prepare the same as No. 29, adding 1 cup blanched, peeled, and grated almonds. When done, brush wafers with egg white, sprinkle liberally with sugar, and stick together in twos.

II. With Cream Filling:

Prepare Almond Wafers as in *I*. Roll each while warm into a cornucopia. Fill with cream whipped with sugar and vanilla to taste.

III. With Pischinger Filling:

¼ lb. bittersweet chocolate	1 tsp. sweet butter
½ cup sugar	1 cup pine nuts (or walnuts)
½ cup sweet cream	

Melt chocolate and sugar, add cream, and simmer a few minutes with butter. Leave half for icing. Combine remainder with chopped nuts. Spread Almond Wafers with the mixture, piling one on top of the next, five layers in all. Simmer remaining chocolate mixture a few minutes longer or until very thick. Ice top and sides of each 5-layer stack, and allow to cool.

31. *MADELEINES* (*Magdalenki*)

2 tsp. grated orange rind	2 cups flour
8 egg yolks	½ lb. melted butter
1 cup sugar	

Sauté orange rind in a little butter until transparent. Cream egg yolks and sugar until white; then continue beating in top of double boiler until mixture thickens. Remove from heat, sift in flour, add butter and orange peel, and beat a few minutes longer. Pour into well-greased, individual pastry shells, filling them a little more than half-full. Bake in 350° oven until nicely brown.

32. HONEY CAKE (*Pierniki Luckie*)

1 tbs. grated orange rind	powdered cloves, to taste
1 tbs. lemon rind (optional)	dash of pepper
2 cups honey	3 cups rye flour
1 oz. pure alcohol	1 scant tbs. baking soda
cinnamon, anise, and	wafer paper (see Index)

Grate orange rind (and lemon, if desired) and simmer in butter until transparent. Combine honey and alcohol and simmer over low heat, skimming off the scum. When clear, add orange rind and spices. Heat the dry flour until it begins to change color, being careful not to scorch. Add baking soda and mix in well. Pour hot liquid into flour gradually, and continue beating with spoon or electric beater for at least 30 minutes, longer if possible. Line

greased baking sheet with wafer paper, and place dough by the
spoonful on the paper, shaping into individual round or oblong
cookies. Bake in 275° oven for 15 to 20 minutes.

33. SPICE CAKE *(Piernik)*

4 cups honey	1 cup citron
5 eggs, separated	2 tbs. finely-chopped orange peel
4 cups flour	¼ tsp. ground cloves
1 tsp. baking soda	½ tsp. cinnamon
1 cup almonds	dash of nutmeg

Heat honey, skim, and simmer until it darkens. Pour into bowl and
work with wooden spoon. When cool, add egg yolks one at a time
and continue creaming. Sift in flour and baking soda and mix thoroughly. Add almonds, citron, and other ingredients, increasing
amounts if a more spicy taste is preferred. Fold in stiffly-beaten egg
whites. Pour into well-greased mold dusted with flour and bake in
slow oven for 1 hour. Best when allowed to stand 10 to 14 days
before using.

34. CHEAP AND EASY HONEY CAKE
(Łatwy i Tani Piernik)

½ cup sugar	1 tbs. baking powder
3 whole eggs, separated	cinnamon, to taste
1 cup ground walnuts	powdered cloves, to taste
2 cups flour	nutmeg, to taste
2 egg whites	
2 cups honey, heated, skimmed, and cooled	

Cream sugar and egg yolks until light. Add nuts and sift in flour.
Add stiffly-beaten egg whites, honey, and baking powder. Add
spices to taste, mix thoroughly, and bake in 250° oven in a greased
mold lined with bread crumbs, for about 1 hour.

35. ALMOND BABA *(Babka Migdałowa)*

10 eggs, separated	juice 1 lemon
1 cup sugar	¼ cup bitter almonds
2 cups potato flour	⅞ cup sweet almonds

Cream egg yolks and sugar until light and cream-colored. Sift in
potato flour and stir for half an hour. Blanch, grate, and mash almonds. Add, with lemon juice, to first mixture and work for 15
minutes longer. Fold in stiffly-beaten egg whites, mix lightly, and
pour at once into greased mold. Bake in 450° oven for 30 to 35
minutes.

Soufflés, Puddings, Strudels, etc.

Soufflés and meringues should be baked in a slow, preheated oven at an even temperature; they must not brown heavily but must be done throughout. A soufflé will fail to rise, or will fall, if heat is not even or if the oven door is opened too soon. Soufflés should be prepared and baked at the last minute: they must not stand around raw, nor can one wait to serve them.

Egg whites should be carefully separated and beaten at high speed. A stiffly-beaten egg white can be cut with a knife. Always fold in egg whites last. Do not stir.

Flour for desserts should be pastry flour, sifted.

When grating lemon or orange rind for desserts, take care to grate only the colored part. The white layer underneath adds a bitter taste.

1. STRUDEL DOUGH

2 cups sifted flour	¼ cup lukewarm water
1 egg	½ tsp. lemon juice
½ tsp. vegetable oil	2–3 tsp. sugar
¼ tsp. salt	½ cup bread crumbs (optional)

Dough for strudel should be elastic, and is therefore best made without any fat or butter. The addition of butter or any kind of shortening makes dough tear easily during stretching. Combine all ingredients, mix quickly with knife or pastry blender, then knead, and finally slap repeatedly against pastry board until bubbles begin to show. Cover with hot bowl and let stand half an hour to warm. Spread a tablecloth on a table at least 3 by 5 feet in size, and sprinkle cloth with flour. Under cloth, in center, place an overturned plate, and place dough on top. Flatten, and begin pulling and stretching dough all around, to cover the table, until dough is transparent. Then allow to dry for about 30 minutes.

Brush dough with melted butter and trim any thick edges. Then
spread evenly with filling, leaving about a quarter of the dough bare.
Sprinkle with bread crumbs if desired. Roll strudel, starting with
the filled part; roll by holding one side of the tablecloth up slightly
so that strudel will roll over and over. Do not use hands or dough
may stick and tear. Brush unfilled part of dough with butter and
continue rolling. Trim edges, twist the roll of strudel, and brush
with the remaining butter. Bake in greased pan in 350° oven for
35 to 45 minutes, or until brown and crisp.

2. STRUDEL FILLINGS

I. *Fruit Filling*

2–3 lbs. tart apples, pared, cored,
and sliced (or equivalent
amount pitted cherries or
prunes)
4 tbs. melted butter

⅔ cup bread crumbs
2–3 tbs. raisins (for apple strudel
only)
½ cup sugar

Fry bread crumbs lightly in butter, mix with fruit and sugar, and
spread over strudel. dough. Roll.

II. *Poppy Seed Filling*

½ lb. poppy seeds, blanched and
crushed
1 tbs. butter
sugar to taste (about ⅓ as
much as poppy seed)

dash of vanilla extract
2–3 tbs. sweet cream

Fry crushed poppy seeds lightly in butter, taking care not to burn.
Combine with sugar to taste, add vanilla extract and sweet cream,
and spread over strudel dough. Roll.

III. *Cheese Filling*

1 lb. farmer or pot cheese
1 tbs. butter
4 eggs, separated
2 tbs. sour cream

2–3 tbs. white raisins
dash of vanilla extract
⅓ cup sugar
½ tsp. lemon rind (optional)

Rub cheese through strainer. Cream butter and egg yolks. Combine.
Add sour cream, raisins, sugar, and vanilla. Fold in stiffly-beaten
egg whites and stir lightly. Spread over strudel dough and roll up.

IV. *Cabbage Filling*

1 med. head cabbage, prepared as
for Pierogi with Cabbage Filling

(see Index)
melted butter

Brush dough with melted butter, spread with cabbage filling, and
roll.

V. *Ham or Meat Filling*

1 lb. minced cooked ham *or* 3 cups
Meat (Beef) Pastry Filling (see
Index)
2 cups sour cream
2 eggs, lightly beaten

salt and pepper to taste
¼ cup bread crumbs (more if necessary)
melted butter

Brush strudel dough with melted butter and spread with minced ham or Meat Pastry Filling. Spread this with sour cream combined with the eggs. Season lightly, sprinkle generously with bread crumbs, and roll. Serve with Madeira Sauce (see Index).

3. CREPES OR PANCAKES *(Naleśniki)*

I.

2 cups whole or skim milk
4 eggs
1 tbs. melted butter

salt to taste
1 cup sifted flour (approx.)

Beat eggs and milk together until well blended. Add melted butter and salt, then as much flour to make a thin, runny batter as the dough will take. Use several skillets at once. Pour a spoonful at a time on a lightly-buttered hot skillet, tilting to allow batter to spread. Brown; then turn and brown on the other side. To keep hot, put one on top of another in warm (not hot) oven or in a bun-warmer. (Batter should be of a much thinner consistency than for ordinary pancakes.) Makes 16 to 20 5-inch cakes.

II.

1 cup milk
1 cup water
4 eggs, separated

salt to taste
4 heaping tbs. flour

Combine milk, water, and lightly-beaten egg yolks. Add flour, beating with fork until smooth. Season. Fold in stiffly-beaten egg whites. Proceed as for *I*.

4. FILLINGS FOR CREPES

I. Use jam, preserves, or a cheese filling prepared as for strudel (see Index). Brown crepes on one side, fill on browned side, and either roll or fold into squares or triangles. Fry on both sides in butter to a golden brown, and sprinkle with sugar. Keep hot in oven until all are ready to serve.

Note: Crepes may be folded without the filling, browned, sprinkled with sugar, and served with sour cream or jam.

II. Almond Filling

1 cup blanched almonds	3 eggs, separated
4–6 bitter almonds	dash of salt
3 tbs. sugar	dash of lemon rind (optional)

Blanch almonds, chop, and grind fine, using either a blender or a grinder. Add egg yolks creamed with the sugar. Season, mix thoroughly, and fold in stiffly-beaten egg whites. Fill crepes and proceed as in *I*.

III. Cream Filling

4 egg yolks	pending on preference)
3 tbs. sugar	dash of vanilla extract
1 tbs. flour	¼ tsp. lemon rind
1 cup sweet or sour cream (de-	

Cream egg yolks and sugar until white. Add flour and cream and continue stirring until thoroughly blended. Place bowl in top of double boiler and beat with whisk until thick. Add vanilla and lemon rind. Allow to cool; then fill crepes and fry lightly in butter. Sprinkle with sugar. This recipe makes filling for 12 generous-sized crepes—4 to 6 portions of dessert.

IV. Prepare like *III*, but use 2 cups sour cream. Do not beat once the ingredients are blended. Fill 12 crepes, arrange them in buttered shallow baking dish lined with bread crumbs, and pour any remaining filling over the top. Spread smoothly and bake in hot oven, 400°, for 30 minutes.

V. Crepes may also be made with any of the fillings for Pirogen (see Index), such as fresh or dried mushrooms, meat, etc. They are then browned in the oven as in *IV*, and served with a sharp sauce such as Caper, Dill, Chive, or Mushroom Sauce (see Index) as a main dish.

5. ROLLED BISCUIT OMELET
(Omlet Zwijany Biszkoptowy)

8 eggs, separated	dash of salt
4 tbs. sugar	jam or jelly for filling
1 cup sifted flour	sugar

Cream egg yolks and sugar; then beat with whisk over heat in top of double boiler until light and fluffy. Remove from heat and slowly add flour, beating constantly. Season with a little salt, and when thoroughly blended, fold in stiffly-beaten egg whites. Pour out on a buttered, floured sheet and bake in 350° oven for half an hour. Fill with jam, jelly, or preserves. Fold, sprinkle with sugar, cut on the bias, and serve with Vanilla Sauce.

6. FRUIT SOUFFLÉ *(Souflet Owocowy)*

6 egg whites, stiffly beaten
6 tbs. sugar
3 tbs. fruit jelly, jam, or preserves
(apricot, raspberry, hawthorne),
or mashed fresh fruit

Add sugar to egg whites and continue beating until stiff. Add jelly and again beat until stiff. Pour into pie dish greased with olive oil, smooth mound with a wet knife, and bake in 350° oven for 20 to 25 minutes, or until lightly brown. Serves 6.

Note: If soufflé is made with apples, bake cooking apples in proportion of one large apple to each egg white. Press through sieve and allow to cool. Place bowl of sieved apples in a bowl of ice, and beat with a whisk until the apple purée is white. Use ½ cup sugar. Proceed as above.

7. COFFEE SOUFFLÉ *(Souflet Kawowy)*

2 cups heavy sweet cream
3 tbs. pulverized coffee (instant
may be used)
6 eggs, separated

¾ cups sugar
1 tbs. potato flour
sugar for sprinkling

Scald cream and combine with coffee. Cover and let stand until cool. Strain through cheesecloth. In the meantime, cream egg yolks and sugar until light and creamy. Combine with coffee and cream mixture, and beat in top of double boiler over boiling water until stiff, taking care not to let mixture cook. Allow to cool again, fold in the stiffly-beaten egg whites combined with potato flour, mix lightly, and pour in a mound on a pie tin rubbed with olive oil. Sprinkle with sugar and bake in a 375° oven for 15 to 20 minutes.

Note: For a chocolate soufflé, use 4 ozs. grated unsweetened chocolate, 4 egg yolks, 3 tbs. sugar, and 6 egg whites. Proceed as for Coffee Soufflé.

8. CHESTNUT SOUFFLÉ *(Souflet z Kasztanów)*

1 lb. chestnuts, parboiled and
peeled
milk to cover
1 tbs. butter
1 tbs. flour

1 cup heavy sweet cream
½ cup sugar
dash of vanilla extract
6 eggs, separated

Parboil chestnuts about 15 minutes. Then drain, shell, and peel, and simmer in enough milk to cover, until soft enough to mash—

another 15 to 20 minutes. Purée by pressing through sieve. Cream butter and flour, slowly add cream, and stir over very low heat until mixture thickens. Cool in a bowl of ice. Combine with chestnut purée, add sugar and vanilla to taste, and stir or beat with whisk until fluffy, adding egg yolks one at a time. Combine with stiffly-beaten egg whites, stir lightly, and pour into shallow baking dish rubbed with butter. Smooth edges of mound with a wet knife and bake in 375° oven for 20 to 25 minutes.

9. ROYAL SOUFFLÉ (Souflet Królewski)

3 sweet rolls	4 eggs, separated
2 tsp. butter	ladyfingers
3 tbs. sugar	2 tbs. jam or marmelade
boiling milk to soak rolls	maraschino or other liqueur—
2 tbs. blanched almonds	about 2 ozs.
2 cups seedless raisins	

Cut up rolls, add butter and sugar, and cover with scalded milk, using only as much milk as rolls will absorb. Press through a sieve. Chop almonds and mash to a pulp. Combine with raisins and egg yolks, and mix thoroughly with roll mush. Finally fold in stiffly-beaten egg whites. Pour half the mixture into well-buttered baking dish. Cover with a layer of ladyfingers, then a layer of jam (which should not be runny), and sprinkle with liqueur. Cover with remaining soufflé mixture and bake in 375° oven for 25 minutes. Serve with Wine or Sherry Sauce (see Index).

10. "MUSHROOM" CAKE OR KAISERSCHMARREN (Grzybek)

1 heaping tbs. butter	5 eggs, separated
1 cup milk	1 cup flour
2 tbs. sugar	2 tbs. seedless raisins
dash of salt	

Melt butter, and add milk, sugar, salt, and egg yolks. Beat lightly. Add flour and stir until thoroughly smooth. Add raisins, and fold in stiffly-beaten egg whites. Pour into well-buttered cake pan and bake in 400° oven for 20 minutes. When lightly brown on both sides, tear (do not cut) with two sharp forks, and sprinkle with sugar flavored with vanilla.

Note: Fresh cherries or plums may be substituted for the raisins. Pit them, cut into small pieces, and sprinkle with sugar an hour before using.

11. CREAM "MUSHROOM" CAKE (*Grzybek Śmietankowy*)

6 eggs, separated
1 tbs. butter
4 tbs. confectioner's sugar
2 cups flour

1 tsp. grated lemon rind
1½ cups sour cream
butter for frying
jam or jelly and sugar

Cream egg yolks, butter, and sugar until very light. Add to flour and blend. Add lemon rind and sour cream and stir thoroughly. Fold in stiffly-beaten egg whites and divide in half. Fry each half separately in hot skillet with butter, turning when nicely brown and browning on other side. Spread one round with jam, cover with second round, and sprinkle with sugar.

12. SAGES OR WISE MEN (*Mądrzyki*)

1 lb. farmer or dry pot cheese
4 eggs, separated
2 tbs. sugar

2–3 tbs. flour
butter or shortening for frying
sour cream and sugar

Mash cheese and press through a sieve. Combine egg yolks and sugar and cream them until white. Add cheese and continue creaming until smooth. Fold in stiffly-beaten egg whites and just enough flour so that dough can be rolled. Roll out on floured board to ¼ inch thickness. Cut crisscross into oblongs about 1 inch by 2 inches, and fry in very hot butter or shortening. Unless the pan is really hot, the cheese will melt instead of frying crisply. Serve at once with sour cream and sugar.

13. YEAST PASTRIES WITH FILLING
(*Pierożki Drożdzowe*)

1 tbs. butter
6 eggs, separated
1 envelope yeast mixed with a little milk
1½ cups sour cream

5½ cups flour, sifted
3 tbs. sugar
grated rind ½ lemon
butter

Filling: see Index for Strudel Fillings

Cream butter and add egg yolks one by one, continuing to stir until light and fluffy. Add yeast, sour cream, and half the flour. Blend well; then add rest of flour (dough should be fairly solid), sugar, and lemon rind. Work for a few minutes, fold in stiffly-beaten egg whites, and let stand at room temperature until dough rises (about 1½ hours). Roll out on greased sheet of paper about ⅜ inch thick, cut into 2½-inch squares, and fill with any of the fillings used for strudel, or meat or cabbage pastries. Roll into cornucopias and bake in 350° oven until brown (about 40 minutes). Discard paper. Serve with drawn butter or sweetened sour cream in separate dish. May also be served cold.

14. FRENCH PASTRIES WITH STRAWBERRIES OR APPLES *(Ciastka Francuskie z Poziomkami lub Jabłkami)*

French Pastry Dough (see Index)

2 cups thinly-sliced apples or strawberries, or equivalent amount of jam

sugar for sprinkling

3–4 ozs. rum

vanilla-flavored sugar (see Index)

Slice apples (cut strawberries in quarters), sprinkle with sugar and rum, and let stand while preparing dough. Divide dough in half, roll out thin, and place one piece on a well-greased pastry sheet. Spread with fruit mixture or jam, cover with remaining dough, and bake in hot oven for 20 minutes. When nicely brown, sprinkle generously with vanilla sugar, cut in squares, and serve hot or cold.

15. CREAM TUBES *(Rurki z Kremem)*

Puff Paste Dough (see Index)
butter

1 whole egg, lightly beaten
sugar

Cut heavy white paper into 3- or 4-inch squares. Roll each square into a tube and secure with thread. Butter the paper, and then cover with Puff Paste rolled out very thin. Press dough firmly together with fingers so that it will stick. Brush with beaten egg, sprinkle with sugar, and bake in 400° oven for 20 minutes on greased cooky sheet. The tubes cook best standing on end. Allow to cool, remove paper, and fill.

Filling:

6 egg whites
1 cup sugar

1 cup water

Beat egg whites stiff. Make a very thick syrup of sugar and water cooked until pearly. Let syrup simmer in top of double boiler and slowly add egg whites, beating constantly. Continue beating for 2 or 3 minutes; then fill tubes. They may also be filled with whipped sweet cream.

16. RICE AND APPLES IN FROTH *(Ryż z Jabłkami Zapiekany z Pianą)*

1 cup rice
4 eggs, separated
3 tbs. sugar
dash of salt
butter and bread crumbs
4 tbs. jam

2–3 apples, pared, sliced thin, and sprinkled with sugar (cinnamon optional)
6 egg whites, stiffly beaten with 2–3 tbs. sugar
confectioner's sugar to taste

Cook rice in milk so that grains separate (see Index). Allow to cool. Cream egg yolks and sugar until light and creamy. Combine with rice, fold in stiffly-beaten egg whites, and bake in buttered cake tin lined with bread crumbs in moderate oven for half an hour. Remove from tin, spread with jam, cover with a layer of the sliced apples, and top with egg whites beaten with sugar. Sprinkle with confectioner's sugar and bake in 400° oven for 15 to 20 minutes, or until top browns lightly.

17. WHIPPED SOUR CREAM FOR BERRIES
(Bita Śmietana do Poziomek lub Truskawek)

2 cups sour cream	¼–½ cup vanilla sugar (according to taste)

Whip sour cream and sugar with rotary egg beater the same as you whip sweet cream, taking care not to overwhip the cream into butter. Serve with berries in season.

18. RICE WITH WHIPPED SOUR CREAM
(Ryż z Bitą Śmietaną)

1 cup rice	¼–½ cup vanilla sugar
¼–½ cup seedless raisins (optional)	jam or jelly for topping
2 cups sour cream	

Cook rice in milk so that grains separate (see Index). Chill in a ring mold or arrange on a platter in the form of a ring, with or without raisins. Whip sour cream and sugar as in No. 17. Fill center of rice ring. Decorate with dabs of jam. Serves 6.

19. CREAM PIE
(Legumina Śmietanowa w Kruchem Cieście)

Pastry Dough made with 1 cup flour (see Index) or prepared pie-crust mix	5 tbs. sugar
	rind ½ lemon, grated
	1 cup sour cream
5 eggs, separated	3 tbs. flour

Cream egg yolks and sugar until light and creamy. Add lemon rind, sour cream, and flour, and mix thoroughly. Fold in stiffly-beaten egg whites. Line pie tin with dough, pour in cream filling, cover with thin layer of the dough, and pinch edges together. Bake 30 to 35 minutes in 350° oven. Serve sprinkled with sugar.

20. CHEESE DOUGH PASTRY (*Legumina z Sera*)

½ lb. farmer cheese or dry pot
    cheese
½ lb. butter
    dash of salt

2 cups flour
vanilla sugar to taste
dash of lemon rind (optional)
beaten egg if made into crescents

Press cheese through a sieve and cream with the butter. Add flour and salt; blend well. Work on a pastry board for a few minutes; then let stand in a cool place for half an hour. Roll out a half-inch thick and cut into shapes with pastry cutter. Sprinkle with sugar and bake on greased cooky sheet in 375° oven until lightly browned, about 20 minutes. Or roll only a quarter-inch thick, cut into small squares, and spread with jam or ground almonds with a little sugar added. Then roll and shape into crescents, brush with beaten egg, and bake in 350° oven until lightly brown.

21. BAKED CHEESE PASTRY
(*Legumina Wypiekana z Sera*)

6 eggs, separated
¼ lb. unsalted butter
¼ lb. pot cheese or cottage
    cheese
½ cup sugar

½ cup blanched almonds
2–3 bitter almonds
3 tbs. bread crumbs
    bread crumbs and butter for
    lining baking dish

Cream egg yolks and butter, add cheese and sugar, and continue mixing until mixture is smooth. Grate almonds, add to mixture, and mix thoroughly. Fold in stiffly-beaten egg whites and then add the 3 tbs. bread crumbs a little at a time. Grease cake tin generously with butter, line with bread crumbs, and pour in cheese and egg mixture. Bake in 350° oven for 30 minutes.

22. POPPY SEED PUFF (*Legumina z Maku*)

1 cup poppy seeds
6 eggs, separated
½ cup sugar
½ cup almonds, blanched and
    chopped fine

4 tbs. bread crumbs
butter and bread crumbs for
    lining baking dish

Blanch and drain poppy seeds and mash. Cream egg yolks and sugar until white and combine with poppy seeds. Add almonds and bread crumbs and mix thoroughly. Fold in stiffly-beaten egg whites. Pour into buttered pastry form lined with bread crumbs. Bake in 350° oven for 30 minutes. Serve with Wine Sauce (see Index).

23. BLACK BREAD PUDDING (Legumina Chlebowa)

6 eggs, separated
6 tbs. sugar
1 cup bread crumbs made from
   black bread (pumpernickel)

¼ tsp. powdered cloves
cinnamon to taste
1 tbs. melted butter
bread crumbs and butter

Cream egg yolks and sugar until white. Add bread crumbs, cinnamon, cloves, and the melted butter. Mix thoroughly and fold in stiffly-beaten egg whites. Line buttered pan with bread crumbs and pour in the mixture. Bake in 350° oven for 25 to 30 minutes. Serve with whipped cream or Whipped Sour Cream (see Index).

24. CHESTNUT PUDDING (Legumina Kasztanowa)

I.

1 lb. chestnuts
   milk to cover
2–3 tbs. vanilla sugar
1 cup mixed dried fruit, soaked

and drained
2 egg whites
sugar to taste

Parboil chestnuts 15 minutes. Shell and peel. Simmer chestnuts in milk until very soft—about 30 minutes. Mash, add sugar, and press through a sieve. Arrange in mound on a baking tin and garnish with the fruit, which has been cut in halves or quarters. Cover with stiffly-beaten egg whites mixed with sugar to taste, and bake in 350° oven for 20 to 25 minutes. Serve hot.

II. Prepare chestnuts as in I. Chill. Whip 1 cup sweet cream with vanilla sugar to taste, pour over chestnut mound, and serve cold.

25. JELLY DOUGHNUTS (Pączki)

2 cups flour
2 cups boiling milk
3½ ozs. yeast
¼ cup lukewarm milk
6 egg yolks

½ cup sugar
½ vanilla bean, ground
1–2 tsp. grated orange rind
¼ lb. butter, melted
flour, jam, deep fat for frying

Sift 1 cup flour into boiling milk, remove from heat, and beat until smooth. Cool. Dissolve yeast in the ¼ cup milk. Add to flour mixture, stir, and let stand half an hour. Cream egg yolks and sugar, add vanilla and orange rind and add to dough when it begins to rise. Add remaining flour and butter, and work with fingers until dough begins to stand away from the hands. Let stand until it has risen to about twice its bulk. Roll out on floured board to thickness of ⅝ inch, and cut out circles with a glass or pastry cutter. Place a teaspoon of jam in center of half the circles (using only fruit, not syrup), cover with remaining circles, press edges together, and let stand in warm place to rise again. Fry a few at a time in deep fat, taking care not to heat the fat so much that the dough will burn. Drain and serve dusted with confectioner's sugar.

26. KINDLING, OR FAVORS *(Chrust Chyli Faworki)*

I.

2 cups unsifted flour	1 egg, lightly beaten
1 tbs. butter, melted	1 tbs. vinegar
2 heaping tbs. sugar	½ cup sour cream (approx.)

Sift flour, combine with butter, sugar, and egg, and stir ingredients together. Add vinegar and sour cream to form dough the consistency of biscuit dough—just solid enough to roll. Divide into four parts. Roll one piece very thin on a floured board, keeping the rest covered to prevent drying. Cut into strips about 1 inch wide and 5 inches long. Cut a short lengthwise slit in the center of each strip, and pass one end of the strip through the slit. Repeat, until all the dough has been used up. Fry in deep fat until golden brown, drain on paper towel, and sprinkle with confectioner's sugar. Serve hot with honey. May also be served cold.

II.

6 egg yolks	2 tbs. rum
6 tbs. sugar	2 cups flour (approx.)
1 cup sweet cream	

Cream egg yolks and sugar until creamy-white. Combine with cream and rum; then add enough flour so that dough can be rolled out very thin (like noodle dough) on floured board. Proceed as in *I.*

Note: A tablespoon of alcohol or a piece of raw potato added to the deep fat will eliminate unpleasant odor of frying.

27. APPLE CHARLOTTE *(Szarlotka z Jablek)*

10 large greenings	2 tbs. apricot jam or apricot
sugar to taste	butter
cinnamon to taste (optional)	2 tbs. seedless raisins
1 tbs. butter	slices of white bread

Core and pare apples and slice them thin. Combine apples, sugar, cinnamon, and butter and simmer, tightly covered, for about 10 minutes. Add jam and raisins and mix thoroughly. Remove crusts from bread, cut in half, and toast. Line a buttered baking dish with slightly overlapping slices of toast, pour in apple mixture, cover top with more toast, and bake in hot oven for 30 to 40 minutes.

Note: The apple mixture can also be baked in a pie shell.

28. APPLES BAKED IN WHIP
(Jabłka Zapiekane w Kremie)

I.

6–8 apples, pared and cored
sugar to taste
3–4 tbs. jam

Whip:
4 eggs, separated
4 tbs. sugar
2 tbs. bread crumbs
1 tsp. grated lemon rind

Parboil apples, being careful not to let them fall apart. Arrange in shallow baking dish, sprinkle with sugar, and fill centers with jam. Cream egg yolks and sugar until white, add bread crumbs and lemon rind, and stir. Fold in stiffly-beaten egg whites and spread mixture over the apples. Bake in moderate oven until top begins to brown (20 to 25 minutes).

II. Prepare like *I*, using 6 egg whites and 6 tbs. sugar. Sprinkle generously with chopped almonds and sugar. Bake in slow oven for 20 minutes.

29. STUFFED APPLES IN WINE
(Jabłka Nadiewane na Winie)

6 greenings, cored and pared
sugar to taste
6 thin strips orange rind
¼ cup blanched almonds

2 tbs. seedless raisins
3 tbs. sugar
1 cup white wine

Arrange apples in heavy casserole, one next to the other in one layer. Sprinkle with sugar to taste. Simmer orange rind in butter until transparent. Combine almonds and orange rind and chop coarsely. Add raisins and sugar and mix. Fill centers of apples, add wine, and bake covered in moderate oven for 30 minutes. Serve with macaroons or ladyfingers.

30. ALMOND PUDDING *(Budyń Migdałowy)*

6 eggs, separated
½ cup sugar
1 cup blanched almonds, chopped
fine

butter and bread crumbs

Cream egg yolks and sugar until white, combine with almonds, fold in stiffly-beaten egg whites, and pour into buttered mold lined with bread crumbs. Cover tightly and cook in steam for 1 hour. Serve with Wine Sauce (see Index).

Note: This recipe may also be made with walnuts or hazelnuts. A third method is to use chestnuts, in which case follow the above recipe but use 1 lb. cooked, peeled chestnuts and add 1 cup whipped sweet cream to the whipped egg whites. Flavor with vanilla if desired.

Dessert Sauces

1. WHITE WINE SAUCE (*Chaudeau z Białego Wina*)

5 egg yolks
5 tbs. sugar

2 cups white wine

Beat sugar and egg yolks until very light. Place over boiling water in double boiler and slowly add the wine, beating constantly with rotary beater. The sauce is done when thick and foamy. Care must be taken not to overcook and curdle. If sauce is to be served hot, prepare directly before serving; otherwise, chill in refrigerator.

2. RED WINE SAUCE (*Chaudeau z Wina Czerwonego*)

2 cups red wine
¼ cup water
lemon juice to taste
piece of lemon rind
2" stick of cinnamon

4–5 cloves
5 tbs. sugar
2 tbs. seedless raisins
1 tbs. potato flour dissolved in 2
tbs. of water

Simmer all ingredients together except raisins. Cooking time depends on how high a flavor is desired—10 minutes will produce a light flavor; longer cooking will bring out the cinnamon, cloves, and lemon oil. Strain sauce, and add raisins.

3. VANILLA SAUCE (*Chaudeau Waniljowe*)

2 cups milk
2" piece vanilla bean

5 egg yolks
5 tbs. sugar

Add vanilla bean to milk, scald, and set aside to cool. In the meantime beat the eggs and sugar until very light. Combine with cooled milk in top of double boiler and continue beating with rotary beater until thick and foamy, taking care not to curdle.

4. PUNCH SAUCE (*Chaudeau Ponczowe*)

2 cups white wine
¼ cup water
juice 1 lemon
juice 1 orange

lemon and orange peel to taste
1 cup sugar
5 egg yolks

288

Combine wine, water, fruit juices, and peel. Simmer 5 to 10 minutes and set aside to cool. Beat sugar and egg yolks until very light and frothy. Combine and proceed as for Vanilla Sauce (No. 3).

5. ALMOND SAUCE *(Chaudeau Migdalowe)*

1 cup sweet almonds	1 tbs. potato flour blended with 2
6 bitter almonds	tbs. of cold milk
2 tbs. sugar	3 egg yolks combined with 3 tbs.
3 cups milk	sugar

Blanch, peel, and chop the almonds. Then pound to a pulp and combine with 2 tbs. sugar. Simmer with milk for 10 minutes. Strain, forcing the almond paste through the sieve. Thicken with potato flour dissolved in cold milk. Beat the egg yolks and remaining sugar until very light, and combine everything in top of double boiler. Proceed as for No. 3.

6. WILD STRAWBERRY SAUCE *(Sos Poziomkowy)*

1 pt. wild strawberries (garden	juice ½ lemon
strawberries, raspberries, or cur-	½ cup white wine
rants may be used)	1 cup sweet cream
1 cup sugar	1 tbs. potato flour

Mash raw fruit through a sieve, combine with other ingredients, and bring to a boil. Serve hot or cold. The cream may be omitted, in which case the potato flour should be blended with 2 tbs. cold water before adding to sauce.

7. SHERRY SAUCE *(Sos Sherry)*

4 egg yolks	¼ cup sherry wine (or more)
2 tbs. sugar	½ cup heavy cream
2 tbs. apricot marmalade	

Beat egg yolks and sugar until very light, and combine with wine and marmalade. Place in top of double boiler and beat vigorously over very low heat until thick. Allow to cool. Whip the cream, combine with rest of the ingredients, whipping until thoroughly blended. Chill in refrigerator.

Party Recipes

Today's electric ice cream freezers, refrigerator freezing compartments, and prepared mixes make ice cream and other frozen desserts extremely simple to make. Hand-freezing is all but obsolete, even though the results, taste-wise, are excellent. The basic technique for hand-freezing is as follows:

The ice should be cracked fine, and mixed with rock salt in the proportion of 8 parts ice to 1 part salt. Pack the freezer ⅓ full of ice and salt, pound down, then add the rest. Fill container or mold only ¾ full, to allow for expansion; cover tightly and either grease the edges or seal with a strip of adhesive tape to prevent the brine from penetrating; place container in freezer; turn slowly at first, then rapidly, until very stiff. The old recipes call for opening the container at 15-minute intervals and scraping the sides and bottom with a wooden spoon to insure even freezing. When ice cream is done, remove container and wipe carefully before opening to avoid penetration of salt.

Bombe Molds are handled similarly to ice cream molds. Fill them only ¾ full. Cover with wax paper, adjust the lid, grease the borders or seal with adhesive tape, place in a bucket packed with ice and salt (1 part salt to 4 parts ice) and allow 3 to 4 hours for freezing.

Both ice cream and *bombes* may be made in a refrigerator freezing compartment. When making ice cream in refrigerator trays, stir frequently while freezing to improve texture. Remove to bowl and beat with wire whisk or electric beater before serving; then return to tray to keep cold. When using prepared mixes, follow directions on the package.

1. VANILLA ICE CREAM *(Lody Waniljowe)*

3 cups cream or milk	5–8 egg yolks
2" piece vanilla bean or 2 tsp. vanilla extract	1 cup sugar (less if desired)

Scald cream or milk with vanilla bean. Cool. Remove vanilla b n. Cream egg yolks and sugar until very light and creamy. If cream is used in recipe, allow 5 egg yolks; if milk, allow 8. Place sugar and egg mixture in top of double boiler and slowly add cream or milk, beating all the time until mixture coats spoon and taking care not to overheat and curdle the eggs. Cool. Pour into mold. Freeze in hand-freezer or freezing compartment of refrigerator, allowing 3 to 4 hours for freezing. Serves 7 to 8.

2. COFFEE ICE CREAM (Lody Kawowe)

Prepare like No. 1, but omit vanilla. Add ¾ cup very strong coffee. Preferably make with heavy cream.

3. BURNT CARAMEL ICE CREAM (Lody Karmelowe)

Prepare the same as No. 1, but reserve ¼ cup of the sugar and 1 cup milk. Melt sugar in dry pan over low heat, and allow to caramelize until dark brown. Dissolve with 1 cup milk and slowly add to egg yolk, sugar, and cream mixture in double boiler.

4. FRUIT ICE CREAM (Lody Owocowe)

4 egg yolks	(strawberries, wild strawberries,
1 cup sugar (scant)	raspberries) *or*
1½ cups cream, scalded and cooled	1 cup fresh fruit juice
1½ cups strained fresh fruit pulp	

Cream egg yolks and sugar until very light and place in top of double boiler. Stir in cooled, scalded cream, beating constantly until thick enough so that mixture coats the spoon. Cool, combine with fruit pulp or fruit juice, and proceed as for Vanilla Ice Cream, No. 1. Serves 6.

5. CHARLOTTE RUSSE

1 cup each of 3 or 4 kinds of ice cream, according to preference	3–4 tbs. jam
½ cup heavy cream, whipped	18 ladyfingers or oblong wafers

Arrange the different kinds of ice cream in layers in mold or freezer tray (ready-made ice cream may be used to advantage here). Allow 2 hours to refreeze. Unmold on platter. Arrange ladyfingers or wafers around the ice cream like a fence. Top with whipped cream and decorate with dabs of jam. Serves 6 to 7.

Bombes (Bomby Chyli Plombiery)

Bombes are another form of ice cream, prepared with the addition of whipped cream. The recipes given here are traditional. The inventive cook will have no trouble making up others to suit herself.

6. COFFEE *BOMBE* (Bombe-Plombière Kawowa)

8 egg yolks	½ cup very strong coffee
1½ cups sugar	4 tbs. dry powdered coffee (more
2 cups heavy cream	if desired)

Cream egg yolks with 1 cup sugar until very light and creamy. Whip cream with remaining sugar. Place the bowl in ice. Slowly add the coffee and powdered coffee to cream, beating all the time. Repeat procedure for adding the egg and sugar mixture. When all the ingredients have been thoroughly blended and mixture is stiff, pour into mold. Follow freezing directions at beginning of chapter. Allow 3 to 4 hours for freezing. Serves 7 to 8.

7. FRUIT *BOMBE* (Bomba Owocowa)

2 cups fruit pulp (strawberries,	2 cups sugar (or less)
raspberries, apricots, etc.)	fresh or candied fruit for
2 cups heavy cream	garnishing

Mash fruit and then press through sieve. Whip cream and sugar until stiff. Place in bowl with ice and continue beating, adding fruit a little at a time. When thoroughly stiff and blended, pour into mold and follow freezing directions at beginning of chapter. Allow 3 to 4 hours for freezing. Unmold and garnish with fruit slices. Serves 8 to 10.

8. *BOMBE À LA REINE* (Bomba à la Reine)
Made with Ready-made Ice Creams

3 cups pineapple ice cream	3 tbs. sugar
Parfait *au Curaçao*, made with	¼ cup Curaçao liqueur
2 cups lemon ice or lemon ice	
cream	candied fruit slices and candied
1 cup heavy cream	orange peel for garnish

Line mold with the pineapple ice cream. Soften lemon ice cream (or lemon ice) and combine with the heavy cream whipped with the sugar and liqueur. Whip again until stiff; then use to fill center of mold. Close, seal, and follow freezing directions at beginning of chapter. Allow 2 to 3 hours for freezing. Unmold, decorate with candied fruit slices around the base, and make a star on top with strips of candied orange peel. Serves 7 to 8.

9. SOUR CREAM MOUSSE *(Krem z Kwaśnej Śmietany)*

1 cup sour cream	⅓ cup rather dry jam
1 cup sweet cream	1 pkg. gelatin, dissolved in ¼ cup
¾ cup sugar	water

Whip sour cream and sweet cream separately, using half the sugar for each. Combine with jam and dissolved gelatin, and pour into mold. Freeze for 2 to 3 hours. Serves 6 to 8.

Note: If possible, spread jam out on flat surface the day before to dry out, or heat in warm oven until syrup evaporates. Cool before using.

10. ORANGE CREAM *(Krem ze Skórką Pomarańczową)*

2 cups heavy cream	3–4 tbs. candied orange peel
½ cup sugar	1 pkg. gelatin

Whip the cream and sugar until stiff. Chop orange peel fine. Dissolve gelatin in ¼ cup of water. Combine all the ingredients, mix thoroughly, and pour into mold. Freeze for 2 to 3 hours. This recipe may also be made with grated lemon rind. Serves 6 to 8.

11. TEA-FLAVORED CREAM *(Krem z Herbaty)*

2 cups light cream	1 cup sugar
2" piece vanilla bean	2 cups heavy cream, whipped
1 tbs. dry tea leaves	¼ cup rum
8 egg yolks	1 pkg. gelatin, dissolved in ¼ cup
	water

Combine light cream, vanilla bean, and tea leaves. Cover and bring to a boil. Cool and strain. Cream egg yolks and sugar until light and creamy, combine with whipped heavy cream, add strained tea-and-cream liquid, the rum, and the dissolved gelatin. Whip again for 5 minutes. Then pour into mold and freeze for 3 to 4 hours. Serves 8 to 10. Recipe may readily be halved for a smaller portion.

12. WINE MOUSSE *(Muss z Wina)*

1 cup sugar	1 pkg. gelatin, dissolved in ¼ cup
1 tsp. grated lemon rind	water
2 cups white wine	5 egg whites
juice 2 lemons	

Make a syrup of the sugar and ¼ cup of water and simmer for 5 minutes with grated lemon rind. Cool, combine with wine, lemon juice, and dissolved gelatin. Mix thoroughly and strain through cheesecloth. Beat with rotary beater or in blender until frothy and white. Combine with stiffly-beaten egg whites and continue beating until stiff. Pour into mold or into individual glasses and chill. Serves 6 to 7.

13. FRUIT CREAM (Kisiel)

A traditional fruit dessert made without gelatin and hence differing considerably in consistency from Jello. It is made with tart berries such as barberries, gooseberries, currants, or cranberries, chilled, and served with sweet cream.

4 cups berries	1 stick cinnamon (2"–3" piece)
4 cups water	3–4 cloves
1½ cups sugar	2 heaping tbs. potato flour

Mash berries, combine with water, boil for 5 minutes, and press through a sieve. Reserve ¼ of the liquid and allow to cool. Combine the rest with the sugar, cinnamon, and cloves and simmer another 10 minutes. Discard vanilla bean and cloves. Dissolve potato flour in the cooled part of the liquid, and when thoroughly blended, pour into the boiling part. Stir continuously for 2 minutes. Wet a mold or bowl, sprinkle with sugar, and pour in kisiel. Chill and allow to thicken for about 2 hours.

14. KISIEL WITH WINE (Kisiel z Winem)

Use gooseberries or tart apples. Follow general directions in No. 13, and add 1 cup white wine and a dash of grated lemon rind for flavoring.

15. VANILLA CREAM (Kisiel Śmietankowy)

2 cups sweet cream	½ cup sugar
3" piece vanilla bean or 2 tsp.	1 heaping tsp. potato flour
vanilla extract	¼ cup cold milk

Combine cream, vanilla bean, and sugar and slowly bring to a boil. Dissolve potato flour in cold milk and add to simmering cream. Stir for 2 minutes, taking care not to scorch the cream. Discard vanilla bean. Wet mold or bowl with water, sprinkle with sugar, and pour in cream mixture. Chill and serve with fruit syrup to taste.

16. CHOCOLATE CREAM (Kisiel Czekoladowy)

Prepare like Vanilla Cream (No. 15), with the addition of 4 ozs. unsweetened chocolate. Semi-sweet or sweet chocolate may be substituted, according to taste. Melt chocolate over very low heat, blending thoroughly with the cream. Serve with heavy sweet cream, plain or whipped.

17. COMPOTES OR STEWED FRUIT *(Kompoty)*

Fruit in season is easy and quick to stew. The basic rules are the same for all fruit; the timing and the amounts of sugar cannot be given accurately since these vary according to the ripeness and sweetness of the fruit and differences in individual taste. Individual taste, too, will determine whether such fruits as apples, pears, plums, peaches, and apricots will be peeled or not. Apples and pears should be cored. Leaving the stones in peaches, apricots, and cherries will give the compote additional tang similar to the flavoring of bitter almonds. Fruit cooked whole in the skin (plums, kumquats, etc.) should be carefully punctured in several places so that the skin will not burst in cooking.

General Proportions: To each 1 lb. fruit, use ½ cup sugar and 1 cup water. Make a syrup of the sugar and water by simmering for 5 minutes. Then add washed fruit, bring to a boil, and simmer covered for 5 to 10 minutes or to desired degree of doneness.

Additional Flavoring: One stick of cinnamon and a few cloves, to be discarded later; grated lemon rind to taste, and a few drops of lemon juice, if desired.

Wine in Fruit Compotes: Prepare according to the general rules, adding 1 cup wine to the syrup when fruit is nearly done. Always keep the cover on after adding wine, for the alcohol content makes flavor evaporate quickly at high temperature. For dark fruit like plums, use red wine. For apples, pears, and peaches, white wine is best. Always use cinnamon, cloves, and a dash of lemon rind when cooking fruit with wine.

Preparation of Berries for Cooking: Always wash first, then hull. If the process is reversed, some of the juices will be washed away. Tart berries like cranberries and currants may require more sugar than called for in the basic directions. Strawberries and raspberries may require less. If too much sugar has been added, add lemon juice.

An excellent fruit compote can also be made of fresh uncooked fruit sweetened to taste, with the addition of ½ to 1 cup of wine or ¼ cup brandy. Fresh sliced orange, melon, or pineapple is best with white wine, sherry, or brandy.

18. QUINCE COMPOTE *(Kompot z Pigw)*

2 lbs. quince	dash grated lemon rind
1 cup sugar	lemon juice to taste

Quinces are extremely hard and therefore difficult to slice. After paring they should be thrown into boiling water and allowed to stand until soft enough to handle easily. Slice, core, and cook in plain water until soft. Reduce water to 2 cups and add sugar, lemon rind, and lemon juice to taste. Allow to boil up several times. Chill and serve.

19. PEACHES OR APRICOTS IN ALCOHOL
(Brzoskwinie lub Morele w Spirytusie)

2 lbs. ripe peaches, skinned	1 cup pure alcohol or distilled
2 cups sugar	white rum, with
1 cup water	½ cup water added

Throw skinned peaches into boiling water and simmer 4 minutes. Drain. Make syrup with sugar and water in proportion of 2 parts sugar to 1 part water, and cook 5 minutes. Add peaches and simmer a few minutes longer. Cool. On the following day pour off syrup, bring to a boil, skim, and pour over fruit. On the third day repeat the process, but add alcohol or rum, diluted with water, to syrup before boiling. Arrange fruit in jars and pour boiling liquid over them. Seal and store.

20. PEARS IN ALCOHOL *(Gruszki w Spirytusie)*

2 lbs. ripe, juicy pears	1 cup pure alcohol or white dis-
juice 1 lemon	tilled rum, with
2 cups sugar	½ cup water added
1 cup water	

The pears must be juicy, for alcohol toughens them. Peel pears but do not cut. Then let stand in cold water with lemon juice for 10 to 15 minutes. This will prevent fruit from discoloring. In the meantime make syrup of sugar and water—2 parts sugar to 1 part water. Drain pears, place in the boiling syrup, and cook a few minutes. Skim and allow to stand overnight. On the following day and the day after, pour off syrup, bring to a boil, and pour back over fruit. On the fourth day repeat the process, adding the alcohol and water before boiling. Arrange fruit in jars, pour in boiling liquid, skim, seal, and store.

21. GREENGAGE PLUMS IN ALCOHOL
(Renklody w Spirytusie)

2 lbs. ripe plums
.juice 2 lemons
½ pkg. spinach
2 cups sugar

1 cup water
1 cup pure alcohol or white dis-
tilled rum, with
⅓ cup water added

Wash plums and puncture skin to prevent breaking. Bring to a boil
enough water to cover the fruit. Add the lemon juice and the spinach, which should be confined in a piece of cheesecloth. (The
spinach will keep fruit from discoloring.) Throw plums into the
boiling water and simmer until they rise to the surface. Drain
and rinse in cold water, drain again, and proceed as for No. 20.

22. QUINCE JAM (Pigwy)

Proceed as for Quince Compote, No. 18. When fruit is soft, drain
and slice thin. Make syrup of 2 parts sugar and 1 part water.
(Allow 1½ times as much sugar as there is fruit: that is, for 2 cups
sliced quince, use 3 cups sugar and 1½ cups water.) Add quince.
Bring to a boil several times, being careful not to overcook or quince
will harden. Pour into jars, seal, and store.

23. HAWTHORNE JAM (Konfitura z Głogu)

Hawthorne berries are picked late in the fall shortly before frost.
They should be dark red in color but still hard. Prepare as follows:
Cut halfway and remove pits with a small fork or a pin. Scoop out
the fibers. Immerse in boiling water and let stand until fruit softens
and is cool enough to handle. Then drain. Cook for about 15 minutes in a light syrup made of equal parts water and sugar. (Allow
same amount of sugar as berries.) Let stand overnight. Reheat
syrup, adding half again as much sugar, and also lemon juice to
taste. Simmer 5 to 10 minutes. Return fruit to syrup and continue
simmering to desired consistency. Seal and store.

24. HAWTHORNE BUTTER (Powidła z Głogu)

Prepare and clean as in No. 23, but do not use any water. Put into
bowl and cover with small saucer, with a weight on top. Let stand
several days until berries are soft enough to mash. Then press
through a sieve, ccmbine with an equal amount of sugar, and simmer in their own juice without water until mixture begins to thicken,
stirring frequently to avoid scorching. Remove from heat before
mixture loses its red color.

25. CANDIED ORANGE PEEL *(Skórka Pomarańczowa)*

3 cups sliced orange peel (packed   ½ cup water
     tight)   sugar for rolling (optional)
2 cups sugar

Cut orange peel in thin strips and simmer in water for 2 to 3 hours
or until tender, changing the water several times. (Or soak in cold
water for several days, changing water every day; this will shorten
cooking time.) Drain and dry. Make syrup of water and sugar,
cook 5 minutes, add orange peel, and simmer for 15 minutes more or
until liquid is thick. Drain orange peel and allow to dry overnight,
reserving syrup. Continue cooking syrup the following day until it
spins. Dip each piece of peel separately and dry in sieve in warm
oven. When peel is dry and the glaze has hardened, it may be
stored. Another method is to roll the peel in granulated sugar while
still warm.

26. GLAZED CHESTNUTS *(Kasztany w Cukrze)*

1 lb. chestnuts, shelled and peeled   ½ cup water
2 cups sugar

Parboil and shell chestnuts according to basic directions (see
Index), taking care to leave nuts whole. Make a thick syrup which
should be simmered until light golden-brown. (Test by dipping
wooden spoon in syrup, then in cold water. Sugar should harden.)
Stick toothpick into each nut and dip separately in syrup, then
immediately in ice water. Spread, well spaced, on greased cooky
sheet to dry. The glaze will not keep longer than 24 to 48 hours;
chestnuts therefore must be prepared for immediate use.

27. GLAZED WALNUTS *(Orzechy Włoskie z Cukrze)*

Prepare like Glazed Chestnuts, No. 26. Walnuts need not be boiled,
but must be shelled very carefully to leave them whole or in halves.
Unsalted shelled nuts may be purchased for glazing. Pecans and
Brazil nuts may be similarly handled.

28. PEARS CANDIED IN HONEY
(Gruszki Smażone w Miodzie)

2 lbs. firm pears   sugar for rolling
2 cups honey

Peel pears, cut in halves, and core. Simmer in water to cover until
tender but not mushy. (Time depends on ripeness and variety of
pear; test with toothpick for doneness.) Drain and let dry while

heating honey. Combine fruit and honey and let stand in cool place for 2 days. Then simmer in a flat pan until honey thickens to a glaze. Allow to cool enough to handle, and roll in sugar. Spread on buttered cooky sheet and dry out in 200° oven.

29. HOT WINE (*Gluhwein*)

1 cup dry red or white wine	1 stick cinnamon
2 tbs. sugar, or less	lemon rind (optional)
2–3 cloves	

Combine all ingredients, bring to a boil, and simmer a few minutes. Always cook wine covered. Strain and serve piping hot. One serving.

30. HOT BEER (*Piwo Grzane*)

4 cups beer	6 egg yolks
1 stick cinnamon	½ cup sugar
4–6 cloves	

Combine beer, cinnamon, and cloves. Cover and bring to a boil. Cream egg yolks and sugar until creamy and light. Strain beer and slowly pour hot liquid into egg yolk mixture, beating constantly to avoid curdling. Beat until frothy. Serve at once.

31. NEW YEAR'S EVE PUNCH (*Poncz Sylwestrowy*)

1 lb. cube sugar, or less	4 cups light white wine
2 oranges	2 cups white rum
2 lemons	

Rub sugar cubes on skins of oranges and lemons. Combine with wine and rum, allow to dissolve, and add strained juice from the oranges and lemons according to taste. Heat, covered, and serve piping hot. If punch is too strong, dilute with a little hot water.

Note: If red wine is used for this punch, substitute dark rum for white.

32. CUCUMBER PUNCH (*Poncz Ogórkowy*)

2 large cucumbers	4 cups lemon ice or ice cream
1 cup dry white wine	(according to taste)
¼ cup distilled white rum	5 egg whites, beaten stiff

Peel cucumbers, grate, and press through a sieve. Combine with wine and rum. Add slightly melted lemon ice, mix well, and fold in stiffly-beaten egg whites. Chill and serve in tall glasses.

33. HOT MEAD *(Krupnik)*

1 cup honey
1 cup water
3–4 cloves
6 sticks cinnamon
  small piece of nutmeg (or ¼
  tsp. fresh ground)

3" piece vanilla bean
¼" strip orange rind
2 cups pure alcohol

Bring honey and water to a boil and carefully remove all scum. Add cloves, cinnamon, nutmeg, vanilla bean, and orange rind. Allow to boil up again, remove from heat and let stand a minute or two, and again bring to a boil. Cover and set aside for at least half an hour to steep. Strain, again bring to a boil, and then pour in the alcohol. Stir well and serve piping hot.

Note: Krupnik is one of the oldest-known drinks in Poland, dating far back into the Middle Ages. References to it are found in literature, folk songs, and poetry. Drunk in large quantities, it was supposed to fell strong warriors and conquer conquerors.

34. LEMON OR ORANGE VODKA
(Wódka Cytrynowa lub Pomarańczowa)

rind of 3 lemons or 2 oranges
1 qt. (4 cups) pure alcohol

2 cups sugar
2 cups water

Peel rind very thin, combine with alcohol, cover, and allow to stand at room temperature for 4 days. Discard rinds. Make a syrup of sugar and water, skim carefully, and pour alcohol into the syrup while it is still hot. Stir very thoroughly, cool, and strain through filter paper or sterile cotton. Bottle, cork tightly, and store. If a weaker vodka is preferred, dilute syrup with more water (1 to 3 more cups may be added), but never dilute once syrup and alcohol have been combined. Allow to stand at least a month before using.

Index